(21)

A

B

Basalt

(22)

a

(23)   (24)

25

(26)

(27)

projects about 60 yards in advance of the general line of cliff. One of its edges, at c, rests on the blue clay, beds of the crag; a, is chalk with flints; b, gravel of broken and half rounded flints; d, leaving atop blue clay; and e, sand and yellow loam.

A lava stream, flowing from the ridge of hills to the east of Olot, descends a considerable slope until it reaches the valley of the river Fluvia. Here, for the first time it comes in contact with running water, which has removed a portion, and laid open its internal structure in a precipice about 130 feet in height, at the edge of which stands the town of Castell Follit. By the junction of the river Fluvia and Fluviol, the basalt has been eaten away on two sides, and the insular mass B [No. 2] has been left, which was probably never so high as the cliff a A, as it may have constituted the lower part of the sloping side of the original current. From an examination of the vertical cliff, it appears that the upper part of the lava on which the town is built is scoriaceous, passing downwards into a spheroidal basalt, some of the huge spheroids being more than six feet in diameter. Below, this is a more compact basalt, with crystals of olivine. There are in all about four distinct ranges of prismatic basalt, separated by thin up beds, not columnar, and some of which are schistose. The whole mass rests on alluvium, some 12 feet in thickness, composed of pebbles of limestone and quartz, but without any intermixture of igneous rocks, in which circumstance alone it appears to differ from the modern gravel of the Fluvia. [Explanation: A, church and town of Castell Follit, over looking basalt precipice. B, small island, on each side of which small branches of the river through flow to meet the Fluvia. c, prismatic of basaltic lava, chiefly columnar. d, recent alluvium, underlying the lava current; e, inclined strata of secondary sandstone.] Fig. 22 is another specimen of the manner in which the rivers cut through the lava currents. It is at the bridge of Cellent, 6 miles east of Olot, called Toxia. a, scoriaceous lava; b, schistose basalt; c, columnar basalt; d, scoria, vegetable soil, and alluvium; e, nummulite limestone; f, micaceous grey sandstone.

The annexed diagram will explain to the reader the manner in which these granite veins often branch off from the principal mass. These are taken from Dr. Macculloch's representations of veins passing thro' the gneiss at Cape Wrath in Scotland. The veins on the left are described by Captain B. Hall as traversing the argillaceous schist of the Table-mountain at Cape of Good Hope. We subjoin another sketch from Dr. Macculloch's interesting representations of the granite veins in Scotland, in which the contrast of colour between the veins & some of the dark varieties of hornblende which associated with the gneiss renders the phenomena more conspicuous

*The
Ruskin
Polygon*

The Ruskin Polygon

*Essays
on the
imagination
of John Ruskin*

JOHN DIXON HUNT
FAITH M. HOLLAND editors

Manchester University Press

Published by Manchester University Press
Oxford Road, Manchester M13 9PL

British Library cataloguing in publication data

The Ruskin polygon.
  1. Ruskin, John – Criticism and interpretation
  I. Hunt, John Dixon   II. Holland, Faith M.
  828'.809   PR5264

  ISBN 0–7190–0834–4

Filmset by August Filmsetting, Stockport, Cheshire
Printed in Great Britain
by Butler & Tanner Ltd, Frome and London

WILLIAM ARROWSMITH is Professor in Classics and the Writing
Seminars at the Johns Hopkins University. Among his works are translations of Aristophanes, Euripides, Sophocles, Petronius, Nietzsche, Pavese, and Montale. In 1978 he received the Award for Literature of the American Academy and the National Institute of Arts and Letters. He is currently at work on a critical study of Eliot's poetry between *Prufrock and The Waste Land*.

STEPHEN BANN is Reader in the Faculty of Humanities at the University of Kent. As editor of *20th Century Studies*, he published a special number of 'Visual Poetics' (December 1976). He has recently edited a supplement on the work of Adrian Stokes for *PN Review 15*, and contributed an essay, 'Abstract art—a language?' to the symposium *Towards a new art* (Tate Gallery, 1980).

J. MORDAUNT CROOK is Reader in Architectural History at the University of London (Bedford College) and President of the Society of Architectural Historians. He was Slade Professor of Fine Art at Oxford, 1979–80. A leading authority on Georgian and Victorian architecture, he had published *The British Museum*, *The Greek Revival* and edited Eastlake's *Gothic Revival*; he was co-author of *The History of the King's Works, 1660–1851*). His book on William Burges is to be published in 1981.

GEORGE L. HERSEY is Professor of the History of Art at Yale University, and the author of several books on both Renaissance and Victorian architecture, including *High Victorian Gothic. A Study in Associationism*.

FAITH M. HOLLAND has done editorial work for Houghton Mifflin and the Woodrow Wilson Foundation; she was an editor of *Strivers' Row* and a research assistant on the Norton Anthology of American Literature; most recently she assisted in the editing of the George A. Lucas diaries for Princeton University Press.

JOHN DIXON HUNT is Professor of English Literature in the University of London (Bedford College). The author of *The Pre-Raphaelite Imagination 1848–1900* and various articles on relations between Victorian literature and the visual arts, he has completed a biography of Ruskin, to be published in 1981 by Dent.

EDWARD N. KAUFMAN was an undergraduate and graduate student at Yale University; he is finishing a dissertation on the architecture of E. B. Lamb.

RICHARD A. MACKSEY is Director of the Humanities Center at the Johns Hopkins University and editor of *M.L.N.*

BRIAN MAIDMENT teaches English at Manchester Polytechnic and has written articles on Ruskin, Victorian publishing and other aspects of Victorian literature. He edits the *Tennyson Research Bulletin*.

MARC A. SIMPSON was an undergraduate at Middlebury College, Vermont, and is now a graduate student in Art History at Yale University.

JEFFREY L. SPEAR is Assistant Professor of English at Princeton University. He discovered and published Ruskin's letter to Acland on his marriage (*TLS*, 10 February 1978); he has written on various aspects of Victorian literature and society and is soon to publish a book, *Realized Romance*, on Ruskin's social criticism. He plans a further study, entitled *Ruskin Reading*.

I never met with a question yet, of any importance, which did not need, for the right solution of it, at least one positive and one negative answer, like an equation of the second degree. Mostly, matters of any consequence are three-sided, or four-sided, or polygonal; and the trotting round a polygon is severe work for people any way stiff in their opinion. [16.187]

In that way John Ruskin explained to a Cambridge audience in 1858 why he hoped that he was 'exceedingly apt to . . . contradict' himself. His conviction that in important matters truth would be discovered by various approaches which might well seem to go against each other is apt for any collection of essays by different hands. But in the case of a writer so various in his interests, so polymathic, as Ruskin the notion is particularly appropriate. He is, it should go without saying, of 'consequence' among Victorian writers, though he has not yet received as much detailed attention as other eminent figures who were his contemporaries. Indeed, though there have been a few honourable exceptions, people still tend to be rather 'stiff in their opinions' about him. We need fresh perspectives, new models of his mind by which to re-view his works and influence; we need, in his words, to trot around the polygon of his imaginative achievement.

The Ruskin polygon, we are certain, has many more sides than this volume can encompass. But the essays collected here are designed to map some of his complexities: they chart his 'set of mind', the efforts he made to manipulate conventional forms for his own imaginative purposes, his strong belief in the interconnections of his life and art and of his different writings, and—above all—the consequences of his intricate mind for our reading of his best texts. This volume sees Ruskin as writer and 'poet' as well as critic of architecture and painting. It focuses closely upon what he wrote and said, and it also observes (to borrow from Auden's elegy for Yeats) how 'The words of a dead man/Are modified in the guts of the living'. For an astonishing part of Ruskin exists in what others made of him and his ideas, just as he had himself absorbed and used previous writers and artists. And finally, *The Ruskin Polygon* offers fresh perspectives upon his life as well as his writings; we take a cue from his own decision to supplement the text of his autobiographical essays in *Praeterita* with the publication of 'primary sources' in its companion volume, *Dilecta*, to provide some most important unpublished materials from Ruskin's correspondence with Charles Eliot Norton; for, again, one of the daunting aspects of the polygon is how much that is vital for an understanding of Ruskin remains unpublished.

Some of these essays originated in a Ruskin symposium, held at the Humanities Center of the Johns Hopkins University in April 1978; those papers, extensively revised for this occasion, are joined by others specially commissioned. With one exception—an earlier version of Dr Crook's essay was delivered as a lecture before the Accademia Nazionale dei Lincei in May 1977 and published in their *Quaderno 241*—none of these essays has appeared before.

All quotations otherwise unidentified are from Ruskin's writings, with references given to the volume and page (thus, 16.187) of *The Works of John Ruskin (The Library Edition)*, ed. E. T. Cook and Alexander

Wedderburn, 39 vols. (1903–12); quotations from the diaries (signalled D.537) are from *The Diaries of John Ruskin 1835–1898*, ed. Joan Evans and John Howard Whitehouse, 3 vols. (Oxford, 1956). Writings by Ruskin still in copyright are quoted by permission of George Allen and Unwin Ltd and of the Ruskin Literary Trustees.

J.D.H.
F.M.H.

Oeuvre and footnote

John Dixon Hunt

My theme is simply how we should read Ruskin. There is, first of all, the sheer bulk of the *oeuvre*—not only the thirty-nine volumes of *The Works*, but close on as many more volumes of subsequently edited diaries, letters and other 'primary materials'. Then there is the problem of how to use all the material that Ruskin's editors, Cook and Wedderburn, crowded into their edition of the *Works*. Against the advice of Charles Eliot Norton, another of Ruskin's literary executors, Wedderburn argued that the Library Edition should be *all* Ruskin, and he and Cook accordingly included all books then available in other editions, all those out of print or available only in private printings; gathered all Ruskin's occasional articles, letters to newspapers and other scattered writings; collated the different editions published by Ruskin; reproduced not only all the illustrations which Ruskin had inserted in his works but also large numbers of his drawings as well as portraits, facsimiles of letters and manuscripts and photographs of Ruskin's 'haunts'; and, finally, for their introductions, footnotes and bibliographical annotations drew upon unpublished MSS, holographs of published books and letters and diaries. The result was and remains probably the richest mine of materials for the study of an English author ever established—yet a mine in parts largely unquarried, for who has not come across uncut pages in any 'Cook and Wedderburn' they have used?[1]

'All Ruskin is in his work,' wrote Robert Furneaux Jordan. 'One must take him whole or not at all.'[2] It is a law for the serious study of any writer, surely, but it would not be special pleading, I think, to claim that Ruskin above all must be taken 'whole'. There are special considerations, which will be more fully explored later, why Ruskin's *oeuvre* requires some overall scrutiny before any part of it is studied and why this is so in a different fashion from other writers— one must be his omnivorous, polymathic mind, which inevitably forged connections between its individual operations; another, less frequently argued but equally crucial, would be the enormous importance of Ruskin's youth, which provided him with all the major concerns of his subsequent career, which has consequently to be read as a continuous elaboration of early ideas and experience.

But even if it were readily acknowledged that Ruskin constitutes a special case, there would still remain the problem of *how* we are to take him whole. As usual, Ruskin himself somehow registered the difficulty. Not only his revisions, by themselves no more unusual than for other self-conscious authors, but his deletions from and additions to the *corpus* of his work represent his own adjudication of what he wished to establish as the core and therefore the structure of his writings: thus in the New Year of 1871:

> Being now fifty-one years old, and little likely to change my mind hereafter on any important subject of thought (unless through weakness of age),[3] I wish to publish a connected series of such parts of my works as now seem to me right. . . .
> The first book of which a new edition is required chances to be 'Sesame and Lilies', from which I now detach the old preface, about the Alps, for use elsewhere; and to which I add a lecture given in Ireland on a subject closely connected with that of the book itself. . . . [18.31]

Of his two major works, *Modern Painters* he came to feel should never be republished 'as a whole' (3.677), but he allowed some selections to be issued in 1875 as *Frondes Agrestes*, to which, however, he added thirty-four notes, and in 1884–85 as *In Montibus Sanctis* and *Coeli Enarrant* he planned to reissue the 'scientific portions' of *Modern Painters* 'on the origin of forms in clouds [and] mountains' (3.678), to which he also added new material as well as cross-references to *Deucalion* and *Proserpina*. With his other great work, *The Stones of Venice*, he was equally if not as radically revisionist: in the 1870s, at the instigation of Prince Leopold, he determined to revise his Venetian study, a project which gave rise immediately to a *Guide to the Principal Pictures in the Academy* (1877), between 1877 and 1884 to the parts of *St Mark's Rest*, subtitled *The History of Venice, written for the help of the few travellers who still care for her monuments*, and to the 'Travellers' Edition' of *Stones*.[4] And if these suggest only the indecisions and 'weaknesses of age', it must be remembered that the pattern of his earliest works was similarly composed of determined directions, then chance indirections, of writing himself into situations where he found he did not know enough to continue, then submitting himself to further research and travel. Thus the first volume of *Modern Painters* was reissued with a new preface before even the second appeared, its lengthy reconsideration of Ruskin's ambitions for the project seeking to accommodate new directions in his reading and thinking, while in the third edition of volume one many modifications were made to the original text; after the second volume of *Modern Painters* he diverted his energies into work that emerged first as *Seven Lamps of Architecture* and then *The Stones of Venice*; his return to the 'main' project with the third and fourth volumes of *Modern Painters* was inevitably a resumption of directions no longer as distinct as they had appeared ten years before with volume two, and indeed before the fifth and final volume could appear in 1860 Ruskin had announced fresh territories for his mind in *The Political Economy of Art* in 1857.

Such a pattern of thinking and writing might be seen to exemplify the idea he announced in a letter to Carlyle on the eve of the New Year, 1853: 'It is the worst of the minor incapacities of human life that one's opinions ought, by rights, to be tested and refitted every five years. They are the soul's clothes—and a healthy soul is always growing too big for its opinions and wanting them to be let out.'[5] The Teufelsdröckhan metaphor, apt enough homage to his correspondent, does not really suit the problem. It does not provide much critical purchase upon the phenomena of Ruskin's intellectual career, I suggest, simply to see him preparing to 'let out' the third and fourth volumes of *Modern Painters* now that the end of *The Stones of Venice* in 1853 is in sight. He himself considered that 'All *Modern Painters* together will be the explanation of a parenthesis in *The Stones of Venice*'.[6] This moves closer to what I would like to suggest as a more profitable approach to Ruskin's mind and writings —the notion of the footnote.

It was Hillis Miller who recognised in passing that Ruskin was 'one of the great masters in English of the footnote'.[7] The perception may be extended: for not only does Ruskin use the footnote and—by extension—the appendix most creatively, but the best model perhaps for describing his *oeuvre* is—paradoxically—the footnote, together with its more magisterial ancestor, the marginal gloss, and its maverick cousins, marginalia. Though Ruskin's own marginalia are not particularly striking,[8] his own exploitation of the footnote is thoroughly creative. A footnote on kingship in *Unto this Last*, for instance, blossoms into larger considerations of that theme in *Munera Pulveris* and *Sesame and Lilies*,[9] while the third chapter of *Munera Pulveris* was almost undermined by its notes, one of which (17.208–16) got elevated into the main text when the essays from *Fraser's Magazine* were issued in book form.

Now there is much to stimulate a reader of Ruskin in Lawrence Lipking's witty and perceptive essay 'The Marginal Gloss'.[10] He reminds us that Burnet's marginal commentary in *Telluris Theoria Sacra* of 1681 was printed as footnotes in eighteenth-century editions, and that such a revision of the habitual spaces of a page signals important intellectual changes. No longer did the Bible and God's other book, of Nature, constitute parallel authorities; a rival relationship of hard or literal fact, established in the main block of text, was set *over* against legend, myth, conjecture, hearsay, even gloss, which were now relegated sceptically to the notes below. But that in the version of 'The Ancient Mariner' which appeared in *Sibylline Leaves* of 1817 Coleridge recovers something of Burnet's original typography in order to harmonise the parts of his poem; for between the mysterious and gnomic verses and the gloss which knows the world makes sense and is not in thrall to the other's perspective there emerges—as the reader 'snakes'[11] back and forth between text and margin—a larger whole.

Now Ruskin seems to me to occupy an interesting position in this history of the gloss and the footnote. Belonging to the scientific age which placed its 'hard facts' in the text above notes which either simply provided sources or inveighed against earlier myth, conjecture and gloss, Ruskin also subscribed to the convictions of a Thomas Burnet that the natural world and the word of the Bible were parallel texts and to Coleridge's confidence in multiple perspectives. It is a vision that at least in the first place was inherited with his Scottish evangelicalism. Its typological structure did not ever really recover the typographical form of Burnet's page, but the strong conviction that Nature is God's book and is to be read side-by-side with the Bible inevitably affected the mode of Ruskin's writing. Furthermore, Bible and natural world are text and gloss (or gloss and text), and Ruskin invoked both as a gloss upon Turner's painting, which was in its turn a gloss upon the divine texts. This multiplicity of 'texts' in *Modern Painters*, texts which are also glosses, makes for difficult reading, no easier for the absence of any typographical help on the printed page; yet it is part of Ruskin's own difficulty that no satisfactory form offers itself to accommodate

his vision—the addition of brief explanatory marginal glosses in a
later edition of *Modern Painters* was rather a clue to the sequence of
thought than a proper recovery of Burnet's layout.[12] Similarly, in
the 1880 edition of *Seven Lamps of Architecture* (hardly the dizziest
of Ruskin's works to fathom) crucial passages were printed in thick
type—glosses on, from, and in the text; Ruskin's first thought had
been to issue some notes on the text separately (see 8.xlvii).

A more interesting mode of gloss/note also associated with the
Seven Lamps was Ruskin's provision of illustrations for its first
edition, an aspect of his books that became a permanent feature after
1848. 'There was never a writer before,' he told his father proudly,
'who could illustrate his own writings.'[13] Among the various manifestations of text-and-gloss/gloss-and-text which Ruskin's life and
works afford, that of word-and-image/image-and-word is central;[14]
even his division of the beauty perceived by the theoretic faculty
seems to cater to his verbal and visual skills—'Typical Beauty'
requiring the literary text as its commentary, 'Vital Beauty' needing
largely the draughtsman's skills (see 4.64). From an early age he was
composing works where visual and verbal languages collaborate,
creating facsimile 'books' after the manner of Rogers's *Italy*; his
picturesque tastes which necessarily brought word and image into
some conjunction were extended in both *Modern Painters* and the
interpolated architectural books by his writing about visual
materials. The provision of illustrations in 1848 for the *Seven
Lamps* gave the illusion of being the provision of objective facts,
upon which Ruskin's prose then served as gloss. Since he always
prided himself upon the accuracy of his drawings, the use of
'illusion' may seem unfair; but it is odd, and not a little begs a
central question in such a book, to offer his own drawings and
engravings of natural and architectural forms as proof of his *analyses*
of their originals. And this method of providing his arguments with
illustrations—even to the extent of his own reworking of details from
paintings of Claude or Turner—has never been discussed: it is, I
suggest, properly a question of text and gloss—are the illustrations
in Ruskin's books simply the 'citation' of sources (as in conventional
footnotes), are they glosses upon his verbal text, or are they the
essential visual text upon which the author writes his commentary?
The answer is that sometimes they are each in turn, sometimes and
more importantly, all together.

This *oeuvre* made up of an incremental series of notes must have
an original 'text' upon which to begin. With Ruskin, as it had been
with Montaigne,[15] this was his own life. His first important publication, the essays which formed *The Poetry of Architecture*, though
they assume a studied air of impersonality, were largely a commentary upon his own travel experiences; where these were insufficient

Ruskin merely indulged in some undergraduate bluffing.[16] The
essays are made up of glosses upon his favourite landscapes and their
indigenous buildings—the word 'gloss', Lipking reminds us, comes
from the Greek for tongue, and in *The Poetry of Architecture* we first
find the distinctive Ruskinian strategy of setting himself up as the
interpreter of the voices or languages of things:

> A mountain . . . does not *tell* this fact to our feelings, or, rather . . . *tells*
> us of no time at which it came into existence . . . But a very old forest
> tree . . . is always *telling* us about the past . . . [1.68][17]

But the essays also give tongue to his experiences of scenery and
architecture. It is also worth observing that as the essays proceed
they steadily lose their careful control of the rigorous enquiry and
acquire another characteristic Ruskinian habit of always needing
more space than had been envisaged for them: and as the subjects
grow and flourish in Ruskin's imagination, so long footnotes are
introduced to accommodate what we may register as central ideas,
but which for the author at that point are too important to waste and
yet not apt for the main text. One of these, by a publishing accident,
actually got itself printed separately (1.80).

The remainder of Ruskin's works after *The Poetry of Architecture*
all derive from the need to give tongue to his own life and contacts.
We in our turn—for no critic of Ruskin has ever escaped being his
biographer as well—are then forced to provide his works with marginal glosses from his life: many opinions and arguments in *Modern
Painters* and *The Stones of Venice* depended entirely on the accidents
of where Ruskin had travelled and what he chose to annotate at that
time. It became an ineluctable mode of his imagination at a very
early age to seize anything that lay to hand as stimulus; in some of
his youthful stories, written so evidently out of personal experience,
we get glimpses of this habit:

> such a fine day that they all got out and walked a good way they had
> intended to walk very quick but they did not for they were attracted by
> such a variety of objects such as the white major convolvulus in the
> hedges the black & white broad beans the butterfly like pea's the
> sparkling rivulets and winding rivers all combined their forces to make
> them walk slowly' [18]

It is, in miniature, a model of both single works and his *oeuvre*;
examples from his adult life would include his discovery of Tintoretto in 1845 or of some Veronese in 1858—'I unexpectedly found
some good Paul Veroneses at Turin' (7.6). The texts of books he
wrote are composed out of these often random encounters. And then
they are re-composed, as he discovers fresh materials and earns new
insights.[19]

Thus his own experiences acquire an ambiguous status as both text and gloss for his ideas (some examples will be examined later). In early books his own experience may be adduced to document his views; later books increasingly refer their readers for further documentation back to previous Ruskin works—professed autodidacts, Lipking suggests, habitually give references to their own writings: his example is Vico, but Ruskin would be another. He can give in one letter to his father a cross-reference to another four years before![20] The first footnote of *Praeterita*, significantly, uses his late work for the St George's Guild as a gloss upon his early visits as a boy to country houses, galleries and gardens (35.7). *Deucalion* resumed ideas first entertained and even written about in 1833 in Chamounix, while *Proserpina* took up some notions first canvassed in a footnote to *The Poetry of Architecture* on the treatment of flowers by Shelley and Shakespeare; both, according to Ruskin, had their source in his youthful poem 'Eudosia'.[21]

This strategy by which his *oeuvre* aspires to the condition of footnote and gloss has at least two distinct causes, though they are also closely related. The first is his lifelong determination to write about things that were for him more important than his own writings—mountains, Turner, Venetian and other Gothic architecture, social and economic health, botany, mineralogy; this sense of priority always meant that he was writing notes upon them. He was driven, he says, 'into literature that I might defend the power of painting' (see *Works*, 3.xxii) and, if we think of *Modern Painters*, into geology and natural history that he might be able to write that literature. The second cause of the note-like structure of his works is that, as the first implies, all his major interests as an adult writer were somehow initiated before he was twenty-one; the result is that many of the mature works are explicitly offered as extensions to, elaborate glosses upon, juvenile texts and his own early life.

Much of this is acknowledged by Ruskin, though the full significance of his tendency to cross-reference has, I think, been neglected. But there is also a hidden, implicit structure of glossing that is also crucial to his imagination, and it revolves around his lifelong determination to create some working relationship between his living self and his writing self. His career, from this perspective, may be seen as a constant effort to establish some liaison between two competing modes of existence: on the one hand, the world of myriad facts, to be carefully gathered and annotated in countless memoranda, an empirical world without end; on the other, the need to organise coherent, general principles. The most widely known version of this competition is *Praeterita*, a recollection of first things, undertaken among the last things that he did and in lucid moments of a steadily encroaching darkness. These *Outlines of Scenes and*

Thoughts perhaps Worthy of Memory in my Past Life, as its subtitle glossed the distancing and lapidary tones of the Latin title, reveal his instinct for myth and fiction and for salvaging some sustaining and healing visions from the world of experience.

An autobiography holds out, especially to a writer, the promise of some congruence between his life and his art. Ruskin was always obsessed by this: in 1852 he wrote to tell his father that 'I shall some day—if I live—write a great essay on Man's work, which will be the work of my life';[22] thirty years later he confessed to Kate Greenaway that 'the truth is my *Life* never went into my books at all. Only my time.'[23] At that point he was indeed putting his life into a book, namely *Praeterita*. Published in twenty-eight instalments, these essays in autobiography have, as we have come to realise,[24] a problematical relationship to the facts of his biography. Ruskin writes them not simply to disclose his early years, but to use these 'first things' as a commentary upon his subsequent career. Yet since, on his own admission, they avoid anything 'disagreeable or querulous' (35.49), they are also an attempt to invent a version of himself that he can live and die with.

Above all, *Praeterita* involves yet another adjudication between accumulation of facts and their glosses. Ruskin had at his disposal a vast archive of family papers. Yet he chose largely to ignore them. In *Praeterita* he told his readers that he knew very little about his parents; yet he had in his house at Brantwood 'all' the material that would establish their story.[25] Furthermore, he actually looked at it— the diary records in February 1885 'a terrible day of chagrins and difficulties; finding my Croydon Grandmothers last letters to my mother. . . .'[26] It is obvious that he simply could not bring himself to review the necessary documents—too painful, but also too formidable a bulk of materials—that would have provided the true basis for his autobiographical work. And, indeed, the pictures that *Praeterita* offers of his childhood—toyless and often joyless, without 'companionable beasts'—and the dismissive version of his time at Oxford ('I learned four dialogues of Plato—of Theology, the Thirty-Nine Articles;—of myself—or the world I was to live in—nothing') —these and much more of *Praeterita* are quite specifically qualified, even contradicted, by the family letters and his own diaries which he could have consulted at Brantwood.[27]

What he did, in fact, was to cannibalise sections of *Fors Clavigera*, re-using them with only minor changes as the initial chapters of *Praeterita*. He had chosen to write such passages in *Fors* because he felt that his wide-ranging coverage of social, economic and spiritual topics needed footnoting with references to his own background. Re-used in *Praeterita*, they had in their turn to be glossed and expanded: 'I fear the sequel may be more trivial, because much is concentrated in the foregoing broad statement, which I have now to continue by slower steps' (35.46); it was partly the changed context, above all its altered tone, that necessitated this extended commentary upon the condensed fragments of autobiography. In *Fors* they had been notes to a larger text; but even supplied with their own gloss in *Praeterita* they could not, in the end, stand by themselves. In 1886, when sixteen chapters of the autobiography had been issued, Ruskin began to publish selections of 'primary materials'—'Correspondence, Diary Notes, and Extracts from Books'—to illustrate and gloss the autobiography in its turn. The completion of both *Praeterita* and *Dilecta* (as this second compendium was called) was never achieved by Ruskin himself; his biographers and critics continue to add, as it were, to both volumes, but material for *Dilecta*—unpublished and published—seems (at least to some of us) infinite.[28] If a *Dilecta* were ever to be completed, it would, as footnotes, overwhelm the text of a finished *Praeterita*; indeed, it would probably become the text, with the chapters of autobiography its glosses.

These rivalries between text and footnote, life and autobiography, which I would suggest are an ineluctable dialogue of Ruskin's career, may be illustrated by one, more local, example. In April 1833, during the family's first major tour on the Continent, Ruskin saw the Alps from Schaffhausen. It had been perhaps a rather desultory Sunday, for the Ruskins on principle never travelled on the sabbath; so that towards sunset they found themselves, almost by accident, walking upon the terrace promenade above the Rhine. From there, for the first time, he saw the Alps, to which, as *Praeterita* put it half a century later, 'my heart and faith return to this day' (35.116). Now we have five ingredients of this crucial experience: the actual moment of sighting the Alps themselves—unrecoverable to Ruskin, let alone to us; a prose account written some time, maybe soon, afterwards; a versification of that, probably written the following winter when the family were back in England; then, many visits to the Alps over many years, recorded in various forms from an early scientific paper on 'Facts and Considerations on the Strata of Mont Blanc', published when Ruskin was fifteen (1.194–6), to sections of later books like *Modern Painters* and *Ethics of the Dust*; finally, *Praeterita*'s version of the original event in the light of Ruskin's subsequent career.

In 1833 the Alps offered themselves as a paradise; in the 1880s they were 'the seen walls of lost Eden' (35.115). In 1833 at Schaffhausen it was a Sunday, much insisted upon in both prose and verse accounts of the immediately succeeding months, and the sabbath aptly provided a 'revelation of the beauty of the earth, the opening of the first page of its volume' (*ibid.*, 116). But the end of his life required a less explicitly theological gloss upon that divine page and so the Alps in *Praeterita* become 'beautiful in their snow, and their humanity'. The text which they had opened for the fourteen-year-old Ruskin on his day of rest needed annotation for years afterwards, filling his days and even spilling over into Sundays that had before been sacrosanct. The poem he wrote in 1833 rather flaccidly announced:

> The Alps! the Alps!—Full far away
> The long successive ranges lay.
> Their fixed solidity of size
> Told that they were not of the skies. [2.367]

That 'told' is among the first of innumerable acknowledgements of a language in things, a gloss or tongue within a text that needs translation: 'not a leaflet', he would write about Gothic ornament, 'but speaks, and speaks far off too' (8.28).

For Ruskin in the late 1830s there were, he thought, two available languages in which to gloss, analogous to the two modes of diary-keeping he noted on 31 March 1840—'I have determined to keep one part of diary for intellect and another for feeling.' During the winter of 1833–34 he tried a studiedly scientific one for his first published paper, on 'The Causes of the Colour of the Water of the Rhone', which appeared in J. C. Loudon's *Magazine of Natural History* in September 1834 (1.191–2). This note upon another 'epiphany' of that summer of 1833 is carefully objective—even similes, for there are no metaphors, invoke scientific analogies. It is simply an 'Enquiry' as to why the Rhone, as it flows out of Lac Léman through the city of Geneva, is 'so transparent, that the bottom can be seen twenty feet below the surface, yet so blue, that you might imagine it to be a solution of indigo'. Ruskin seems to be submitting his fascination with the rush of water, at once headlong in its speed but seemingly a stationary mass, to the need for scientific explanation, though he himself provides no answers. Although he did not apparently treat of the Rhone in any alternative language, from his verses at the time it is obvious that a sub-Byronic effusion in the manner of *Childe Harold's Pilgrimage*—we have seen four verses of this sort on the Alps from Schaffhausen—would have served to accommodate the 'feeling' as opposed to 'intellectual' response.

Years later he returned in *Praeterita* to the topic he had so narrowly treated in the *Magazine of Natural History*. There is still some suggestion of 'technical work', the careful discrimination of optical and physical effects. But there is also a passionate refusal to be limited by the language of such considerations—at one point the autobiography actually uses the idea, specifically rejected in 1834, that the Rhone is blue because it obtains the colours of the glaciers whence it flows. That covert allusion makes the famous *Praeterita* passage an intricate gloss upon fifty years of 'text'; its opening implies a crucial contrast between natural jewels, like the river, and the work of the jeweller Bautte, in whose shop 'twenty steps' from the water Ruskin had bought his wife a bracelet in 1849:[29]

> For all other rivers there is a surface, and an underneath, and a vaguely displeasing idea of the bottom. But the Rhone flows like one lambent jewel; its surface is nowhere, its ethereal self is everywhere, the iridescent rush and translucent strength of it blue to the shore, and radiant to the depth.
>
> Fifteen feet thick, of not flowing, but flying water; not water, neither,—melted glacier, rather, one should call it; the force of the ice is with it, and the wreathing of the clouds, the gladness of the sky, and the continuance of Time.
>
> Waves of clear sea are, indeed, lovely to watch, but they are always coming or gone, never in any taken shape to be seen for a second. But here was one mighty wave that was always itself, and every fluted swirl of it, constant as the wreathing of a shell. No wasting away of the fallen foam, no pause for gathering of power, no helpless ebb of discouraged recoil; but alike through bright day and lulling night, the never-pausing plunge, and never-fading flash, and never-hushing whisper, and, while the sun was up, the ever-answering glow of unearthly aquamarine, ultra-marine, violet-blue, gentian-blue, peacock-blue, river-of-paradise blue, glass of a painted window melted in the sun and the witch of the Alps flinging the spun tresses of it for ever from her snow. [35.326-7]

If we respond to that visionary passage of water and prose, it is not because it is 'fine writing', but because we register in its language a tongue or gloss that articulates Ruskin's mind. It is partly that such careful apprehensions of the natural world are somehow cognate with self-apprehension; as *Praeterita* puts it some pages later, 'minute knowledge and acute sensation throw us back into ourselves' (*ibid.*, 404).

Both the larger example of *Praeterita*'s composition, intricately related to other works like *Fors* and *Dilecta*, and the smaller instance of his commentaries upon two important events of the 1833 Continental tour (themselves, in fact, linked—as alp and river are one) may serve as paradigms of Ruskin's mind and method of work. The dependence of all subsequent texts upon a first, usually the 'text' of himself, initiated a sequence of writings the status of which was always ambiguous.

At the centre of this complexity of *oeuvre*, I think, is the 'digression' into architectural work for *Seven Lamps*, which in its turn led to *Stones*. Something of Ruskin's scope is emblemised in the advertisement in the first edition of *Seven Lamps* for the next book: it tells us that there is 'In preparation' (though nothing is said of three volumes, nor of publication over two years) *The Stones of Venice*, which is 'uniform' with *The Seven Lamps of Architecture* and by the author of *Modern Painters*. One of the 'uniformities', of course, is Ruskin's conviction of the 'brotherhood between the cathedral and the alp'[30] and that the Gothic craftsman looked to other stones and natural things for inspiration. The stones of Chamounix and the stones of Venice were parallel texts. From an early age, owing partly to his picturesque tastes which endorsed his scrutiny of particulars and partly to his mineralising, Ruskin had attended to details, whether of mountains or of buildings; so that the ornaments of Venetian buildings, to which he devotes the majority of his space in *Stones* and which we might think of as something like marginalia on a building, become the main text for him, which he reads and glosses as he did natural phenomena in *Modern Painters I*.

At the stage in his son's work when *Modern Painters* was losing ground to the architectural work for *Seven Lamps* John James Ruskin wrote (on 25 May 1846) to his old friend and literary advisor, W. H. Harrison, from Venice:

> He is cultivating art at present, searching for real knowledge, but to you and me this is at present a sealed book. It will neither take the shape of picture nor poetry. It is gathered in scraps hardly wrought, for he is drawing perpetually, but no drawing such as in former days you or I might compliment in the usual way by saying it deserved a frame; but fragments of everything from a Cupola to a Cart-wheel, but in such bits that it is to the common eye a mass of Hieroglyphics —all true—truth itself, but Truth in mosaic. [8.xxiii]

And some eight years later, writing and still researching the second and third volumes of *The Stones*, Ruskin himself wrote to his father twice on the same day (18 January 1852) to confess his own frustration, even panic, with what his work entailed. First, he simply laid out the problem—that he had had only twelve months 'to examine piece by piece—buildings covering five square miles of ground—to read—or glance at—some forty volumes of history and chronicles—to make elaborate drawings . . . and to compose *my own book*'.[31] But then in the second letter he announced more revealingly:

> There is something burdensome in the vast breadth of the subject at present—It is all weighing on my brains at once, and I cannot devote my full mind to any part of it. As soon as I have it all down on paper— out of *danger* as it were—and well in sight, I can take up any part and finish it as highly as I like, but as soon as I begin to dwell on any bit carefully, thoughts come into my head about other parts—unfinished —which I am afraid of losing and then I go away and touch upon them.[32]

What is written down is, significantly, 'out of danger' and somehow controllable. What is as yet only projected threatens with its details and ramifications as yet uncoded and unrelated, one bit tempting the writer from another in an endless series of fragmentary rushes and *essais*. In 1877 he was still involved in the same problems, issuing the first supplement to *St Mark's Rest* with the prefatory advice that 'The following (too imperfect) account of the pictures by Carpaccio in the chapel of San Giorgio de' Schiavoni, is properly a supplement to the part of "St Mark's Rest" in which I propose to examine the religious mind of Venice in the fifteenth century' (24.335n). Supplements to work in progress but as yet unavailable are entirely typical of a temperament that in the 1830s was accurately described by Margaret Ruskin as spoiling 'a good beginning from not taking the trouble to think and concluding in a hurry'.[33] Hurried conclusions, in their turn, would often necessitate clarifications, either public or private, though by the time of *Fors* such distinctions seem to have been deliberately blurred. Indeed, *Fors Clavigera* as a whole should perhaps be read as Ruskin's last attempt to establish a form flexible enough to accommodate the writings of his life and mind. Its very title acknowledges the chances that direct his writing.

Something of Ruskin's imaginative skill at shaping his various texts can be examined best at the point where he brings *Modern Painters* to a conclusion. He had interrupted this work after two volumes, letting his architectural books—*Seven Lamps* and *The Stones of Venice*—expand upon the consideration of early Christian art in *Modern Painters II*.[34] But when he resumed *Modern Painters* those architectural writings seemed (increasingly to Ruskin) to be metamorphosed from gloss to crucial text, to which later volumes of what started as the defence of Turner assume the status of notes in their turn. As he brings *Modern Painters* to its conclusion with lengthy expositions of Turner's *Garden of the Hesperides* and *The Python Slain by Apollo* (see figs. 7 and 9) and their coda, the very last[35] chapter entitled 'Peace', Ruskin strives to draw all his experience and work into their pages. Despite the cumbersome segment of text involved (7.389–460), it is worth examining its structures more carefully.

In the first place, we may notice how the footnotes proliferate as Ruskin tries to gather in the work of seventeen years: they refer readers to other works, to 'various statements made respecting colour in different parts of my works' now collected into a 'system' in one huge footnote to the second painting discussed,[36] to Ruskin's redrawing of Turner details, to now altered facts of European topography ('the railroad bridge over the Falls of Schaffhausen') which have been crucial to him, to *projected* work on 'benevolent and helpful action towards the lower classes', or to work on Turner 'being as yet impossible'. Then the second painting is invoked to serve as a commentary upon the first: 'The [second] picture is at once the type, and the first expression of a great change which was passing in Turner's mind' (one of the many places here when I feel that what Ruskin writes about Turner is covertly or unconsciously a gloss upon his own history). Further, and most important, the defence of Turner that has been the ostensible *raison d'être* of *Modern Painters* is intertwined with the cultural history of Venice that was narrated in *The Stones* so that each text may serve as gloss upon the other. This intertwining bears unravelling.

The titles of the two chapters devoted to Turner paintings ('The Nereid's Guard' and 'The Hesperid Aeglé') announce only gnomic-ally how Ruskin will gloss their images; thus they are a type of the pictures themselves. He refers the reader first to his *Notes on the Turner Collection* and singles out his emphasis there on Turner's 'generally gloomy tendency of mind', with which he is 'only' con-cerned in the following sixty pages. Turner's temperament is a gloss on (tongue for) the condition of England, but to understand the full implications of this Ruskin must first invoke the Greek myths which Turner is said to paint (though it soon becomes un-clear whether picture or myth is text or gloss):

> How far he had really found out for himself the collateral bearings of the Hesperid tradition I know not; but that he had got the main clue of it, and knew who the Dragon was, there can be no doubt; the strange thing is, that his conception of it throughout, down to the minutest detail, fits every one of the circumstances of the Greek tradition.

To elucidate these traditions requires a text from Hesiod, which Ruskin translates and footnotes—he is, as Hillis Miller observed,[37] an 'interrogator of origins', which explains his determination to 'look to the precise meaning of Hesiod's words'. Collateral texts from Dante and Spenser, equally in need of glossing, threaten to extend the materials indefinitely (but 'We must yet keep to Dante, however'), The typologies that Ruskin establishes are, of course, a series of parallel texts, each as authoritative as the others; this structure of meaning authorises further parallels—the dragon's body in Turner's *Hesperides* is a nearly perfect representation of glacier movement; the mythologies of sea recall Venetian history; the sea dragon parallels the serpent in Eden (Ruskin refers us to his earlier genealogies of dragons[38]) and thus is a type of all corruptions of paradise; this sea dragon, Geryon, is the 'evil spirit of wealth', and the implied comparison with Venetian history then surfaces clearly when the Goddess of Discord, present in Turner's *Hesper-ides*, is glossed by Ruskin's allusion to his own discussion of the Ducal Palace—'remember the inscription there, *Discordia sum, discordans*'. And so via evil wealth and disharmony in the Venetian paradise we begin to see how Turner's England ('a paradise of smoke . . . the Assumption of the Dragon') and the early Christian worlds of which Venice was a type are connected; both feature St George, and Turner, contrary to *Modern Painters III*, is now acknowledged to have been 'educated under the influence of Gothic art'.

The following chapter extends and ultimately clarifies that connection; the destinies of England and Venice are once again compared, as they had been at the very start of *The Stones* ('. . . the thrones of Tyre, Venice and England'). Turner's second painting images the 'worm of decay'; his vision is increasingly, we are told, of 'Ruin, and twilight'—a long passage on Turner's attraction to English ruins distantly recalls the 'ruin' of Venice, also adumbrated at the very start of *Stones*. And via Turner's own obsession with the fate of Tyre we arrive, finally, at Turner's intense imaginative response to Venice herself, the type of that 'death which attends the vain pursuit of beauty':

> How strangely significative, thus understood, those last Venetian dreams of his become, themselves so beautiful and so frail; wrecks of all that they were once—twilights of twilight!

The scarlet colour which Turner 'dared' to paint and a discussion of which rather inexplicably filled the opening pages of this chapter is now glossed by Giorgione's scarlet frescoes on the Fondaco dei Tedeschi ('sanguigna e fiammeggiante, per cui le pitture cominciarono con dolce violenza a rapire il cuore delli genti'); seen by Ruskin ten years before, and already fading then, the frescoes are an emblem of Venice—decaying; yet by the Sea Sybil, Deiphobe, who has twice appeared in preceeding pages, Venice's 'enchanted voice' will for ever tell of 'faithful light and truth'. Now, in a footnote to his very last paragraph, Ruskin explains the engraving of a Giorgione woman, placed without explanation at the start of the chapter:

> My impression is that the ground of the flesh in these Giorgione frescoes had been pure vermilion; little else was left in the figure I saw. Therefore, not knowing what power the painter intended to personify by the figure at the commencement of this chapter, I have called her, from her glowing colour, Hesperid Aeglé.

As prose explication of Turner's visual images Ruskin's chapters are hardly lucid. But his verbal imagination—this is, significantly, juxtaposed to Turner's 'silence'—subsumes the paintings into a larger meditation, difficult in its allusions and intricate patterns of analogy and gloss, on the histories of England and Venice, Turner and Giorgione. We are dealing, in fact, with a verbal fabric that has all the density and elliptic structures of poetry, in much the way that

Ruskin himself expatiates on 'the Real Nature of Greatness of Style' in *Modern Painters III*:

> Let us therefore look into the facts of the thing, not with any meta-physical, or otherwise vain and troublesome effort at acuteness, but in a plain way; for the facts themselves are plain enough, and may be plainly stated, only the difficulty is, that out of these facts, right and left, the different forms of misapprehension branch into grievous complexity, and branch so far and wide, that if once we try to follow them, they will lead us quite from our mark into other separate, though not less interesting, discussions. [5.48]

That the misapprehensions ('not less interesting') are connected to the plain facts by some organic growth makes the task of distinguishing them problematical for Ruskin and for the reader. It ensures, too, as Hillis Miller remarked, that any one of Ruskin's books is in fact potentially endless.[39] One end to which these final sections of *Modern Painters* that I have been examining gesture is Ruskin himself; they have often the strength of personal identification, not only by involvement in their topic, but by a sub-stratum of personal metaphor discovered in other materials. This is initiated in the reader's mind, first, by the cross-references Ruskin supplies to his other writings and by the allusions to other obsessions like geology, climate and marriage; then, by his stress upon Turner's 'Education amidst country possessing architectural remains of some noble kind', which so evidently accounts for Ruskin's own work from *The Poetry of Architecture* to *The Stones of Venice*. Finally, when he treats of 'Rose and cankerworm', I hear in his celebration of the former his awareness that its 'loveliness and kindness' have already found their embodiment in Rose La Touche, first encountered in the autumn of 1858.[40]

The last chapter, 'Peace', is Ruskin's exorcism of the daemon that has kept him at work on *Modern Painters* through seventeen years and five other collateral volumes: 'Looking back over what I have written, I find that I have only now the power of ending this work,— it being time that it should end, but not of "concluding" it; for it has led me into fields of infinite inquiry, where it is only possible to break off with such imperfect result as may, at any given moment, have been attained.' To which might be added—and which at any moment may be resumed. For this is exactly the difficulty of reading Ruskin 'whole': that even as he ends he is aware both of beginnings and of future work; that he realises nothing can stand alone (this partly because he was such a polymath) and that each text requires and represents the notation of others, finished or yet unbegun.

By now it is perhaps clear how singularly inappropriate are the conventional criticisms of Ruskin's propensity to be led away from 'one' topic by 'digressions'; yet from his mother onwards commentators have looked askance at what Townsend, for example, calls Ruskin's 'inability to avoid digressions' or his being 'constitutionally unfitted to avoid digressions'.[41] As early as *The Poetry of Architecture* 'digressions' and footnotes announced his typical absorption in many things simultaneously or at random—footnotes at least evade writing's usual insistence upon sequence and permit two texts almost equal status on the same page. Ruskin was even encouraged by his editor, J. C. Loudon, who said he could not be too diffusive![42]

But it is important to insist that this tendency was creative rather than just pathological. When he excuses his modes of proceeding in *Modern Painters*—'they will lead us quite from our mark into other separate, though not less interesting, discussions' (5.48)—he is in fact attempting to establish connections between things generally considered to be different. His later writings especially have this tendency to synthesise 'separate branches of knowledge into "grammars" for the schools of the Guild of St George'.[43] Indeed, a perfect emblem of Ruskin's imaginative energy in relating the disparate objects of his study would be the museum that he started to establish for the Guild, which had its prototypes in his collections for the Oxford Drawing Schools, his dream in 1852 of an ideal Turner Gallery, and the Oxford Museum ('my habits of system could only be of use if I took the thing wholly in hand'[44]). But, like everything else in Ruskin's career, this idea of a museum in which wide-ranging interests might be accommodated without needing to give priority to any one was encountered very early in his life, at the famous Crosthwaite's Museum in Keswick during the family tour of the Lakes in 1830.[45] In this bewilderingly eclectic display were presented, *inter alia*, 'several old manuscript books, written before printing', 'the rib of a man, 21 feet high!!' and some 'musical stones' of the sort that Ruskin was to have made for himself in the 1880s. Faced with such an indiscriminate profusion of objects collected and displayed by one man and received with the same spread of interest by the Ruskins, it is difficult to talk of incoherence, irrelevance or digression. The same dedication to a seemingly inchoate mass of items, ideas and pursuits never ceased to enthral Ruskin. He was a true, old-fashioned virtuoso, the keeper certainly in spirit and often in fact of one of those cabinets of curiosities where each item has equal authority with any other, where coherence lies simply in the *tout ensemble*. Thus it is, I suggest, that the Ruskin Museum at Coniston, with its early Ruskin manuscripts 'written before printing', its mineral cases, stone harmonicum, local history display, model of Ruskin's boat and so on, is an absolutely authentic memorial of him. It lacks only his own imaginative framework, a coherence in which text and note are one—and the other.

NOTES   1 For a further discussion of related aspects of the bibliographical status of Ruskin's *oeuvre* see the second section of the chapter by B. E. Maidment in this volume.

2 *Victorian Architecture* (1966), p. 170.

3 Yet see the remark in a letter to Carlyle quoted below, p. 3 and note 5, which expresses a contrary viewpoint and one that I would find truer of Ruskin's *lifelong* instincts towards his past work.

4 For further material on these versions of *The Stones* see the relevant bibliographical sections of *Works*: namely 9.liii–lx and (for *St Mark's Rest*) 24.143–4, 195–9 and the general introduction to the whole volume. In the Beinecke Library at Yale (MS Vault/Shelves/Ruskin) are some pages of the 1874 edition of *Stones* showing Ruskin's reworking of them for the Travellers' Edition.

5 Letter to Carlyle, National Library of Scotland, 2624.

6 10.xlvii. The parenthesis he refers to is that which explains the modern taste in landscape painting as compensation for the loss of picturesque architecture (10.207). But Ruskin has various other ways of explaining the connection between these works: in 1852 he wrote that 'The last part of this book [*Stones*] will be an introduction to the last of *Modern Painters*' (10.208n).

7 'Myth as "Hieroglyph" in Ruskin', *Studies in the Literary Imagination*, VIII (1975), p. 15.

8 Some of them may be consulted in 34. Robert Hewison has drawn attention to the marginalia in Ruskin's copy of Mill's *Principles of Political Economy*, now in the British Library.

9 The point is made by Robert Hewison, *John Ruskin. The Argument of the Eye* (1976), pp. 151 and 154.

10 *Critical Inquiry*, III (1977), pp. 609–55.

11 Coleridge himself invokes the serpent (Lipking, *loc. cit.*, p. 620), but Lipking glosses this in his turn with Valéry's invocation of the snake of intellect or self-consciousness and his association of the mind's return upon itself with the need to discover variant expressions.

12 Most readily available in the frequently found 'edition in small form' (and in dark green binding) of *Modern Painters*, published by George Allen in 1897.

13 *Ruskin's Letters from Venice 1851–52*, ed. J. L. Bradley (New Haven, 1955), p. 199.

14 I have explored this more fully in my '*Ut pictura poesis*, the picturesque, and John Ruskin', *M.L.N.*, XCII (1978), pp. 794–818; see also the relevant section of Richard L. Stein, *The Ritual of Interpretation* (Cambridge, Mass., 1975) and George Hersey's chapter in this volume.

15 'And finding my selfe afterward wholy unprovided of subject, and void of other matter; I have presented my selfe unto my selfe for a subject to write, and argument to descant upon', in 'Of the Affection of Fathers to their Children'.

16 For he implies that he knows the south of Italy and Spain, when in fact at that time he had not been south of Milan.

17 My italics. For more on this emphasis of Ruskin's see my essay cited in note 14.

18 Beinecke Library, Yale University, Poetry Notebooks III, f. 6.

19 Thus in the 1870s he can say, 'I find so much more beauty than I

used to [in Venice], because I had never time to look for it rightly, doing the technical work of the *Stones*' (24.xxxvii). And in 1877 he told a lecture audience that he could now see that 'the essential business' of *Modern Painters* went 'beyond' Turner (22.512).

20 *Letters from Venice*, p. 254.

21 For *Deucalion* see 26.97, *inter alia*; for *Proserpina*, 25; there are many references in both these books to his earlier work. For *The Poetry of Architecture* see 1.157–8; for 'Eudosia', 2.269–71.

22 *Letters from Venice*, p. 177.

23 Pierpont Morgan Library, MS 2010, 429.

24 This is discussed by Helen Gill Viljoen, *Ruskin's Scottish Heritage* (Urbana, Illinois, 1956) and in *The Ruskin Family Letters*, ed. Van Akin Burd, 2 vols. (New York, 1973).

25 So he told his later editor, Cook: see 35.lv.

26 D.1099—the experience was 'humiliating and grievous', he noted.

27 The references to *Praeterita* are 35.20, 36 and 610. Even a brief consultation of *The Family Letters* will reveal how much either proposition is untrue.

28 See the letters edited in this volume by Jeffrey Spear for a few more contributions to this infinite *Dilecta*.

29 Mary Lutyens, *The Ruskins and the Greys* (1972), p. 191.

30 10.188, but see also 9.xxii, D.450 and 453, and *Letters from Venice*, pp. 54 (where he compares the Campanile to the Aiguille Dru!), 71 and 163. The comparison is evidently an older, eighteenth-century commonplace, for, as Denis Lambin has kindly pointed out to me, it occurs in William Windham II of Felbrigg's *Account of the Glaciers or Ice Alps in Savoy* (1741), p. 8: 'These Valleys, although at the Top of a high Mountain, are surrounded with other Mountains; the Tops of which being naked and craggy Rocks, shoot up immensely high; something resembling old *Gothic* Buildings or Ruines.'

31 *Letters from Venice*, p. 140, my italics—to suggest that he saw Venice as a prior book; cf. 'The idea of reading a building as we would read Milton or Dante' (10.206).

32 *Letters from Venice*, p. 141. Some letters he wrote for the *Times* (but his father would not send) on taxation, franchise and education were done 'because I want to be able to refer to them in the future [*ibid.*, p. 219].

33 *The Ruskin Family Letters*, p. 187.

34 See 10.xlvii *ff.* for Ruskin's own sense of this expansion.

35 Last, that is, until the 'Epilogue', added in 1888. And he added another gloss on Turner's python in a footnote to his preface for *The Economist of Xenophon* (31.13). For another discussion of these passages from *Modern Painters V* see Marc Simpson's chapter below, where there are some further quotations from this long section on Turner's paintings.

36 For commentary on Ruskin's ideas of colour see the chapter by Stephen Bann in this volume.

37 *Loc. cit.* (see note 7), p. 17.

38 As the reader here is invited to consult Marc Simpson's chapter below.

39 *Loc. cit.*, p. 16.

40 See the introduction to *John Ruskin and Rose La Touche. Her unpublished Diaries of 1861 and 1867*, ed. Van Akin Burd (Oxford, 1980).

41 F. G. Townsend, *Ruskin and the Landscape Feeling* (Urbana, Illinois, 1951), pp. 4 and 5. Cook and Wedderburn, too, make similar complaints: see 8.xix and xxvii and 10.xlv. For Ruskin's own, more astute, view ('I'm digressive when I do but talk of digression') see *Iteriad*, ed. J. S. Dearden (Newcastle-upon-Tyne, 1969), p. 99.

42 *The Ruskin Family Letters*, p. 521.

43 Hewison, *op. cit.* (see note 9), p. 177.

44 Bodleian Library MS Eng. Letts. C.36, f. 94. See also fig. 16 below. I discuss Ruskin's career-long involvement with the idea of museums and the consequences for his imagination in a forthcoming paper for the British Society of Comparative Literature. But see also George L. Hersey's chapter below.

45 For more details of Crosthwaite's Museum see both *Iteriad, ed. cit.*, pp. 74–5, and the relevant pages of my forthcoming biography of Ruskin, *The Wider Sea*.

The dream of the dragon: Ruskin's serpent imagery

MARC A. SIMPSON

January 22 Thursday. Calm lake and clearing sky. . . . [P]lanned for lecture—on snakes. The seer—ophis—that sees and holds its tongue—the lark—latet alauda, latet anguis—one, mute, the other heavenly voiced. The speechless forked tongue?—a double tongue never *can* say anything—Basilisk sight. The Evil Eye. If thine eye be evil! *Robin* without an eye in modern science—so owl!—Then Rod and Serpent slavery of rod—or of subtlety? Cadmus—teeth—then Two Horse Guards! Q[uestion] of fangs? of London! Dive to Duck—coo into quack. Woodwalk into ground waddle,—and water dabble—

Then the colours. Hunts doves—Turners. Duck variegation—vulgar violent.—But the main point Speckle—Stigma. Spot. Clouding. Wings like a dove—*you* don't want wings and rest—you want bellies—and lots of going on them.[1]

This allusive passage from the Brantwood diary, with the hurried dash almost the sole punctuation, served John Ruskin as an outline for a lecture which he titled 'A Caution to Snakes', and which he delivered, appropriately enough, on St Patrick's Day, 1880. The event was an inspired piece of showmanship, at one point including two reluctant officials at opposite ends of the stage with the skin of a boa constrictor stretched between them while Ruskin, having leaped nimbly upon his lecture table, described the predatory action of the giant snake, 'with appropriate gesture', to the delight and applause of his startled audience.[2] Later printed with illustrations (see fig. 8) as 'Living Waves', a chapter in *Deucalion, Volume II*, this lecture contains Ruskin's most concentrated treatment of the serpent. Yet even a cursory examination of his remaining works reveals a surprising quantity of serpentine references and allusions (fig. 1) which not only span his entire career but continually shift in their message and import.

The cryptic catalogue of snake-inspired associations entered in the Brantwood diary evolved finally, in Ruskin's word, into comic 'badinage'.[3] Only rarely did he find the topic this playful. More often the image of the serpent was rife with disturbing resonances, particularly (though by no means solely) as it appeared in the more private prose of his letters, diaries and unpublished manuscripts. Ruskin himself, however, in his examination of Keat's *Lamia*, excuses our prying interest in these patches of horror:

I
John Ruskin,
Study of a carved
dragon

A healthy and practical farmer, meeting a viper in his field, regards it simply as one of the creatures ranged under the general term of 'vermin'—kills it—throws it over the hedge out of his way, and pro-

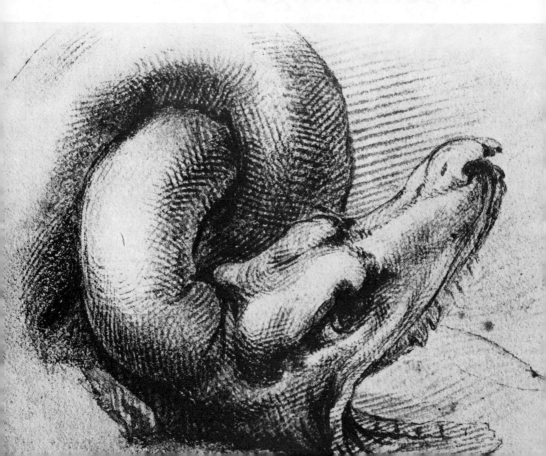

ceeds in his walk—whistling. A sick and sorrowful poet, meeting the same creature, pauses—watches, follows, irritates it—takes a strange pleasure in looking into its eyes, and hearing it hiss; and measuring the concentric circles of its prepared coil. Presently it uncoils itself and glides away. The youth watches the waving of the long grass over its body—. . . half fascinated and wishing to be bitten. Goes home, and dreams of it, intensified into a fiery serpent by his mistress's last frown —rises utterly ill and miserable, and writes 'Lamia'. . . .

It will follow from these general considerations, that so far as a mind of pure make, and powerful imagination is either (1) affected by a noble, but doubtful and faithless compassion for the agony of world— or (2) by remorse for carnal sin, and by weakness of body, it will be liable to fits of fear, and correspondent visions of terrible things . . . which at first sight it will be difficult to distinguish from the perpetual and base horror of wicked men. If we do not find [great men] doing this . . . we may be sure they are disguising something from us—hiding their fear, and not speaking from their hearts—in other words, that they are verily not great men, though we thought them so. [4.379–80]

Prompted initially by his consideration of Keats's transformation of the everyday serpent into the vehicle of artistic expression, Ruskin sought to utilise comparable 'pieces of horror' as criteria for his analyses of naturalist paintings. But these same two explanations of darkness within a moral man's work, propensity to carnal sin and compassion for the misery of the world, are in fact two crucial elements of Ruskin's own biography. And, in a fashion analogous to Keats, it is sometimes Ruskin's probing into and utilisation of this horror of the serpent that, through his art, reveal these two elements to us. As he wrote in *Modern Painters V*, '. . . all great and beautiful work has come of first gazing without shrinking into the darkness. . . . the dragon breath of it' (7.271).

Of course, with a writer as prolific as Ruskin, we must not be surprised at the occasional appearance of neutral references to the serpent. In the diaries, as early as 1835, the young Ruskin records seeing mottled green and yellow snakes at Aosta and Vevey (D.34), and such relatively harmless narratives recur until at least 1884 (D.1073). Indeed, in *The Eagle's Nest* (1872) he tells of meeting a rather charming grey serpent whom he praises for its 'calculating wisdom . . . exquisite grace, strength, and precision of the action' (22.197). As late as 1887, a metaphoric serpent could find a comfortable place in the old man's fondest memories of childhood. Writing of an early home:

. . . the windows of it, fortunately for me, commanded a view of a marvellous iron post, out of which the water-carts were filled through beautiful little trapdoors, by pipes like boa-constrictors; and I was never weary of contemplating that mystery, and the delicious dripping consequent. . . . [35.15–6]

Moreover Ruskin supported a scholarly interest in the serpent, as evidenced by his citations from contemporary ophiological works such as Richard Owen's *On The Anatomy of Vertebrates, Vol. 1, Fishes & Reptiles* (1866), Thomas Bell's *History of British Reptiles* (2nd ed., 1849), *The Thanatophidia of India* by J. Fayrer (2nd ed., 1874), and Albert Günther's *The Reptiles of British India* (1864), among others (19.363, 26.296–7). It was, after all, the 'fortuitous hearing' of a lecture on snakes delivered by T. H. Huxley at the London Institution on 1 December 1879 that induced Ruskin to deliver the already mentioned 'A Caution to Snakes' in place of his scheduled lecture on geology (26.296).

Sometimes Ruskin's use of the serpent image betrays an ambivalent attitude. In his account of Greek mythology in *The Queen of the Air* (1869) he elaborated on the positive, chthonic powers attributed to the serpent by the ancients, including its association with Aesculapius and Hygieia as a healing spirit, and as carrier of the gods' wisdom at Delphi. Throughout the passage Ruskin characterised the serpent as emblematic of the accepting, generative and purifying power of the earth (19.364).4 He compromised this positive tone, however, by prefacing these comments with terse pronouncements of the serpent's evil:

> But it is the strength of the base element that is so dreadful in the serpent; it is the very omnipotence of the earth. . . . the clothed power of the dust . . . the grasp and sting of death. [19.362–3]

Ruskin summarised the 'continual change in the interpretation put upon [the serpent] in various religions' (19.363) four years later in *Fors Clavigera* (February 1873):

> That it [the dragon/serpent] is an indisputably living and venomous creature, materially, has been the marvel of the world, innocent and guilty, not knowing what to think of the terrible worm; nor whether to worship it, as the Rod of their lawgiver, or to abhor it as the visible symbol of the everlasting Disobedience. [27.483]

As this small sample indicates, Ruskin's writings encompass many facets of the snake's reputation. Yet it is the negative references that dominate in his works. As early as 1846, in *Modern Painters II*, he asserted the primal evil of the symbolic serpent in a beautiful passage saying, 'No man's soul is alone; Laocoon or Tobit, the serpent has it by the heart or the angel by the hand' (4.281). This antagonism to the serpent was, moreover, a feeling which became ever more violent as time passed. The process of this thought appears in Ruskin's reaction to medieval art. In 1851 he wrote of the dragon form admiringly, as evocative of the sublime:

The forms of the serpent and lizard exhibit almost every element of beauty and horror in strange combination; the horror, which in an imitation is felt only as a pleasurable excitement, has rendered them favourite subjects in all periods of art . . . the unity of both lizard and serpent in the ideal dragon, the most picturesque and powerful of all animal forms, and of peculiar symbolical interest to the Christian mind, is perhaps the principal of all the materials of mediaeval picturesque sculpture. . . . The best and most natural representations of mere viper or snake are to be found interlaced among their confused groups of meaningless objects. The real power and horror of the snake-head has, however, been rarely reached. I shall give one example from Verona of the twelfth century. [9.276–7][5]

But by 1869 he had hardened his viewpoint and attacked the serpent with virulence:

. . . in its best times there were deep corruptions . . . infecting Christianity . . . with fatal terror of doctrine, and ghastliness of symbolic conception, passing through fear into frenzied grotesque, and thence into sensuality.

In the Psalter of St. Louis itself,[6] half of its letters are twisted snakes; there is scarcely a wreathed ornament, employed in Christian dress, or architecture, which cannot be traced back to the serpent's coil; and there is rarely a piece of monkish decorated writing in the world, that is not tainted with some ill-meant vileness of grotesque. [19.365]

The change is dramatic. Rather than the ambivalent tone of the 1851 passage there is an explosion of condemnatory expletives: fatal terror, frenzied grotesque, sensuality, vileness. Ruskin's view of the serpent's evil culminated in 'Living Waves':

And again, whatever may be the doubtful meanings of the legends invented among all those nations of the earth who have ever seen a serpent alive, one thing is certain, that they have all felt it to represent to them, in a way quite inevitably instructive, the state of an entirely degraded and malignant human life. [26.324]

What are the sources of this progressive, unequivocal hatred of the serpent?

For Ruskin, raised on the Bible, passages from Genesis were his earliest acquaintance with the serpent tribe, an introduction on the whole unflattering to the snake: "Now the serpent was more subtil than any beast of the field which the LORD God had made" (Gen. 3:1). Eve and the serpent enter into conversation, the fatal fruit is plucked, enjoyed, shared. As Orestes Brownson wrote in 1873, 'It was through the seductions of the woman, herself seduced by the serpent, that man fell.'[7] According to Genesis:

And the man said, The woman whom thou gavest to be with me, she gave me of the tree, and I did eat. And the LORD God said unto the woman, What is this that thou hast done? And the woman said, The serpent beguiled me, and I did eat. And the LORD God said unto the serpent, Because thou hast done this, thou art cursed above all cattle, and every beast of the field; upon thy belly shalt thou go, and dust shalt thou eat all the days of thy life: And I will put enmity between thee and the woman, and between thy seed and her seed; it shall bruise thy head, and thou shalt bruise his heel. [Gen. 3:12-15]

And that serpent is none other than Satan, the arch-enemy of God and man, as revealed in Revelation 12:9:

And the great dragon was cast out, that old serpent, called the Devil, and Satan, which deceiveth the whole world: he was cast out into the earth, and his angels were cast out with him.

The nature of the original sin, as Brownson intimates, was assumed to be carnal. C. Staniland Wake, author of *Serpent Worship and Other Essays with a Chapter on Totemism*, observed in 1888, '... the "eating of the forbidden fruit" was simply a figurative mode of expressing the performance of the act necessary to the perpetuation of the human race'.[8] The serpent is thus associated with dangerous sensuality. For example, the *Eclectic Review* of 1806 warned its readers of the dangers lurking within Thomas Moore's poetry in a review which equates the serpent with sensual sin, complete with alliteration and onomatopoetic sibillants:

If, then, in the perusal of these voluptuous volumes, [the reader] finds himself fascinated with their beauty, let him tremble, let him fly; it is the beauty, it is the fascination of the serpent, of the Old Serpent, which ought to inspire terror and repugnance, while it is tempting, attracting, delighting him into destruction. . . . The danger lies in dallying with sin, and with sensual sin above all other: it works, it winds, it wins its way with imperceptible, with irresistible insinuation.[9]

Ruskin himself said essentially the same thing, if less snakily:

Now the things which are the proper subjects of human fear are twofold: those which have the power of Death, and those which have the nature of Sin . . . [T]he serpent . . . appears to unite the deathful and sinful natures in the most clearly visible and intelligible form. [11.166]

Serpent, sin, death and sensuality—the four elements twine together, marking the serpent, for Ruskin, as 'the divine hieroglyph of the demoniac power of the earth,—of the entire earthly nature' (19.363). Lurking within the serpent's flesh, 'clumsy and vile—a mere morbid secretion and phosphatus prop of flesh', lies 'the grasp and sting of death' (19.61; 19.363).

If the Old Testament serpent carries the weight of man's sexual guilt, nonetheless the entire burden cannot rest upon a serpentine form. For many of us, owing in large part to pictorial conventions,[10] the serpent in the Garden is a hybrid, part human and part snake. Ruskin wrote of the creature as it appears in Michelangelo's Sistine Ceiling:

> ... the serpent with the human head, and body twisted round the tree, was the universally-accepted symbol of the evil angel, from the dawn of art up to Michel Angelo. [5.261]

Nor is it enough to say merely human without specifying gender, for this and a vast number of examples conflate the serpent's trunk with the torso and head of a beautiful woman. In another context Ruskin specifically mentioned this configuration:

> ... half-maiden, half-serpent; ... she is the spirit of all the fatallest evil, veiled in gentleness; or, in one word, treachery;—having dominion over many gentle things;—and chiefly over a kiss. [7.399]

This association of woman and viper becomes a recurrent theme in Ruskin's literary and visual works, as well as appearing often in his recorded dreams. But the merging of female and reptile is no mere symbol from the past, a carrier of literary meaning. Rather, in a highly disturbing fashion, the characters of the literal or metaphoric hybrid are Ruskin's contemporaries, its setting is the present.

2
J. E. Millais, *Sketches for 'Natural Ornament', following a suggestion by John Ruskin*, c.1853, pen and sepia ink

One of the earliest of these hybrids appeared in a letter which Ruskin wrote to his father from Italy on 12 September 1858:

> One of the finest things I saw at Turin was a group of neglected children at play on a heap of sand—one girl of about ten, with her black hair over her eyes and half-naked, bare-limbed to above the knees, and beautifully limbed, lying on the sand like a snake. [36.291]

This girl's body, like Veronese's *Solomon and the Queen of Sheba*, acted on Ruskin as a revelation of the physical world. His prose celebrations of both these sights marked his break with Evangelicalism and his corollary conversion to the world.[11]

Some foretaste of this conjunction of woman and snake is present in a John Millais drawing of Effie Ruskin wearing a costume suggested by Ruskin's theories of natural ornament (fig. 2). Here Effie calmly bears rats and reptiles as part of her garb: salamanders climb her arm; squirrels roost on her hair and breast; beneath the bat-winged owl a giant snake makes a partial appearance.[12]

But the easy, positive association of woman and serpent in these examples, part of Ruskin's homage to unbridled exuberance and sensuality, was short-lived. By 1867 he would write of a twelve-year-old girl's dance:

> A dance, so called, which consisted only in a series of short, sharp contractions and jerks of the body . . . made to the sound of two instruments . . . [reminding one] partly of the deadened quivering and intense continuousness of the alarm of the rattlesnake. [17.343]

The girl's tenuous connection with the rattlesnake damns her in Ruskin's eyes, marking her a nymphet Lilith.[13]

Occurring chronologically between these two extremes are the 1866 lectures entitled *The Ethics of the Dust*, written for the young girls of Winnington School. These latter also evidently had, in Ruskin's view, highly ambiguous snake-like qualities. In one passage the dialogue describes the Valley of Diamonds, a curiously corrupt paradise:

> LECTURER: [T]he berries there are the blackest you ever saw; and wherever they fall, they stain a deep red; and nothing ever washes it out again; . . . And the boughs of the trees are twisted, as if in pain . . . And it is in these forests that the serpents are; but nobody is afraid of them . . . They have fine crimson crests, and they are wreathed about the wild branches, one in every tree, nearly; and they are singing serpents, for the serpents are, in this forest, what birds are in ours.
> FLORRIE: Oh, I don't want to go there at all, now.
> LECTURER: You would like it very much indeed, Florrie, if only you were there. The serpents would not bite you; the only fear would be of your turning into one! [18.213–14]

We might well agree with Florrie when she replies, 'But that's worse!' The lecturer here baldly, albeit through the screen of a fairy-tale, tells little English girls that they might some day turn into snakes. And not mere snakes of simile, like the Torinese child in the passage of 1858, but jaded, bejewelled beasts singing siren-like in a forest where even the trees writhe in pain.[14]

Occasionally Ruskin seems to anticipate the transformation which he mentioned to poor Florrie. A drawing of his from 1876 (fig. 3) forces the viewer momentarily to share in a confusion of serpentine and feminine attributes. The finely detailed coil immediately suggests a serpent's skeleton; it is only the drawing's title, *Lily's Dress Necklace*, which indicates the correct reading, and even then the two meanings of the depiction, skeleton and necklace, continue to co-exist in an uneasy balance.[15] The serpentine aspects of the form loom forth with particular clarity when viewed in the light both of Millais's drawing of Effie wearing natural ornament (fig. 2), and of mid-Victorian taste in jewellery, which could easily dictate a gold, turquoise, ruby and diamond snake twined about a lady's neck and wrist as the height of fashion.[16]

The most virulent example of Ruskin's association of woman and snake may well appear in the discussion of what was for him the

3
John Ruskin,
Lily's Dress
Necklace, 1876,
pencil

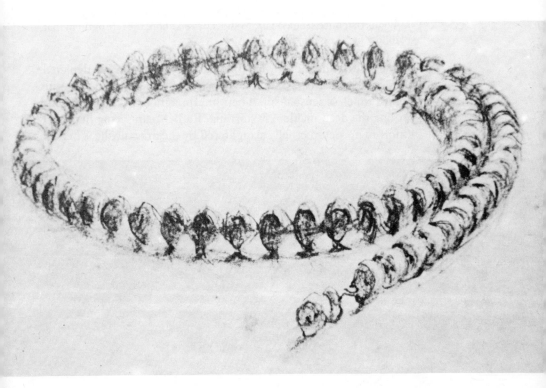

noblest depiction of St George's battle with the dragon, the version painted about 1507 by Vittorio Carpaccio (fig. 4). Ruskin wrote of this knight and dragon as 'perfect, each in its own kind' (24.340–1).[17] A full explanation of the painting, written not by Ruskin but by his disciple, James Reddie Anderson, is in chapter 11 of *St Mark's Rest* (1878). Undoubtedly, however, it reflects and amplifies Ruskin's thought, for in his preface to the chapter Ruskin writes of 'our result', 'our originality', 'both of us', and concludes, 'I know myself to be a true master, because my pupils are well on the way to do better than I have done' (24.371). Anderson's description of the painting is revealing of his sentiments:

> The Dragon is bearded like a goat . . . Every ridge of his body, wings, and head, bristles with long spines . . . an acknowledged symbol of the lust of the flesh, whose defeat the artist has here set himself to paint . . . Behind the dragon lie, naked, with dead faces turned heavenwards, two corpses—a youth's and a girl's. . . . The girl's face—seen in profile —is quiet and still beautiful; her long hair is heaped as for a pillow under her head. It does not grow, like St George's, in living ripples, but lies in fantastic folds, that have about them a savour, not of death only, but of corruption. For all its pale gold, they at once carry back one's mind to Turner's *Python*, where the arrow of Apollo strikes him in the midst, and, piercing, reveals his foulness. Round her throat cling a few torn rags, these only remaining of the white garment that clothed her once . . . [Carpaccio] meant here to reveal in true dragon aspect the Venus that once seemed fair, to show by this shore the fate of them that follow her. [24.386–8]

For Anderson, and presumably Ruskin, Carpaccio has depicted no mere hagiologic narration but the struggle of the moral George against timeless sensual sin. Their interpretation, particularly concerning the dead maiden, is startling. Rather than seeing her as an unfortunate victim cruelly slaughtered by the dragon, she is herself

4
Vittorio
Carpaccio, *St
George Slaying the
Dragon*, *c*.1507, oil

associated with the vicious serpent of myth, Python; she is then
characterised as a corrupt and licentious seductress whose torn and
mangled body reveals her 'true dragon aspect'. Ruskin's *Study of
Carpaccio's St George Slaying the Dragon* further skews the role of
the woman in Carpaccio's painting (fig. 5). Carpaccio's original has
three nearly equal focuses, each emphasised with visually compelling red paint: the dragon, the mounted knight and the princess.
Ruskin has dramatically modified this composition by centring attention, with detail rather than colour, solely on the struggle of
knight and dragon. Like Anderson, who did not speak of the undeniably virtuous princess until an almost apologetic coda at the
very end of his interpretation, Ruskin too nearly obliterates her from
the scene. Only roughly sketched in, she is a faceless form barely
distinguishable from the landscape. More tellingly, she and the back
half of the horse are on a separate sheet of paper from the rest of the
drawing, as if she were an unnecessary addendum or regretted con-
cession to completeness. The only female clearly depicted in Ruskin's
copy is the dead maiden vilified by Anderson. Her head is sheltered
by the dragon's head and neck. Crawling toward her gaping torso,
rather than Carpaccio's plump lizard, Ruskin has placed a slithering
serpent form. By denying the virtuous princess and framing the
maiden's corpse between dragon and snake, Ruskin's drawing
promotes the same interpretation as Anderson's verbal misreading
of the scene.

The horror of the woman-snake was very real for Ruskin. From
among a series of dreams recorded in his diary, the entry of 1
November 1869, is especially telling:

> Got restless—taste in mouth—and had the most horrible serpent
> dream I ever had yet in my life. The deadliest came out into the room
> under a door. It rose up like a Cobra—with horrible round eyes, and
> had woman's, or at least Medusa's, breasts. It was coming after me,

5
John Ruskin,
*Study of Carpaccio's
St George slaying
the Dragon*, from
Works, 24, plate LX

out of one room, like our back drawing room at Herne Hill, into
another; but I got some pieces of marble off a table and threw at it, and
that cowed it and it went back; but another small one fastened on my
neck like a leech, and nothing would pull it off. [D.685]

The dream beasts perhaps had their marble prototypes in Michelangelo's tomb of Lorenzo de Medici in the New Sacristy of San
Lorenzo (fig. 6). The mature Ruskin had visited the Medici Chapel
briefly as early as 1845,[18] and the writings contain several references
to Michelangelo's work there. A particularly striking passage in this
context comes from the seventh Oxford lecture of 1870–71:

But the form of Michael Angelo's Night is not one which he delighted
to see in women. He gave it her, because he thought it was fine, and
that he would be admired for reaching so lofty an ideal.*

*He had, indeed, other and more solemn thoughts of the Night
than Correggio; and these he tried to express by distorting form, and
making her partly Medusa-like. [22.96–7]

For Ruskin Medusa-like forms inhabited the chapel, either in the
decorative reliefs of the Lorenzo tomb, in the sculpture of Night at
the base of Giuliano's, or perhaps in a synthesis of the two that
would feminise the heads of the eel creatures and add serpentine
forms to the Night. Whether or not the creatures in Ruskin's dream
took the form of Michelangelo's hybrids, their image clarifies for us
the terror which must have engulfed the man pursued by such serpents, their repellent nature intensified by the travesty of their
pendulous female breasts.

But Ruskin's references to the serpent do not solely relate it to the

6
Michelangelo,
detail of tomb of
Lorenzo, Medici
Chapel, Florence

sensual female. Rather, a number of prose passages suggest that the serpent image became self-referential and masturbatory. In his 1880 lecture 'Living Waves' he lamented:

> In the deepest and most literal sense, to those who allow the tempt-ations of our natural passions their full sway, the curse, fabulously (if you will) spoken on the serpent, is fatally and to the full accomplished upon ourselves. [26.324]

That is to say, Ruskin substitutes his own sensual, guilt-ridden self for the serpent in the pronouncement 'I will put enmity between you and the woman.' Most likely, this is a reference to the troubled, consuming passion which he vainly felt for Rose La Touche.

The relationship of these two disturbed individuals has been chronicled in numerous biographies and need not be related here.[19] One decisive incident is significant for this discussion. After long months of self-imposed silence, Rose failed to write to Ruskin on Christmas Day, 1867. The effect on him was devastating. He wrote several months later:

> What the effect on my mind has been—if she cares to know it—is this —that my idea of womanhood is destroyed—and irrevocably—that my love and tenderness to all men is greatly deadened—my own personal happiness in *any* love, destroyed.[20]

The exact cause of Rose's silence is unknown, but Ruskin's per-ception of the problem can be gleaned from a letter which he wrote on 2 June 1868 from Denmark Hill to Mrs Cowper-Temple:

> Her [Rose's] words are fearful—I can only imagine one meaning to them—which I will meet at once—come of it what may. Have I not often told you that I was another Rousseau?— . . . but redeemed from the evil that was its death. . . . She will find me—if she comes to me— all that she has thought. She will save me *only* from sorrow—from Sin I am saved already. . . . But it was not so always. There was that in my early life which is indeed past as the night.[21]

Most commentators have linked this passage of sin and Rousseau, veiled though it is, to the habit of masturbation.[22] We must read the letter to Mrs Cowper-Temple in this sense, as also the letter to his mother of 1866 where he wrote that 'the intense resemblance be-tween me and Rousseau, in mind, and even in many of the chances of life, increases upon my mind more and more' (18.xxxviii).

If, then, in 1868 the innocent and pure Rose should reject Ruskin, if, in fulfilment of the Lord's curse upon the serpent, there be enmity between him and the woman, Ruskin could but blame it upon his own past transgressions, upon his ready capitulation to venomous, infectious, irrecoverable sin. The biblical texts transcribed in his diary for 1867 are, for Rosenberg, suggestive:

> Blessed is the man that endureth temptation. . . .
> Oh remember not the sins and offenses of my youth . . .
> I will wash my hands in innocency, Oh Lord. . . . [D 618, 622][23]

Recorded dreams of this time suggest Ruskin's identification of serpent with masturbation. On 9 March 1868 he wrote of one of them:[24]

> I took too much wine. Dreamed of walk with Joan and Connie, in which I took all the short cuts over the fields, and sent them round by the road, and then came back with them jumping up and down banks of earth, which I saw at last were washed away below by a stream. Then of showing Joanna a beautiful snake, which I told her was an innocent one; it had a slender neck and a green ring round it, and I made her feel its scales. Then she made me feel it, and it became a fat thing, like a leech, and adhered to my hand, so that I could hardly pull it off—and so I woke. Vermilion dawn, today. [D.644]

This dream, in addition to the obvious terror of the metamorphosis, again contains the juxtaposition of girl and snake which we have noted previously. Now, however, the woman's touching of the snake evokes no response; it is only after Ruskin strokes its scales that it grows in size, attaches itself to him and, 'like a leech', sucks blood from the horrified man.[25]

The obsessive guilt registered by such dreams over the 'solitary vice' is today perplexing; masturbation is no longer reputed to fill asylums and cemeteries with the weak, sickly indulgent. Yet in the nineteenth century books and pamphlets decrying the spread of the sin proliferated, each couched in obfuscatory, opaque language.[26] One of the most respected writers on these matters was Dr William Acton. In his most famous work, *The Functions and Disorders of the Reproductive Organs* (1857), Acton wrote of masturbation in a manner that, if he happened upon it, would surely have compounded Ruskin's already enflamed sense of guilt:

> [The youth] does not know that to his immature frame every sexual indulgence is unmitigated evil. He does not think that to his inexperienced mind and heart every illicit pleasure is a degradation, to be bitterly regretted hereafter—a link in a chain that does not need many to be too strong to break.[27]

Particularly applicable to Ruskin was the following:

> [A]s anyone may observe, it is not the strong athletic boy, fond of healthy exercise, who thus early shows marks of sexual desires, but your puny exotic, whose intellectual education has been fostered at the expense of his physical development.[28]

Not only any confessed misdeeds but his own precocity could weigh upon the saddened Ruskin of these years just prior to 1870.

Ruskin's guilt over his onanistic practices was thus largely confirmed by his society. Masturbation, whether known as the great corrupter of youth, the secret sin, or personal pollution, was seen as an addictive, debilitating habit that would destroy the moral and physical well-being of the young, leading to lunacy and (amid many other terrors) death.[29] The language of the moral reformers and polemicists finds a striking resonance within *Modern Painters V* (1860). The last of Turner's paintings to be dealt with at length was not, as we might expect, one of the landscapes which had motivated the entire project, but the *Apollo and Python* (fig. 7). Apollo, god of light, rationality, calm and order, has struck down Python, child of Hera, beloved of the earth and of the cool darkness. For Ruskin the meaning of the painting was clear:

> [The beast at the side of the golden youth is] no merely devouring dragon—no mere wild beast with scales and claws. It must possess some more terrible character to make conquest over it so glorious. Consider the meaning of its name, 'THE CORRUPTER'. . . . This is the treasure destroyer . . . the worm of eternal decay.
>
> Apollo's contest with him is the strife of purity with pollution; of life with forgetfulness; of love, with the grave.
>
> I believe this great battle stood, in the Greek mind, for the type of the struggle of youth and manhood with deadly sin—venomous, infectious, irrecoverable sin. In virtue of his victory over this corruption, Apollo becomes thenceforward the guide; the witness; the purifying and helpful God . . . the conqueror of death . . . the healer of the people. [7.420]

7
J. M. W. Turner,
Apollo and Python,
*c.*1811, oil

It is nothing less than the struggle of the bright and pure moral man against his dark, earth-bound, sensual nature.[30]

One further category of association suggests itself. In Ruskin's writings on snakes, the terms light and darkness, sight and blindness, carry more than metaphoric value. In the February 1873 *Fors Clavigera* he wrote on the etymologies of the serpent's names:

> The word 'Dragon' means 'the Seeing Creature,' and I believe the Greeks had the same notion in their other word for serpent, 'ophis.' There were many other creeping, and crawling, and rampant things; the olive stem and the ivy were serpentine enough, blindly; but here was a creeping thing that saw! [27.483–4]

Not only did the snake have and use its eyes, but the very nature of these eyes, the 'deadly cleft in the iris' (22.200), would repel the writer who has been called 'an optical self'[31] (fig. 8). For Ruskin, next in ugliness to the eyes of animals which have no expression in them 'come the eyes that gain in vitality indeed, but only in the expression of intense malignity, as in the serpent' (4.158).

Even more terrible was an event which he recorded in 1880, in his lecture on snakes, the outline for which opened this chapter. Ruskin wrote about two soldiers in India who, at one o'clock in the morning, were bitten by the small *cobra di morte*, the most venomous of the Indian reptiles:

> [T]he first died at seven in the morning, the second at noon; in both, the powers of sight gradually failing, and they became entirely blind before death. The snake described as of a dark straw colour, with two

8
John Ruskin,
Studies of Vipera Elegans, from
Works, 26 plate
XIX

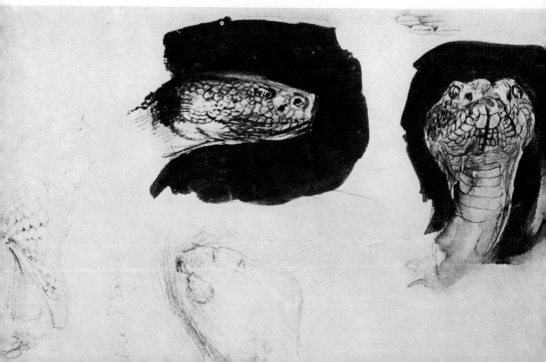

black lines behind the head; small flat head, with *eyes that shone like diamonds*. [26.321–2]

Great indeed would be the intense horror of this fate for Ruskin, the man who wrote:

[T]he greatest thing a human soul ever does in this world is to *see* something, and tell what it *saw* in a plain way. Hundreds of people can talk for one who can think, but thousands can think for one who can see. To see clearly is poetry, prophecy, and religion,—all in one. [5.333]

Not only did the serpent sully the beauty of vision by its malignant misapplication of it, but here was a creature which could rob from man the most precious of gifts—the power of sight.

If Ruskin's references to serpents were confined to innocent narratives, a phobia of losing his sight, or reactions to his troubled sexual identity, then their interest for us would be limited indeed. But in a grand fashion he was able to utilise this disturbing personal image to expound on far broader social issues. The damnation lent by association with the serpent covered all that was degraded in human society:

And truly, it seems to me, as I gather in my mind the evidences of insane religion, degraded art, merciless war, sullen toil, detestable pleasure, and vain or vile hope . . . [it is] as if the [human] race itself were still half-serpent, not extricated yet from its clay; a lacertine breed of bitterness—the glory of it emaciate with cruel hunger, and blotted with venomous stain: and the track of it, on the leaf a glittering slime, and in the sand a useless furrow. [19.365][32]

Perhaps the foremost example of insane religion and sullen toil presented to Ruskin's eye was industrialism's worship of and greed for money at the expense of 'workers' healthful and natural labour' (7.427). The process through which his thought came to identify this burgeoning industrialism as a fiery dragon may be followed by reviewing his discussion of the dragon in Turner's *The Goddess of Discord in the Garden of the Hesperides* (fig. 9). After deprecating Turner's youthful work in many of its details, in 1856 Ruskin wrote of it:

There is, however, one image in the landscape which, in its kind, is as noble as may be—the dragon that guards and darkens it; a goodly watch-tower he has; and a goodly pharos he will make of it at midnight, when the fire glares hottest from the eyes of the ghastly sentinel. There is something very wonderful, it seems to me, in this antici-pation, by Turner, of . . . very nearly an exact . . . model of the Iguano-don [at the Crystal Palace]. [13.117–18]

9
J. M. W. Turner,
*The Goddess of
Discord choosing the
Apple of Contention
in the Garden of the
Hesperides, c.*1806,
oil

Ruskin goes on to celebrate 'the mighty articulation of his body,
rolling in great iron waves, a cataract of coiling strength', and 'the
skeleton glacier of him' (7.118). At this point the dragon inspires
admiring thoughts of dinosaurs and long-past ice ages. Writing in
Modern Painters V, in 1860, Ruskin began by tracing the mytho-
logical origins of the Hesperian dragon and ended with a faint echo
of his earlier comment: 'I know no published engraving of glacier
breaking over a rocky brow so like the truth as these dragon's
shoulders would be' (7.402). But elsewhere in the discussion he
dissected the moral significance of the dragon as 'the consuming
(poisonous and volcanic) passions—the "flame-backed dragon,"
uniting the powers of poison, and instant destruction' (7.397–8),
'the demon of all evil passions connected with covetousness; that is
to say, essentially of fraud, rage, and gloom' (7.401), 'the evil spirit
of wealth' (7.403). Rather than a coiling cataract of strength, as in
the 1856 passage, the dragon:

> drags the weight of [its body] forward by his claws, not being able to
> lift himself from the ground ('Mammon, the least erected spirit that
> fell'). [7.402]

The quotation from Milton, drawing a direct line between the
dragon and Mammon, solidifies the identification of the beast as
money-worshipping industrialism. Ruskin closed the chapter with
an ironic apotheosis of this dragon:

Such then is our English painter's first great religious picture; and
exponent of our English faith. A sad–coloured work . . . in a sulphurous
hue, as relating to a paradise of smoke. That power, it appears, on the
hill-top, is our British Madonna . . . the Assumption of the Dragon.
No St George any more heard of; no more dragon slaying possible.
[7.407–8]

In later years his use of this serpent of wealth is coloured with
increasing self-reference and sadness. In the preface to *The Queen of
the Air* (1869) he abstracted the serpent's thick, coiled form to vivify
for his readers the defilement of the Earth caused by 'masters of
modern science' (19.294):

In that half of the permitted life of man, I have seen strange evil
brought upon every scene that I best loved. . . . [T]he air which once
inlaid the clefts of all [the Alp's] golden crags with azure is now defiled
with languid coils of smoke, belched from worse than volcanic
fires. [19.293]

In a famous passage from the same work Ruskin firmly established
the association of the serpent image with the increasing poverty of
the workers who crowded into London's slums:

There is more poison in an ill-kept drain,—in a pool of dish-washings
at a cottage door,—than in the deadliest asp of the Nile. Every back-
yard which you look down into from the railway, as it carries you out
by Vauxhall or Deptford, holds its coiled serpent: all the walls of those
ghastly suburbs are enclosures of tank temples for serpent worship . . .
[19.362]

The rich capitalists and landowners whose practical economics
fostered the 'ghastly suburbs' were 'only the claws of my Dragon'
(28.396).

When Ruskin wrote in *Modern Painters V* of 'No St George any
more heard of; no more dragon slaying possible' he of course spoke
too soon. In 1871, twelve years after his gloomy observation,
another St George did appear to do battle with the inflated dragon of
covetous wealth and social sin. Ruskin himself, as founder and
principal benefactor of St George's Guild, joined in battle against
the evil beast. The dragon was a mighty enemy, as we can sense even
in the monogram of Ruskin's publisher, where St George is engulfed
by the encircling worm (fig. 10). The raging struggle eventually
consumed his idealism, perhaps even his sanity, yet the need for the
battle was clear. He aptly summarised it in 1872:

Physical purity . . . That, you will find, is the meaning of Apollo's war
with the Python—of your own St George's war with the dragon.
[22.204]

10
George Allen
monogram

NOTES   1 Helen Gill Viljoen, ed., *The Brantwood Diary of John Ruskin* (New Haven, 1971), pp. 221–2. This paper originated at Yale University in the spring of 1978 at a seminar led by George L. Hersey, whom I would like to thank for encouragement and suggestions offered in the course of my study.

2 Moncure Daniel Conway, *Autobiography. Memories and Experiences of Moncure Daniel Conway* (Boston and New York, 1904), II, p. 122. I would like to thank Catherine Lynn for bringing this source to my attention. See also Viljoen, *loc. cit.*, p. 208, where she records the lecture as 'so amusingly effective that he was requested to repeat it on the 23rd, with the demand for tickets on each occasion out-running the supply'.

3 Viljoen, *loc. cit.*, p. 208.

4 On the latter function, Cook and Wedderburn (19.364) suggest that Ruskin, always the topical writer, was here alluding to the Rev. Henry Moule's newly invented (1860) system of dry-earth sanitation (i.e. a new, improved outhouse).

5 As noted by Cook and Wedderburn (9.277n.1), the twelfth-century example from Verona intended to accompany this passage was never given. I would suggest, however, that a drawing now at the John Ruskin Museum, Coniston, may provide Ruskin's reference. This is drawing No. 933 (38.260); it is illustrated in Terence Mullaly, *Ruskin a Verona* (Verona, 1966), fig. 55a.

6 Ruskin, who had purchased the Psalter of St Louis (*c.*1260–70, now in the Fitzwilliam Museum, Cambridge) in 1854, considered it to be his 'greatest treasure'; for it to be seen as containing vileness reveals the strength of Ruskin's distaste for the coiling, serpentine forms. On this psalter see James S. Dearden, 'John Ruskin, the Collector', *The Library*, 5th series, XXI, No. 2 (June 1966), 125, 134.

7 Quoted in Martin Seymour-Smith, *Sex and Society* (1975), p. 87.

8 C. Staniland Wake, *Serpent Worship, and Other Essays, with a Chapter on Totemism* (1888), p. 16.

9 *The Methodist Eclectic Review* (1806), quoted in Eric Trudgill, *Madonnas and Magdalens. The Origins and Development of Victorian Sexual Attitudes* (New York, 1976), p. 15.

10 See, for example, J. B. Trapp, 'The Iconography of the Fall of Man', in *Approaches to 'Paradise Lost'*, ed. C. A. Patrides (1968), pp. 223–65.

11 See *Letters of John Ruskin to Charles Eliot Norton*, ed. C. E. Norton (Boston, 1905), I, 67.

12 It may be that, for Ruskin, Effie had once before been associated with serpentine forms. A major factor that persuaded Ruskin's parents to allow his marriage was the mental strain he suffered in 1847, chronicled in a letter to his father (27 June, 1847): 'I cannot look at anything as I used to do and the evening sky is covered with swimming strings and eels' (quoted in Joan Evans, *John Ruskin*, New York, 1954, p. 125).

13 Later, in 1870, Ruskin again linked the serpent and the girl through association. In his 'Lecture on the Relation of Art to Religion' he wrote of the two: '. . . it may be possible to show the necessities of structure which groove the fang and depress the brow of the asp, and which distinguish the character of its head from that of the face of the young girl' (20.53). An ostensible contrast, but the choice of comparison merits scrutiny in

this context.

14 Ruskin was not, obviously, alone in this writing of the metamorphosis of woman into snake. In 1878 C. Hartley Smith anonymously published *The Serpent of Cos*, a poem which relates to Ruskin's imagery:

I have heard thy tale; now listen unto mine.
I have a serpent met ere now,
Not with thy fearful form and horrid brow,
But clothed in woman's loveliest mould,
With voice as sweet as bird that ever sung,
And words smoother than from the serpent tongue;
One that round my heart did twine,
And crushed it in its fold,
And into madness stung;
Blasted my manhood's golden prime,
Stained me with its serpent slime,
And made me an outcast and a man of crime.'

It is uncertain whether Ruskin ever saw *The Serpent of Cos*, but the same transformations occur in a more important (historically and aesthetically) work with which Ruskin was familiar, Keats's 1820 retelling of the tale *Lamia*. In love with the youth Lycius of Corinth, the serpent Lamia gains maiden form through the intervention of Hermes. Together Lamia and Lycius retire to a 'purple lined palace of sweet sin'. A marriage is planned, but at the feast Lycius's tutor denounces her:

'A serpent!' echoed he; no sooner said,
Then with a frightful scream she vanished:
And Lycius' arms were empty of delight . . .

Lycius dies of grief that evening. Here, as in Smith's poem, the serpent in woman's guise is closely aligned with sensual pleasure, and brings ruin, even death, to the man with whom she associates.

15 Writing of this drawing, Paul Walton noted that 'the effect is not entirely tranquil. His subjects often seem to tremble with an alien and sometimes menacing life that imbues them with personal significance' (*The Drawings of John Ruskin*, Oxford, 1972, p. 99). It is the serpent within the necklace, I believe, that Walton senses here.

16 For examples see Nancy Armstrong, *Victorian Jewelry* (New York, 1976), pp. 78, 97.

17 For Ruskin's chief discussion of the St George legend see 27.473–88.

18 Harold I. Schapiro, ed., *Ruskin in Italy. Letters to his parents, 1845* (Oxford, 1972), p. 92.

19 Most recently and fully in Van Akin Burd's *John Ruskin and Rose La Touche* (Oxford, 1980). In this context see especially where Ruskin glosses Mrs La Touche's nickname, Lacerta, as meaning that she 'had the grace and wisdom of the serpent, without its poison' (p. 49), and where, in a letter to Mrs Cowper-Temple, he says of Mrs La Touche that she is like a Lamia (p. 117).

20 Quoted in Evans, *John Ruskin*, p. 300.

21 Quoted in John Lewis Bradley, ed., *The Letters of John Ruskin to Lord and Lady Mount-Temple* (Columbus, Ohio, 1964), p. 167.

22 See, for example, Evans, *John Ruskin*, p. 291; Peter Quennell, *John Ruskin. The Portrait of a Prophet* (New York, 1949), pp. 202–3; John D.

Rosenberg, *The Darkening Glass. A Portrait of Ruskin's Genius* (New York and London, 1961), p. 169.

One link with Rousseau is through the second *Dialogue*, wherein Rousseau not only admits to but praises the practice of masturbation. See Lester G. Crocker, *Jean-Jacques Rousseau. The Quest (1712–1758)* (New York, 1968), especially pp. 67–8.

23 Rosenberg, *op. cit.*, p. 169.

24 See also D.642.

25 By November his mind had regained some peace, at least externally. He wrote in his diary on the 27th: 'Some one said something, of which I only remember the words "six inches." . . . Singularly I have had no disgusting or serpent dreams lately' (D.661).

26 Many modern analyses of Victorian sexual attitudes exist. Steven Marcus, *The Other Victorians. A Study of Sexuality and Pornography in Mid-nineteenth Century England* (New York, 1966), Seymour-Smith, *Sex and Society*, and Trudgill, *Madonnas and Magdalens*, have discussions of attitudes toward masturbation; Ronald Pearsall, *The Worm in the Bud. The World of Victorian Sexuality* (n.p., 1969) includes many specific references to Ruskin, as well as a separate section entitled 'Ruskin's Dream World'. In spite of the American emphasis, G. J. Barker-Benfield, *The Horrors of the Half-Known Life; Male Attitudes toward Women and Sexuality in Nineteenth-century America* (New York, 1976), is particularly enlightening, especially in the discussion of the Rev. John Todd, whose anti-masturbatory book *The Student's Manual* went through twenty-four editions from 1835 to 1854, and whose bibliography includes the (apt for this discussion) title *Serpents in the Dove's Nest* (1867).

27 Quoted in Marcus, *op. cit.*, p. 16.

28 Quoted in *ibid.*, p. 18. Ruskin anticipated Acton in espying the susceptibility of intellectuals to terror: 'Evidently also mere weakness of physical health, especially if resulting from over exertion of the mind, and irregular habits of life, will tend to produce painful visions, just as fever does, literally visions, not merely gloomy thoughts, but frightful spectra' (4.379).

29 Marcus, *op. cit.*, pp. 16–17. Marcus quotes from Acton that 'self-indulgence, long pursued, tends ultimately, if carried far enough, to early death or self-destruction'.

30 The tragedy of the struggle is its futility, relating perhaps to what Acton called a 'natural propensity [towards] the violation of [man's] sanctity' quoted in Seymour-Smith, *Sex and Society*, p. 21. For Ruskin clearly sees that, again referring to the Turner painting, '. . . this dragon of decay is a mere colossal worm: wounded, he bursts asunder in the midst, and melts to pieces, rather than dies, vomiting smoke—a smaller serpent worm rising out of his blood' (7.420).

31 Jay Fellows, *The Failing Distance. The Autobiographical Impulse in John Ruskin* (Baltimore, 1975), p. 1.

32 See Van Akin Burd, ed., *John Ruskin and Rose La Touche*, pp. 117–18, for Rose's personal interpretation of this passage. In 'Living Waves' Ruskin drew an even closer parallel between the snake and the evil human individual: expressions in animals 'are delightful or dreadful to us exactly in the degree in which they resemble the contours of the human countenance given to it by virtue and vice'; then, speaking perhaps of fig 9, he continued, 'and this head of the cerastes, and that of the rattle-snake, are in reality more terrific to you than the others, not because they are more snaky, but because they are more human,—because the one has in it the ghastliest expression of malignant avarice, and the other of malignant pride' (26.324).

Ruskin as an optical thinker

GEORGE L. HERSEY

1 A watercolour self-portrait of Ruskin dating from 1874 and now belonging to Wellesley College reveals some fascinating facts about the great man (fig. 11). The sketch is very broadly brushed in with large, damp, cloudy strokes of greyish umber for the hair and background. The face is modelled like a mountain, some of its protuberances made jagged with cobalt shadows, while the rest of the flesh is varied with inlays of pink and faint brown. The blue-green neckcloth that forms the base of the sketch is, in colour, almost a vignette of a river or lake. In other words, the drawing can be looked upon as a portrait of the artist as landscape.

A photograph of Ruskin tells us something else. In fig. 12 he is the man on the left. It was taken almost twenty years after the Wellesley sketch, when he had grown his long hair and longer beard. (He is with his friend Dr Henry Acland, his collaborator on the campaign to erect the Science Museum at Oxford.)

The two images suggest my theme: first, Ruskin as the intense starer at himself and his world, a contemplator who tended to dissolve his vision of the human self into one of landscape, or even one

11
John Ruskin,
self-portrait, 1874,
watercolour

of abstract strokes of atmospheric colour. The photograph, on the
other hand, makes Ruskin look rather like Leonardo, especially as
Leonardo was portrayed in the nineteenth century (fig. 13). Did he
consciously adopt a Leonardesque persona? Certainly one can say
that he attempted to fuse art, optics and the scientific study of
Nature in a Leonardesque way. Ruskin has something else in
common with Leonardo: both were copious writers on art whose
writings have been called chaotic and incomplete; and as with
Leonardo so with Ruskin this has led to an irresistible urge on the
part of many writers to explain what he really meant.[1]

There is another bond between Leonardo and Ruskin, and
another possible view as to what constitutes coherence of thought.
This involves writing (or speaking) that I will call visual or optical
rather than verbal. A verbal writer may be defined as one who is

interested in sequence, consequence, action, the passage of time. He avoids gaps, too many branchings-off, and the like. He wants to get the reader from point A to point B. A visual writer on the other hand is almost the reverse. He is interested in juxtaposition rather than sequence, simultaneity rather than consequence, appearance rather than time. He delights in colour, aura, texture, nearness, distance. He does not see thought as a form of transport from A to B.

A number of writers on Ruskin have sensed this quality in him. One is Robert Hewison in *John Ruskin. The Argument of the Eye* (1976). Hewison quotes one of the most familiar statements by Ruskin himself about the visual nature of his work—and of his mission:

> the greatest thing a human soul ever does in this world is to *see* something, and tell what it *saw* in a plain way. Hundreds of people can talk for one who can think, but thousands can think for one who can see. To see clearly is poetry, prophecy, and religion,—all in one. [5.333]

However, after making this the exordium of his book, Hewison simply presents us with one more Ruskin biography. It is perfectly good but certainly no 'argument of the eye'. Something similar may be said of Richard Stein's *The Ritual of Interpretation* (1972). This is

12 left
Photograph of Ruskin (left) and Dr Henry Acland, 1893

13 right
Giovanni Baggi, after an earlier drawing, *Portrait of Leonardo da Vinci*, from Leonardo, *Trattato della Pittura* (Milan, 1804)

in part devoted to Ruskin, and shows how the early books, *Modern Painters* and *The Stones of Venice*, are in large part guided tours. In them Ruskin conducts his readers along imaginary galleries of pictures or of specimens, or along the canals of Venice, or through mountain passes. Yet Stein does not really anatomise the notion visually. Though he sees Ruskin as a visual writer in the sense I have defined, in the end, like almost everyone else who has written on the subject, he is himself verbal and verbal only. He does not attempt to visualise what Ruskin says. He does not seek out what it was that Ruskin was looking at. He does not check up on him. He does not ask where Ruskin saw truly and where falsely. He does not ask if there was a strategy behind the true and the false seeing.

Two years after Stein's book Jay Fellows, in *The Failing Distance. The Autobiographical Impulse in John Ruskin* (1975), rose more nobly to the occasion. Fellows's book is tough going, and accordingly some critics have been hard on it.[2] But he is on a right track that so far as I know no one else has followed. He interprets Ruskin's writings as forms of vision, or perspective. In Ruskin's prose vistas he sees distance, viewpoint, the elimination of foreground, a movement from near to far. The distance which fails is the ever-converging co-ordinates of the one-point perspective into which Ruskin's future moved. Fellows locates Ruskin's logic in space rather than in time. He reveals to us a thinker whose mind has the simultaneity of a landscape, a palace, a gallery, rather than a mind concerned with process and action.

In thus characterising Ruskin as 'visual' Fellows is not simply applying to him the categories of Rudolph Arnheim, Ernst Gombrich and other writers on perception theory. Fellows is not interested in how ordinary people see physically, nor in how they perceive, interpret and remember what they see. If I understand him correctly he is saying that the visual world, and especially the prolonged, energetic contemplation of landscape, and of works of art, can generate in certain elect minds a system of thought, of logic, of arrangement, that is very different from the systems of thought, logic and arrangement generated by those who are immersed in a purely verbal culture. This is the task Ruskin mentions, that of the rare soul who has the greatness to see clearly.

We have Ruskin's own authority, just quoted, for some of this. As he says, seeing—truly seeing—is rare, and a higher act than telling. In *Fiction Fair and Foul* he claimed that only four other men in recent history had had the sense of material beauty—i.e. of aesthetic sight—that he possessed (34.343).[3] That is why the high, rare, 'great' seer must tell what he sees to those who cannot or cannot yet see. For Ruskin, one senses, a visual thing descends into a verbal one much as Neoplatonic idea descends into its temporary material embodiment. He was thus a practitioner of ecphrasis, for that word means first of all 'a plain declaration' and secondly, in literature, the verbal description of some great visual work such as the shield of Achilles or Pygmalion's statue.⁴ Chronologically and verbally Ruskin stands with his immediate predecessors and successors, like Hazlitt or Pater. But in his vision-filled soul he belongs with the ecphrastic describers, with Ficino, Bruno, Marino, Spenser; or for that matter with the more near-by Keats and (as a Pre-Raphaelite ecphrasist) Tennyson. The writings of these men are animated by sequences and arrangements of details, colours, outlines, textures, symmetries, of seen forms. They claim that empire of powerfully worded visual experience which those of us who are visually receptive enjoy, and of which Ruskin conquered so extensive a part.

We are willing to grant with Richard Stein, then, that the reader of *Modern Painters* and *The Stones of Venice* is stationed on a sort of promontory, or in a great imaginary hall filled with images.⁵ The seen things are endlessly expounded, spotlighted, analysed, compared, accepted, rejected by our guide. Or, in the same way, in *The Stones of Venice I* Ruskin lets us watch as he builds before our eyes a Gothic palace. He quarries the stone for us, places block on block for us, carves the detail.⁶ These books of Ruskin's are in fact Victorian theatres of memory, developments of the humanist tradition of the universal compendium as a described architectural, garden or landscape space. But they are not so vaguely imagined as are humanist theatres of memory. They have the tactile immediacy of a set of surfaces deeply and relentlessly studied.

11   But Ruskin was no Renaissance or baroque humanist; his visions are Victorian. He not merely sees greatly but describes plainly—a statement that can hardly be made about Bruno or Marino. This plainness takes the form of sharpness, brilliance, overwhelmingness of detail and texture. It involves physical closeness to the seen object. Ruskin tells us in the preface to the second edition of *The Seven Lamps of Architecture* that

'architecture should be taken, not merely when it presents itself under picturesque general forms, but stone by stone, and sculpture by sculpture; seizing every opportunity afforded by scaffolding to approach it closely, and putting the camera in any position that will command the sculpture. [8.13]

We see that closeness, detail and brilliance in the tympanum he illustrates in *The Stones of Venice* (fig. 14). This is seen, and drawn, stone by stone and piece by piece, like a coloured diagram or working drawing. In short the Claude glass of the eighteenth century is replaced, with Ruskin, by the magnifying glass, by the optical

14
John Ruskin, Archivolt in the Duomo at Murano, from *The Stones of Venice* (1851–53)

15
Photograph of the upper room of the Cottage at Walkley, Sheffield, *c.*1876

16 above
Oxford,
University
Museum, the Glass
Court, Deane and
Woodward,
architects, 1855–59

17 right
John Ruskin,
drawing of Sta
Maria della Spina,
Pisa, 1845

18
John Ruskin,
drawing of Sta
Maria della Spina,
Pisa, 1840

machine, by the camera. Our man is not a Horace Walpole but, bending over a tiny flower, or examining Tintoretto's brush strokes, or staring at the marks of rain in mud, he is an anticipation of Sherlock Holmes. And that is why I call him not merely a visual but an optical thinker. Furthermore he remembers and writes down what he sees; for what describer of things seen was ever more copious than Ruskin? He also admires, adores, what he so carefully transcribes. In this sense his collections of daguerreotypes, of drawings, of shells, bones, feathers, plaster casts, and so on, are instructive—in every sense. I would instance the Museum of the Guild of St George at Walkley, Sheffield (fig. 15), whose rooms were lined with such juxtaposed things or images: watercolour vignettes of campaniles, genre paintings, plaster casts after the antique, plant specimens, lithographs of Gothic mouldings, copies of old masters, rocks, medals—almost a re-creation of a Renaissance *Wunderkabinett*, and hence another connection between Ruskin and the humanist tradition. The schemes for the Glass Court at the Oxford Museum (fig. 16), though not Ruskin's, were Ruskinian in that they constituted a three-dimensional map of the flora and fauna of the British Isles.[7] But the collections at Walkley, at Oxford and elsewhere were only the tip of the written iceberg. And that written iceberg of image and note, or of text and gloss, was in turn only the tip of Ruskin's mental iceberg: his colossal collection of optical memories.

The Victorian visual image could be soft but in its normative state it was 'photographic' in the commonest sense. It was an image with high resolution, sharply bounded tonal separation, powerfully distinct detail, uniform brightness, high acuity. Space, depth, silhouette, air or aura were eliminated. Stefan Muthesius has shown the difference that this sort of daguerreotype image made for Ruskin's own seeing and drawing. In 1840 Ruskin made one of his typical early Prout-like sketches (now in the Courtauld Gallery) of the church of Santa Maria della Spina, Pisa (fig. 18). In 1845 he made a second drawing of the same building, a drawing now at Sheffield (fig. 17). Muthesius notes that Ruskin's conception of the architecture itself changed over these five years. In the earlier version the church is rich, picturesque, decayed; in the second it is brilliantly coloured, flat-surfaced, articulated into powerfully outlined facets. Muthesius adds, almost by the way, that the 1845 drawing is said to have been based on a daguerreotype and that when Ruskin came to Venice in that year he found this sort of photography 'blessed' because 'every chip of stone is here'.[8] What Muthesius does not say is what Eve Blau added in a talk at the Frick Collection, New York, in 1975:[9] that Ruskin accepted and exploited the sharp limitations imposed by the acceptance angle of the camera

lens as it was set up in the narrow defile between Via Sant' Antonio
and Via La Maddalena. And because the camera had to be so near,
the outline of the church was vigorously cropped. One sees only a
bay or two plus the famous gabled portal. The rules of picturesque
composition as practised in the early nineteenth century are broken.
The building does not sit back in space but crowds forward on to
the picture plane. There is no foreground repoussoir, there are no
dark corners. By the standards Ruskin had learned in his watercolour lessons the recession on the right is jarringly sharp. There are
no emphasis and de-emphasis, no fading out and fading in as in the
earlier scene, no principal and subsidiary lights. There are, however,
in the 1845 drawing, an attention, a power of optical admiration and
a thirst for the exactitude of irregularity that are missing in the
earlier drawing. The 1845 version of the church undoubtedly
reproduces the hard, sharp, continuous, corner-to-corner detail—
'every chip of stone'—of the daguerreotype on which it was based.
Ruskin was now 'seeing' optically this overall precision, this close
surface articulation, and was willing to lose—was willing *not* to see
—all the information about the building's shape, siting and relation
to its surroundings that the earlier sketch contained. The 1845
seeing, or re-seeing, of the Pisan church belongs with a new sensibility for hard detail, for arduous field trips, for botanising and
geologising, whose growth we can trace in *The Poetry of Architecture*
and throughout *Modern Painters*. Indeed, the 1845 drawing is a
Victorian image not only in appearance but in that it is an optical
correction of the earlier drawing, a critical re-seeing of the church.

It is often remarked that Holman Hunt's watercolours and

19
Holman Hunt,
Apple Harvest—
Valley of the Rhine,
Rogaz, 1883–84(?),
watercolour

landscapes have the resolution, detail, overall lighting, flat planar
structure, wilful baldness and suppression of framing and repoussoir elements that are found in this sort of Victorian photography.
In short, Hunt's work has the qualities that in the 1850s Ruskin
tended to equate with optical truth.[10] Indeed, in such later works as
the watercolour painting of 1883–84 entitled *Apple Harvest—
Valley of the Rhine* (fig. 19) Hunt considerably outdistances even
Ruskin in these respects. In fact Ruskin, at least when placed in the
company of Hunt, remains in part a prisoner of his early training
under J. D. Harding and Samuel Prout. While Hunt's drawings
and paintings have the hardest, closest optical imagery, Ruskin
was never really able to expunge the sweet early Victorian light-
drenched quality from his own work that we see in figs. 17 and 18.
But as we are also about to see, he made up for it by railing against
juiciness in the work of other artists whom he did not like.

Ruskinian 'optical truth' may be traced to a more unexpected III
quarter: Rossetti. We do not think of Rossetti as being particularly
under the spell of Ruskin's ideas—though of course Ruskin had
been Rossetti's friend and patron in the 1850s. Ruskin's ambivalence
about Rossetti is patent. They were friends, yet not friends. Ruskin
once impetuously declared that Rossetti was the greatest of living
painters.[11] But he obviously liked only Rossetti's early work. One
can well imagine that Rossetti's more sensuous pictures, with their
highly sexed yet curiously embalmed-looking sibyls and magdalens
would not have gratified Ruskin in any way he could approve of.[12]
And yet Rossetti's later works are Ruskinian. Rossetti looked at a
woman much as Ruskin looked at an alpine flower or a geological
layer: with overwhelming closeness, minute transcription, scientific
honesty, optical devotion. *The Day-dream* (1880), now in the Victoria and Albert Museum (fig. 20), is an example. We do not have
Holman Hunt's daguerreotype detail, it is true. But we do have a
scene at life size, studied with passion, with almost no depth or
perspective, and plainly and completely told. In structure it is a
relief like a carved tympanum. Each leaf, each bough, we learn, is a
portrait of a leaf and a bough brought fresh to the studio.[13] The
sitter, Jane Morris, is no mere model but one whom the painter
truly studied and loved, as Ruskin loved the marble tendril on a
Venetian window frame. Rossetti never painted except what was
physically before him, whether lute, hair, leaf or hand; and as he
painted he admired and it is not too much to say adored every eye-
lash, every curl, every jewel, every fingernail. As the picture progressed and the seasons changed the original snowdrops that Jane
had held gave place to honeysuckle flowers. Rossetti, then, not only
painted plants as they actually were but the very act of painting

them had to occur during the plant's proper season. But above all, everything in the picture was transcribed from a reality that had been physically established in the studio. In these ways, and in his own way, Rossetti was also a Ruskinian optical seer and a plain sayer.

Indeed, when one looks at the plain saying, or fancy poem, that Rossetti wrote to go with *The Day-dream*, and which makes it half of a double work of art, one can go further. Just as Ruskin describes and moralises on the Val d'Aosta or the Scrovegni Chapel, so Rossetti's sonnet describes and moralises on this picture. Jane Morris has turned from the light, aimless dreams of never-ending summer to penetrate with deep gaze her lover's eyes:

> The thronged boughs of the shadowy sycamore
>   Still bear young leaflets half the summer through;
>   From when the robin 'gainst the unhidden blue
> Perched dark, till now, deep in the leafy core,
> The embowered throstle's urgent wood-notes soar
>   Through summer silence. Still the leaves come new;

20
Dante Gabriel
Rossetti, sketch for
The Day-dream,
1880

21 *facing*
Dante Gabriel
Rossetti, *The Day-
dream*, 1880

Yet never rose-sheathed as those which drew
Their spired tongues from spring-buds heretofore.

Within the branching shade of Reverie
   Dreams may spring till autumn; yet none be
Like woman's budding day-dream spirit-fann'd.
Lo: tow'rd deep skies, not deeper than her look,
   She dreams; till now on her forgotten book
Drops the forgotten blossom from her hand.[14]

The daydreams of summer are like sycamore leaves, always rebudding as the months go by, from robin's song in early leafless spring to that of the throstle in high summer. But only the buds of very early spring have rosy sheaths and spiral tongues. So too is woman's first spring daydream. She dreams out of her bower into the deepest of skies.

Throughout the poem the woman's form is fragmented and absorbed into bower-foliage and landscape; her eyes become skies, her dress is gradually overgrown (compare the chopped, denuded boughs of the preliminary drawing (fig. 21) with the abundant foliage of the picture) and smothered in leaves, her book covered with the honeysuckle blossoms. And the woman's blue dress, like her blue eyes, becomes a sky.[15]

Hence, though the spiritual and sexual relationship between painter and model was anything but Ruskinian, their optical relationship was precisely that. Rossetti creates a Ruskinian botanical landscape—colour at full intensity, every form crystal-clear; a true optical picture, for all the softness of the facture. But, more important, and in a yet more Ruskinian way, the poem almost forgets the human figure. The woman is transmuted into a look, a stare, into skies not deeper than her look. And those deep skies outside the picture are, of course, her lover-painter's eyes. The poem turns the partly Ruskinian picture into a fully Ruskinian landscape.

We often see Ruskin doing something similar with his own 'poetry'. To Ruskin the living body of Nature at her most sublime was a physique, a vast personage, reflected back and forth from heaven to earth, from sky to forest, as Rossetti's Jane was reflected in her lover's eyes and into boughs and blossoms. The plains of earth, in Ruskin's vaster scheme, are like skies and this makes the skies themselves sorts of skins, while earth's mountains are breasts and arms:

from the inactive plain, sleeping like the firmament, with cities for stars, to the fiery peaks, which, with heaving bosoms and exulting limbs, with the clouds drifting like hair from their bright foreheads, lift up their Titan hands to heaven, saying, 'I live for ever!' [3.427]

One part of Ruskin's and of Ruskinian optical thought, then, IV involves the image within that thought: this image, with its completeness, its fixed limits, sharpness and shallowness, governed the way he and his followers saw, what they scrutinised, what they omitted. Another part of Ruskin's optical thought leads to the 'plain telling' of the thing seen, and as we shall see also of the thing mis-seen and of the thing not plainly but falsely told. In other words we turn from Ruskin's art and his influence on artists to his criticism. Here we must deal with a new phenomenon. Ruskin's great aim in *Modern Painters* was not only to set Turner on the slopes of Parnassus, it was also to remove entirely from that mountain, where they had reigned so long, the great landscape painters of the Continental Baroque—especially Claude, Gaspar Dughet and Dutch artists like Aelbert Cuyp. To achieve this removal Ruskin became what I will call the first great negative critic in the history of art. Before him art critics, in so far as they may be said to have existed as a separate species, principally concerned themselves with what they considered to be good art. Ruskin concerned himself equally with the good and with what he felt, perhaps even more passionately, to be bad.

An example occurs in *Modern Painters II*, where Ruskin quotes William Hazlitt's praise of a painting by Cuyp (fig. 22):

> Again, look at the large Cuyp in the Dulwich Gallery, which Mr Hazlitt considers 'the finest in the world,' and of which he very complimentarily says, 'The tender green of the valleys, the gleaming lake, the purple light of the hills, have an effect like the *down* on an unripe nectarine!' I ought to have apologized before now, for not having studied sufficiently in Covent Garden to be provided with terms of correct and classical criticism. One of my friends begged me to observe the other day, that Claude was 'pulpy'; another added the yet more gratifying information that he was 'juicy'; and it now is happily discovered that Cuyp is 'downy'. Now I dare say that the sky of this first-rate Cuyp is very like an unripe nectarine: all that I have to say about it is, that it is exceedingly unlike a sky. The blue remains unchanged and ungraduated over three-fourths of it, down to the horizon; while the sun, in the left-hand corner, is surrounded with a halo, first of yellow, and then of crude pink, both being separated from each other, and the last from the blue, as sharply as the belts of a rainbow . . . [3.349–50][16]

Ruskin has done three things in this passage. First, he has belaboured Hazlitt for making an unworthy or undignified comparison between scenery and fruit, thus confusing, in a way that an earlier critic like Félibien would not have approved of, the higher genre of landscape with the lower one of still life. He has attacked Hazlitt, that is, on Hazlitt's own art-critical grounds. Ironically enough,

22
Aelbert Cuyp,
*Cattle and Figures
near a River, with
Mountains*

he has done this with a Hazlittean phrase, 'correct and classical criticism'. Secondly, he has criticised Hazlitt for likening one part of nature to another part that ought to be irrelevant to it—a confusion not of genres of painting, that is, but of the realms of Nature herself. A painted sky must be like a real sky, he is saying, and a painted nectarine like a real nectarine; but a painted sky should *not* be like a real nectarine. (This in no way prohibits Ruskin from saying that mountains are like breasts, however, as we have just seen.)

The third thing Ruskin has done in this passage is the most important. He has brought us into his fascinating looking-glass world of strategic misprision. Hazlitt's comparison, we recall, was of the unripe nectarine to Cuyp's valleys, lake and hills. So Ruskin is criticising a comparison between nectarine and sky that Hazlitt never actually made. But never mind; such misprision lies at the heart of Ruskin's critical method. Incensed at Hazlitt's transformation of hills and lake into fruit, he completes the ruin of Cuyp's landscape, as it were, by transforming its sky into an archery target: the sun, and its halo of sharp belts of yellow, pink, then blue.

But Ruskin's critical job is only half done. He now proceeds to an even deeper strategy. He describes, very beautifully, a true sunset:

> that sunset purple which invariably extends its influence to the zenith, so that there is no pure blue anywhere, but a purple increasing in purity gradually down to its point of greatest intensity (about forty-

five degrees from the horizon), and then melting imperceptibly into the gold, the three colours extending their influence over the whole sky; so that throughout the whole sweep of the heaven, there is no one spot where the colour is not in an equal state of transition, passing from gold into orange, from that into rose, from that into purple, from that into blue, with absolute equality of change, so that in no place can it be said, 'Here it changes,' and in no place, 'Here it is unchanging.' This is invariably the case. There is no such thing—there never was, and never will be such a thing, while God's heaven remains as it is made—as a serene, sunset sky, with its purple and rose in *belts* about the sun [3.350–1]

Now in fact this description of Nature optically seen—of God's heaven—is a fine and accurate description of a Cuyp sunset. There are many such pictures and they *do* give us just this sunset purple extending its influence to the zenith, melting imperceptibly into gold. Ruskin has simply detached this description from Cuyp and attached it to God. Such are the complexities of visual thinking in Ruskin; of the soul's seeing, and of plain or in this case fancy and even downright false telling.

The vision of a sunset is, as noted, optical. It is beautiful, a typical Ruskin purple passage, but it is constructed out of meteorological and technical colour language. It talks of zeniths, and degrees, of sweeps of heaven, of pure blue, of equal transition, and so on. It is oriented towards the observations and equipment needed for the study and measurement of colour and air. The final point of the exercise, however, is that Ruskin's beautiful close description is to be posed against Hazlitt's meagre, grotesque, vague one:

> The tender green of the valleys, the gleaming lake, the purple light of the hills, have an effect like the down on an unripe nectarine.

From all this we learn the following: if we read the whole passage in *Modern Painters II* without visualising Ruskin's images, and without actually looking at Cuyp, then the passage means that Cuyp mis-sees a scene, and that Hazlitt compounds this mis-seeing by misunderstanding it. We may note, also on this purely verbal level, that Ruskin adds his own misreading to the pile by transferring the fruit-piece from the lower to the upper part of Cuyp's picture.

But if, instead of merely reading Ruskin, we also look closely at Cuyp; if we practise visual or optical thinking on our own—then an entirely different meaning emerges. The passage is 'about' Cuyp only in a very peculiar way. What is really happening is that Ruskin is seeking to establish himself as a great optical-scientific critic, while Hazlitt cuts a poor figure as a loquacious dilettante. Cuyp, the painter, is only the victim, sacrificed in the struggle between the two critics.

But Ruskin can bring his negative-critical cannon to bear on guilty v
as well as on innocent targets. If he is unfair to Cuyp we have to
admit that he is right about Gaspar Dughet (fig. 23):

> 'Storms' indeed, as the innocent public persist in calling such abuses
> of nature and abortions of art as the two windy Gaspars in our
> National Gallery, are common enough; massive concretions of ink and
> indigo, wrung and twisted very hard, apparently in a vain effort to get
> some moisture out of them; bearing up courageously and successfully
> against a wind whose effects on the trees in the foreground can be
> accounted for only on the supposition that they are all of the India-
> rubber species. [3.396]

And, looking at the absolute uniformity of the curves of these
branches, their calligraphic sameness, all independent of thickness,
placement, length, and the like, we have to admit that Ruskin is
right. What tree *does* look like this? Or, in the interests of optical
truth, compare the India-rubber tree with a magnificent photograph
by Fox Talbot made in the early 1840s (fig. 24). Here, in Fox
Talbot's own phrase, Nature paints.[17] With what a difference:
Nature gives us a powerfully resourceful set of possibilities for the
jointing, branching, direction, thickness, curvature, density, refinement, power and indeed sublimity—of a tree. Compared with

this, poor Gaspar's bough does indeed look insecure and repetitive, and feathery rather than tree-like.

24
Fox Talbot,
photograph of tree,
early 1840s

Another example: Dughet's National Gallery picture *A View near Albano* (fig. 25):

> This latter is a representation of an ornamental group of elephants' tusks, with feathers tied to the ends of them. Not the wildest imagination could ever conjure up in it the remotest resemblance to the bough of a tree. It might be the claws of a witch, the talons of an eagle, the horns of a fiend; but it is a full assemblage of every conceivable falsehood which can be told respecting foliage, a piece of work so barbarous in every way, that one glance at it ought to prove the complete charlatanism and trickery of the whole system of the old landscape painters. [3.577–78]

Ruskin, then, bases both his positive and his negative criticism on comparisons between what he sees in a painting—or says he sees in a painting—and what amounts to a gallery, collection or file of optical memories collected from his notes and experiences of skies, mountains, flowers, feathers, tusks. (Nectarines are excluded only for purposes of rhetoric.) And, of course, it is precisely in that it seriously studies puddles along with lakes, feathers along with trees—and not just for the sake of negative criticism but for their

25
Gaspar Dughet,
View near Albano

own sake—that *Modern Painters* differs so profoundly from earlier treatises on painting, except of course Leonardo's.

At the beginning of this chapter I commented on the Leonardesque appearance of the elderly Ruskin. I do not suggest that he was consciously adopting the persona of his great predecessor. But we also noted that, like Leonardo, he left behind a massive, flawed, magnificent treatise on painting in which all Nature and the world were ultimately to be encompassed; that both studied nature, in twig and mountain, crystal and river, with a scientist's passion. The very titles of some of Ruskin's chapters—'Of Leaf Beauty', 'Of Cloud Beauty', 'Of Mountain Beauty'—are almost quotations from Leonardo ('Della polvere', 'Del fiume', etc.). Chapter CLI in the edition of the treatise available to Ruskin, 'Da che nasce l'azzurro nell'aria', might have been drawn on for the sunset description quoted above.[18] To these likenesses between the two we can add the one discussed earlier: both, more than any other great writers on painting, fused their subject with optics. From Leonardo's fusion there emerged a new, strong, light-and-shadow-drenched art, that of the High Renaissance. From Ruskin's fusion there emerged a new art criticism replacing an old one that had been drawn from literary genres such as the travel book, the exhibition review and the biography. In this new criticism optical and scientific tests were administered to the Old Masters. Thus did Ruskin see himself, in the passages we have analysed and in many others like them, as a great critic. And, indeed, what earlier writer *has* brought a more sustained power of seeing, and, equally important, of strategic mis-seeing, to the act of criticism? Not Vasari, not Baldinucci, not Félibien, not Diderot, not Stendhal, not Baudelaire; and for that matter what subsequent critic has done so?

1 A detailed reinterpretation of *Modern Painters* in terms of Leonardo's NOTES *Trattato* is in order. Apparently at one time Ruskin was seriously reading the *Trattato* in Italian. (He was probably using the edition published in Milan in 1804 by Giusti Ferrario, which has a biography of the artist by Carlo Amoretti and the portrait reproduced in fig. 3.) There is a letter now in the Princeton University Library (AM 20669), dated 7 March (no year), from Ruskin at Denmark Hill to Rossetti asking for help in translating certain passages from the *Trattato*.
2 For example Garry Wills, 'The Augustinian Ruskin', *New York Review of Books*, 7 August 1975.
3 The others were Rousseau, Shelley, Byron and Turner. See also John D. Rosenberg, *The Darkening Glass. A Portrait of Ruskin's Genius* (New York and London, 1961), p. 4.
4 For this see Jean H. Hagstrum, *The Sister Arts. The Tradition of Literary Pictorialism and English Poetry from Dryden to Gray* (Chicago, 1948), p. 20, and Murray Krieger, *The Play and Place of Criticism* (Baltimore, 1967), pp. 105–28.
5 Here again Rosenberg, *Darkening Glass*, p. xii, is *à propos*: 'One seems to have wandered without a guide into a vast gallery where finished masterpieces hang alongside hasty sketches, titles of objects are misleading, the rooms arranged at random and the partitions dividing them arbitrarily placed.' I agree with everything except that the reader is without a guide. Rather he is *with* one of the most overbearing of guides—one who confuses through his copiousness, not through his absence from the scene.
6 I refer to the first thirty chapters of *The Stones of Venice* (Cook and Wedderburn, vol. 9), which have titles such as 'The Quarry', 'The Wall Veil', 'The Wall Cornice', 'The Pier Base', etc., and which then move through shaft, cap, arch and so on to roof and ornamental carving.
7 See G. L. Hersey, *High Victorian Gothic. A Study in Associationism* (Baltimore and London, 1972), pp. 196–8.
8 Stefan Muthesius, *The High Victorian Movement in Architecture, 1850–1870* (1972), p. 29.
9 The talk was entitled 'Ruskin and Victorian Architectural Drawing' and was given on Friday, 18 April 1975.
10 See particularly 33.272–3 (*The Art of England*), 35.404 (*Praeterita*), 37.83 (letter of 1874 to J. A. Froude).
11 Ruskin 34.493 (*Arrows of the Chace*). For the Ruskin–Rossetti friendship see also 36.xliii–li.
12 Rossetti seems, however, to have owned quite a number of Ruskin's books—mostly courtesy of their author. For Rossetti's library see Helen S. Culler, 'Studies in Rossetti's Reading', Ph.D. dissertation, Yale University, 1943.

13 Virginia Surtees, *The Paintings and Drawings of Dante Gabriel Rossetti, 1828–1882* (Oxford, 1971), I, Nos. 259, 259A.

14 *The Collected Works* (1890), I, 304.

15 See my 'Rossetti's "Jenny": a Realist Altarpiece', *Yale Review*, LXIX (1979), pp. 17–32, especially p. 24.

16 Ruskin is slightly misquoting Hazlitt's *Criticisms on Art and Sketches of the Picture Galleries of England* (1843), p. 24. Hazlitt writes 'beyond' after 'valleys'.

17 See William Henry Fox Talbot, *The Pencil of Nature* (1844). The title refers to the new process.

18 Leonardo, *Trattato* (see above, note 1), pp. 90–1.

Ruskinian Gothic

J. Mordaunt Crook

In 1765 Edward Gibbon, that most Augustan historian, visited
Venice. 'Of all the towns in Italy,' he wrote, 'I am least satisfied with
Venice.... Old, and in general, ill-built houses, ruined pictures, and
stinking ditches, dignified with the pompous denominations of
canals, a fine bridge spoilt by two rows of houses upon it, and a
large square decorated with some of the worst architecture I ever
saw.'[1] About one hundred years later Dickie Doyle's hilarious
Foreign Tour of Messrs Brown, Jones and Robinson includes a
caricature of three English tourists lolling blissfully in a gondola on
the Lagoon. 'Oh,' says one, 'if there be an elysium on earth, it is this,
it is this!'[2]

Between those two events occurred that great revolution in taste
which we call the Gothic Revival. Now the earlier, or Georgian,
phases of this movement—first the Rococo and then the Picturesque
—had been, with significant exceptions, largely indigenous to Britain. It was only the later, or Victorian phases—first the Ecclesiological and then the Eclectic—which assumed a fully international
flavour. So it was not until the late 1840s that Britain's Gothic

Revival began to look outside Britain for its sources of inspiration. And the man who is traditionally held to be responsible for this novel expansion of our national aesthetic is, of course, John Ruskin. Something called 'Ruskinian Gothic' is supposed to have swept across mid-Victorian England. But the more closely one examines that concept the more nebulous it seems. Ruskin certainly had an immense influence.[3] But what we find, when we dissect High Victorian Gothic, is a series of interlocking aesthetic factors, of which Ruskinian or Italian influence is only one. What I shall try to do here is to pick out that distinctive Italian accent amid a veritable babel of conflicting voices in the 1850s and the 1860s.

In 1849 two London churches were the talk of fashionable architectural circles. They were similar in that both were sponsored by the Cambridge Camden Society. They were different in that they represented successive and distinct phases in the search for an ecclesiological archetype. The first was St Mary Magdalen, Munster Square (1842–52), designed by R. C. Carpenter. Its style was fourteenth-century Decorated, its material Kentish ragstone. It was a country church incongruously marooned in the metropolis. Its design was precise, painstaking and dull. The second was All Saints, Margaret Street (1849–59), designed by William Butterfield, conceived as a town church, built of brick, and Continental in its inspiration.[4] Now the date of its design—1849—is also the date of the publication of Ruskin's *The Seven Lamps of Architecture*. And All Saints has often been presumed to be the morning star of Ruskinian Gothic. But its exterior is hardly Italian: it is much more reminiscent of north Germany—Frieburg, Breisach or Lubeck, for example. And its interior was not exactly to Ruskin's liking. The only time he mentioned All Saints was to remark in *The Stones of Venice*: 'I do not altogether like the arrangements of colour in the brickwork' (11.229). Maybe Italy was in Butterfield's mind, Assisi and Orvieto perhaps. But his abstract polychromy—developed here in 1850–51—owed as much to Matthew Digby Wyatt's book on mosaics[5] as it did to Ruskin's theories of design. And throughout his career Butterfield's details are more often English—from East Anglia and the Midlands[6]—than Italian. That is certainly true of his greatest work, Keble College, Oxford (1868–82) (fig. 26).[7] There the pattern—if not the scale—of his brickwork is closer to Norfolk than to north Italy. So Butterfield is only in part a Ruskinian Goth. And in fact neither Ruskin nor Butterfield was the first to propagate Continental brick prototypes.

Before All Saints, Margaret Street, there had been several prominent English examples of ecclesiastical designs which were consciously Continental in tone. Pugin's St Chad's, Birmingham (1839–41), looked to Lubeck. T. H. Wyatt's church at Wilton,

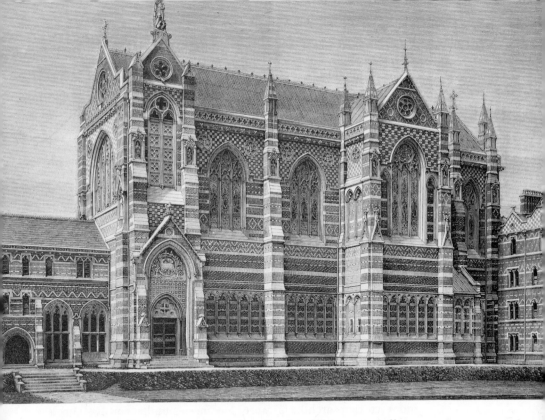

Wiltshire (1840–42), looked to Lombardy. That extraordinary building is of stone rather than brick, but its interior is perhaps the earliest example of the new Italian polychromy. James Wild's Christ Church, Streatham (1840), is something of a freak, anticipating High Victorian attitudes to colour, style and material by more than a decade. Both Wild and Wyatt were working in a pre-Renaissance, 'round-arched' style—what art historians call 'rundbogenstil'—a mixture of Early Christian, Lombard and Romanesque. This tentative, early Victorian synthesis in the Lombardic manner prepares us for the full-blown eclecticism of High Victorian Italian Gothic: Venetian, Veronese, Pisan and Florentine.

It was in 1835 that Professor Robert Willis—in some ways England's greatest architectural historian—began the process of rescuing Italian medieval architecture from 'contempt' and 'undeserved neglect'.[8] But English Gothic revivalists only began to show a serious interest in Italy from 1845 onwards. That was the year in which Benjamin Webb, secretary of the Ecclesiological Society, came back from north Italy, singing the praises of Italian Gothic: its colour, its massiveness of form, its simplicity of detail.[9] Webb's report was quickly followed by Thomas James's pamphlet on *Ecclesiastical Brickwork in Italy* (1847).[10] In the previous decade English publications on medieval Italy—by Thomas Hope, Robert Willis or Gally Knight—had been concerned with history, typology and structure.[11] Now the accent was on materials, on decoration, on

26
William Butterfield, The Chapel, Keble College, Oxford, 1868–82

colour. And all the old stereotypes of taste were overturned. Willis had drawn the line at Siena Cathedral: he thought zebra stripes were utterly 'destructive of architectural grandeur'.[12] Gally Knight had found it merely 'peculiar'.[13] But when Webb entered he felt as if he were in Westminster Abbey.[14] Knight found S. Zenone at Verona in parts 'ludicrous' and in general 'curious'.[15] But for Webb it was a building 'of prodigious interest'.[16] And the most that Knight could say about St Mark's, Venice, was that it seemed 'venerable and picturesque'.[17] For Webb its style was 'unique' and its 'gorgeousness of construction quite beyond description'.[18] So during the 1840s English attitudes towards Italian Gothic were beginning to change dramatically.

In 1849 this new aesthetic religion received its first instalment of Holy Writ: Ruskin's *Seven Lamps*. The next three instalments— that is, the volumes of *The Stones of Venice*—appeared in 1851–53. Finally, as if to demonstrate to all art historians the interaction of aesthetic and socio-economic factors, the tax on bricks was repealed in 1850.[19] The scene was set for High Victorian polychromy.

But what form was the new Victorian style to take? The choice of style was complicated by the interaction of two aesthetic factors: mid-Victorian architects were looking—simultaneously—for a style which embodied the beauties of the past *and* expressed the materials and necessities of the present. They wanted a style which was both old and new. Theirs was the dilemma of eclecticism, a dilemma compounded by historicist forms of design and associationist modes of thinking.

In 1849 Ruskin argued, in the *Seven Lamps*, for the rejection of styles and the pursuit of style: 'We want no new style in architecture. . . . But we want *some* style' (8.252). Once a single style had become universally accepted, its adaptation would eventually produce a new style suitable to a new world. Unfortunately, however, Ruskin recommended not one style but a choice of four: Pisan Romanesque, as in the Baptistry and Cathedral at Pisa; Early Gothic of the western Italian republics, as at Sta. Croce, Florence; Venetian Gothic—Sta. Maria dell'Orto, for example; and early English Decorated, as in the north transept at Lincoln. Of these four, he claimed to favour the last (8.258). But in practice his influence was all in favour of the third possibility: Venetian Gothic.

Now Ruskin's reputation as the apostle of Venetian Gothic was something he did his level best to shake off. In the 1855 edition of *Seven Lamps* he went out of his way to deny his supposed commitment to Venetian Gothic. 'The Gothic of Verona', he wrote, 'is far nobler than that of Venice; and that of Florence nobler than that of Verona. [But] For our own immediate purposes that of Notre-Dame of Paris is noblest of all' (8.13). In 1859 he announced that

Chartres was ten times as fine as St Mark's, Venice (16.469). But in vain. Ruskin and Venice were for ever linked. The phrase 'Ruskinian Gothic' had entered the English language.

Ruskin's contribution to the search for style was, anyhow, confused. In June 1853 he was invited to read a paper in Oxford on 'the Uses of Gothic'. He accepted. But he found himself too tired after finishing *The Stones of Venice*, so instead he set off on that ill-fated tour of the Highlands. His wife Effie noted: 'he wants rest, and has not time to prepare a Lecture. I think he is very wise, as for Oxford he ought to be perfectly got up.'[20] In fact the 'Uses of Gothic'— that is, the adaptability of Gothic to the Victorian age—was the ultimate problem of nineteenth-century architecture. Not an easy subject for a lecture, and one that Ruskin himself was never very clear about. Anyway, a few weeks later, in Scotland, he set to work on a New Style (fig. 27), using Millais as his *alter ego*. Millais wrote eagerly to Holman Hunt and Charles Collins, describing the operation.

27
Ruskin and Millais, A New Style of Architecture, 1853

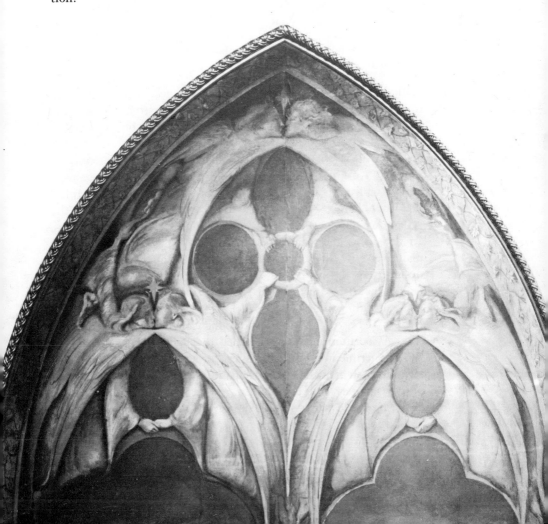

Ruskin and myself are deep in the design of novel architecture. He is quite astonished and delighted at my designs—he thought that we were simply capable of copying nature, and that we had no invention. Now he admits that he was awfully mistaken. . . . I have promised to design doors, arches, and windows for Churches. . . . It is the most amusing occupation and it comes quite easily and naturally to my hand. . . . Ruskin is beside himself with pleasure as he has been groaning for years about the lost feeling for Architecture. When I make a design he slaps his hands together in pleasure. He draws the arches and frames the mouldings for me to fill up. The Church which will be designed *entirely by me* (excepting the ground plan) will *for certain* be executed shortly as Ruskin is mad that it should be begun as soon as the drawings are made . . . Ruskin believes now that I have almost mistaken my vocation and that I was born to restore Architecture. Please say nothing about this, as we don't wish it to become public that we are working in consort. . . . I have made several drawings for the Church, among others a cloister on which are to be cut in stone all the vices and virtues opposed to each other. The windows I have finished represent eternal happiness and the struggle for life. To give you a notion of how they are designed (for they are unlike any other windows ever thought of) the figures form the shape of the windows [that is, the] figures are bended into [the] form of the porch, or window, instead of the rotten old notion of having flowers (which are naturally frail) to support walls.[21]

'Millais has done me a beautiful design of angels,' Ruskin reported to his father. And Ruskin's father was 'thunderstruck' by it. 'It is the most beautiful Painting/Fresco I ever set eyes on,' he gasped. . . . 'This is pure sublimity.'

Now Millais's painting was not only a design. It was intended to illustrate Ruskin's Edinburgh lectures. Ominously, all the angels have Effie Ruskin's profile. And when Effie left Ruskin for Millais the whole project collapsed. Interestingly, Ruskin regarded the scheme as so important that it transcended mere marital troubles. In 1854, *after* the scandal had broken, he was still writing, rather plaintively, to Millais, 'Have you given up all thought of *architectural* design?'[22]

Alas, neither Millais nor Ruskin ever found the New Style. In fact, soon afterwards, Ruskin decided it was wiser to stop looking. In 1857 he bravely addressed the young iconoclasts of the Architectural Association on what he called their chief 'head-problem in these experimental days': the quest for a style 'worthy of modern civilisation in general, and of England in particular; a style worthy of our engines and telegraphs; as expansive as steam, and as sparkling as electricity'. With the aim of a skilled debater he fired straight at their Achilles heel. What exactly was to be the form of this New Style? And, anyway, who was to form it, and for how long? Was each 'inventive architect' to 'invent a new style for himself, and have a county set aside for his conceptions, or a province for his practice? Or must every architect invent a little piece of the new style, and all put it together at last like a dissected map?' Anyway, what next? 'I will grant you this Eldorado of imagination—but can you have more than one Columbus? Or, if you sail in company . . . who is to come after your clustered Columbuses? . . . When our desired style is invented, will not the best we can all do be simply— to build in it?—and cannot you now do that in styles that are known?' Whatever happens, that New Style will not be final.

> You shall draw out your plates of glass and beat out your bars of iron till you have encompassed us all—if your style is of the practical kind— with endless perspective of black skeleton and blinding square—or if your style is to be of the ideal kind—you shall wreathe your streets with ductile leafage, and roof them with variegated crystal—you shall put, if you will, all London under one blazing dome of many colours that shall light the clouds round it with its flashing, as far as to the sea. And still, I ask you, What after this? . . . if you cannot rest content with Palladio, neither will you with Paxton. . . .

No, Ruskin concludes,

> If you think over this quietly by yourselves, and can get the noise out of your ears of the perpetual, empty, idle, incomparably idiotic talk about the necessity of some novelty in architecture, you will soon see that the very essence of a Style, properly so called, is that it should be practised *for ages*, and applied to all purposes; and that so long as any given style is in practice, all that is left for individual imagination to accomplish must be within the scope of that style, not in the invention of a new one. [16.348–9]

That was well said. But the public remained confused. In effect, Ruskin had lent the sanction of his name to a particular form of eclecticism: Anglo-Venetian Gothic. Very few mid-Victorian buildings followed Venetian Gothic prototypes with any degree of precision. One of the few architects who set out to translate medieval Venice into Victorian England was George Somers Clarke snr (1825–82). His office building for the General Credit and Discount Company (1866–68) at 7 Lothbury, next to the Bank of England, was described by the *Building News* as 'perhaps the nearest reproduction of the Venetian Gothic manner that has yet been made' (fig. 28). But the same journal went on to remark: 'Of course the exactitude of the reproduction detracts greatly from the *art-character* of the work.'[23] Even the chimney pots were laden with archaeology. Such exact imitation was perhaps curious, even fascinating; but ultimately it was aesthetically indefensible. In 1861 the same architect produced the Merchant Seamen's Orphan Asylum, now Wanstead Hospital (fig. 29). Here the scale is grander

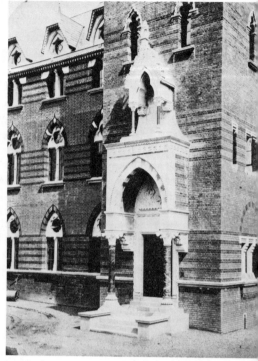

and the materials are cheaper, but the level of replication is much the same. Indeed, some of the details—mostly Venetian or Veronese —produce a sense of *déjà vu* which is almost uncanny.

But it was not in mimicry like this that the future of Victorian Gothic lay. Its destiny was a broader, more flexible eclecticism. And in this respect the work of three architects is particularly instructive: Benjamin Woodward, George Edmund Street and Sir Gilbert Scott.

Benjamin Woodward (1815–61)[24] was junior partner in a firm of Irish architects known as Deane and Woodward who came to prominence in 1853 with their new Museum—later the Engineering School—at Trinity College, Dublin. Thomas Deane (1792–1871) was a builder, and the son and grandson of a builder, from County Cork.[25] A man of energy and talent, he became Sir Thomas Deane, Lord Mayor of Cork, at the age of thirty-eight, in 1830. Thereupon he took up architecture, first as a Neo-classicist and then as a Gothic Revivalist. His son, Thomas Newenham Deane (1828–99), was educated at Rugby and Trinity College, Dublin, and joined his father's firm in Cork in 1850.[26] Two years later the firm's architectural style was transformed by the arrival of a third partner, Benjamin Woodward. Woodward's early years are still something of a mystery. He also came from County Cork, perhaps from the family of Dr Richard Woodward (d. 1794), Bishop of Cloyne.[27] During the 1840s he was working in Thomas Deane's office and travelling—almost certainly—in Italy. It was Woodward who launched Ruskinian Gothic: on Dublin in 1853; on Oxford in 1854; and on London in 1856. With offices in Cork, Dublin and London,[28] the firm of Deane and Woodward, sponsored by Ruskin and Rossetti, became almost an architectural branch of the Pre-Raphaelite Brotherhood.[29] But in 1861 Woodward, a frail, tubercular genius, died of consumption, and the fire went out of the firm.[30] Thomas Deane lived on until 1871. Thomas Newenham Deane became the architectural doyen of Victorian Dublin, and was himself knighted in 1890. His son Thomas Manley Deane (1851–1933) —the fifth generation of the family—maintained the firm's reputation into the twentieth century.[31] But it was Woodward who had been—in Rossetti's words—the firm's 'quickening spirit'.[32]

Certainly Woodward must take most of the credit for winning the Dublin competition of 1853. Ruskin congratulated him on the design and seems to have encouraged him to enter for the Oxford Museum competition in 1854.[33] Again he was the winner, and Ruskin introduced his young protégé—'one of my truest and most loving friends' (18.150)—to all the leading Pre-Raphaelites. That winter Rossetti first met Woodward at dinner at Ruskin's, found him 'gentle' and 'quiet', and fell in love with him 'for life'.[34] The following summer William Allingham wrote to Rossetti, 'Yesterday in Dublin I saw but hastily the part-finished building in Trinity College, which is after Ruskin's own heart. Style early Venetian (I suppose) with numberless capitals delicately carved over with holly leaves, shamrocks, various flowers, birds and so on. . . . [No doubt] all you *cognoscenti* will be rushing over to examine the Stones of Dublin.'[35] Outside, Venetian Byzantine-Renaissance with touches of French Romanesque; inside, polychrome Morisco-Gothic (fig. 30): the building was certainly a monument to the new eclecticism.[36] It was also an eloquent advertisement for Ruskin's theories of design: 'the first realisation I had the joy to see, of the principles I had . . . been endeavouring to teach' (18.141–50)—that is, truth to nature, truth to materials, constructional polychromy, significant ornament, and the creative autonomy of the craftsman.

Then came the Oxford Museum (1854–60) (figs. 31 and 16).[37] Not only an essay in Ruskinian Gothic, but a full-blown experiment in progressive design: an attempt to combine historic forms with the materials of the railway age, cast and wrought iron. Its design brought together very different sources: Venetian fenestration, Veronese mouldings, Byzantine carving and a Netherlandish roof line with echoes of Ypres or Nuremburg; a quadrangular plan on traditional Oxford collegiate lines; and, finally, an octagonal

30 right
T. N. Deane and Benjamin Woodward, staircase, Engineering Schools, Trinity College, Dublin, 1853–57

31 below
T. N. Deane and Benjamin Woodward, The University Museum, Oxford, 1854–60

laboratory whose ancestor—a very long way back—was the monastic kitchen at Glastonbury. Its construction was a drama played out with wildly different characters in the leading roles: the eloquent Ruskin, the silent Woodward and the mercurial Irish stonemason James O'Shea. On the periphery were a shoal of young Pre-Raphaelites playing subsidiary parts: Morris and Burne-Jones, still undergraduates at Exeter College; Thomas Woolner the sculptor; Millais and Rossetti.

One Oxford man remembered the scene. 'Into our midst came Woodward, architect of the museum, a man of rare genius and deep artistic knowledge, beautiful in face and character but with the shadow of an early death already stealing over him.'[38] Rossetti's brother noted that 'he was the very reverse of what Irishmen are . . . assumed to be . . . modest, retiring . . . taciturn . . . gentle and courteous'.[39] Acland called him 'refined . . . fastidious . . . almost a recluse'.[40] 'His life,' wrote Thomas Woolner, 'looks as weak as a little candle in the open air. He is the most splendid genius we have in architecture, and his loss would not be made up in a hurry.'[41] 'Woodward brought with him his Dublin pupils, drew round him eager Oxonians. . . . The lovely museum rose before us like an exhalation, its every detail, down to panels and footboards, gas-burners and door-handles, an object lesson in art, stamped with Woodward's Picturesque inventiveness and refinement. Not before had ironwork been so plastically trained as by Skidmore in the chestnut boughs and foliage which sustained the transparent roof. . . . Every morning came the handsome red-haired Irish brothers O'Shea bearing plants from the Botanic Garden to reappear under their chisels in the rough-hewn capitals of the pillars. . . . Ruskin himself hovered about to bless the . . . work, to offer cheques, and to suggest improvements, which silent Woodward sometimes smiling-ly put by.'[42]

It was the O'Shea family—the O'Sheas of Balyhooly,[43] Nature's own Pre-Raphaelites—who stole the show. Beginning each day with a prayer; lectured to by Ruskin on political economy in the evening; they were the embodiment of the hypothetical Ruskinian artisan. On another occasion Woolner described James O'Shea at work: 'O'Shea is doing his work like a man, and the corbels are bursting forth into violets, roses, thistles, ivies and other things lovelier than their names . . . such rapidity of workmanship I never saw. He does three corbels a day! I thought he would take a day each.'[44] 'Your Museum,' Ruskin told Acland, 'is literally the first building raised in England since the close of the fifteenth century which has fearlessly put to new trial this old faith in nature, and in the genius of the unassisted workman, who gathered out of nature the materials he needed'; it is 'the first exponent of the recovered truth' (16.231,234). Ruskin even helped to design one of the windows himself, besides paying for several more.⁴⁵

But, alas, the autonomy of the inspired artisan was an expensive luxury. Convocation starved the project of funds. The sculptured porch designed by Hungerford Pollen for Thomas Woolner was never built.⁴⁶ O'Shea ended up carving caricatures of his academic superiors in the guise of parrots and owls.⁴⁷ And eventually even Ruskin came to see the whole building as 'a failure': Skidmore's ironwork failed to turn the new material into a new style—his wrought iron supports had even to be replaced by cast iron;⁴⁸ the walls inside were never frescoed and remained 'built of common brickbats'; most of the carving remained unfinished, and even those sections which had been carved were the work not of a revived school of artists but merely of one 'lively Irishman' (20.524–5; 16.lxii).⁴⁹

In the long run it is doubtful whether Ruskin received any greater pleasure from Deane and Woodward's other Oxford buildings— the Oxford Union (1857)⁵⁰ and Meadow Buildings, Christ Church (1862–66)⁵¹—still less the bricky villas of north Oxford,⁵² though he would have recognised the talent in the carving designed by Hungerford Pollen at 62 Banbury Road (1864–65) (fig. 33).⁵³ Pollen was one of the major talents produced by the Ruskinian phase. His University Chaplaincy for the National University in Dublin (1855–56) is perhaps the most extraordinary instance of Byzantine-Romanesque taste in the whole history of the Gothic Revival.⁵⁴

Meanwhile Ruskinian Gothic had reached London in the shape of two insurance offices—long since demolished—in New Bridge Street, Blackfriars (1855–57) and Fleet Street (1862–65) (fig. 32). The first of these was visible from Rossetti's studio. He called it 'the most perfect piece of domestic architecture of the new school that I have seen in London. I never cease to look at it with delight.'⁵⁵ Both buildings were the product of the same team of artists and craftsmen: Ruskin, Woodward, Deane, O'Shea, Whelan and Pollen. Their polychrome features—Sicilian marble in red and green; white Portland stone; buff Caen stone; red, black and grey-blue granite—were hailed as a breakthrough in urban design. Such exoticism represented an escape from 'the beaten track of stereotyped monotony in our street architecture'.⁵⁶ As for the style, some contemporaries called it 'Italio-Gothic', others Pisan-Romanesque, Veronese or Venetian Gothic. Perhaps we should just settle for Ruskinian.⁵⁷ Whatever it is, it is eclectic.

Back in Ireland, the Kildare Street Club (1858–59) erupted amid the monochrome terraces of Georgian Dublin. Its brickwork was vermilion pink, its voussoirs striped grey-blue. And some of the

carving—monkeys playing billiards, for example, by young C. W. Harrison—outdid even O'Shea.[58] After Woodward's death T. N. Deane more than maintained the Byzantine-Gothic banner. 'We are glad to hear,' noted one journal, that 'Mr. T. N. Deane is . . . about to desecrate "the plain straight lines" [of Dublin] by giving the inhabitants . . . a taste of Medievalism.'[59] His Munster Bank (1870–73) in Dame Street (fig. 34) is the most striking surviving instance of this new commercial idiom in the British Isles. Partly because of its corner site, there is no sense of incongruity. Not so at Kilkenny Castle. There Woodward's Venetian balconies of 1859 look a little out of place in the feudal stronghold of the Butlers.[60]

Apart from Woodward, the only architect Ruskin regularly praised was George Edmund Street. Street's loyalties were first and foremost to Early French Gothic. He ranked Chartres and Amiens with the Parthenon as 'the noblest and most masculine . . . architecture in the world; in Paris, Notre Dame was 'supreme' and the Ste Chapelle a 'work of inspired genius'.[61] As regards Italian Gothic, therefore, Street's book on *Brick and Marble in the Middle Ages* (1855) maintains a level of cool, astringent criticism which makes a refreshing contrast with Ruskin's glowing enthusiasms.

Street went on an elaborate tour of north Italy in 1853. The high points of his journey were as follows: in Bergamo, Sta Maria Maggiore;[62] in Verona, San Zenone, S. Fermo Maggiore and the tombs of the Scaligeri;[63] in Padua, the Arena Chapel;[64] in Venice, St Mark's and the Ducal Palace;[65] at Cremona, the Cathedral and the Palace of the Jurisconsults;[66] at Pavia, the Castle of the Visconti;[67] at Milan, the interior of the Cathedral;[68] at Vercelli, the interior of Sant' Andrea;[69] and at Como, the exterior of the Broletto.[70] He saw much to admire and much to condemn.

Street admitted openly that North Italian Gothic was by no means perfect. It lacked the 'completeness in . . . development' of English and French Gothic.[71] It lacked the visible engineering— the buttresses, the multiple vaulting, the petrified science—of North European Gothic.[72] It never entirely shook off the incubus of antique classicism: hence its hybridity in plan and form.[73] It was the product of many nationalities: 'the Italians employed Greeks, Moors, Frenchmen, Germans, Catalonians. . . .' The result was 'very eclectic'.[74] It even embodied alien influences from the East, hence 'the Venetian love for the ogee arch . . . a most vitiated perversion'.[75] On the other hand, it was exactly this synthesis which made it so appealing as a model for the eclecticism of the nineteenth century.[76] And although its workmanship was 'inferior' to the Gothic of France and England, the professionalism which created it —and its application, in particular, to secular, urban domestic and public buildings—made it peculiarly relevant to the problems of

33 *left*
J. Hungerford
Pollen, porch, 62
Banbury Road,
Oxford, 1864–65

34 *below*
T. N. Deane,
Munster Bank,
Dame Street,
Dublin, 1870–73

Victorian architects.[77] Most of all, 'in . . . the introduction of colour in construction . . . Italian architecture of the Middle Ages teaches us', says Street, 'more than any other architecture since the commencement of the world'.[78] Polychromy—whether incrusted in the Venetian manner, or constructional in the manner of Bergamo, Cremona or Como—polychromy was the answer to the inhibiting puritan aesthetic of north European Protestantism.[79] The average Englishman's 'insane hatred of bright colours' was best cured by a holiday in Italy.[80] And that holiday should have as its climax the wondrous triple church of Assisi.[81]

Italian Gothic, therefore, was not a prototype worthy of precise imitation—that privilege was reserved for Early French—but an inspiration and a stimulus, a key ingredient in the creation of a new synthesis. And Street's version of that synthesis is seen at its most complex in his greatest building, the Law Courts in London (1868–82). Having passed through a first phase[82]—Puginian, English and Picturesque—and a second phase (fig. 35)—Ruskinian, Italian and Sublime—Street settled in middle age on a personal synthesis which owed something to England and Italy, something to Spain and the Netherlands, but most of all to France.[83] His Law Courts, therefore, are the culmination of this eclectic progression: Pevsner calls it English; Hitchcock calls it French;[84] but we might

35 below
George Edmund Street, St James the Less, Thorndyke Street, Westminster, 1860–61

36 right
George Edmund Street, the Law Courts, London, 1868–82

equally call it Italian—especially the Carey Street front (fig. 36). For it is all three: English, French and Italian: eclectic and triply so—even if, from a compositional point of view—its parts are greater than their sum. The most striking exterior unit in the design —the Sienese tower on the Carey Street front—must seem strangely familiar to Roman eyes. It strongly recalls the tower Street designed for the American Church in Rome (1873–76). Here Italian Gothic was returning to the land of its origin: a prodigal returned, but a prodigal prodigiously transformed.

In their different ways Woodward and Street were both trying to do the same thing: to call in the Gothic of southern Europe—its colour, its variety, its fire—to rejuvenate the Gothic of the north. So was Gilbert Scott. The title page of Scott's *Secular and Domestic Architecture, Past and Future* (1858) sums up his own philosophy: an imaginary town square, where the Doge's Palace of Venice faces the Cloth Hall at Ypres in happy fellowship.

Being slightly older than Woodward and Street, Scott began his career very much in the Puginian mould. His Martyrs' Memorial at Oxford (1841–43) is still English in form, modelled on the Eleanor Crosses of the thirteenth century. But by the end of his career, at the Albert Memorial (1863–72) in London—inspired by Orcagna's shrine at Or San Michele in Florence—he was fully absorbed the form and spirit of Italian Gothic. Scott always re-garded Pugin as 'the great hero'.[85] But as his career advanced he looked more and more beyond England, to Flanders, France, Germany and Italy. This 'progressive eclecticism' was a doctrine he borrowed from Beresford-Hope, the high priest of ecclesiology, to whom Scott's *Secular and Domestic Architecture* was dedicated. Hope's advice to the eclectic was: sin boldly.[86] Scott was ready to oblige.

Scott's tour of Italy, in 1851–52, was conducted at helter-skelter pace. In Venice he was initially put off by Benjamin Ferrey mutter-ing at his elbow, 'Batty Langley, Batty Langley.' But he did meet Ruskin there, and after tea one evening they had a 'great architec-tural séance' (10.xxxiii). In Florence he spent only three days— 'three days of the purest delight'—and was in such a rush that he forgot to see S. Miniato. In Siena he spent only three hours: 'the hardest three hours' work in my life'. In Pisa his 'unalloyed delight' was limited to 'one working day and a Sunday'. In Genoa he thought the west front of the cathedral the best Gothic he had seen in Italy, and therefore probably by a Frenchman. Rushing to beat the Alpine snow, he spent only one day in Milan, and didn't stop at all at Pavia. 'I must say,' he wrote years later, 'that I gained very much by this journey. . . . I was convinced, however, that Italian Gothic, as such, must not be used in England, but I was equally convinced, and am so still, that the study of it is necessary to the perfecting of our revival.'[87] 'I never,' he concludes, 'fell into . . . the Italian mania.'[88]

On the face of it, Italian Gothic seemed to compromise two of the Gothic Revivalists' trump cards: it was foreign, not national; and it was decorative rather than constructional. Indeed, Scott—like Street—had no illusions at all about its inferiority. It constituted a quarry, to be used with caution.[89] Its polychromy was its great attraction.[90] Its danger was its standing encouragement to 'unbridled eclecticism'.[91]

Scott's eclectic style begins with his Whitehall competition scheme of 1856; develops with Kelham Hall, Notts. (1858–62);[92] continues with Preston Town Hall (1862–67), Beckett's [now Westminster] Bank, Leeds (1864–66) and Hafodunos, near Llanrwst, North Wales (1861–66); and culminates at St Pancras station and hotel (1868–74).[93]

In designing the Foreign and War Office in 1856 Scott tells us, 'I did not aim at making my style "Italian Gothic"; my ideas ran much more upon the French, to which for some years I had devoted my chief study. I did, however, aim at gathering a few hints from Italy, such as the pillar mullion, the use of differently coloured materials, and of inlaying. I also aimed at another thing which people consider Italian—I mean a certain squareness and horizontality of outline. This I consider pre-eminently suited to the street front of a public building. I combined this, however, with gables, high-pitched roofs, and dormers.'[94] Scott's design had no buttresses, plenty of polychromy in colonnettes and voussoirs, elaborate Italian Gothic porches, and broad sash windows divided by colonnettes. 'My style,' he told the judges, 'is, generally speaking, more columnar and more thoroughly arcuated than has been usual in the modern treatment of the style.'[95]

Scott's design became the centre of a famous controversy. It was immediately christened 'the great Gothic design' to distinguish it from also-rans like those of Street and Woodward.[96] By comparison, Street's design seemed tame and disjointed and Woodward's a mere 'Venetian jumble', more suitable for 'the Doge and Senate' than for the government of 'the English commonwealth'.[97] J. H. Parker of Oxford thought Scott's design had an equally mixed and 'foreign' look.[98] But then, Parker was an early Victorian, and a Puginian at heart. What he failed to realise was that it was precisely the eclecticism of Italian Gothic which appealed to the mid-Victorian mind. A revival of Pugin's 'true thing' was no longer enough. High Victorian architectects were looking to the eclecticism of the past to provide them with a basis for an eclecticism of the future. As it happened, however, Prime Minister Palmerston belonged to an older generation still: he vetoed both Scott's Gothic design and a variant Byzantine scheme which the architect produced in desperation.[99] In the end, much against his will, Scott was compelled to produce the present mixed Renaissance Foreign Office, with assistance from Matthew Digby Wyatt.

At St Pancras, however, Scott got his chance. This time he decided to play down the Italian element somewhat. The polychromy is still there. But the skyline is no longer rectangular but syncopated, no longer Italian but Dutch or Flemish; and some of the details are Early English and Early French. The Cloth Hall at Ypres is the origin of the station entrance tower; Oudenarde town hall probably supplied the inspiration for his gabled and pinnacled hotel entrance;

the mouldings around the great portals are Early French; the first-floor oriel windows incorporate distant echoes of Bishop Bridport's tomb at Salisbury Cathedral; other windows, just as clearly, are Anglicised Venetian. With a pedigree like that no wonder Scott thought his design almost '*too good* for its purpose'.[100] Eclecticism had become the *lingua franca* of High Victorian Gothic. 'This is not copybook stuff,' Sir John Summerson concludes, 'it is improvisation on to the drawing board. To fail to appreciate this is to fail hopelessly to understand Victorian architecture.'[101]

37
Col. St Clair
Wilkins, R.E.,
Public Works
Office, Bombay,
1869–72

Such eclecticism could be, and was, exported all over the world. To India, for instance, where Bombay still boasts formidable examples of Anglo-Venetian Victorian, such as the Public Works Offices (fig. 37).[102] And America, where the Harvard Memorial Hall, by Ware and Van Brunt (1867), confirmed the acceptability of Ruskinian Gothic in New England,[103] and makes a fleeting appearance in Henry James's *The Bostonians* (1886).[104]

Eclecticism, however, also required skill and restraint. And Scott readily admitted the dangers of its popularity. Just 'as we were generating a secular style peculiarly suited to our wants', he complained in the later 1860s, it fell into the hands of 'an ignorant and untutored rabble'.[105]

Ruskinism, such as would make Ruskin's very hair stand on end [Memorial Hall, Manchester, 1864–66, by Thomas Worthington]; Butterfieldism, gone mad with its endless strippings of red and black bricks [houses in Banbury, Oxon., 1866, by W. Wilkinson]; architecture so French that a Frenchman would not know it, out-Heroding Herod himself [Tavistock, Devon, church by Henry Clutton, 1865]; Byzantine in all forms but those used by the Byzantines [Dublin, university chaplaincy, by Hungerford Pollen, 1855–56]; mixtures of all or some of these; 'original' styles founded upon knowledge of old styles, or upon ignorance of them . . .; violent strainings after something very strange, and great successes in producing something very weak; attempts at beauty resulting in ugliness, and attempts at ugliness attended with unhoped for success [Vinegar Warehouses, 33–5 Eastcheap, London, 1868, by R. L. Roumieu]. All these have given a wild absurdity to much of the architecture of the last seven or eight years, which one cannot but deplore: but at the same time it must be allowed that much of the best, the most nervous, and the most original results of the revival, have been arrived at within the same period [Elvetham, Hants., by Samuel Sanders Teulon, 1859–60].[106]

It was indeed a precarious balance, poised between originality and absurdity. As G. E. Street put it, 'this hot taste is dangerous'.[107]

Ruskin certainly had much to be responsible for. Twenty years after the publication of *The Stones of Venice* he was still bitterly regretting the popularity of Venetian Gothic. Living in suburban London, near the Crystal Palace, he saw himself surrounded by Anglo-Italian Gothic villas—'Frankenstein monsters' of his own making, like 107 Tulse Hill, built to designs by Charles Hambridge in 1865. No wonder he fled to the Lake District.[108]

39 left
J. and J. Belcher, Mansion House Buildings, Poultry, London, 1870

40 below
G. Aitchison, 56–61 Mark Lane, London, 1864

Nevertheless, Ruskinian Gothic also had its triumphs, and in ways which Ruskin, no doubt, least expected. 'Remember,' he wrote, 'that it is the glory of Gothic architecture that it can do *anything*' (12.78). That dictum came nearest to fulfilment in the unlikely shape of the High Victorian warehouse and multi-storey office building.

Bristol, Manchester and London were the three urban centres which best exploited this Ruskinian medium in a commercial context. And nowhere more strikingly than Bristol, the city which once vied with Amsterdam as the Venice of the North. 'Bristol Byzantine' was a style which reached its apogee with one very remarkable warehouse: the Granary, Welsh Back (fig. 38).[109] This was designed by a local firm, Ponton and Gough, for local clients, Messrs Wait and Jones,[110] with distinctly North Italian imagery—'looking, in some lights', as Sir John Summerson puts it, 'like the palace of an eccentric doge with a prophetic passion for skyscrapers'.[111] Ten stories high; £6,000 worth of brick, iron, timber and concrete; mechanically operated, with hydraulic lifts in each corner, feeding sliding containers which disgorged their contents—12,000 quarters of wheat—through multicoloured portholes. The North Italian prototypes have been industrialised, synthesised, abstracted.

Manchester and London never quite matched that. But they still possess a number of effective examples. Business premises like 109 Princess Street, Manchester (1863), by Clegg and Knowles; factories like Lavers and Barraud's stained glass works in Endell Street, London, designed by R. J. Withers in 1859; warehouses like those at 18–20 St John Street, London;[112] or offices like several in the City of London: in Throgmorton Street, by J. Chatfield Clarke (1869), or in Poultry, by J. and J. Belcher (1870) (fig. 39) and R. H. Moore (1869). Anglo-Venetian Gothic lent itself admirably to the multiplied grid formation of urban commercial properties. The grid could be chopped into sections, or extended indefinitely, or even wrapped round corners, as at Albert Buildings in Queen Victoria Street, London, by F. J. Ward (1871).[113]

It was left to George Aitchison, who as a young man had travelled with Burges in Italy, to carry the flexibility of the new style to its logical conclusion. At 56–61 Mark Lane in the City of London (fig. 40) Aitchison designed a façade in 1864 consisting of the three tiers of Byzantine-Gothic arches decorated with bands of inlaid black mastic. Behind, and independent of, the serried colonnettes are plate-glass windows. And behind, and independent of, the whole façade is an autonomous, fireproof structure of cast iron.[114] Ruskin's theory of the wall-veil—the façade as an expressive skin, an idea derived from medieval Italy—had been turned to novel advantage. The future development of the Chicago skyscraper had been foreshadowed, in miniature, in a London City back street.

By the late 1860s, therefore, Italian or Ruskinian influence on Victorian Gothic was scarcely identifiable as such: it had been absorbed into the mainstream of eclectic historicism. By 1884 Beresford-Hope could look back on the days when Woodward's Oxford Museum was 'hailed as an architectural revelation' as utterly remote: 'as remote as the days of Chambers and the Adam family, perhaps more so'.[115] The hey day of Ruskinian Gothic was indeed brief. And even in its heyday it was diluted by other influences, particularly English, Flemish and French Gothic. The more one looks at the Italian medieval sources of High Victorian Gothic, the more one realises that the inspiration is very rarely direct. Compared with the precise archaeology of Georgian and Regency Neo-classicism, High Victorian Gothic is consciously imprecise. During the 1850s and the 1860s Italian Gothic is merely one of several streams of inspiration mingled in a veritable ocean of eclecticism. The prototypes are transfigured by the eclectic process into a style which is frequently individual, often idiosyncratic, but always identifiably Victorian.

1 R. E. Prothero, ed., *Private Letters of Edward Gibbon*, I (1896), p. 75.   NOTES

2 R. Doyle, *The Foreign Tour of Messrs Brown, Jones and Robinson* (1854), 1904 ed., p. 69.

3 Goodhart-Rendel's love of paradox caused him seriously to undervalue Ruskin's influence (H. S. Goodhart-Rendel, *English Architecture since the Regency* (1953), pp. 135, 142). Contemporary architectural periodicals confirm that influence beyond doubt.

4 P. Thompson, 'All Saints, Margaret Street, Reconsidered', *Architectural History*, VIII (1965), 73–87.

5 M. D. Wyatt, *Specimens of the Geometrical Mosaics of the Middle Ages* (1849).

6 As a precedent for the carved bosses at All Saints, Thompson points to Warmington, Northants.

7 In 1875 Palgrave, author of Murray's *Handbook to North Italy*, called it 'the most beautiful church built within my knowledge—proportions, details equally lovely and original; the whole with a shrine-like air, yet also with a look of size and power most rarely united' (G. F. Palgrave, ed. *F. T. Palgrave*, 1899, p. 139).

8 R. Willis, *Remarks on the Architecture of the Middle Ages, especially of Italy* (1835), I, p. iii.

9 Webb was there in 1844, and reported in 1845 'On Pointed Architecture as adapted to Tropical Climates', *Trans. Eccles. Soc.* (1845), 199–218. His findings were definitively presented in *Sketches of Continental Ecclesiology* (1848), for which Butterfield prepared the illustrations. Webb's ectasy in north Italy is already Ruskinian: he called Verona 'dream-like' and Venice 'the realisation of a dream' (*ibid.*, pp. 242, 299).

10 'On the use of Brick in Ecclesiastical Architecture', *Fourth Report of the Architectural Society of . . . Northampton*, pp. 25–37.

11 T. Hope, *Historical Essay on Architecture* (1835); Willis, *op. cit.*; H. Gally Knight, *Ecclesiastical Architecture of Italy from the Time of Constantine to the Fifteenth Century* (1842–44).

12 Willis, *op. cit.*, p. 12.

13 Knight, *op. cit.*, p. xxiv.

14 Webb. *op. cit.*, p. 381.

15 Knight, *op. cit.*, pp. vi, vii.

16 Webb, *op. cit.*, p. 251.

17 Knight, *op. cit.*, p. xxxi.

18 Webb, *op. cit.*, pp. 268–9.

19 A. Clifton-Taylor, *Patterns of English Building* (1962).

20 Mary Lutyens, *Millais and the Ruskins* (1967), pp. 40, 44.

21 *Ibid.*, pp. 80–2n, 147.

22 *Ibid.*, p. 247.

23 *Building News*, XXIV (1866), 679, 792. So narrow was the site that much of the decoration was almost invisible: an 'exemplification of "sacrifice" that [amounted to] torture' for the spectator. See also *ibid.*, XV (1868), 11, 29, 147.

24 W. Papworth, ed., *Dictionary of Architecture* (1852–92); *Builder*, xix (1861), 436; *Irish Builder*, III (1861), 563; D. S. Richardson, 'Gothic Revival Architecture in Ireland' (Ph.D., Yale, 1974).

25 *Builder*, XXIX (1871), 804, obituary.

26 *Builder*, LXXVII (1899), 471, obituary; *British Architect*, lii (1899) 343, obituary; *R.I.B.A. Journal*, 3rd series, VII (1899), 48–9; obituary by Thomas Drew.

27 C. P. Curran, 'B. Woodward, Ruskin and the O'Sheas', *Studies* (Dublin), XXIX (1940), 255–68. [See also Eve Blau, *Ruskinian Gothic. The Architecture of Deane and Woodward, 1845–1861* (Princeton, forth-coming).—Eds.]

28 3 Upper Marrion Street, Dublin; 88 St James's Street, London.

29 The three partners made a curious trio. Rossetti called Woodward 'the stillest creature that ever breathed out of an oyster shell' (J. W. Mackail, *William Morris*, I (1899), p. 122). The elder Deane was an incurable chatterbox, and the son had an embarrassing stammer; one don remarked, 'One won't talk, one can't talk, and one never stops talking' (Vice-chancellor Jeune, quoted in W. Tuckwell, *Reminiscences of Oxford*, 1907, pp. 51–2).

30 He died at Lyons, having previously wintered at Hyères in Algeria: 'such a lonely deathbed . . . [he was] unutterably devoted to . . . the Art which he loved, I am sure more dearly than his life' (D.G. Rossetti, *Letters*, ed. O. Doughty and J. R. Wahl, II (1965), pp. 404–11).

31 He became a pupil of William Burges in 1872, and travelled abroad on a Royal Academy fellowship in 1876–78 (*Builder* LXXVII, 1899, 471).

32 Rossetti, *Letters*, *loc. cit.*

33 This persistent legend has yet to be confirmed by primary evidence.

34 Rossetti, *Letters*, *loc. cit.*

35 Quoted in Ruskin, 16.xliv.

36 'One of the greatest masterpieces of the Gothic Revival, the finest secular building the movement ever produced' (Osbert Lancaster, *Cornhill Magazine*, May 1944). For contemporary praise see *Dublin Builder*, III (1861), 563. Some of the motifs derive from Palazzo Dario

and Casa Visetti, Venice (*Builder*, XI, 1853, 420).

37 H. M. and K. D. Vernon, *A History of the Oxford Museum* (Oxford, 1909).

38 Tuckwell, *loc. cit.*

39 W. M. Rossetti, *D. G. Rossetti. Letters, etc.*, I (1895), p. 195.

40 H. W. Acland and J. Ruskin, *Oxford Museum* (1859).

41 A. Woolner, ed., *Thomas Woolner. Life and Letters* (1917), p. 156.

42 Tuckwell, *loc. cit.*

43 *Builder*, XIV (1856), 171. James O'Shea, his brother John, and his nephew Edward Whelan or Whelland.

44 Woolner to Palgrave, 1861, describing his new studio at 29 Welbeck Street (Woolner, *op. cit.*, pp. 205, 213).

45 Acland and Ruskin, *op. cit.*, pp. 106. He also seems to have designed part of Skidmore's metal bracketing.

46 Woolner, *op. cit.*, pp. 194; see Ruskin, 16.lii and 28.366.

47 This famous episode is described at length in 16.xlix. The university authorities seem to have objected to 'the unnecessary introduction of cats' (*Aratra Pentelici*: 16.231).

48 Vernon, *op. cit.*, p. 70.

49 See 20.16. The interior capitals were eventually completed by two carvers called Mills and Holt, working for Farmer and Brindley in 1906–15 (Vernon, *op. cit.*, pp. 85–6).

50 The story of the Pre-Raphaelite decoration of the interior has often been told. See Georgiana Burne-Jones, *Memorials of Sir Edward Burne-Jones* (1904).

51 This was the work of T. N. Deane alone. The carvings by Whelan were never finished. Critics received it 'without . . . any violent expressions of admiration' (*Builder*, XXIV, 1866, 346–7).

52 Mostly designed by Wilkinson and Codd; see N. Pevsner and Jennifer Sherwood, *Oxfordshire* (1974), pp. 317–22.

53 Designed by E. G. Bruton (*ibid.*, pp. 271).

54 For Pollen see Anne Pollen, *John Hungerford Pollen* (1912).

55 Rossetti, *Letters*, *op. cit.*, II (1965), pp. 404–11.

56 *Building News*, IV (1858), 723, 725; XII (1865), 438–9, 447. See also *Illustrated Builders' Journal*, I (1865), 85–6.

57 H.-R. Hitchcock, 'Monuments of Commerce', *Architectural Review*, CV (1949), 66.

58 Members rejected both circular and pointed windows, so Woodward compromised with segmental openings and slim colonnettes which did not impede the sashes. The total cost was some £25,000, of which less than £800 was spent on carving (*Dublin Builder*, III, 1861, 600).

59 *Building News*, XII (1865), 442, with reference to the Crown Assurance Office.

60 Here Woodward was responsible for a new picture gallery, with polychrome walls, and hammerbeam roof. In the near-by cathedral of St Canice, restored by T. N. Deane, there is a stained glass window in Woodward's memory.

61 G. E. Street, *Brick and Marble in the Middle Ages. Notes of Tours in the North of Italy* (1874 ed.), pp. 4, 9.

62 *Ibid.*, frontispiece.

63 Respectively, *ibid.*, pp. 111–12 ('This noble church'), ills., 117;

pp. 121–2 ('the best details of brickwork in all Italy'), ills. *ibid.*; pp. 102–3, ills.

64 *Ibid.*, p. 139, ill.

65 Respectively *ibid.*, pp. 153–5: ('Very outré. . . . It is quite in vain to describe this in formal architectural terms. The colour is so magnificent that one troubles oneself but little about the architecture . . . all architectural lines of moulding are entirely lost, and nothing but a soft swelling and undulating sea of colour is perceived . . . yet the mystery of colour does for it even more than the mystery of size does for Köln or Beauvais, Milan, Toledo, or Bourges') and pp. 197–210: ('The very best and truest specimen of Gothic . . . South of the Alps . . . [but] not properly to be placed in the first class . . . in some respects of almost unparallelled beauty, but at the same time of unequal merit').

66 *Ibid.*, pp. 266, ill., and 269, ill., respectively.

67 *Ibid.*, pp. 277–8, ills.: 'Refined and delicate almost beyond . . . any brickwork that I know elsewhere.'

68 *Ibid.*, p. 321: 'amazement . . . and delight that anything so magnificent and so perfect should ever have been reared on the Southern slopes of the Alps, to exhibit, to the eyes as it were of enemies, the full majesty and power of the pointed architecture of the North . . . one of the grandest interiors in the world'.

69 *Ibid.*, p. 332, ill.: 'So good that I found myself in the rare state of mind (in an Italian church) of admiring without grumbling!'

70 *Ibid.*, p. 340, ill., 380.

71 *Ibid.*, p. 366. 'I am not by any means a blind enthusiast about Italian architecture.' Italian Gothic 'never produced anything perfect both in detail and mass; and one always finds it necessary to make excuses for even the best works'. Compared with the Gothic of northern Europe, 'undoubtedly there is very much less external grandeur' (*ibid.*, p. 381).

72 *Ibid.*, p. 361.

73 *Ibid.*, p. 363. 'Their lingering fondness for old Classic forms' (*ibid.*, p. 369). For plans see *ibid.*, pp. 370–1.

74 Street's Royal Academy lecture 'Thirteenth Century Architecture: Italy', reprinted in A. E. Street, *Memoir of G. E. Street* (1888), pp. 397–8.

75 Street, *Brick and Marble, op. cit.*, p. 367. 'I did not find one finial in Venice which was satisfying' (*ibid.*, p. 218); 'I have only seen one good Gothic staircase in Venice. This is in the Casa Galdini' (*ibid.*, p. 223, ill.).

76 *Ibid.*, p. 365.

77 *Ibid.*, p. 368–9.

78 *Ibid.*, p. 380.

79 'Our buildings are, in nine cases out of ten, cold, colourless, insipid, academical studies. . . . The puritanical uniformity of our coats and all our garments is but a reflection from the prevailing lack of love of art or colour of any kind. A rich colour is thought vulgar, and that only is refined which is neutral, plain and ugly' (*ibid.*, pp. 400, 406).

80 *Ibid.*, p. 20.

81 R. A. lecture, *op. cit.*, p. 399.

82 E.g. Cuddlesdon College, Oxon. (1853–54).

83 'By-and-by, Street's candid mind and clear intellect realized that workaday Italian Gothic was for England a caprice, and he bravely returned to the purity and elasticity of the Edwardian [Gothic] style, only

retaining . . . the greater variety of materials in marble and brick and mosaic which modern commerce and processes had made available' (A. J. Beresford-Hope, obituary of Street, *R.I.B.A. Transactions*, 1883–84, 199–203).

84 N. Pevsner, *London*, *I* (1973 ed.), p. 321, and H.-R. Hitchcock, *Architecture: Nineteenth and Twentieth Centuries* (1963 ed.), p. 186.

85 Scott, *Lectures on Medieval Architecture*, II (1879), p. 318.

86 He favoured 'Cismontane Gothic for Cismarine England'. 'The absolute Gothic of Italy is surely out of court,' on climatic grounds. But 'its diversity of materials, and . . . colour' were there for the taking, thanks to 'the conjoint action of chemistry and commerce, and the increased facilities of transport and working'. Let not the architect 'be afraid of the new colours which God had given' him. Instead, let him 'make proof of his daring'. The Gothic of the future would be northern in origin—Hope preferred Decorated or Middle Pointed ('the golden mean') to early French; Early English he thought too 'prim'—but enriched by the diversity and colour of southern types (Hope, *The English Cathedral of the Nineteenth Century*, 1891 ed., pp. 33, 44, 62).

87 Scott, *Professional and Personal Recollections* (1879), pp. 157–63.

88 *Ibid.*, pp. 204, 373.

89 'Italian Pointed, though replete with beauty, is *per se* very inferior as an architectural style to the contemporary architecture of England, and especially of France. Its details are so mixed with reminiscences of classic antiquity, and its construction falls so far short of carrying out fully the great principles of Pointed architecture, that it must ever be considered as a far less perfect development of the style than those of Northern Europe. . . . The principle I am advocating [is] of enriching Northern Gothic with Italian ideas, but doing so without infringing upon its essential characteristics.' In particular, Italian urban Gothic had much to teach the Victorians: its 'square, corniced street fronts' might well prove a useful alternative to the multi-gabled houses of medieval England (*Secular and Domestic*, *op. cit.*, pp. 282, 285).

90 Scott admired the Cathedral and Baptistery at Florence; the south and east fronts of Siena Cathedral; the marble columns in the nave arcades and western portals of the Cathedral at Genoa; the brickwork of Verona, the Cathedral and Old Palace at Mantua; the Mercanzia and S. Petronius at Bologna; and the interiors of the Arena Chapel at Padua, the apse of Sta Croce at Florence, the chapel of S. Felice in S. Antonio at Padua, and the chapel of St John under the east end of Siena Cathedral (*Secular and Domestic*, pp. 283–9).

91 *Ibid.*, pp. 280, 290. See also Scott, *Medieval Architecture*, I (1879), pp. 212–13.

92 'Modified Venetian Gothic' (C. L. Eastlake, *History of the Gothic Revival*, 1872, ed. J. Mordaunt Crook, Leicester, 1978, appendix 156). See also M. Girouard in *Country Life*, 13 and 20 May 1967.

93 J. Simmons, *St Pancras Station* (1968).

94 Scott, *Recollections*, *op. cit.*, p. 178. Scott's premiated design (No. 116A) is illustrated in *Building News*, III (1857), 855, along with his explanatory justification.

95 *Illustrated London News*, 12 September 1857, p. 276.

96 *Building News*, III (1857), 626. For Street's design see *Illustrated*

London News, 24 October 1857, p. 412, ill.

97 *Building News*, III (1857), 501, 615.

98 'It is true that the medieval palaces of Italy are very tempting models, or rather storehouses to furnish ideas, because there is more street architecture of the Middle Ages remaining in Italy than in the Northern countries, and these Italian palaces are very beautiful examples in their way; but the Gothic of Italy differs very much from our own Northern Gothic, and is generally late work copied from Northern buildings, and a jumble of all the styles: mouldings and details of the 12th century, such as the cable and billet, with trefoil cornices or corbel-tables of the 13th century, and windows with tracery of the 14th century; all jumbled together in the same palace really built in the 15th century. However beautiful such buildings may be in their proper place, they will never be satisfactory to English eyes in England' (*Building News*, iii, 1857, 724–5). Parker preferred Verona to Venice—and north Germany to Verona—as a precedent for brick Gothic, citing publications by Street and, long before, by Repton (*Archaeologia*, XXI, pp. 158–9).

99 Scott had experimented with 'a sort of early Basilican style' at St Michael, Cornhill, London, and Lord Hill's chapel at Hawkstone, Salop. When Palmerston rejected Gothic, Scott 'conceived the idea of generating what would be strictly an Italian style out of . . . the Byzantine of the early Venetian palaces, and . . . the earliest renaissance of Venice . . . Byzantine, in fact, toned into a more modern and usable form.' Palmerston called it a 'regular mongrel affair' and insisted on 'ordinary Italian' (*Recollections, op. cit.*, pp. 192–9).

100 *Recollections, op. cit.*, p. 271.

101 J. Summerson, *Victorian Architecture. Four Studies in Evaluation* (1970), p. 42. Girouard justly calls St Pancras 'a masterpiece in spite of its absurdities' (*Country Life*, 13 May 1967, p. 1233). For contemporary criticisms see *Building News*, XXI (1871), 96–7; XXVI (1874), 437; XXIV (1875), 133.

102 *Builder*, XXXII (1874), 437, 439, ills.; G. Stamp, 'Victorian Bombay', *A.A.R.P.* (1977), pp. 22–7.

103 H.-R. Hitchcock, 'Ruskin and American Architecture', in J. Summerson, ed., *Concerning Architecture* (1967), pp. 166–208.

104 Basil Ransome 'had heard of the great Mediaeval Hall . . . the ornate, overtopping structure, which was the finest piece of architecture he had ever seen [he had of course yet to visit Europe] . . . He thought there was rather too much brick about it, but it was buttressed, cloistered, turreted, dedicated, superscribed, as he had never seen anything; though it didn't look old, it looked significant' (Penguin ed., p. 209).

105 *Recollections, op. cit.*, p. 228.

106 *Ibid.*, p. 210.

107 *Ecclesiologist*, XXII, new series, XIX (1861), 354; XXIII, new series XX (1862), 16.

108 'I am proud enough to hope . . . that I have had some direct influence on Mr Street. But I have had indirect influence on nearly every cheap villa builder between [Denmark Hill] and Bromley; and there is scarcely a public house near the Crystal Palace but sells its gin and bitters under pseudo-Venetian capitals copied from the Church of the Madonna of Health or of Miracles. And one of my principal notions for leaving my present house [and fleeing to Brantwood] is that it is surrounded every-where by the accursed Frankenstein monsters of, *in*directly, my own making. . . . For Venetian architecture developed out of British moral consciousness I decline to be responsible' (10.458–9, 16 March 1872). This statement was made in reply to a review in the *Pall Mall Gazette* by Coventry Patmore. Patmore had suggested that Ruskin's direct influence was bad: 'a preference for Venetian over English Gothic . . . the under-rating of expressional character in architecture, and the overrating of sculptural ornament, especially of a naturalistic and imitative character, and . . . an exclusiveness which limited the due influence of some . . . noble styles of architecture'. He thought Ruskin's indirect influence—what Graham Hough has called the Ruskinian 'revolution in sensibility'—was, however, beneficial (G. Hough, *The Listener*, 30 May 1963, p. 921). In the preface to the third edition of *Seven Lamps* (1874) Ruskin wrote: 'I would rather . . . that no architects had ever condescended to adopt one of the views suggested in this book, than that any should have made the partial use of it which has mottled our manufactory chimneys with black and red brick, dignified our banks and drapers shops with Venetian tracery, and pinched our parish churches into dark and slippery arrangements for the advertisement of cheap coloured glass and pantiles.' In particular he cited a public house in Ealing: 'the modern brickwork would have been in no discord with the tomb of the Can Grande, had it been set beside it in Verona. But this good and true piece of brickwork was the porch of a public house, and its total motive was the provocation of thirst, and the encouragement of idleness' (10.11–12).

109 *Builder*, XXIX (1871), 426–7.

110 For details see A. Gomme, M. Jenner and B. Little, *Bristol. An Architectural History* (1979).

111 *The Listener*, XL (1948), 857–8.

112 Compare warehouses in similar vein by Burges and Edis.

113 Like 'a Victorian Gothic river steam-boat' (Hitchcock, 'Monu-ments of Commerce', *loc. cit.*).

114 *Ibid*,; N. Taylor, *Monuments of Commerce* (1968), pp. 50–5.

115 *R.I.B.A. Transactions*, 1883–84, pp. 202.

'The weight and vigour of their masses': mid-Victorian country churches and 'The Lamp of Power'

EDWARD N. KAUFMAN

The years about 1850 marked a crucial stage in the Gothic Revival. For if the 1840s had seen the emergence and consolidation of an ideology based on the triple creed of liturgical, archaeological and structural truth, the 1850s saw the simultaneous triumph and fragmentation of that doctrine. After Butterfield's great church of All Saints, Margaret Street, it was no longer possible to uphold the image of the fourteenth-century English parish church as an ideal of universal applicability. Now, each kind of church called for a particular treatment according to its condition: urban minster, cathedral, colonial mission, country church.[1]

Not all these programmatic types were inventions of the new decade, but only one, the country church, already had a distinguished record of architectural achievement. It had been in the vanguard of the ecclesiological Gothic movement during the 1840s, and for two reasons: first because Pugin, preaching the vernacular values of rough textures, thick walls, honest (as opposed to clever) construction, had succeeded to some degree in shifting critical interest from the great cathedrals to the humble parish churches of the Middle Ages; and second because the enthusiasm of rich landowners and country clerics, moved by the religious and architectural fervour emanating from Oxford and Cambridge, had ensured that the country would be one of the chief fields of ecclesiological action. The style which resulted—one of low walls and high roofs, rough textures and picturesque articulation, all controlled by a more or less faithful adherence to the style of the early fourteenth century—gradually gained ground during the second half of the decade and persisted in the hands of some architects until well past the middle of the century.

Yet the country church did not escape the ferment of the years around 1850. There was a growing restlessness among young architects, a mounting frustration with the strict discipline of ecclesiology, a stirring for novelty and experimentation. Then too, there was an urgent need, imposed by the success of the urban minster, to reassess the programme of the country church. And then there was Ruskin. And out of these varied stirrings arose a new style of country church, quite different from that of the 1840s but different also from the urban minster of the 1850s.

It is this new country church style which this chapter sets itself to explore. Rather than chronicling its year-by-year evolution, however, it aims to do two things: to sum up its leading characteristics, and to suggest a general interpretation, one capable of accounting for its specific programmatic nature without losing sight of its broader stylistic connections. The country church, however, was much less extensively glossed than the urban minster or the cathedral, and I have had to draw inferentially for architectural support on a variety of general architectural treatises of the period, and most of all on the third chapter of Ruskin's *Seven Lamps of Architecture* (1849), 'The Lamp of Power'. This calls for a note of explanation. Ruskin's influence on the architectural theorists of the 1850s is demonstrable, but his influence on architecture remains, outside a few key instances,[2] a moot point. One can say for certain only that many (if not most) advanced Gothicists read Ruskin and were moved by him, and that their work is nonetheless irreducible by any known process to an illustration of what they read. I have relied on Ruskin not for his putative influence but for his interpretive eloquence.

If the first monument of the urban minster style was Butterfield's Church of All Saints, Margaret Street, the first monument of the new country church style was not a building but a book, George Truefitt's *Designs for Country Churches*, published in 1850. Calling his designs '*attempts to think* in "Gothic," exclusive of actual authority'.[3] Truefitt opened his book with a bold call for liberation from the shackles of copyism. His fourth design is a good example

41
George Truefitt,
*Designs for Country
Churches*, 1850, No.
IV

of what he had in mind (fig. 41). It looks like no fourteenth-century
English church. One cannot fail to notice that it lacks that most
essential adjunct of a correct country church, a porch. Nor is it the
least bit humble or picturesque: it is compact, angular and assertive,
and its high, broad walls reprove the dappled textures and broken
outlines beloved of the ecclesiologists. But, most of all, it is massive
—not in the loose sense in which the sturdy rubble walls of the
1840s are often called massive, for they always remained space-
enclosing planes, however thick—but in a more sculptural sense.
Truefitt's compact shapes, resting on a broadly battered base and
culminating in a tower so deeply bevelled as to deny the existence
of space within, seem to have been not built up in courses but
hewn from blocks of stone.

The feeling for broad surfaces and angular masses manifested in
Truefitt's designs became characteristic of many areas of mid-
Victorian architecture, but in no other type of building were the
possibilities of mass so thoroughly explored. In city churches,
houses, public buildings, architects may have been constrained
by complex programmes or circumscribed sites. Not so in the
country church. Here architects were free to compose sculpturally,[4]
and they did so, often with breathtaking power. At times, indeed, it
seems that they were striving towards an ideal of pure mass, unattainable in architecture except on the level of metaphor. Truefitt
bevelled his tower so as to deny its hollowness; Scott piled the

weighty masses of his at Leafield so as to crush out any space below; Street, Pearson and Bodley made theirs great solid blocks of masonry, standing independent of the churches they seem to guard (figs. 41–5). Nor is it only towers that testify to the solidity and power of mass. Truefitt's decision to excise the entrance porch, a course frequently followed over the next fifteen years, was a step towards the suppression of features expressive of hollowness or permeability. Clutton's sombre cliff of Woburn, its ribbed walls forbiddingly blank until far above eye-level, and enterable through a single door placed under the compression of a 200 ft tower and spire, reached perhaps the acme of inaccessibility. Windows, too, usually the strongest of features indicating space or permeability, were subverted to tell of matter instead of void. Street, for instance, often treated his windows as cut-aways through the wall, diagramming their thickness and consistency (fig. 46). Truefitt's windows—the deepset tower windows of his fifteenth design, for instance—forced with evident difficulty through the unyielding stone, become the permanent record of its impermeable weight and substance.

To the metaphorical suppression of voids in furtherance of an ideal of pure solidity the architectural literature of the 1850s offers many parallels.[5] Indeed, it is clear that a major revaluation of mass and space had taken place in the mere decade or so since Pugin had completed the last of his early churches—churches in which he had sought to enclose luminous volumes of space within brittle envelopes of structure. In 1843 Pugin himself, turning from a rationalistic appreciation of the excellence of Gothic structure at its most daring to a more materialist and primitivist appreciation of its 'honesty' at its most unassuming, had repudiated these churches,[6] and he now led the way towards the reassessment of breadth, weight and texture. The concept of mass began to emerge and to be invoked with increasing favour in architectural criticism;[7] yet it was only about 1850 that it came to the forefront of aesthetic discourse as a palpable quality, endowed furthermore with a wide range of specific and positive associations. The crucial text in this transformation was Ruskin's 'The Lamp of Power'.

> For there is a crust about the impressible part of men's minds, which must be pierced through before they can be touched to the quick; and though we may prick at it and scratch it in a thousand separate places, we might as well have let it alone if we do not come through somewhere with a deep thrust. . . . And mere weight will do this; it is a clumsy way of doing it, but an effectual one, too; and the apathy which cannot be pierced through by a small steeple, nor shone through by a small window, can be broken through in a moment by the mere weight of a great wall. [8.105]

No stronger claim for the aesthetic efficacy of mass could be made than this. Like Burke, Ruskin found that mass fulfilled the central requirement of the sublime—it induced an extreme sensation of awe or terror. Indeed, the concept of mass played a leading role throughout 'The Lamp of Power' as a fundamental attribute of sublimity.

> . . . the relative majesty of buildings depends more on the weight and vigour of their masses, than on any other attribute of their design: mass of everything, of bulk, of light, of darkness, of colour, not mere sum of any of these, but breadth of them; not broken light, nor scattered darkness, nor divided weight, but solid stone, broad sunshine, starless shade. [8.134]

42 below
Sir George Gilbert Scott, St Michael, Leafield, Oxon., 1859

43 right
George Edmund Street, St John the Evangelist, Whitwell-on-the-Hill, North Yorks., 1858–60

Here Ruskin defined mass in broader, more painterly terms, as an attribute of immaterial as well as material phenomena. Far from devaluing material mass, however, this had the effect of drawing a sharper distinction between phenomena of mass and phenomena of thinness or linearity. A bi-polar system of values resulted, in which mass was sublime, its opposite contemptible or even sub-human. Thus Ruskin could anathematise English architecture in the following terms: '. . . all that we do is small and mean, if not worse—thin, and wasted, and unsubstantial . . . we have built like frogs and mice since the thirteenth century (except only in our castles)'

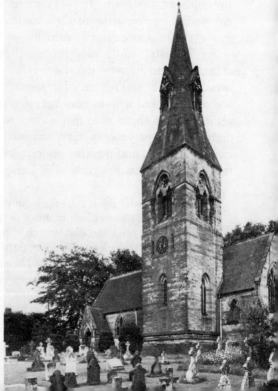

(8.135–6). Sublimity, however, was not to be found in mass alone: 'but as regards abstract power and awfulness, there is no question; without breadth of surface it is in vain to seek them . . . the light of heaven upon it, and the weight of earth in it, are all we need . . .' (8.109). Thus sublimity was to be sought through a combination of substance and surface. And not only breadth but also angularity was called for, to produce effects of 'broad sunshine' and 'starless shade' through sudden shifts of direction.

These aspects of the sublime were further explored by Edward Garbett, who found that the 'severe and grand character' of rocky scenery was largely attributable to 'the sharply contrasted light and shade arising from the prevalence of plane surfaces and cuboidal nooks and edges'.[8] This aesthetic principle Garbett called the beauty of 'contrast'; and he said that, of the two classes of beauty (the other being 'gradation'), 'there can be not a moment's doubt which approaches nearest the character of sublimity: in fact, the beauty depending on contrast seems to require only magnitude of scale to render it sublime; and it can be rendered so by a far less amplification than is necessary with the other class of beauty. . . .'[9]

Here Garbett introduced an idea of particular importance for the country church: a special application of the theory of sublimity to small buildings. Admitting that true sublimity was unattainable without great size, Garbett nonetheless argued that its principles

44 left
John Loughborough Pearson, Christ Church, Appleton-le-Moors, North Yorks., 1862–65

45 below
George Frederick Bodley, All Saints, Selsley, Glos., 1858–62

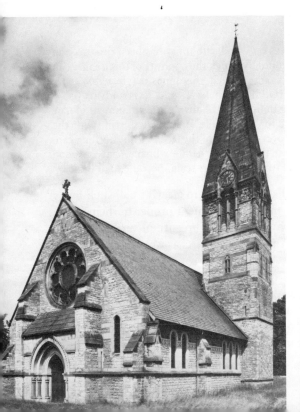

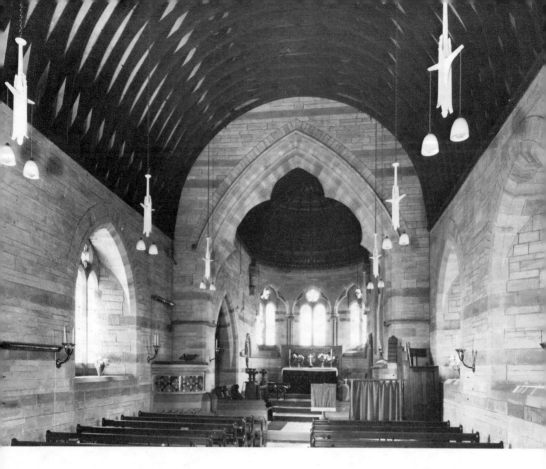

were all the more worthy of study when magnitude could not be obtained:

> ... for the same principles by which sublimity has been produced in great works, are the only ones by which the opposite of this quality can be avoided in small works; and, indeed, this opposite (viz. *meanness*) is the very worst fault a building can have, and its avoidance is, if possible, more important in little works, than is the attainment of true sublimity in great ones; for magnitude and richness will, with the many, always suffice to cover the want of the latter; while nothing can, in small buildings, stand in the stead of that for which we have no good name, but which would, if increased in scale, be called sublimity.[10]

William White spelled this out even more clearly: 'All such lowly churches ought to have a mode of treatment proper to themselves. ... Effect must be given by masses and breadth of surface and not by height of detail or multiplication of parts as would be the case in buildings of a loftier type.'[11]

So, at the beginning of the 1850s, mass, breadth and angularity were firmly established as the characteristic expression of sublimity, particularly in small buildings—a dictum amply born out by Selsley, Appleton-le-Moors, or Leafield (figs. 42, 44, 45). But mass carried other positive connotations as well, some of which are most clearly revealed through their opposites. For James Fergusson, Beauvais was the most 'unsatisfactory' of Gothic cathedrals. 'Though it has stood the test of centuries, it looks so frail, requires so many props to keep it up, and is so evidently an overstrained exercise of mechanical cleverness, that though it may excite wonder as an architectural *tour de force*, it never can satisfy the mind of the true artist, or please to the same extent as less ambitious examples.'[12] Fergusson was an enemy of mechanical cleverness not only because it suggested deceits and expedients but because it made the architect a slave to utilitarian considerations. '. . . The satisfactory architectural effect of a building is nearly in the inverse ratio to the mechanical cleverness displayed in its construction.'[13] The design of French Gothic vaults had been determined by engineering necessities, and they were ugly. The English designer, working with a wider margin of strength, could design his for beauty. Superabundant mass and demonstrable over-structuring, then, were a guarantee of stability and structural honesty and a sign that the designer had risen above utilitarianism.

Mass also guarded against another kind of deceit, that of ostentatious poverty. The 'honesty' of medieval churches contrasted with the 'spurious architectural pretension' of many modern ones. '*They* never made their walls a foot thinner, or their buttresses a foot shallower, or their roofs lower and less substantial, than they ought to be, that they might expend a larger sum upon a fine doorway, or a superfluous arcade, or a richly decorated font.' In the medieval church all was 'real, genuine, and natural'.[14] So a generous expenditure on mass was a guarantee that ornament would not be mere pretension. If budgetary constraint made it necessary to choose between the two, honesty demanded the former.

Pugin also perceived antithetical meanings in money spent on mass and ornament. 'I have passed my life in thinking of fine things, designing and realizing very poor ones,' he said in 1850, going on to blame his failure on his patrons, whose calculating meanness had shrunken his ground plans, lowered his roofs, shrivelled his walls. 'Both the collegiate chapels I have erected have been spoilt for want of a sufficient sum expended in the first instance, on *thick* walls and *stout buttresses*, omissions which no subsequent amount of enrichment or expenditure can redeem.'[15] Thus his patrons' meanness would be recorded through all time by the thinness of the walls they built, just as their generosity might have been signified by their mass. More than this, it was Pugin's own spirit of generous enthusiasm, so different from the calculating coldness of professionalism, which he always opposed, that sought expression in a plenitude of substance.

There is a seeming paradox here. If the country churches of the

47
George Frederick
Bodley, All Saints,
Selsley, Glos.,
1858–60

1850s were open-handed with mass, they were often niggardly
with form. To the approaching visitor Selsley turns a visage of the
most withdrawn austerity (fig. 47): just two smooth stone bars, one
horizontal, the other vertical, each finished off with a prism—a
wealth of mass but no wealth of forms. Appleton-le-Moors and
Leafield are, *mutatis mutandis*, the same (figs. 44, 48). Their hard,
featureless surfaces seem to repress the mental luxury of fancy as
sternly as, inside, they deny the physical luxury of comfort.

Yet the paradox is only apparent, for both sides are but the
different manifestations of a single phenomenon, an austere and
uncompromising primitivism which swept over English architecture in the 1850s, leaving its deepest mark on the country church.
Primitivism was not, of course, a new factor in English architecture.
Most recently there had been an element of it in the vernacular
Gothicism of the 1840s. But the new primitivism was bolder and
more resourceful. It banished both the charming rusticity of the
rubble wall and the finished beauty of Decorated detailing. What
replaced them was a tough, forthright expression of structural
forces (fig. 49) and a more distant range of stylistic association—
more distant in both time and place. The new primitivism turned
to the Italian medieval and the Early French Gothic styles, especially the latter, which had, according to A. J. B. Beresford Hope,
'boldness, breadth, strength, sternness, virility'[16]—all eminently
primitive virtues—and was especially suited for adoption in country
churches. The universal emblem of the Early French at its most

austere and righteous came to be plate tracery, and especially the wheel window, which looks down from the facades of countless churches of the late '50s and early '60s. The wheel window (figs. 44, 45, 48) was bold and direct, made strong geometrical patterns of light and shade while eschewing the use of line, allowed the architect to punch out his voids without compromising the depth or breadth of his substance.

The wheel window, then, and the Early French in general, derived their primitive allure from a combination of association and formal qualities—not just a vigorous, crude style of carving but also copious massiveness and a strong, forthright geometry. Beresford Hope singled out its 'dispendious use of matter'[17] as a potent primitivising factor, and James Fergusson had also admiringly identified massiveness as a sign of the unsophisticated state of Norman and Early Gothic architecture. It 'arose more from clumsiness and want of constructive skill than from design', but 'its effect is always grand, and the rude Norman nave often surpasses in grandeur the elegant choir which was afterwards added to it'.[18] Ruskin too had endowed mass with a primitive virtue, requiring no tuition: 'There are few men in the world . . . who could design a

48 left
Sir George Gilbert Scott, St Michael, Leafield, Oxon., 1859

49 below
George Edmund Street, St Mary, Westcott, Bucks., 1863–67

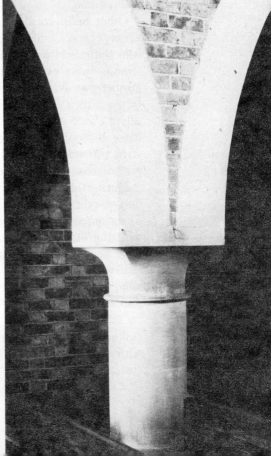

Palladian front, or a flamboyant pediment; many who could build a square mass like the Strozzi Palace' (8.135n).

It was this consideration, or more precisely the search for a mode of expression untainted by historical erudition, which above all else gave the mid-Victorian country church its characteristic savour of primitivism expressed through the formal perfection of geometry. Truefitt's '*attempts to think* in "Gothic," exclusive of actual authority' were perhaps its first manifestation. For in looking forward to a day when 'nothing but *design* in its strictest sense will be admitted' Truefitt was also looking backward to a day when the slate of historical memory had not yet been written on.[19] He proposed to cleanse it so that forward progress could again ensue along the lines of first principles, and not precedents.

Truefitt's designs show that he did not envision jettisoning the historicist's entire freight of forms and motifs. He asserted the possibility of designing ahistorically on a deeper level, that of composition, and it was largely the organising power of geometry, supplanting that of antiquarianism, which made it possible for him to do so.[20] His naves, towers and stair turrets crystallised into geometric solids whose abstract formal authority superseded historical example and whose vigorously clashing angles constituted composition.

Other architects also employed geometry during the 1850s in a variety of ways, but always with the aim of evading the toils of copyism. Butterfield used it simply and forthrightly to give point to a strong, direct expression of structure; Street used a crystalline geometry at Wheatley or Whitwell-on-the-Hill (fig. 43) to purify forms of their close dependence on medieval precedent; or a scintillating geometry at Howsham to give point to an eclectic assemblage of motifs drawn from Early French, Italian, and Decorated styles; Brandon used a dramatic geometry at Datchet (fig. 50) to give contrast and movement to weighty bulk of a tower.

During the following decade geometry became an instrument not only of stylistic liberation but also of a more severe formal reduction. The geometric playfulness of Howsham gave way to an austere condensation of shape and composition in which the rudimentary solids, those based directly on square, circle and triangle, assumed an increased prominence. At Westcott the precision with which Street handled surface and material in the interior served to articulate a geometrical armature of perfect purity and completeness: cylindrical columns, cubical abaci, equilateral arches (fig. 49). At the east end of Appleton-le-Moors Pearson countered the cylindrical apse with a square tower (fig. 51). The two forms stand for ever equal, abstract and unreconcilable. Here the extreme statement of primitivist reductivism became the pure expression of sublimity: for, as

Ruskin put it 'the square and circle are pre-eminently the areas of power . . .; and these, with their relative solids, the cube and the sphere, and the relative solids of progression, . . . the square and cylindrical column, are the elements of utmost power in all architectural arrangements' (8.110).[21]

Behind the sublime primitivism of the country church lay an activist conception of its moral role in society, born of an intense preoccupation with decay and a fundamentally pessimistic view of civilisation. Street saw his own age as 'darker times',[22] above which architecture could rise only by ministering the truths of religion and preparing the way for a brighter future. This view contributed most directly to the programme of the urban minster, but it operated equally in the country church, and with results which were as distinct from the urban minster as from the morally reticent country church of the 1840s. Beresford Hope thought that, while middle-pointed was the appropriate style of the urban minster, the country church's 'missionary vocation' could best be discharged by a more primitive style like the Early French, which was indeed 'exactly suited to supply the crying deficiencies of the age': 'The grave, strong Early French will be adduced as the preacher of righteousness, truth, and simplicity to a luxurious and a crooked generation.[23]

Let us, then, approach an Early French country church, St Michael's, Leafield, and pay heed to the sermon (fig. 48). The majestically simple tower rears up over the foliage, demonstrating the strength of religion and broadcasting its message over the landscape. Its 'dispendious use of material' helps 'to give cogency to the sermon';[24] its weighty sublimity awes the visitor into an impressible state of humility and wonder; its piled masses inculcate truthfulness and generosity. The angular yet flat facade looms at the visitor, as if to say, in the unsoftened punchings of its windows, Here are forthrightness and manly vigour, and, in the unornamented severity of its plane surfaces, Here is renunciation.

The awareness of having renounced something in the splendid simplicities of the country church was central to their primitive mission, which owed as much to the fear of decadence as to the love of virtue. The urgent necessity of renunciation was a consequence of a deeply pessimistic model of history. Civilisations rose and declined in endless cycles, for ever without hope of redemption. The corollary, implicitly accepted by most mid-century architectural writers, though occasionally conflicting with their activist view, was that architecture, as civilisation's most legible expression, would follow the same curve. In 'The Lamp of Power' Ruskin clothed this historical schema with a garment of forms simply by mapping it on to his formal diagram of thick–thin: massive architecture belonged to early periods, thin and linear to late ones.[25] The transition from

one to the other constituted decadence. 'It was the substitution of
the *line* for the *mass*, as the element of decoration' in Gothic tracery
that heralded its decay. The brief moment of perfection just before
the fall was 'the great watershed of Gothic art. Before it, all had been
ascent; after it, all was decline . . .' (8.90 and 89).

If Ruskin developed the outlines of a historical machine, Garbett
made it work. In place of Ruskin's simple binary system of forms he
postulated a system of five formal classes, evenly graduated from the
weighty and angular through the thin and curvilinear, in which he
then introduced an inherent imbalance. The weightier classes of
form were sterner and more worthy, but the lighter ones were
indisputably the most beautiful in themselves'. Therefore, whenever architecture was 'in a progressive state', there was 'far more
danger of their encroaching on the domains of the graver classes,
than there is of the contrary evil'.[26] The historical movement thus
initiated was, in every case, a decline from the virtuous to the
attractive, and, since the imbalance which caused it was inherent in
the nature of forms, history would always repeat itself. 'Accordingly,
it was in this way that the Greek, the Gothic, and the Italian systems
all declined and fell after their perfection had been reached'[27]—and
not these three only. 'In the decline of taste, in all countries and in all

51
John
Loughborough
Pearson, Christ
Church, Appleton-
le-Moors, North
Yorks, 1862–65

50 facing
Raphael
Brandon, St Mary,
Datchet, Bucks.,
church 1857–58,
tower 1860

arts alike, everything is ornament, if not fritter, and no beauty is seen in the pure noble breadth and simplicity of the earlier productions.'[28]

The pessimism of Garbett's historical vision needs no emphasis, except to underline the sense of urgency it imparted to the primitivist programme. Once instate architecture in a 'progressive state' (which was, after all, the aim of all who would return it to first principles) and it would be only a matter of time before the lighter and less worthy forms began to exercise their dangerous attractions, thinning, linearising, ornamenting. Only one civilisation had escaped the fate of the Greek, the Gothic and the Italian: the Venetian. 'That architecture began with the luxuriance in which all others expired . . . and laying aside its ornaments, one by one, while it fixed its forms by laws more and more severe . . .' stood forth, at last, so grand that no other architecture had 'so stern a claim to our our reverence' (8.130). It had achieved its nobility, reversing the tides of history, through renunciation. '[T]he fourteenth century Venetian had cast away, one by one, for a succession of centuries, every splendour that art and wealth could give it . . . once capricious and fantastic, it had bound itself by laws inviolable and serene as those of Nature herself. It retained nothing but its beauty and its power; both the highest, but both restrained' (8.130–1). If, then, deeply distrustful of their own age, and faced with a prophecy of decay, the architects of the mid-Victorian country church chose to immure themselves behind rugged, unfeatured masses of stone, should not their action be considered the renunciation of all that was attractive and pleasant in architecture, and an heroic attempt to stem the tide of history?

At once aggressive and withdrawn, the hard stone forms of Leafield, Selsley or Appleton-le-Moors manifestly belong to a different world from the foliage through which their forms erupt (figs. 48, 45, 44), just as they belong to a different world from the humble, rustic churches of the 1840s. Those churches were 'natural', blending with their surroundings, catching the dappled tints of the forest in their rubble-textured walls. These assert their own irreducible identity, rejecting the naturalism of pictorial assimilation.

Yet the mid-Victorian country church was as intimately linked with the forms and images of nature as its predecessor, though it was with a nature differently interpreted, a geological nature. The hard substance and faceted geometry of their towers often call to mind the forms of crystals (figs. 43, 50); the rugged slopes of Leafield, those of a mountainside (fig. 42); their interiors, caves—rock-walled, dark-roofed and dim, with a glitter of coloured marble and semi-precious stones. These are only images; yet the geological naturalism of the mid-Victorian country church rested on broader foundations.

The imagery of geological nature, above all of mountains, dominated the architectural imagination of the 1850s and '60s. Architects were avid students of practical geology and mineralogy; more, there was a 'love of savage scenery, of wild, severe association, rife at the present day', which Beresford Hope believed was 'the spontaneous expression of the age', its 'protest . . . against the luxury and mammon-worship of the time'.[29] Thus the path to primitivism also led to the mountains; and indeed, some professed to see in the Early French an 'identity of its principle with that principle of beauty which forms the charm of Alpine scenery'.[30] Garbett also responded to the primitive allure of mountains, calling them the 'Doric works' of nature.[31]

The majestic image of the mountains was omnipresent too in 'The Lamp of Power', was indeed its illuminating force, for Ruskin believed that the most sublime creations of nature were mountains, and that sublime architecture was that which captured their essence. He discerned a 'sympathy in the forms of noble building, with what is most sublime in natural things', and called for 'the expression of abstract power . . . of a consciousness that, in this primal art of man, there is room for the marking of his relations with the mightiest, as well as the fairest, works of God (8.102). At intervals throughout 'The Lamp of Power' Ruskin set out strings of correspondences between architectural and geological forms: he hymned, for instance, the hermit spirit which '. . . . raised into ordered spires the wild rocks of the Norman sea; which gave to the temple gate the depth and darkness of Elijah's Horeb cave; and lifted, out of the populous city, grey cliffs of lonely stone, into the midst of sailing birds and silent air' (8.137).

As a literary device metaphors like these were not entirely un-precedented—how many times had the vaults of a Gothic cathedral been compared with those of a forest[32]—but what is new and arrest-ing is the range and precision of Ruskin's imagery. The entire spec-trum of architectural form passed through his metamorphic lens, emerging as natural imagery and passing back again. Thus a cliff became a Cyclopean wall, the pinnacles of a rocky promontory fortress towers, a distant mountain cone a tumulus (8.103). All these were sublime images. In contrast, architecture which was based on the principle of 'tracery of line' found its natural counterpart in the 'woods and thickets'; a branch became 'a twisted tower' or a 'twisted spire' (7.34). And further down the scale the same transforming process was turned to satiric purpose: the starved portals of Salis-bury Cathedral became 'pitiful little pigeon-holes' or 'entrances to a beehive or a wasp's nest' (8.136). These images, vivid and varied, indicate that for Ruskin the suggestive capacity of architectural forms to call up the imagery of nature was a matter of fact. Their range and density, furthermore, made it possible to express the entire range of architectural sentiment through the language of natural equivalents.

The sympathy between noble buildings and mountains, however, was based on something more substantial than their capacity to suggest each other. The architect could study the mountains as a book. 'Send him to our hills,' said Ruskin, 'and let him study there what nature understands by a buttress, and what by a dome' (8.136). The advice, admittedly, seemed insufficiently precise to some; but one example of the mountain's teaching, recorded in *The Stones of Venice*, stands out for its topicality. Ruskin had observed that Mont Cervin was largely built of soft stone. This was bound together by 'a course of living rock, of quartz as white as the snow that encircles it, and harder than a bed of steel. . . . It is one only of a thousand iron bands that knit the strength of the mighty mountain' (9.87–8). From this Ruskin drew the lesson for the architect that into a wall of loose stone it was necessary 'to introduce courses of more solid material. . . . A banded structure, almost stratification of the wall, is thus produced (9.81), which would somewhat resemble the cliff-like, though diminutive banded, face of Truefitt's eighteenth design.

This kind of banding, however, did not become popular: it suffered from the rejection of all soft-textured materials after 1850. But another kind of banding, with colour instead of texture, was widely adopted, most notably by G. E. Street (fig. 46).[33] This Ruskin also linked with geology: the bands were 'valuable in their suggestion of the natural courses of rocks, and beds of the earth itself' (9.347).

But stratification was not the most important of Mont Cervin's lessons: this is conveyed by Ruskin's illustration from *Modern Painters IV* better than by any description (fig. 52). It is an image completely devoid of circumstantial detail, whether of situation, scale or local texture. It shows a mountain which appears to be an asymmetrical crystal, a pure solid form of perfect hardness, breadth and angularity.

This stark, abstract image of the 'most noble cliff in Europe' (9.88) encapsulated a lesson which could be learned only through a laborious course of observation and analysis. That process of learning was based on the academic concept of imitation of nature. Garbett explained it well:

Is a building or a member, then, required to have a particular character or expression [i.e. sublimity or beauty]? There is only one way of giving it, viz. by collectively examining all, or as many as possible, of those works of nature which have this particular character,— . . . by analyzing them and extracting that which they have in common, carefully rejecting everything in which they differ; for, in whatever points they *differ*, these are proved by that very difference to be things

non-essential to the character required; but in whatever points they *agree*, these constitute nature's mode of expressing that particular character, and it is *the only mode*. When thoroughly eliminated and refined from all things not essential to it, then, and *not till then*, it may be pushed further than in any work of nature . . .[34]

What nature's mode of expressing sublimity or power was, the reader will by now anticipate. 'It is by a particular application of this principle that we discover *angularity* to be an important part of nature's mode of expressing *force*,—and *reflexed curvature* to be part of her mode of expressing *delicacy*. . . .' Similarly, the 'severe and grand character of rocky scenery' stemmed from its 'plane surfaces and cuboidal nooks and edges'.[35] But, above all, mountains taught how to 'conceive and deal with breadth and solidity (8.136). That is why Ruskin sent the architect to the hills; that is what he meant when he said, of the 'thin, and wasted, and unsubstantial' quality of English architecture, 'I know not how it is, unless that our English hearts have more oak than stone in them, and have more filial sympathy with acorns than Alps . . .' (8.135).

The object of studying nature in this way was to apply her principles, and this the country church did: it distilled the principles of the mountains and could thus claim to express the closest bond of sympathy with them. Selsley and Appleton-le-Moors are abstract representations of mountains, seen in terms of their most typical qualities. But the bond was physical as well as abstract, for into the body of the church were incorporated the very substance and texture of the mountain. In *The Poetry of Architecture* Ruskin had said of a roughly built stone cottage that one could trace in its stones 'the presence of an Almighty hand'; 'we dwell upon every bend of the rough roof and every hollow of the loose wall, feeling it to be a design which no architect on earth could ever equal, sculptured by a chisel of unimaginable delicacy ...' (1.48). In 'The Lamp of Power' he said further that the uncut stones of a wall conveyed 'a stern expression of brotherhood with the mountain heart from which it has been rent' (8.114–15).

To the eye attuned to the picturesque naturalism of the 1840s this may seem inapplicable to the country church of the 1850s, whose hardness of surface is one of the strongest marks of its alienness. But what was the cleavage of a mountain that was both natural and sublime? It was not rubble-faced—not the soft majority of Mont Cervin, but the iron-hard substance of its bands, or of Ruskin's illustration. Rough walling was perhaps natural, but not sublime; it could convey only ideas of weakness.

> Do not think that Nature rusticates her foundations. Smooth sheets of rock, glistening like sea waves, and that ring under the hammer like a brazen bell,—that is her preparation for first stories [9.350–1]

Nature did rusticate sometimes, but not to express sublime power: 'Then she seeks the polished surface and the iron heart, not rough looks and incoherent substance' (9.351). The 'polished surface and the iron heart' could well stand as an epitome of the proud geological naturalism of the mid-Victorian country church; 'rough looks and incoherent substance' as an impatient dismissal of the humble forest naturalism of the 1840s.

To capture the essence of the mountain in the forms of a church was a reasonable exercise, because the mountain epitomised an important (and a threatened) article of belief for the mid-nineteenth century: that the wonders of nature testified to the truth of religion. William Buckland's Bridgewater Treatise on *Geology and Minera-logy considered with Reference to Natural Theology* (1836) had put this differently. Its frontispiece proclaimed 'the Power, Wisdom and Goodness of God as Manifested in the Creation';[36] and the faith therein exampled, in a nature which bore the impress of divine intent, became part of the structure of belief for many—not least for Ruskin, who had studied geology with Buckland at Oxford and had easily harmonised his teaching with the doctrines of his own fundamentalist upbringing. That faith Ruskin reinvented for himself later, at Fontainebleau, where the discovery of unexpected beauty in a humble aspen tree had led him to an overwhelming awareness that God's power of design was omnipresent in nature. 'He hath made everything beautiful in his time,' became for me thenceforward the interpretation of the bond between the human mind and all visible things' (35.315). Even in the very stones one could trace, 'as in the crags of the mountain-side, the presence of an Almighty hand' (1.48). But it was the mountains that communicated most powerfully the divinity of creation: they 'seem to have been built for the human race, as at once their schools and cathedrals'; they are 'glorious in holiness for the worshipper' (6.425); 'To fill the thirst of the human heart for the beauty of God's working,—to startle its lethargy with the deep and pure agitation of astonishment, —are their higher missions' (6.118).

The architect J. P. Seddon said of Ruskin's dictum that the architect must look to nature for inspiration, that 'it reminded us of our mission as her disciples and expounders'.[37] This is the lesson which had to be expounded. And if the wonders of nature testified to the divinity of creation, could not architecture testify in its turn by sharing in those wonders? It could distill the essence of mountain form in its outlines and surfaces; suggest the layers of the earth and rock in its strata; incorporate the very weight and substance of the mountain in its walls; inlay the glowing marbles and minerals of the earth in its font, pulpit or reredos.

Some of these things even the urban minster did, but it was the province of the country church to expound most fully the doctrine of nature. And it did something more. Underlying the structure of physico-theological faith was the mystery of the Creation; the wonder not simply of the beauty of nature but of the power that brought it forth. To this the country church bore witness, its abstraction warmed by the beauty of emergent life. At Souldrop (fig. 53) the geometrically chamfered mullions of the vestry blossom upwards into abstract buds; the jambs of the side aisle progress further, sprouting crude but recognisable leaves; finally, by the porch door, a fully formed, tiny but succulent leaf uncurls from behind the shadow of a capital. Everywhere inanimate matter gives way to life. At Howsham primitive wreaths festoon a rerodos of sparkling minerals, while at Selsley bands of primeval vegetation wave above the shining granite cylinders of the arcade (fig. 54). The country church became a tableau of creation, not merely primitive but primeval.

The act of creation was at once that which separated and that which linked God and man; and it was human creation, as well as divine, which lay at the heart of 'The Lamp of Power'. What 'depends for its dignity upon arrangement and government received from human mind, becomes the expression of the power of that mind, and receives a sublimity high in proportion to the power expressed' (8.101–2)' This was the other side of sublime architecture, for the value of architecture depended 'on two distinct characters: the one, the impression it receives from human power; the other, the image it bears of the natural creation' (8.138). The two characters were not entirely opposed, for if mountains were the earth's 'natural cathedrals' (6.457), architecture was man's act of creation; and man, in striving to mark 'his relations with the mightiest, as well as the fairest, works of God', was driven by a spirit of rivalry as much as veneration.

The country church became the testament of this sublime rivalry. In using geometry to break the 'tyranny of antiquarianism'[38] it was the exemplar of an architecture whose forms originated not in copyism but in the inventive power of the human mind. It demonstrated man's ability to create form, his capacity for "composition and invention . . . the highest elements of Power in architecture' (8.134). The architect could go further: he could give voice to his forms. The country church was a richly communicative artefact, and in the act of communicating it testified not only to the divinity of creation but also to man's life-giving power over matter. 'Building materials, in the hands of a religious designer, acquire a vital property, and

53 below
Henry Clutton,
All Saints,
Souldrop, Beds.,
1861

54 right
George Frederick
Bodley, All Saints,
Selsley, Glos.,
1858–60

afford an artistical translation of God's words in addition to the sublime doctrine we already possess in our own tongue.' Thus the act of giving voice to matter was akin to giving it life, and G. R. Lewis went on to ask:

> Then why in these days should not an ecclesiastical designer speak through his works in an intellible [sic] language—a language of his own making derived from nature, and in which every one will be conversant? . . . If life can be given to inanimate matter, it should be given, and not suffered to remain dead to the world.[39]

The country church evidenced not only man's power as a creator but more generally his status as the highest of God's creatures. Its massiveness demonstrated his capacity to rise above utilitarian concerns of 'convenience and stability', and it was that capacity which proved that men had 'been made men, and not bees nor termites' (9.451). Its communicative power was proof of his articulacy and intelligence, and it was 'man's power of articulate speech' and his 'gift of reason'[40] that distinguished him from the lower animals.

Finally, the country church proclaimed man's dominion over the rest of creation. Its knowing renunciation of ornamental luxury, its sternly repressive action on the imagination, its relentless control over the imagery of nature, all spelled not only man's moral control but also his universal domination, just as the renunciatory abstraction of Venetian ornament had spelled for Ruskin both 'the temperance of man' and 'the command of Adam over creation':

> I do not know so magnificent a marking of human authority as the iron grasp of the Venetian over his own exuberance of imagination; the calm and solemn restraint with which, his mind filled with thoughts of flowing leafage and fiery life, he gives those thoughts expression for an instant, and then withdraws within those massy bars and levelled cusps of stone.

The ornament of the Venetian 'embraced, while it governed, all vegetable and animal forms' (8.131).

But one does not have to read so deep. The proud masses of Leafield, Selsley or Appleton-le-Moors assert man's authority and presence in the landscape with ruthless emphasis—yet not so ruthless that they came up to the architect's ideal in this respect. Their drawings—Bodley's first design for Selsley, or Pritchard and Seddon's for Tynant—show the church as its architect wished it to be seen: (fig. 55) in steep perspective, its weight pressing down upon the earth and its spire piercing the heavens, a gesture of challenge flung out to the very hills.

Yet this was no blasphemous gesture. Along with his articulacy and his reason it was 'man's derived supremacy over the earth' that

55
John Pritchard
and John Pollard
Seddon, *Design for
Tynant Church,
Glamorgan*, not
executed,
watercolour, 1854

Bishop Samuel Wilberforce listed first among the theological truths threatened by Darwin's 'degrading notion of the brute origin of him who was created in the image of God. . . .'[41] Man's supremacy over nature was derived from God. Without it there would have been neither sublimity nor reverence.

1 On the Gothic Revival in the 1840s and 1850s see Charles Lock NOTES Eastlake, *A History of the Gothic Revival* (1872; ed. J. M. Crook, Leicester, 1970); Georg Germann, *The Gothic Revival in Europe and Britain. Sources, Influences, and Ideas* (1972); George L. Hersey, *High Victorian Gothic. A Study in Associationism* (Baltimore and London, 1972); Henry-Russell Hitchcock, *Early Victorian Architecture in Britain*, 2 vols. (New Haven and London, 1954); Stefan Muthesius, *The High Victorian Movement in Architecture, 1850–1870* (London and Boston, 1972); Nikolaus Pevsner, *Some Architectural Writers of the Nineteenth Century* (Oxford, 1972); Phoebe Stanton, *The Gothic Revival and American Church Architecture. An Episode in Taste, 1840–1856* (Baltimore, 1968); James F. White, *The Cambridge Movement, the Ecclesiologists and the Gothic Revival* (Cambridge, 1962). On individual architects and writers see, for Butterfield: John Summerson, 'William Butterfield, or the Glory of Ugliness', *Heavenly Mansions and other Essays on Architecture* (1949), pp. 159–76; Paul Thompson, *William Butterfield* (1971); Paul Thompson, 'All Saints' Church, Margaret Street, Reconsidered', *Architectural History*, VIII (1965), 73–94; for Bodley: David Verey, 'George Frederick Bodley: climax of the Gothic Revival', in Jane Fawcett, ed., *Seven Victorian Architects* (1976), pp. 66–83; for Fergusson and Garbett: Maurice Craig, 'James Fergusson', in John Summerson, ed., *Concerning Architecture. Essays on Architectural Writers and Writing presented to Nikolaus Pevsner* (1968), pp. 140–52; Robert R. Winter, 'Fergusson and Garbett in American Architectural Theory', *Journal of the Society of Architectural Historians*, XVII (1958), 4, 25–30; for Pearson: Anthony Quiney, *John Loughborough Pearson* (New Haven and London, 1979); David Lloyd, 'John Loughborough Pearson: noble seriousness', in Jane Fawcett, ed., *op. cit.*, pp. 66–83; for Pugin: Phoebe Stanton, *Pugin* (1971); *id.*, 'Pugin: Principles of Design versus Revivalism', *Journal of the Society of Architectural Historians*, XII (1954) 20–5; for Street: Henry-Russell Hitchcock, 'G. E. Street in the 1850s', *ibid.*, XIX, (1960), 145–71; Basil F. L. Clarke and John Piper, 'Street's Yorkshire Churches and Contemporary Criticism', in John Summerson, ed., *op. cit.*, pp. 209–25; for Truefitt: obituary, *Journal of the Royal Institute of British Architects*, 3rd series, IX (1902), 461–2; for White: Paul Thompson, 'The Writings of William White', *ibid.*, 226–37.

2 For Ruskin's association with the architects Deane and Woodward, for instance, see Eve Blau, *Ruskinian Gothic. The Architecture of Deane and Woodward* (Princeton, University Press, forthcoming).

3 George Truefitt, *Designs for Country Churches* (1850), p. 7.

4 '. . . When effect is sought [i.e. when utility poses no constraints], it is almost impossible for an architect to err in giving too much solidity to his building.' (James Fergusson, *The Illustrated Handbook to Architecture*, 1855, I, p. xxxii.).

5 Edward Garbett, for instance, criticising the apparent thinness of the facade of Westminster New Palace, focused on the expressive value of windows. 'In the original perspective views of its famous river front (to judge from engravings), the windows were recessed at least *three feet* from the plane of the wall, but, as executed, they do not seem to be *one* foot therefrom; that is to say (taking the extent of the front in round numbers at 800 feet by 70 [*sic*], the glass has been so advanced as to rob the exterior of 112,000 cubic feet of apparent solidity'—a loss which might 'make *all* the difference between a sublime building and a mean one . . .'. Garbett includes the areas of the facade occupied by voids in his calculation of mass. (Edward Garbett, *Rudimentary Treatise on the Principles of Design in Architecture as Deducible from Nature and Exemplified in the Works of the Greek and Gothic Architects*, 1850, p. 103.) James Fergusson compiled a table of sixteen famous buildings, listing their total area, area covered by 'solids' or 'points of support', and ratios between the two (expressed decimally and in fractions). The ratio of solids to total area in the Hypostyle Hall at Karnak is 0·496, or about 1/2; at the Parthenon, 0·148, or about 1/7; at Milan Cathedral, 0·107, or about 1/10. Fergusson concluded that the buildings with the highest ratio of solid to total area (i.e. those which were most nearly solid) were the most aesthetically satisfying. Similarly, he found no building in England 'more aesthetically satisfying than the nave at Winchester', where 'the width of the pillars exceeds that of the aisles'. This ideal vision of buildings which approached the condition of solidity retreated, however, whenever it came into obvious conflict with practicality. (Fergusson, *op. cit.*, I, pp. xxxli, xxxvi–xxxvii.)

6 A. W. Pugin, *An Apology for the Revival of Christian Architecture in England*, (1843), p. 15 n. 11.

7 Massiveness was seen to be the primary quality of Albi Cathedral, for instance: '. . . . solid and huge, it possesses neither transepts, nor aisles, but side chapels merely, of considerable size indeed, but excavated out of the immense thickness of the walls . . .'. Thus space is hollowed out of the walls but has no independent interest, e.g. '. . . the monotony of so vast an area . . .' (Anon., 'Albi Cathedral (S. Cecilia)', *Ecclesiologist*, VI, 1846, 100.) Even this late, however, the concept of mass could be applied imprecisely and with negate connotations: the original south porch of Wymeswold church, Leics., was described as 'a massive stone cavern, built for convenience, in all ages, of no style. . . . I doubt whether the country could furnish two less comely or more grotesque entrances to a parish church.' (anon., *A History and Description of the Restored Parish Church of Saint Mary, Wymeswold*, 1846, p. 3.) The development of mass as a concept, and of a preference for low, massive shapes, in the 1840s, is discussed by Muthesius, *op. cit.*, pp. 13–15. Paul Thompson notes Butterfield's increasing feeling for mass in the mid-1840s but also at times calls it, confusingly, a 'feeling for volume'. (Paul Thompson, *William Butterfield*, 1971, p. 275.)

8 Garbett, *op. cit.*, p. 76. His views on the correlations between angularity and strength, curvilinearity and weakness, are derived from Alison, whom he quotes extensively, e.g. on pp. 64–8, 69–74. He also quotes with approval Ruskin's comments on the sublimity of mass (pp. 101–2).

9 *Ibid.*, p. 99; and for the principle of contrast see also pp. 57–8, 75 ff.

10 *Ibid.*, p. 98. Here Garbett is pursuing a disagreement with Archibald Alison, the Scots philosopher; he maintains that sublimity does not stem from association or perceived extent but is an inherent quality in some forms.

11 William White, 'Upon some Causes and Points of Failure in Modern Design', *The Ecclesiologist*, XII (1851), 313. For similar views see the same author's 'On some of the Principles of Design in Churches', *Transactions of the Exeter Diocesan Architectural Society*, V (n.d.), p. 178.

12 Fergusson, *op. cit.*, I, p. xxxii.

13 *Ibid.*, p. xxxvi.

14 Anon., 'On Simplicity of Composition, especially in Churches of the Early-English Style', *Ecclesiologist*, II (1843), 118–19.

15 A. W. N. Pugin, *Some Remarks on Articles which have recently appeared in the 'Rambler'*, quoted in *The Builder*, VIII (1850), 109.

16 A. J. B. Beresford Hope, *The English Cathedral of the Nineteenth Century* (1861), p. 45. Beresford Hope is here (and in all subsequent quotations) for the adoption of Middle Pointed for the urban minster. He puts the case for Early French on behalf of its proponents, accepting for his own part its appropriateness for the country but not the city.

17 *Ibid.*, p. 59.

18 Fergusson, *op. cit.*, I, p. xxxii.

19 Truefitt, *op. cit.*, p. 10. For Truefitt's opinions on antiquarianism and progress see also his 'A few Words, Antiquarian and Architectural', *Associated Architectural Societies, Reports and Papers*, III, Part 2 (1855), pp. 366–9. G. E. Street, arguing for an intelligent electicism, also rebelled against the copyism of the 1840s, saying that it would justify the accusation that 'our first endeavours as revivers of the ancient art are to stifle originality, and to insist on pure copyism, on careful and endless reference to books of "Authorities," as they are quaintly called, instead of being (as they should be) marked by a desire to discover the principles on which our art was founded, and then fairly and legitimately to work out those principles. . . .' (G. E. Street, 'The True Principles of Architecture and the Possibilities of Development', *Ecclesiologist*, XIII, 1852, 249.) Street was also aware of the constraints exercised by historical knowledge: he attributed the high development of the Gothic style in England, but not in Italy, to the lack of classical ruins in the north; 'men worked, therefore, freely, and in their own way, and apparently quite untramelled with the suspicion even that there had been another style brought to perfection. . . .. (G. E. Street, *Brick and Marble in the Middle Ages. Notes of a Tour in the North of Italy* (1855), p. 254.

20 The notion that geometry has functioned periodically through history as an escape from historicism was developed by Charles Handley-Read, who identified a distinct 'geometric style' within the spectrum of mid-Victorian architecture and especially design, the most representative examples of which are perhaps the patterned wall treatments and liturgical artefacts of Butterfield and Street. The earliest of these, e.g. Butterfield's font at Ottery St Mary, Devon, and the walls of All Saints, Margaret Street, were exactly contemporary with Truefitt's *Designs*. For a survey of the 'geometric style' see Simon Jervis, *High Victorian Design* (Ottawa, 1974), catalogue of an exhibition organised by the Victoria and Albert Museum for the National Gallery of Canada.

21 Ruskin also instanced Pisa as 'not perhaps the fairest, but the mightiest type of form which the mind has ever conceived'; it was 'based exclusively on associations of the circle and the square', not only in minor forms but also in plan and elevation (8.112). Butterfield's churches showed a sharp change from octagonal and clustered piers in the 1840s to cylindrical piers in the 1850s, which Paul Thompson linked with Ruskin's views on the sublimity of the circle. (Paul Thompson, *William Butterfield*, 1971, p. 288.)

22 G. E. Street, 'On the Proper Characteristics of a Town Church', *Ecclesiologist*, XI (1850), 231.

23 Beresford Hope, *op. cit.*, p. 59.

24 *Ibid.*

25 For instance: '. . . Of the many broad divisions under which architecture may be considered, none appears to me more significant than that into buildings whose interest is in their walls, and those whose interest is in the lines dividing their walls . . . in French Flamboyant, and in our detestable Perpendicular, the object is to get rid of the wall surface, and to keep the eye altogether on tracery of line; in Romanesque work and Egyptian, the wall is a confessed and honored member. . . .' (8.108–9). The same point—that early architecture is thick, late architecture thin—emerges from Fergusson's table of historic buildings (see above, note 5).

26 Garbett, *op. cit.*, p. 97. For his system of formal classes see also p. 85

27 *Ibid.*, p. 97.

28 *Ibid.*, p. 164.

29 Beresford Hope, *op. cit.*, p. 61.

30 *Ibid.*

31 Garbett, *op. cit.*, p. 165.

32 [See above, p. 21, note 30.—*Eds.*]

33 For Street's advocacy of banded construction see 'The True Principles of Architecture and the Possibilities of Development', *The Ecclesiologist*, XIII (1852), 255; and 'On Colour as applied to Architecture', *Associated Architectural Societies, Reports and Papers*, III, Part 2, 1855, p. 355.

34 Garbett, *op. cit.*, p. 114. Garbett's elucidation of the distinction between imitation (generalised) and copyism (specific) is explicitly based on academic concepts; both Quatremere de Quincy and Reynolds are quoted in support (pp. 110–11; and see also pp. 74–5). The distinction was fundamental to Gothic Revival theory in the 1850s, complementing the distinction between imitation of Gothic principles and copyism of Gothic forms. Fergusson: 'It is generally assumed that in architecture we ought to copy natural objects as we see them, whereas the truth seems to be that we ought always to copy the processes, never the forms of Nature' (*op. cit.*, I, pp. l–li). J. P. Seddon: architecture is 'essentially conventional: it works rather with the principles than with the forms of nature' ('Progress in Architecture', *The Builder*, VIII, 1850, 124).

35 Garbett, *op. cit.*, p. 114.

36 William Buckland, *Geology and Mineralogy considered with Reference to Natural Theology*, 2 vols. (1836). The 'Bridgewater Treatises on the Power Wisdom and Goodness of God as Manifested in the Creation', as the frontispiece of each volume describes them, were commissioned by the Royal Society following a clause in the Earl of Bridgewater's will. For their place in the history of religion see Owen Chadwick, *The Victorian Church* (1966), I, pp. 558–68. From the extensive literature on the relationship between science and religion in the nineteenth century see especially Charles Coulston Gillispie, *Genesis and Geology. A Study in the Relations of Scientific Thought, Natural Theology and Social Opinion in Great Britain, 1790–1850* (Cambridge, Mass., 1951). For the role of geology within Ruskin's aesthetic and religious beliefs, and for his loss of faith, see George P. Landow, *The Aesthetic and Critical Theories of John Ruskin* (Princeton, 1971), especially pp. 243–44, 266–7, 281–6, 329–31.

37 Seddon, *op. cit.*, p. 124.

38 *Ibid.*

39 G. R. Lewis, *Illustrations of Kilpeck Church, Herefordshire. In a Series of Drawings made on the Spot. With an Essay on Ecclesiastical Design, and a Descriptive Interpretation* (1842), pp. xi and xiv.

40 [Samuel Wilberforce], 'Darwin's *Origin of Species*', *Quarterly Review*, CVII, (1860), 258.

41 *Ibid.*

The colour
in the text :
Ruskin's basket
of strawberries

Stephen Bann

This chapter does not attempt anything so ambitious (or dubious) as a demonstration of Ruskin's theory of colour. It will, on the contrary, develop the argument that his frequent and suggestive references to colour are an indication of failure to develop a coherent theory of representation within which the powerful stimulus of colour would have its allotted and determined place. But such a failure might be seen, from another point of view, as one of the most interesting aspects of Ruskin's criticism. It will be argued that the problem of colour, as it exists for Ruskin the writer and critic, is a remarkably telling index of the equivocal role which colour has played in the theoretical and practical development of post-Renaissance art in Europe. Ruskin's text is a litmus paper which records, not the state of colour theory in the nineteenth century, but the resistance of prevalent views of representation to the concrete *experience* of colour in the visual arts. Moreover, in its very theoretical confusion, Ruskin's writing on colour points towards the specific field of practice within which the artists of the Modern Movement were to seek to close this gap between experience and theory.

Such a claim is not easy to sustain in a short space. But it is surely supported by the evidence of one of the most original of recent writings on Ruskin: John Unrau's *Looking at Architecture with Ruskin*. In the last chapter of his study Unrau tackles the question of colour with an initial, frank admission:

> Colour has proved a continual embarrassment to architectural writers concerned that their study of buildings should be strictly accurate and systematic, for it is difficult—perhaps ultimately impossible—to reduce the visual complexities introduced by colour to categories that lend themselves to analysis.[1]

Such a statement is indeed strongly supported by the succeeding quotation which Unrau takes from a leading architectural writer of Ruskin's day, who is 'not inclined to assert that the colour of a building in a landscape is unimportant to the general effect of that landscape' but does not hesitate to say that colours are 'of minor consequence in relation to our art'.[2] Against these uneasy double negatives Ruskin does indeed, as Unrau emphasises, make an unequivocal assertion:

> The perception of colour is a gift just as definitely granted to one person, and denied to another, as an ear for music; and the very first requisite for true judgment of St Mark's, is the perfection of that colour-faculty which few people ever set themselves seriously to find out whether they possess or not. For it is on its value as a piece of perfect and unchangeable colouring, that the claims of this edifice to our respect are finally rested. . . . [10.97–8]

Yet Ruskin perhaps leads his sympathetic exegete astray when he writes of the 'colour-faculty' and places the issue squarely on the ground of 'perception of colour'. As Unrau himself admits, the study of colour perception as a branch of experimental aesthetics has made very little progress between Ruskin's time and our own.[3] But this fact may not be strictly relevant to the 'embarrassment' of successive architectural writers, or to the determined stand which Ruskin makes upon the principle of colour. In order to appreciate Ruskin's originality (and no doubt to add a small piece to the jigsaw of modern art), we should recognise that the denial of colour is itself an important aspect of the economy of post-Renaissance representation. In other words, it is not our inability to theorise about the experimental data of colour perception that is of significance here. It is the role of colour within a representational system, its uneasy role, that determines the originality, and indeed the excess, of Ruskin's text.

Two extracts from contemporary French critics, both closely concerned with the problem of colour, will help to clarify the distinction that I am making. In his essay 'Split colour/blur' Jean-Louis

Schefer draws a broad distinction between Western attitudes to colour and those of other civilisations:

> ... The West can perceive colour but (contrary to India, China, Africa, South American Indians, etc.) cannot think in colour; and for another reason, that because of its closed economics the figurative system can never introduce elements that it is not capable of engendering. Plato, Aristotle, Malebranche . . . all engender colour for perception, that is to say, in the general economics of 'reasonable' cost to the subject—which guarantees the subject/the world/philosophy.[4]

Schefer is here referring to the subordinate role which colour perception has played within the dominant tradition of Western philosophy—a point which is perhaps curiously echoed by Ruskin himself when he accuses the 'metaphysical Germans' of being prone 'to see things without colour' (6.67). But he clearly views the development of theory of perspective at the time of the Renaissance as the most telling sign of the primacy of 'figure' over 'colour'—a primacy which Leonardo celebrates by stressing that colour differences are merely an aid to the correct definition of receding bodies in perspectival space. For Schefer, the Western tradition locates colour only as an attribute or accident of the figurative system: 'what is unthinkable in all this is the fact that objects might be seen as attributes or accidents of pure colour (which Leonardo only ever refers to as a fog): that is, that these things should be produced within the picture is unthinkable'.[5] A necessary corollary of this position, however, is the assertion that contemporary art, at least since Cézanne, has made the unthinkable something to be contemplated and achieved. Marcelin Pleynet draws the two threads together succinctly in his critical and theoretical programme:

> As opposed to the metaphysical role of the sign which, for the humanist of the Renaissance, overdetermines line as the bearer of a meaning which colour succeeds in filling out (and the impossibility of moving from there to the investigation of subjective or sexual positions), I shall emphasise Cézanne's 'mad' obstinacy in the face of the motif, Matisse's 'drawing with scissors, cutting directly into colour', the insistence with which some contemporary artists consider the 'problem' of colour, and . . . the wish for 'colour' no longer to colour in between lines, or to be cut out in colour, but for colour to produce line.[6]

What place has Ruskin in this grand design? I suggest that in many important respects he anticipates the 'spilling' of colour out of its Renaissance straitjacket. Even if, as is inevitable, he is continually drawn back within the 'economics' of the perspectival system, he is nonetheless able to discern and promote the *productivity* of colour, as opposed to its merely distinctive and differential properties. Yet this conspicuous prescience is most of all observable in the texts where Ruskin comes closest to incoherence: in the texts where Pleynet's 'subjective or sexual positions' come most clearly into view. Cézanne's '"mad" obstinacy' has its correlative in the manic eruptions of Ruskin's late prose.

An extraordinary footnote to the chapter on 'The Hesperid Aeglé', in the last volume of *Modern Painters*, makes the intense contradictions in his position only too apparent. The note unequivocally dismisses the pretensions of colour, as exemplified in the Roman school: 'Its colour is not subordinate. It is BAD.' Nevertheless, Ruskin hastens to add, the perfection of colour improves even the most excellent achievements of form and figure: 'Had Leonardo and Raphael coloured like Giorgione, their work would have been greater, not less, than it is now' (7.415). A certain amount of further equilibration between the claims of colour and of form, with particular reference to Turner, leads to a further and firmer restatement of the issue—as if colour had simply refused to lie down:

> Colour, as stated in the text, is the purifying or sanctifying element of material beauty.
>
> If so, how less important than form? Because, on form depends existence; on colour, only purity. Under the Levitical law, neither scarlet nor hyssop could purify the deformed. So, under all natural law, there must be rightly shaped members first; then sanctifying colour and fire in them.
>
> Nevertheless, there are several great difficulties and oppositions of aspect in this matter, which I must try to reconcile now clearly and finally. As colour is the type of Love, it resembles it in all its modes of operation; and in practical work of human hands, it sustains changes of worthiness precisely like those of human sexual love. That love, when true, faithful, well-fixed, is eminently the sanctifying element of human life: without it, the soul cannot reach its fullest height or holiness. But if shallow, faithless, misdirected, it is also one of the strongest corrupting and degrading elements of life. . . .
>
> So it is with the type of Love—colour. Followed rashly, coarsely, untruly, for the mere pleasure of it, with no reverence, it becomes a temptation, and leads to corruption. Followed faithfully, with intense but reverent passion, it is the holiest of all aspects of material things.
> [7.417]

The modern reader can scarcely fail to note the tensions within this passage—within this inordinately prolonged footnote, which dramatises the return of the repressed. Ruskin salvages the idealist viewpoint only at the expense of indicating the libidinal bases of colour perception. Not surprisingly, the same chapter concludes with a paean to colour which is intended to stress, once again, the primacy of the ideal over the material:

> But ten years ago, I saw the last traces of the greatest works of Giorgione yet glowing like a scarlet cloud, on the Fondaco de' Tedeschi. And though that scarlet cloud (sanguigna e fiammeggiante, per cui le pitture cominciarono con dolce violenza a rapire il cuore delli genti) may, indeed, melt away into paleness of night, and Venice herself waste from her islands as a wreath of wind-driven foam fades from their weedy beach;—that which she won of faithful light and truth shall never pass away. [7.438–39]

It is worth mentioning here that Ruskin's initial reaction to the Giorgione frescoes on the Fondaco dei Tedeschi was a more muted one. On 4 October 1845 he wrote to his father from Venice that he regretted the passing of fresco painting from the exteriors of the buildings in most cases, but mentioned the persistence of 'a fragment or two of Giorgione . . . purple and scarlet, more like a sunset than a painting'.7 In the passage of time such vestiges were thus claimed, inexplicably, for Giorgione's 'greatest works', while the deprecatory simile of the sunset became converted into a powerful metaphor of the decline of the great maritime city. But there are other things, as well, at work in the text. Just as Ruskin confines the discussion of colour and 'sexual love' to a footnote, so he here restricts Zanetti's powerful evocation of the 'soft violence' of colour to a bracketed section—and to the relative obscurity of a foreign language. And he reserves for a final footnote the 'impression that the ground of the flesh in these Giorgione frescoes had been pure vermilion'.

Purple . . . scarlet . . . vermilion . . . What exactly is involved in this shifting of colour descriptions? Before this question is answered, it is worth adding yet another qualification of the vanishing frescoes which appears in Walter Pater's essay on 'The School of Giorgione', published for the first time in 1877. Pater asserts, in sharp contrast to Ruskin:

> Much of the work on which Giorgione's immediate fame depended, work done for instantaneous effect, in all probability passed away almost within his own age, like the frescoes on the facade of the *Fondaco dei Tedeschi* at Venice, some crimson traces of which, however, still give a strange additional touch of splendour to the scene of the *Rialto*.

One suspects, with regard to this passage, that the confutation of Ruskin is Pater's primary though unstated purpose. Ruskin makes the imaginative leap of proclaiming these vanished frescoes to have been Giorgione's 'greatest works'. Pater dismisses them as 'done for immediate effect'. Ruskin speaks of a 'scarlet cloud' (rejecting his earlier alternative of 'purple'), and hypothesises that the ground was once 'pure vermilion'. Pater prefers 'crimson traces'. The nuances of discrimination used in relation to this vestigial work should alert us to some of the paradoxes of colour attribution in art criticism. For—quite apart from the weight that might be placed on Pater's need to modify Ruskin's original colour description—we must reckon with the fact that the two alternative colour adjectives are in fact derived from the same root! The word 'crimson' is a variant of the Arab 'kermes', which denotes a small insect whose shell once served in the processes of dyeing. And 'scarlet' also relates to this insect, being the word which describes the shell itself. Of course the fact that scarlet is originally a kind of metonymy of crimson need not lead us to dismiss the difference which usage has conferred upon the two types of red. But the very scantiness of the evidence on which the colour descriptions are based in this case leads us to press further than the conventions of usage would normally allow. We begin to see the operation in Ruskin's text—and, *a contrario*, in that of Pater—of a kind of colour code whose terms are not conventional but hermetic. Colour is not so much denotative as richly connotative, and the field of connotation is within the Ruskin text.

This being so, we might frame an answer to the question 'Why does Ruskin pick scarlet rather than crimson?' in the following way. Colour, for Ruskin, is mediated by the particular use which the great painters, and pre-eminently Turner, have made of it.[9] And crimson, in the work of Turner, has an extremely specific connotative charge: 'He was very definitely in the habit of indicating the association of any subject with circumstances of death, especially the death of multitudes, by placing it under one of his most deeply *crimsoned* sunset skies. The colour of blood is thus taken for the leading tone in the storm-clouds above the "Slave Ship"' (6.381). This connotative chain of crimson/sunset/blood/death, which Ruskin also identifies with the 'setting sun, red "like the colour he predicts"' in Byron's *Sardanapalus*, becomes additionally charged in the references to scarlet in *Modern Painters V*:

> Note with respect to this matter, that the peculiar innovation of Turner was the perfection of the colour chord by means of *scarlet* . . . Now, this scarlet colour,—or pure red, intensified by expression of light,—is, of all the three primitive colours, that which is most distinctive . . . Observe, farther, that it is this colour which the sunbeams take in passing through the *earth's atmosphere*. The rose of dawn and sunset is the hue of the rays passing close over the earth. It is also concentrated in the blood of man. [7.413–14]

Scarlet, therefore, the 'pure red', both subsumes and exceeds crimson. To the chain of connotations already cited it adds additional, ambivalent terms: not sunset/blood/death but 'rose of dawn and sunset'/blood and *life*. To refer to Giorgione's frescoes as a 'scarlet cloud' is thus to pick up the Turner motif ('No man hitherto had painted the clouds scarlet'), and implicitly to deny the deathly connotations of crimson. But here we may have to reckon with a definite shift in usage between the writing of volumes IV and V of *Modern Painters* (a shift whose significance is emphasised by the appearance of 'rose' in the later text, as we shall shortly see). In the earlier volume Ruskin quite evidently maintains a working distinction between scarlet and crimson, referring for example to the presence of both colours in Turner's drawing of Goldau (6.381). In the later volume, however, he writes at one point as if the two terms were synonymous. We should expect the term scarlet to be picked up at the moment when he records—ironically, of course—'Crimson is impure and vile; let us paint in black if we would be virtuous' (7.413). Is it that Ruskin could not bring himself to refer, even ironically, to scarlet as 'impure and vile'? Certainly our impression is that he has been labouring to set up, within the terms of colour differentiation, a good red and a bad red—a paradigm of purity against the threat of impurity. Such an aim predominates, by this point at any rate, over any more objective purpose of description.

Furthermore, there is the question of 'pure vermilion'. Here we are dealing not simply with a descriptive term but with a chemically fixed pigment.[10] Consequently, the word vermilion is not so much an alternative within the register of crimson/scarlet as a supplement: the colour effect brought down to the material determinants of the painter's practice. After writing of the effect of scarlet reflection, Ruskin adds the gloss: 'Turner habitually, in his later sketches, used vermilion for his pen outline in effects of sun.' In relation to the Giorgione frescoes, the impression conveyed in the footnote that 'the ground of the flesh . . . had been pure vermilion' is thus an intriguing link between Turner and the Venetian painter. Giorgione is retrospectively associated, on the faith of Ruskin's 'impression', with the supreme colourist of modern times. Small wonder that, in this not unimportant detail, Pater makes his second decisive shift from Ruskin's essay, associating the 'flesh' of Giorgione's painting with an idealised landscape effect quite contrary to Ruskin's advocacy:

> Only, in Italy all natural things are as it were woven through and through with gold thread, even the cypress revealing it among the folds of its blackness. And it is with gold dust, or gold thread, that these Venetian painters seem to work, spinning its fine filaments, through the solemn human flesh, away into the white plastered walls of the thatched huts.[11]

The contrast between this carefully colour-coded passage and

those which have been drawn from Ruskin shows that colour is
indeed the bearer of a burden beyond description. Pater has produced an effect of total sublimation, in which the gold 'filaments'
permeate and dematerialise that 'solemn human flesh'. Ruskin has
allowed the almost vanished frescoes to serve as a pretext for the
resurrection of that flesh (we might almost say)—through the insistent chain of meaning which carries us from scarlet to vermilion.
One further term requires to be placed within this chain, if we are to
appreciate the full psychological dimension of his use of colour
terms, particularly within the register of reds. In the following
passage all the connotations are taken from the field which has
already been explored. But the apparently casual reference to the
'rose of dawn' is supplanted by a much stronger equation between
the colour and the flower:

> Perhaps few people have ever asked themselves why they admire a rose
> so much more than all other flowers. If they consider, they will find,
> first, that red is, in a delicately gradated state, the loveliest of all pure
> colours; and secondly, that in the rose there is *no shadow*, except what
> is composed of colour. [6.62]

The purest of reds (which is, we remember, scarlet) is thus exemplified by the rose. (And the fact that there are roses of other colours is
curiously suppressed in the confident equation!) Despite Ruskin's
later assertion that 'neither scarlet nor hyssop could purify the de-
formed', we seem to glimpse here, in the rose which has *'no shadow'*,
an absolute and purifying principle. Yet the guarantee of this
principle lies ultimately elsewhere than in Ruskin's text, or rather it
lies in what the French psychiatrist André Green has called the 'text
of the life'. Rose La Touche, the young girl to whom Ruskin formed
his most passionate attachment, cannot be seen as merely external to
his life as a writer, so numerous are the instances where the name
'Rose' is overdetermined in these later years by the sad history of
their liaison.[12] 'Rose' is the signifier which (like the 'pure vermilion'
ground of the Giorgione frescoes) promises love as the 'sanctifying
element of human life'; love as the purification of the material world
and the material body. But if 'Rose' is therefore the final condensation of Ruskin's desire, the equation within the text which draws
together the manifold meanings of red, it points back at the same
time to a biographical history which prepares and prefigures the
eventual result. Adrian Stokes has sympathetically retraced the
story in Part II of *The Painting of our Time*. Ruskin is first of all
portrayed in his youth, taken away from his Oxford college because
of an illness in which he spat blood, and seeking to restore his health
through a trip to the Continent. In *Praeterita* he recounts how this
period of illness and depression was terminated by a series of inci-

dents, the first being the present of 'a little basket of wild strawberries' (35.313) which was brought to him in the inn at Fontainebleau. As Stokes puts it, his immediately subsequent success in
drawing a 'a little aspen tree' was prepared by this innocent gift:

> ... in the forms of an exterior perception Ruskin regained the measure
> of a good incorporated object and of potency feeling, focused by the
> integrated body of the aspen tree. The occasion was nearest prepared
> by the manic impact upon him of the basket of strawberries: we cannot
> doubt it.[13]

Nearly thirty years later, on the night of 11–12 November 1869,
Ruskin was to record a dream of '"a friend of mine" running a race,
who asked for a basket of strawberries from a girl walking in front.
"So I ran and caught her, and she had four little baskets of strawberries, all stuck together and I couldn't choose which basket to
take."' Stokes explains: 'Poor Ruskin's good objects, at that time,
particularly the wild strawberries of the child, Rose La Touche,
were the centre of unceasing conflict.'[14]

Even in the bare lineaments of this biographical sketch, which
establishes the link between the youthful illness (and cure) and the
conflicts of old age, we have the deep underpinning—so it would
seem—of the colour vocabulary which we have been considering.
On the one hand there is the gift of strawberries, a gift which
counteracts the (perhaps delayed) effects of a state of illness characterised by spitting of blood, and enables Ruskin to rehabilitate the
'integrated body' of the aspen tree. (It is worth noting that the
incident takes place in the early stages of a journey to Switzerland.
No doubt Switzerland, rather than Italy, represented for Ruskin the
'rested mother'[15] of Stoke's autobiography. Nevertheless Venice,
like Siena at the close of *Praeterita*, seems to have prefigured intermittently the possibility of that maternal identification, and never
more so than in the evocation of the Hesperid Aeglé.) On the other
hand—towards the other end of his life—there is the dream of
strawberries: both a recurrence of the earlier experience and an
indication of how much his equilibrium was bound up, by this time,
in the passionate futility of his love for Rose. But in the dream
Ruskin is no longer the receiver of the basket of strawberries; on the
contrary, he is asked to make a present of them to Rose, and cannot
choose between four baskets 'all stuck together'. Is it too fanciful to
see in Ruskin's gift to Rose—the gift which he cannot make up his
mind to choose—the same ambiguity as resides in the colour coding
of the reds, in *Modern Painters V* particularly? The four alternative
baskets might almost be seen as the four variants of red which Ruskin brings into play: purple, scarlet, crimson, vermilion. To be
unable to choose between them would be to represent symbolically

the conflict which we have seen to be implicit in his usage of colour terms: to be fixated upon the 'changes of worthiness precisely like those of human sexual love' in which his maimed desires could find their correlative.

I have said little, up to this point, of the fourth variety of red: purple. Ruskin uses it as an alternative to scarlet in the letter of 1845. In the later texts which have been cited he does not allow it to bear the same weight as scarlet or crimson. Nevertheless, in the very year of the dream of baskets of strawberries, he published a series of lectures entitled *The Queen of the Air* in which the colour purple became the pretext for an astonishing display of subtlety and erudition. *The Queen of the Air* reverberates from the start with the anxiety of definition; Ruskin rebels against the linearity of writing which compels him to represent plurality of meanings through strict succession: 'I am compelled, for clearness' sake, to mark only one meaning at a time. Athena's helmet is sometimes a mask—sometimes a sign of anger—sometimes of the highest light of aether: but I cannot speak of all this at once' (19.307n). Seen in relation to this *cri de coeur*, the passage on purple is indeed a prodigy of compression, in which 'clearness' is all but sacrificed to the principle of plural meaning; in which almost all the images and aspects of the discussion up to this point recur as incidents in the connotative chain of this one colour. The passage is long, but can only be quoted *in extenso*:

> As far as I can trace the colour perception of the Greeks, I find it all founded primarily on the degree of connection between colour and light; the most important fact to them in the colour of red being its connection with fire and sunshine; so that 'purple' is, in its original sense, 'fire-colour', and the scarlet, or orange, of dawn, more than any other, fire-colour. I was long puzzled by Homer's calling the sea purple; and misled into thinking he meant the colour of cloud shadows on green sea; whereas he really means the gleaming blaze of the waves under wide light. Aristotle's idea (partly true) is that light, subdued by blackness, becomes red; and blackness heated or lighted, also becomes red. Thus, a colour may be called purple because it is light subdued (and so death is called 'purple' or 'shadowy' death); or else it may be called purple as being shade kindled by fire, and thus said of the lighted sea; or even of the sun itself, when it is thought of as a red luminary opposed to the whiteness of the moon; 'purpureos inter soles, et candida lunae sidera'; or of golden hair: 'pro purpureo poenam solvens scelerata capillo'; while both ideas are modified by the influence of an earlier form of the word, which has nothing to do with fire at all, but only with mixing or staining; and then, to make the whole group of thoughts inextricably complex, yet rich and subtle in proportion to their intricacy, the various rose and crimson colours of the murex-dye,—the crimson and purple of the poppy, and fruit of the palm—and the association of all these with the hue of blood;—partly

direct, partly through a confusion between the word signifying 'slaughter' and 'palm-fruit colour', mingle themselves in, and renew the whole nature of the old word; so that, in later literature, it means a different colour, or emotion of colour, in almost every place where it occurs; and casts around for ever the reflection of all that has been dipped in its dyes.

So that the word is really a liquid prism, and stream of opal. And then, last of all, to keep the whole history of it in the fantastic course of a dream, warped here and there into wild grotesque, we moderns, who have preferred to rule over coal-mines instead of the sea . . . have actually got our purple out of coal instead of the sea! And thus, grotesquely, we have had enforced on us the doubt that held the old word between blackness and fire, and have completed the shadow, and the fear of it, by giving it a name from battle, 'Magenta'. [19.379–80]

Ruskin's fantasia on the etymology of purple indeed retains and multiplies the ambiguities which we have noted in the case of the other colour variants of red: purple is either 'light subdued' ('shadowy' death) or 'shade kindled with fire'; from 'fire-colour', the colour of dawn, it has descended to the base and terrifying role of canalising the blood spilt at the battle of Magenta. If we are to argue that it is this disturbance of the colour signifier—precisely its oscillation between high and low, noble and base, life and death— that betrays its suppressed links with sexuality, then we shall have an unexpected confirmation in the poetry of Thomas Hardy. Strangely enough, Donald Davie does not mention, in his brilliant article on 'Hardy's Virgilian Purples', the possible influence of *The Queen of the Air*. But what he writes after pursuing his own etymo- logical and poetic investigation through the uses of the word purple might almost serve for Ruskin himself: 'This clinches it: the pur- ples which prink the main as seen from Beeny Cliff are the spiritual light of sexual love—as indeed we should have guessed, for what but sexual passion is so likely to terrify and irradiate alternately or at the same time?'[16]

The foregoing passages may seem to have brought the issue of Ruskin's colour vocabulary unequivocally on to the territory of biography. But such is not my primary intention. In order to under- stand the obsessional recurrence of these colour terms, we must, I believe, explore the determinations exercised by the images of Ruskin's life: the spitting of blood, the basket of strawberries and the rose with no shadow. But such a strategy does not simply abandon the issues of art criticism for the lusher pastures of psycho- sexual exploration. As I explained at the outset, Ruskin's proble- matic use of colour adjectives should be seen against the background of post-Renaissance representational norms: if, in Pleynet's terms, the sign 'for the humanist of the Renaissance overdetermines line as the bearer of a meaning which colour succeeds in filling out', then Ruskin is the anti-humanist who precisely 'overdetermines' colour as the bearer of meaning. If the Renaissance position prevents any recourse 'to the investigation of subjective or sexual positions', then Ruskin, through his reiterated use of the variants of red, brings the issue of these positions uncomfortably, but undeniably, into the foreground. The general point can therefore be made without equivocation. Ruskin's colour in the text is not a contribution to the dissipation of the 'complexities of colour' through the solvent of experimental aesthetics. It is an index of the way in which the 'problem' of colour continues to arise in modern art, indissolubly linked as it is with the oral and libidinal bases of perception.[17]

I should finally anticipate the accusation of having imported into this study of Ruskin concepts from the psycho-analytic arsenal of Freud and Melanie Klein, to which the name of Adrian Stokes may have alerted the reader. Indeed, it would be absurd to claim that the general position which I have associated with the names of Schefer and Pleynet is not heavily indebted to psychoanalysis in its reading of the history of representation. Colour as the return of the repressed in modern painting may appear a crude and overtly ideological slogan. But its possible contribution to the imperfect state of our knowledge, not least in the matter of our hopelessly banal distinction between the 'abstract' and the 'figurative', is in my opinion very considerable. Ruskin wrote *The Queen of the Air* over thirty years before Freud published *The Interpretation of Dreams.* Yet Ruskin's tracing of the history of purple through 'the fantastic course of a dream' shows to what extent he anticipated the discovery of the mechanisms of condensation and displacement, and how lightly he is able to dispense with the logic of non-contradiction.[18] Similarly, his very equivocations in the discussion of colour and 'love' help us to identify and understand the historical bases of figuration in the post-Renaissance tradition. Jean-Louis Schefer, in his study of Uccello, shows how colour may override the supposed abstract/figurative dichotomy in an important way—he writes of 'bodies . . . cut out in colour' and colour as 'a fundamental prerequisite of figure'.[19] It is the force of this inversion of customary strategies which Ruskin faithfully indicates through the very excessiveness of colour in the text.

1 John Unrau, *Looking at Architecture with John Ruskin* (1978), p. 140. NOTES

2 *Ibid*. The extract is from Joseph Gwilt, *Encyclopedia of Architecture* (1842).

3 *Ibid*., p. 171: 'Clearly the visual psychologists are still a long way from being able to supply information that might be useful to the architectural critic in analysis of a colour scheme of any complexity'. A recent research thesis on 'Chromo-audition'—the association of colours with sounds—suggests that this is a lively direction in contemporary experimental psychology, which may shortly produce results. ('Continuing research . . . tends to suggest a physiological basis . . . will soon be found': John Duffield, 'A personal investigation of Chromo-audition', M.A. dissertation submitted to the School of Art Education, Birmingham Polytechnic, 1979, II, p. 199.) However, the relevance of such experimental findings to visual representation cannot be taken for granted.

4 Jean-Louis Schefer, 'Split colour/blur' (trans. Paul Smith), in *Twentieth Century Studies*, 15–16, December 1976, p. 92.

5 *Ibid.*, p. 86.

6 Marcelin Pleynet, 'De pictura' (trans. Stephen Bann), *ibid.*, pp. 112–13. For further indications of the role of Cézanne's 'petite sensation colorante' and its neglect by artists and historians see Pleynet, 'La lettre de l'incarnation', in *Documents Sur*, 2–3, October 1978, p. 87. A notable example of the reconsideration of colour and sexuality in Cézanne's painting can be found in Lawrence Gowing's article 'The Logic of Organized Sensations', in William Rubin (ed.), *Cezanne. The Late Work* (1978). Gowing writes, 'It seems rather that the brilliant vibration of red, emerald and violet, repeating in every combination across the great sheet reflects an absolute intoxication with colour contrasts as an order of reality in itself, a complete world. He finds in it a morphology of its own, endowing the stems that pass through it with a sexual thrust. Colour contrasts become the internal life of art' (p. 61).

7 *Ruskin in Italy. Letters to his Parents, 1845*, ed. Harold I. Shapiro (Oxford, 1972), p. 219.

8 Walter Pater, *The Renaissance* (1925), p. 149. For further information on the uneasy relationship of Pater to Ruskin see Michael Levey, *The Case of Walter Pater* (1978), Levey writes, with regard to the 'Notes on Leonardo da Vinci' first published in November 1869, 'Whether or not news of that appointment [Ruskin's to the Slade Chair of Fine Art at Oxford in 1869] caused Pater to feel any spurt of irritation or envy, or even prompted an urge to challenge the implied official recognition of Ruskin as *the* English authority on art, he could certainly have found no clearer way to proclaim alternatives to Ruskin's views than by this article' (p. 123).

9 It is also at least possible that Ruskin's thoughts on colour were influenced by those of Goethe, despite the professed contempt which he shows for the German writer. Goethe's colour theory, rightly dismissed by Wittgenstein as no theory at all, insists upon the view that red is the first colour that children recognise and show affection towards; it also suggests a link between the 'purple' pigment derived from sea creatures and the origins of human blood; finally it stresses the struggle between light and shadow as the decisive element in the engenderment of colours. (See especially Jacqueline Lesschaeve, 'Comment parler à la couleur', in *Documents Sur*, 4–5, June 1979, pp. 78–80.)

10 The word vermilion is derived from the Latin *vermiculus*, an alternative title for the *kermes*. But by the nineteenth century it had become associated with the chemical product red sulphur of mercury. Ruskin was not alone in using the terms denoting pigments in his descriptions of works by Turner. In 1840 the young Thackeray referred to the

'Slave Ship' in terms of 'rocks of gamboge . . . flakes of white laid on with a trowel; Bladders of vermillion [*sic*]' (*Turner, 1775–1851*, Tate Gallery exhibition catalogue, 1975, p. 145).

11 Pater, *op. cit.*, p. 159.

12 Ruskin first met Rose La Touche in 1858, when he had not yet completed the fifth volume of *Modern Painters*. Numerous letters referring to her are to be found in John Lewis Bradley, ed., *The Letters of John Ruskin and Lord and Lady Mount-Temple* (Columbus, Ohio, 1964). A sympathetic and revealing account is to be found in Robert Hewison, *John Ruskin. The Argument of the Eye* (1976).

13 Adrian Stokes, *Critical Writings*, ed. Lawrence Gowing (1978), III, p. 173. Stokes has in fact conflated two journeys to the Continent: that of winter 1840–41 which indeed followed the incidents of spitting of blood, and that of 1842, when the basket of wild strawberries was presented to him at the inn at Fontainebleau (cf. 35.259–60 and 35.313). The motif of the wild strawberries recurs at least twice in *Praeterita*, with varying effects. On one occasion, after climbing the Fer-à-cheval near Geneva, he finds 'the wild strawberries there to taste of slate' and returns 'rather penitently down to Geneva again' (35.336). On another, he finds at Chamounix 'some wild strawberries which were a consolation' (35.455)'

14 Stokes, *loc. cit.*

15 Stokes, *op. cit.*, II, p. 153.

16 Donald Davie, 'Hardy's Virgilian Purples', in *Agenda*, Thomas Hardy special issue (spring–summer 1972), p. 140.

17 For an effective illustration of the problematic nature of colour in modern art and criticism see Brandon Taylor, 'Abstract Colour Painting in England—the case of Patrick Heron', in *Artlog*, 4 (1980), unpaginated. Taylor writes with reference to post-war American painting: 'Within such a programme, with its exclusive appeal to the scientific concepts of hue and value variation, there is no room for any significance to be accorded to the influence of shape or texture upon colour, and indeed no room either for the description of the sensory effect of one particular colour arrangement on the spectator. Indeed the descriptions of dialectical modernism are entirely general and entirely lacking in any reference to the spectator or the artist as thinking, perceiving beings.'

18 The justification for this *rapprochement* is succinctly made by Emil Benveniste: 'What Freud looked for in vain from "historical" language, he could to a certain extent have found in the language of myth and poetry. Certain forms of poetry are able to adapt themselves to the dream, suggesting the same type of structuration and introducing the same suspension of sense into normal forms of language that the dream projects into our actions' (translated from 'Remarques sur la fonction du langage dans la découverte freudienne', in *Problémes de linguistique générale* (Paris, 1966), and quoted in Paul Rodgers, 'Discourse of Modern Art', in *Artlog*, 5, 1980, unpaginated).

19 See Gérard-Georges Lemaire's interview with Schefer in *Opus*, 70–71 (winter 1979), p. 40. Another striking formulation of the connection between colour and the 'body' can be found in Schefer's recent essay on the contemporary painter Titina Maselli: 'La couleur n'est pas un site: elle saisit ici un corps lorsqu'il se détourne' (*Titina Maselli. Trajets lumineux*, Paris, 1978, p. 5). And an acutely Ruskinian note is sounded in

the extended study of Uccello's 'The Flood', to which reference has already been made: 'Aucun de ces corps n'a jamais stationné dans la peinture; on semble assister à un etrange déshabillage du corps figuratif au milieu de la chrétienté: que porte-t-il? rien, il est une nuée, un pli dans la couleur' (*Le Déluge—La Peste—Paolo Uccello*, Paris, 1976, p. 87).

'These *are the Furies of Phlegethon'*: *Ruskin's set of mind and the creation of* Fors Clavigera

Jeffrey L. Spear

The biggest temptation to the scholar engaged in the rehabilitation of an historical figure is the lure of prophecy, the urge to isolate, if not exaggerate, aspects of the subject's thought that seem to anticipate dominant trends in later generations. Certainly it is easy to find in Ruskin the social thinker a prophet of the Welfare State. After all, a whole programme of social welfare legislation can be abstracted from his works: free public education and vocational training; public works employment for the jobless; public assistance, housing and fuel for the aged and destitute; a graduated income tax; fixed minimum wages for workers and income ceilings for the wealthy; guaranteed medical care for the needy; 'green belts' around urban areas and protection of the environment through the regulation of economic development; limitation of what is now called 'defence spending'; the creation of a National Store that would include grain reserves to prevent starvation or the exploitation of shortages for financial advantage in years of bad harvests. Now that "ecology" is the word of the day one could add to the list Ruskin's proposals for flood control in Italy, his desire to substitute power generated by the forces of wind and water for the combustion of coal that fouls the air. One could even argue that a line of influence on contemporary thinking in these matters runs from Ruskin through Patrick Geddes to Lewis Mumford; from Ruskin through John Hobson to the economist K. William Kapp, whose work *The Social Costs of Private Enterprise* Barry Commoner cites with approval in his ecological study *The Closing Circle*.[1] Just as such a contemporary reading presents Ruskin as a progressive, so did a rather different selection of his proposals in the 1930s and '40s place him, with Carlyle and Matthew Arnold, among the *Victorian Critics of Democracy*.[2] These abstractions from Ruskin's works demonstrate how a Tory of the old school of Homer and Sir Walter Scott could have had so positive an influence on the founders of the Labour Party. However, that a gathering of scattered references from *Unto this Last, Munera Pulveris, Time and Tide* and *Fors Clavigera* suggests a legislative programme from one who had scant faith in legislation tells us remarkably little about what Ruskin actually thought. The habit of mind that lay behind these proposals, while typically Victorian in most of its components, was in its totality uniquely Ruskin's; nor was that mind, for all its dogmatism, a simple one. As he himself predicted, there have been, despite his wide influence, no real 'Ruskinians'.

It has been the biographers and critics who approach Ruskin from a background in the study of art and literature who have done the most to define the peculiarities of his thinking. Studies of Ruskin's economic and social criticism have been more resolutely focused upon his relation to his predecessors and contemporaries, particularly the classical economists. When driven to some consideration of his mind, students of his social thought have tended to draw *ad hoc* upon the work of others, particularly in recent years on John Rosenberg's influential study *The Darkening Glass*.[3]

But some overview of Ruskin's categories of thought seems essential if one is to explain, for example, the fact that he can attack Mill's economics in the body of *Unto this Last* with as scrupulous a regard for the text of the first edition of *The Principles of Political Economy* as one could expect from a hostile polemicist, but then unfairly assault Mill in the Preface added to that work and in *Fors Clavigera*. What kind of mind is it that can at one moment argue against the specific points of a Mill or Huxley and the next use the man's name as a symbol of false belief rather than as the advocate of a false argument? One may 'marvel at Ruskin's blindness in attributing to Mill a particularly rigid adherence to the policy [of *laissez faire*]' but why should such blindness be intermittent?[4] What kind of mind is it that wants to determine carefully whether Lord Derby has written anything before referring to him as 'an "*unscholarly* blockhead"'.[5] Such questions, it seems to me, cannot be fairly addressed by consideration of the sources of Ruskin's ideas alone, nor need they entail a wholesale flight into historical psycho-biography, but they must involve demonstrable influences upon the structure of his thought.

The relation of Ruskin's set of mind to his social thought is a problem that arises most acutely in consideration of *Fors Clavigera*, the multi-volume letter to the world which he produced monthly between 1871 and his mental breakdown in 1878 and intermittently thereafter. Inadequate consideration of Ruskin's frame of reference is one reason why *Fors* has been the least satisfactorily treated of his writings on social issues and the source of so many misstatements of his positions—statements based on apparently unambiguous quotations that, when returned to their context, are transformed in the acid of Ruskin's irony. Thus one social historian writes that on the declaration of the Paris Commune, 'John Ruskin himself for a moment was inspired to declare himself a communist: "reddest of the red"—only to lose sympathy when persuaded the communards were laying waste to Paris'[6]—a point of view that is at least complicated, as we shall see, by the fact that Ruskin's principal comrade is not Karl Marx but Sir Thomas More. Whatever else *Fors* may have been, the constant encounter between Ruskin's fixed frame of reference and the random events which *Fors* records was the most extensive example of sustained ironic writing in English prose since Jonathan Swift, with whom Ruskin felt a powerful affinity in the years of its production.

Ruskin's intellectual interests and the categories of his thought were set at a remarkably early age, and the most important shaping influence was the evangelical Christianity in which he was raised. The well known annual review of the Bible and the Scottish paraphrases conducted by Margaret Ruskin was accompanied by an interpretive bias that he could reproduce in elaborate summaries of sermons by the age of nine. The fundamental assumption of the teaching he absorbed in childhood was the literal truth of scripture, the belief in its verbal inspiration, and the accompanying practice of typological interpretation which had the function of harmonising the doctrine of the Old and New Testaments. Typology reconciled literal reading and figurative interpretation because both type and antitype were believed to be historical actualities and thus distinct from allegorical fiction. Typology in the strictest sense, ritual or legal typology, was restricted to the prefigurations of gospel events in the Mosaic law, but historical typology was applied to prophecies extending beyond New Testament times forming, wrote the Rev. Patrick Fairbairn in 1852, a double prophecy—a prediction in type, more general and indefinite because only embodying the great truths and principles, which were to be developed in the antitype, accompanied by a prediction in words, disclosing in express terms what was afterwards to be accomplished, and these terms suggested by the corresponding typical events, with which the prophecy was connected.[7]

It is easy to picture typical acts as moments of arrested action: Abraham, at the point of slaying Isaac, seeing the ram caught in the thicket; Joseph being sold by his brothers, a prefiguration of the Judas kiss. From early childhood on, Ruskin delighted in transforming abstract concepts into images. 'Papa, is time a figure or a sense?' he asked in one of his first poems. Deciding in favour of figure, Ruskin, not yet eight, went on for more than thirty lines describing and interpreting scythe-bearing Father Time, and time as Saturn.[8] Typological interpretations not only reconciled the visual and literary aspects of his youthful imagination under religious sanction but gave the 'Oxford Graduate' a ready-made critical tool when he turned to the analysis of religious painting. In fact it was Ruskin's typological interpretation of Tintoretto's *Annunciation* as much as the advocacy of fidelity to nature that led the young Holman Hunt to praise his ability to reveal a painting to the reader's inner sight and gave him his influence upon the first-generation Pre-Raphaelites.[9] In his description of the *Annunciation* Ruskin focuses the reader's attention on the corner-stone of the ruined building in which the Virgin sits, because it 'sufficiently explains the typical character of the whole'.

The ruined house is the Jewish dispensation; that obscurely arising in the dawning of the sky is the Christian; but the corner-stone of the old building remains, though the builders' tools lie idle beside it, and the stone which the builders refused is become the Headstone of the Corner. [4.265] cf. Psalm 118:22.

Strict typology is not, however, the single key to Ruskin's critical method, for while it is useful in certain cases, as George Landow has amply demonstrated,[10] Ruskin was not, even in his evangelical days, concerned as a theologian would have been to distinguish typological readings from symbolical or allegorical ones. Rather, I stress the effect of typology on his habit of mind, for two of its salient characistics permeate Ruskin's thinking. First, although a type can be said to symbolise its antitype, both type and antitype are historical actualities; neither is simply an abstraction. Second, type and antitype must be somehow analogous. In the course of a typical event time and eternity momentarily interpenetrate. Thus a biblical man or woman, confined in the chronological time of the fallen world, performs an action that is simultaneously an event in his or her own

time and in providential or *kairos* time: the action is simply part of
the individual's life, yet has its completion in a later historical occur-
rence as part of a progress towards that divine event to which all
creation moves. The doctrine did not demand that—to take an
example dear to Margaret Ruskin in giving thanks for the child for
whom she had so fervently prayed—Hannah should know that her
words applied equally to her own child and the coming Messiah: the
first event does not cause the second, but their connection is pre-
ordained.

It is this habit of thinking in terms of historical analogues,
connected, yet not causally connected, that leads Ruskin for example
to suggest that the fate of Tyre lamented in Ezekiel prophesied that
of Venice, which may in turn anticipate the fate of an unrepentant
England; to analyse the effect of the corruption of city life upon the
artist by contrasting the boyhoods of Giorgione and Turner; even,
in *Fors*, to draw conclusions about the English national character by
analysing that of Richard Coeur-de-Lion. The historical and
literalistic bias of Evangelicalism naturally carried over from strict
typology into the reading of prophecy, and Ruskin remained particularly sensitive to the manifestations in life of the images of
prophecy, which retained their imaginative potency for him far
longer than any sectarian interpretation of them. Thus the sight of
the face of a Venetian boy selling 'half-rotten figs, shaken down,
untimely, by the midsummer storms' before the Ducal Palace was a
kind of epiphany.

> His face brought the tears into my eyes, so open, and sweet, and
> capable it was; and so sad. I gave him three very small halfpence, but
> took no figs, to his surprise: he little thought how cheap the sight of
> him and his basket was to me, at the money; not what this fruit 'that
> could not be eaten, it was so evil,' sold cheap before the palace of the
> Dukes of Venice, meant, to any one who could read signs, either in
> earth, or her heaven and sea. [27.336]

Like a biblical type figure the boy acts without awareness of the
symbolic significance of his action, at least in the eyes of his peculiar
customer. But we as readers of *Fors* must have in mind the references to vile figs in Jeremiah, Amos and Revelation in order to
understand the sign Ruskin is reading, and what it is doing in a
chapter devoted to the topic of blessing and cursing. For these figs in
Jeremiah 24:10 are the evil portion of Israel that God will curse 'till
they be consumed from off the land'; and the sin for which in these
latter days judgement is to fall is suggested by the tree of Revelation
6:13 casting 'her untimely figs' and the verses following the reference to figs in Amos 8:4–6, though Ruskin never specifically alludes
to them. It is the curse upon those who 'swallow up the needy', who

'buy the poor for silver, and the needy for a pair of shoes; *yea*, and sell the refuse of the wheat'. These verses lie behind the paragraph following the encounter with the fig seller in which Ruskin accuses the Churches of having lost the will either to provide material help to the poor or to curse their exploiters.[11]

The starkest aspect of evangelical dualism is the final distinction between the saved and the damned, the elect and the reprobate. From the time of the first social contacts recorded in *Praeterita* that took him beyond the family circle where he, the only begotten son, was the centre of the universe, Ruskin persistently saw himself as an outsider. The courtly manners for which he was famous papered over a fundamental insecurity in unfamiliar company that can only have been intensified when the scandal that accompanied the collapse of his marriage made him for a season a public curiosity and topic of gossip. The rhetoric of the evangelical clergy stressing the virtue of an elect but outcast minority inspired to carry the word of salvation even to their oppressors would almost inevitably be congenial to someone assured of his special genius within the family but nevertheless shy outside it. As Ruskin matured he increasingly regretted the sectarian narrowness of such early works as *The Seven Lamps of Architecture* and rebelled against the obscurity of biblical prophecy, insisting that a religion postulating rewards and punishments was obliged to make explicit to the ordinary human understanding the beliefs and particularly the behaviour that assured the one and excluded the other.[12] He came to despise that modern Protestantism which, he said, 'consists in an assured belief in the Divine forgiveness of all your sins, and the Divine correctness of all your opinions' (22.81); nevertheless, the role of the scorned prophet was too deeply rooted in his personality to be cast off with his sectarian faith. While Ruskin grew more tolerant of other faiths— thinking almost any better than none—and became increasingly sympathetic in his middle years to the 'old Greek' religion (38.384) —desiring only half in jest 'to get some substantial hope of seeing Diana in the pure glades'[13] in the years after he lost his faith—an evangelical, prophetic strain of dogmatic self-righteousness runs through his criticism from first to last.

From his earliest days he attempted to buttress the truths of faith with those of science. Ruskin's enthusiasm for mathematics and science has been generally slighted—perhaps because its late efflorescence in such works as *Proserpina* and *Love's Meinie* has embarrassed commentators eager to make a case for Ruskin in the face of scorn or neglect. In fact geometry was his best academic subject. The only recollection of his Oxford education he records in *Praeterita* with pride untinged by irony is his initial rejection of the diagrams passed out with the Euclid examination paper. 'I could then, and can still, dictate blindfold the demonstration of any problem, with any letters, at any of its points' (35.201). Certainly his skill in geometry contributed to his fondness for arguing from what he took to be the aesthetic equivalent of axioms, postulates and theorums, with corollaries applicable to the representations of nature in art and architecture, and the proper relationship of men to nature and to their fellows.

The science Ruskin knew best was, of course, geology. In his youth he had reconciled the evangelical conviction that nature was God's second book with the indwelling spirit celebrated by Words-worth and with the sentiment of Byron's Childe Harold in the Alps that 'high mountains are a feeling'. The 'visible forms of things' became to Ruskin expressive of their inner glory so that, he said:

> they talk to us about God, and the changeful and typical aspects by which they witness to us of holy truth, and fill us with obedient, joyful, and thankful emotion. [5.386]

He received, at his own request, a copy of H. B. de Saussure's *Voyages dans les Alpes* for his fourteenth birthday, and the French-man's combination of scientific observations, sketches of minerals, glaciers and geological formations, comments on the relationship of the people of the Alpine regions to their environment, together with his aesthetic response to the awesomeness of the peaks themselves, have obvious echoes in his work.

When he began the formal study of geology at Oxford under the Rev. William Buckland the methods did not conflict with the premises of his own thought or with what he had learned from de Saussure. Dr Buckland's science was firmly within the Aristotelian tradition of description and classification that had long been recon-ciled with Christianity. It was science in what Karl Popper calls the tradition of methodological essentialism as opposed to methodo-logical nominalism: the science that asks, for example, what an atom is, rather than, say, under what conditions does an atom radiate light.[14]

Buckland, like others of the so-called Catastrophist school of geology, attempted to square the ever-accumulating evidence of the great antiquity of the earth with the Genesis account of the Creation by such *ad hoc* rationalisations as the assertion that 'millions and millions of years may have occupied the indefinite interval between the beginning in which God created the heaven and the earth, and the evening of the first day of the Mosaic narrative'.[15] But to Ruskin a literal interpretation of scripture had to be just that. He preferred even mystery to rationalisation, and while he seems for a time to have uneasily accepted both Lyell and progressionism he reluctantly conceded the greater plausibility of developmentalism in its

Darwinian form. So to his concern over the obscurity of the Bible text on points seemingly essential for salvation was added the distress of finding faith and scientific fact, the twin supports of his most confident and systematic early writings, at odds.

In the end science carried the day but Ruskin never altered the paradigm that underlay the scientific work he had begun as a child and continued under Dr Buckland. Even in his periods of greatest religious doubt he remained a teleological thinker and an essentialist, convinced that both the moral and the physical universe were governed by purposeful laws even though the law-giver himself seemed to have mysteriously retreated into an obscurity from which he apparently viewed all life, from midge to man, with equal indifference.[16] With the loss of faith that culminated in his 'unconversion' in 1858, Ruskin was left in the uncomfortable position of believing in the literal truth of biblical ethics, but not in the verbal inspiration of the biblical text; in the significance of response, or lack of response, to what is beautiful or awesome in nature as a moral indicator, but not in the immanence of a deity; in a universe organised purposefully, but by an unknown final cause. In short, he became an unwilling fatalist—a circumstance reflected in the very title *Fors Clavigera*, Fors by turns Force, Fortitude or Fate, bearing in its different manifestations the club of Hercules, the key of Patience or the iron nails of Necessity.[17]

If Ruskin did not change the underlying structure of his thought as his faith faded, he did change its focus. While continuing to grant that so great an artist of penetrative imagination as Turner could capture the essence of things as well as their external appearance, he increasingly concentrated upon what he called the 'science of aspects', of surfaces, and defended that interest as truly scientific, arguing that

> it is as much a fact to be noted in their constitution, that [things] produce such and such an effect upon the eye or heart (as, for instance, that minor scales of sound should cause melancholy), as that they are made up of certain atoms or vibrations of matter. [5.387]

Surfaces still expressed the essence of the object even if the essence itself had become undefinable. Similarly, Ruskin's faith in the literal truth of the word was gradually transformed into reliance upon the science of language, particularly upon etymologies, as the basis of continued faith in the essential meaning of key terms, so that, for example, 'economy' (as in political economy) meant 'house-law' as surely as 'astronomy' meant 'star law'. Contemporary philology as presented first by his friend F. J. Furnivall (who sent him a copy of R. C. Trench's *The Study of Words* in 1853) and then, more importantly, by F. Max Müller, who was to be a friend and colleague during Ruskin's Oxford professorship, also served to confirm his preference for the pagan tendency to animate nature in response to its surfaces over the (to Ruskin) post-Christian tendency to take a mechanical nature apart in search of its basic constituents. In Max Müller's account of the development of religion the ancient Aryans were said to have animated nature metaphorically and then given birth to religion by taking their personifications literally.[18] Whereas to Max Müller this process meant that mythology was a disease of language, to Ruskin it was a glory of language, for like Bacon he considered mythology not as a superstitious distortion of reality but as occult teaching. Ruskin found

> 'myths'—allegorical fables or stories . . . 'incomparably *truer*' than the Darwinian—or . . . any other conceivable materialistic theory—because they are the instinctive products of the natural human mind, conscious of certain facts relating to its fate and peace; and as unerring in that instinct as all other living creatures are in the discovery of what is necessary for their life. [26.336]

All science, whether social or physical, devoted to facts without regard to ends, was truly, so far as he was concerned, turned away from life and devoted to death.

Ruskin's severe dualism, which would make of holistic, essentialistic science a science of life and of atomistic, nominalistic science a science of death, reflects the persistent influence of his childhood religion on the pattern of his thought and brings us to the central myth in his own work: the conviction that moral and physical law are ultimately the same, and together form a law of light in perpetual conflict with anarchic forces of destruction.[19] Through all stages of his religious belief Ruskin held firm to the conviction that there was a link between the laws of nature and the principles of right conduct; that he could read both the face of the sky and the signs of the times, and indeed, each in the other. 'All up and down my later books,' he wrote in *Fors*,

> . . . you will find references to the practical connection between physical and spiritual light—of which now I would fain state, in the most unmistakable terms, this sum: that you cannot love the real sun, that is to say physical light and colour, rightly, unless you love the spiritual sun, that is to say justice and truth, rightly. That for unjust and untrue persons, there is no real joy in physical light, so that they don't even know what the word means. That the entire system of modern life is corrupted with the ghastliest forms of injustice and untruth, carried to the point of not recognizing themselves as either—for as long as Bill Sykes knows that he is a robber, and Jeremy Diddler that he is a rascal, there is still some of Heaven's light left for both—but when everybody steals, cheats, and goes to church, complacently, and the light of their whole body is darkness, how great is that darkness! And that the

physical result of that mental vileness is a total carelessness of the beauty of sky, or the cleanness of streams, or the life of animals and flowers: and I believe that the powers of Nature are depressed or perverted, together with the Spirit of Man . . . [28.614-15]

The changes that unfolded in Ruskin's career, from the defence of Turner, through the history of art and architecture and their relation to the society that produced them, on through social reform and the redefinition of political economy, to the wayward natural science of his last years, were not to him the absolute changes of field that they seem in relation to the number of modern academic boundaries they cross. Rather they involved defence of a never completely articulated science of nature against the trend of the times towards ever-increasing specialisation and fragmentation: against the breakdown of natural philosophy into discrete natural sciences; against the development of separate social sciences; against the divorce of economics from ethics, and of scientific from religious thought; against atomistic, analytic explanations as opposed to holistic, systemic ones. Even as in his own religious life he groped for a new basis for his faith in a unitary science of nature and sought in the science of language a partial substitute for the holy word he had trusted in his youth, he resisted the trend towards compartmentalised study. While his love of Turner led him first to apply a combination of essential definitions and what became the science of aspects to the study of art, he came to feel it morally imperative to apply his syncretic thought to the field of political economy in order to resist the evil perpetrated by the substitution of an abstract and, by definition, selfish economic man, motivated solely by rational, pecuniary self-interest, for the older concept of man as a basically social being with a life inseparable from that of his community. The central definition of Ruskin's economics, 'there is no Wealth but Life', was meant not merely as a moral sentiment but as an essential scientific definition, an axiom from which certain propositions would necessarily follow. It implies, for example, that the richest country is that with 'the greatest number of noble and happy human beings'; that the material constituents of wealth are not merely things that can be used but things that avail life; that the opposite of wealth is not poverty but what Ruskin calls 'illth', death-dealing things that, regardless of the money to be made in their manufacture and sale, do more damage than their consumption gives benefit—the ultimate example being the military hardware whose consumption *is* death (17.105 ff). 'Science,' argued Ruskin, invoking the law of the conservation of energy, tells us '. . . that all mortal strength is from the Sun,' and thus we have 'arithmetical and measurable assurance that men vitally active are living sunshine' (28.541). It followed as the night the day that an economic system built upon the dual exploitation of nature and of human workmen would produce an illth in the form of air pollution that obscured the sun, the source of life, which is wealth.

As all students of Ruskin know, his attempts to teach natural political economy to his countrymen directly without an art-historical coating were not well received. The world was not, in the words of one reviewer, 'to be preached to death by a mad governess' (17.xxviii). After being driven from the pages of *Fraser's Magazine*, *Unto this Last* in book form fell stillborn from the press despite being offered at a mere 3/6d. When another public outcry stopped the publication of the *Munera Pulveris* essays in the *Cornhill* Ruskin did not even attempt to publish them in book form until his work at Oxford and the reception of *Fors* paved the way for them. Although discouraged by the neglect not only of cherished ideas but of what, in the case of *Unto this Last*, he rightly considered some of his best prose, he nevertheless persisted in his attempts to bring his social ideas before the public, working them into lectures regardless of the ostensible subject, giving public testimony, writing to daily papers ranging from the *Times* to *Tit Bits*. At the time of the debate over the Second Reform Bill, Ruskin gathered from their scattered publication in twenty-five newspapers the letters that became *Time and Tide*, letters written to Thomas Dixon, whom he calls 'a working man of Sunderland'.[20] It was in the lectures and letters of the 1860s that he forged the epistolary style of *Fors* which has the range of reference of *Munera Pulveris*, without what he came to see as its affected concentration of language, and an informality that allows, as in a personal letter, a movement from topic to topic sustained as much by the personality of the writer as by the orderly succession of ideas one would expect of an essayist.

In the sixty-first letter Ruskin described *Fors* as 'a bywork to quiet my conscience,' and ever since his editors, elaborating on the comment, described *Fors* as 'a payment of ransom' it has been commonly considered a compulsive work in its very conception: a guilty response to his position as a man of wealth in an impoverished world, a guilty reaction to his prestigious professorship. *Fors* was begun a year after his first lecture as Slade Professor of Fine Art at Oxford, and the fact that its years of publication coincided with this appointment does suggest a connection between the two. But the constant association of *Fors* with personal guilt has opened the way to looting that work for evidence of impending insanity, programmatic suggestions of the sort I cited at the outset, and examples of style lifted from their context. Protestations about what he would be doing were it not for conscience and obligation are scattered throughout *Fors*. While not entirely disingenuous, such remarks are one of Ruskin's standard rhetorical gambits: an appeal to ethos, an attempt to establish himself as a disinterested commentator acting on the promptings of conscience in opposition to the advocates of self-interest. Little even of the autobiography in *Fors* is there solely for its own sake irrespective of argument.

It is certainly true that as his breakdown approaches the letters do show signs of tension and collapse of which, indeed, Ruskin is partially aware. In 1876 he said to readers who thought he wrote in jest that 'if I took off the Harlequin's mask for a moment, you would say I was simply mad' (28.513), and at times the mask slips. There are passages in which he assumes knowledge of his private life and personal thoughts so intimate as to lose contact with his audience; passages in which the increasing irritability that always preceded his attacks of mania boils over into print in a manner he came to regret, as in the unfortunate quarrel with his disciple, the housing reformer Octavia Hill (29.354 ff). More broadly, the serio-comic history recorded in *Fors* of the establishment of the Guild of St George is part of Ruskin's attempt not merely to escape the personal tensions and anguish of his private life by burying himself in his work (as, indeed, he had from the time of his youth) but to escape those private sorrows by living entirely for his public life, by virtually turning himself into a public institution. To explore these matters would lead to psychological speculation, into analysis of his response to the death of his parents, to the pathetic story of his love for Rose La Touche—a ground of pain against which the figures of Ruskin's late work are drawn. But already I hear the siren song of biographical reduction. Resisting that music, I will move on to argue that, like his earlier work, most of *Fors* subsumes its biographical elements within a larger and rationally comprehensible purpose. As Ruskin himself explained in 1877 with eighty issues of *Fors* behind him:

> *Fors is a letter*, and written as a letter should be written, frankly, and as the mood, or topic, chances; . . . True, the play of it (and much of it is a kind of bitter play) has always, . . . as stern [a] final purpose as Morgiana's dance; but the gesture . . . must be as the humour takes me. [29.197][21]
> . . . *Fors Clavigera* is not, in any wise, intended as counsel adapted to the present state of the public mind, but it is the assertion of the code of Eternal Laws which the public mind *must* eventually submit itself to, or die; and I have really no more to do with the manners, customs, feelings, or modified conditions of piety in the modern England which I have to warn of the accelerated approach either of Revolution or Destruction, than poor Jonah had with the qualifying amiabilities which might have been found in the Nineveh whose overthrow he was ordered to foretell, in forty days. That I should rejoice, instead of mourning, over the falseness of such prophecy, does not at all make it at present less passionate in tone. [29.197–8]

When Ruskin heard of his appointment as Slade Professor in 1869 he immediately wrote to his mother that '. . . it will enable me to obtain attention, and attention is all that I want to enable me to say what is entirely useful instead of what is merely pretty or entertaining' (19.lix). Four days later he was writing to his friend and champion at Oxford, Dr Henry Acland, that the doctor will be surprised at how he will 'avoid saying anything *with the University authority* which may be either questionable by, or offensive to, even persons who know little of my subject, and at the generally quiet tone to which I shall reduce myself in all public duty' (20.xix; italics mine). One way Ruskin could capitalise upon the prestige of his appointment in order to say what he thought useful and, as best as he was able, still keep his promise to Acland, was to complement his university lectures with a separate popular forum for the presentation of his more controversial views—a forum that would not be subject to constraint by the proprieties of professorship, the pressures of subscribers, or even constraints of commercial publication.

Ruskin watched the press for reports of his appointment and his lectures and, as he seems to have anticipated, accounts of his activities began to appear in the news and feature pages as well as the book review columns. Additional encouragement to proceed with his journal came with the receipt in the summer of 1870 of a series of articles by Joseph Lawton, the editor of a small, virtually one-man newspaper in Shropshire, who was writing Ruskinian pieces on the condition of the working class and comparable subjects.[22] Lawton's success may well have influenced Ruskin's decision to handle the publication and distribution of *Fors* himself through the agency of George Allen, his former pupil at the Working Men's College.[23]

The aim of *Fors* was to continue the description of the natural political state of man begun in *Time and Tide* and, in the process, gather around Ruskin a group of contributors to what became the St George's Fund in the attempt to realise, at least partially, through a St George's Company, his neo-feudal ideal kingdom; to begin the transformation of English society that would bring it into conformity with what he believed to be the moral laws of Nature. Whatever one may think of the practicality of Ruskin's intentions, they were a logical complement to his art teaching. He was firmly convinced, as he told his Oxford undergraduates, that '*you cannot have a landscape by Turner, without a country for him to paint; you cannot have a portrait by Titian, without a man to be portrayed*' (20.107). While Ruskin's hope of transforming his country was doomed to failure, his propaganda efforts did lead to the successful reissuing of *Unto this Last*, the publication of *Munera Pulveris* and, in sum, largely paved the way for what influence he has had on modern economic and social thought.

As fate, or what Ruskin called in those years the third Fors, would have it, the early numbers of the new venture coincided with the Prussian siege of Paris, the rise and fall of the Commune, the birth throes of yet another French republic to replace the sorry empire of the third Napoleon, of whom he had once entertained some hopes. Ruskin's name (and it is another indication of his public standing in 1871) was linked with such prominent men as Archbishop Manning, the banker and M.P. Sir John Lubbock, T. H. Huxley, the Archbishop of London and the Lord Mayor on a committee to raise food for the relief of Paris in the very month *Fors* first appeared. But even without his personal involvement in the relief effort he would have felt the need to comment on the events in Paris. So potent an example of what he feared would come to pass in England took precedence over the orderly exposition of what he hoped might be done to prevent it. As a disciple of Carlyle's, forming with him a society of two in opposition to the political economists, Ruskin was tempted, even more than most Englishmen, to read French revolutions through Carlylean spectacles as portents of the probable future of an unregenerate England.

War and revolution were catastrophes that he saw as logical consequences of the social and scientific trends of his century, and the warning signs were very much in the public eye. By balloon post during the siege and by conventional transport thereafter came not only news stories but pictures—sketches commissioned for engravings by such weeklies as the *Illustrated London News* and *Graphic*. If we read through the magazines week by week the story progresses in images that assimilate the progress of events to graphic and narrative conventions. From the image of the heroic Frenchman off to defend home and country we move to the shell-torn rubble of a

French home where children play even as parents despair. We see the arrogant Prussians, self-crowned victors in the Tuileries, contrasted with the generous English, distributors of food (collected by Ruskin's Mansion House Committee) to the starving Parisians.

After the declaration of the Commune comes a change in sympathy. We see the mob building barricades, National Guards on the loose, the women of Paris as Carlyle's insurrection of woman reborn (fig. 56). Finally we have death on the barricades (fig. 57); and, at the end of May, Paris in Flames (fig. 58); summary justice for the accused fire bombers, the alleged *pétroleuse* (fig. 59); glimpses of the Versailles government's reprisals (fig. 60); and a moralised conclusion, 'Justice Satisfied' (fig. 61)—though, as we shall see, Ruskin thought the class of person looking so pensively, even pityingly, into the mass grave was in fact primarily responsible for it.

These pictures of war and revolution ran concurrently with the ordinary stuff of English life as though the two had nothing in common. Ruskin asks his readers to recall a picture of the Queen's concert in the *Graphic* of August 1871 (fig. 62), and interprets it for them thusly:

> All the fine ladies sitting so trimly, and looking so sweet, and doing the whole duty of woman—wearing their fine clothes gracefully; and the pretty singer, white-throated, warbling 'Home, sweet home' to them, so morally, and melodiously! . . . Surely we are safe back with our virtues in satin slippers and lace veils;—and our Kingdom of Heaven is come again, *with* observation, . . . Cherubim and Seraphim in toilettes de Paris . . . and vulgar Hell reserved for the canaille, as heretofore! Vulgar Hell shall be didactically pourtrayed accordingly . . . —Wickedness going its way to *its* poor Home—bitter-sweet. Ouvrier and pétroleuse—prisoners at last—glaring wild on their way to die. [Fig. 63]

58 left
Burning of the Hôtel de Ville, Paris; *Illustrated London News*, 10 June 1871

59 below
The End of the Commune— Execution of a Pétroleuse; *The Graphic*, 10 June 1871

Alas! of these divided races, of whom one was appointed to teach and guide the other, which has indeed sinned deepest—the unteaching, or the untaught?—which now are guiltiest—these, who perish, or those—who forget? [27.137–8]

The ruling classes of England listening to 'Home, Sweet Home' while working people of Paris are led off to be shot Ruskin links without so much as a transition to the French upper classes, those 'swine of the five per cent', as he calls them, who, back in power, will not tolerate what they call the 'inquisition' of an income tax. He promptly places them in the fourth circle of Dante's Hell, where spendthrift and miser suffer together, both classes of the ungrateful in life indistinguishable in death.

While he rarely makes so direct a reference to the illustrated papers, many of the events which Fors, or chance, presents to him in the columns of the newspapers as instances of his arguments are

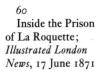

60
Inside the Prison
of La Roquette;
*Illustrated London
News*, 17 June 1871

61
Justice is
Satisfied—A Scene
in the Cemetery of
Père La Chaise;
The Graphic, 24
June 1871

actual illustrations in the weeklies. Ruskin is certainly aware that while he contrasts picture-making and munitions-making in the first *Fors* as patronage industries that, in terms of material wealth, only rob Peter to pay Paul, and decides in favour of painting, the papers are carrying pictures of French homes destroyed by Prussian shells.

If you have done no good by painting, at least you have done no serious mischief. A bad picture is indeed a dull thing to have in a house ... but it won't blow the roof off. Whereas, of most things which the English,

French, and Germans are paid for making nowadays,—cartridges, cannon, and the like,—you know the best thing we can possibly hope is that they *may* be useless, and the net result of them, zero. [27.21]

'During the last eight hundred years', he writes in the second *Fors*,

the upper classes of Europe have been one large Picnic Party [fig. 64]. Most of them have been religious also; and in sitting down, by companies, upon the green grass, in parks, gardens, and the like, have considered themselves commanded into that position by Divine authority . . . [27.39–40]

They might at little expense have taught the people some science and art, but instead have spent hundreds of millions of pounds to teach 'the peasants of Europe—to pull each other's hair. With *this* result . . .' and he quotes from the *Daily Telegraph* of 17 January 1871:

65 below
The 35 Ton Gun, Called 'The Woolwich Infant'; *Illustrated London News*, 11 February 1871

Each demolished house has its own legend of sorrow, of pain, and horror; . . . of weeping women and trembling children running away in awful fear, abandoning the home that saw their birth . . . of startled men seizing quickly under each arm their most valued goods, and rushing, heavily laden, after their wives and babes . . . [27.41]

66 right
Envy, from Giotto's Arena Chapel, Padua; photogravure reproduced in letter 6 of *Fors Clavigera*, from *Works*, 27, facing p. 111

In England meanwhile the *Pall Mall Gazette* gives Ruskin a vivid description of filth, hunger and disease in overcrowded slum dwellings in a London founded 'on the eternal laws of Supply and Demand' while the '35-ton gun called the 'Woolwich Infant' [fig. 65] . . . is fed with 700-pound shot, and 130 pounds of gunpowder at one mouthful; not at all like the Wapping infants, starving on a half-chance meal a day' (27.42–3).

As we see, in the early numbers of *Fors* Ruskin is himself writing an illustrated monthly. But his pictures, unlike those recording events in the regular press, are meant to illustrate the eternal principles that should guide our understanding of transitory events, to manifest the natural laws of human relations whose violation leads to the horrors of 1871 on both sides of the Channel. Writing in May during the last days of the Commune, Ruskin says:

> (... I waited before finishing my letter, to see if the Sainte Chapelle would follow the Vendôme Column), the sin of it, I tell you, is not that poor rabble's, spade and pickaxe in hand among the dead ... round the barricades, and the ruins, of the Street of Peace.
>
> This cruelty has been done by the kindest of us, and the most honourable ... who through their happy and, as they thought, holy lives, have sought ... only 'the entertainment of the hour.'
>
> [They are worshippers of] Covetousness, lady of Competition and of deadly Care ... I have given you the picture of her ... as Giotto saw her: dominant in prosperous Italy as in prosperous England, ... and having her hands, clawed then, as now, so that she can only clutch, not work.... [27.111–12]

The opposite of Envy, (fig. 66) and the virtue under whose aegis Ruskin gives his most complete analysis of the Commune, is Charity, who tramples on bags of gold while giving food and flowers. Because Ruskin saw industrial capitalism as the incarnate opposite of Charity, his analysis of the underlying causes of the war in Europe is as radical as that of a Marxist, emphasising class over nationality. It is not overt theft by the insurrectionists that lies at the root of the problem, but 'occult' theft.

> And the guilty Thieves of Europe, the real sources of all deadly war in it, are the Capitalists—that is to say, people who live by percentages on the labour of others; instead of by fair wages for their own. The *Real* war in Europe, of which this fighting in Paris is the Inauguration, is between these and the workman, such as these have made him. They have kept him poor, ignorant, and sinful, that they might, without his knowledge, gather for themselves the produce of his toil. At last, a dim insight into the fact of this dawns upon him; and such as they have made him he meets them, and *will* meet. [27.127]

But radical as it may be, this analysis is hardly that of a Marxist; it is, as he says, that of a communist of the old school of Sir Thomas More, who in *Utopia* denounced enclosures, satirised the idle priest and gentleman, and invented a government that organised labour and promoted common wealth over private fortune. If Ruskin calls himself 'reddest of the red' it has more to do with the fact that red is the colour of Dante's Charity, who is 'so red of hue / She'd scarce be noted in the furnace flame',[24] than with a sudden, and momentary, conversion to the workers' cause.

The hue of Charity has its demonic counterpart in Phlegethon, the fiery river of blood that borders Dante's nether Hell, where Ruskin confines not the avaricious man but the capitalist usurer under the dominion of the Minotaur which has become, he says, 'precisely the general type of the English nation to-day' (27.428).

> There is one lust and one anger of the flesh only; these, all men must feel; rightly feel, if in temperance; wrongly, if in excess; but even then, not necessarily to the destruction of their souls. But there is another lust, and another anger, of the heart; and *these* are the Furies of Phlegethon—wholly ruinous. Lord of these, on the shattered rocks, lies couched the Infamy of Crete. For when the heart, as well as the flesh desires what it should not, and the heart, as well as the flesh, consents and kindles to its wrath, the whole man is corrupted, and his heart's blood is fed in its veins from the lake of fire. [27.424–5]

Of the covert lust and violence of industrial capitalism Ruskin can acquit himself—he can defeat that aspect of the Minotaur. But like Theseus returning from Crete he has in his own life 'lost love's hope and help'. It was, he says, in mourning for Ariadne and not out of mere forgetfulness that Theseus hoisted over his returning ship the fatal black sail that precipitated his father's death.

> Of which the meaning is, that we must not mourn for *ourselves*, lest a worse thing happen to us,[25]—a Greek lesson much to be remembered by Christians about to send expensive orders to the undertaker: unless . . . they mean by their black vestments to tell the world that they think their friends are in hell. If in Heaven, with Ariadne and the gods, are we to mourn? And if they were fit for Heaven, are we, for ourselves, ever to leave off mourning? [27.429]

The personal note is so strong in this passage that it must have been felt even by readers who did not know that Ruskin was writing within a month of the first anniversary of his mother's death and after another wrenching separation from Rose La Touche, whose own mental and physical decline had become manifest.

Much of the imagery of *Fors Clavigera* is Janus-faced, one aspect addressing a public problem, the other Ruskin's own. I have stressed the public face while acknowledging the other to avoid collapsing the conceptual aspect of Ruskin's mind into the merely personal, let alone the pathological. For out of the eclectic materials of his early training in religion, science and art he constructed a place of vision apart from those of his contemporaries, a prospect that enabled him to see what most of them could not about the condition of England. The example of the Commune and illustrations from the weeklies demonstrates how vivid and powerful he could make the encounter between the random flow of events and his peculiar point of view. That Ruskin's point of view *was* peculiar, and constructed in opposition to most of the intellectual trends of the time, meant that while he could convince many that things were wrong, and some of why they were wrong, he could persuade very few to adopt his ideas of what might be done to set things right. His public frustration in *Fors* is that of a man crying, 'See, can't you see?' to people who, if they can be made to see the same thing at all, will see it with different eyes.

Eventually Ruskin's world collapsed, folded in on itself, and he found more terribly than Yeats that lust and rage, the very furies of Phlegethon, can 'dance attention upon old age'. The tension between the battle within and the battle without that permeates *Fors Clavigera* became a psychomachia; the war between an external light and darkness was reduced to a battle between angels and devils, waged within. Method became madness. But his power as a social critic did not come because he projected darkness, fragmentation and collapse upon the world, but because, like the literalist and typologist he was raised to be, he found them concretely embodied there.

1 See, for example, Geddes's 'John Ruskin', in *The Round Table* NOTES *Series*, ed. H. Bellyse Baildon (Edinburgh, 1887); Mumford's *Technics and Civilization* (New York, 1934); Hobson's *Work and Wealth* (New York, 1914) and *John Ruskin* (Boston, 1898); Kapp's *Social Costs* (Cambridge, Mass., 1950); Commoner's *The Closing Circle* (New York, 1971), particularly chapter 12, 'The Economic Meaning of Ecology'.

2 Benjamin E. Lippincott (Minneapolis, 1938).

3 New York, 1961.

4 James C. Sherburne, *John Ruskin, or the Ambiguities of Abundance* (Cambridge, Mass, 1972), p. 11. Sherburne's is the most exhaustive study of Ruskin's social and economic criticism in relation to his sources and the work of his contemporaries. Ruskin read not blindly but selectively and, like many polemicists, tended to save the chaff and throw away the wheat when quoting opponents. Moreover, like his 'papa' Carlyle, he not only personified abstractions but gave some of them the names of actual individuals. Ruskin was quite capable of supporting the man John Stuart Mill as a candidate for Parliament in 1865 while writing of the author of *On Liberty* and *The Principles of Political Economy* as if he were a devil incarnate.

5 Ruskin to William Cowper-Temple, April 1873. *The Letters of John Ruskin to Lord and Lady Mount-Temple* (Columbus, Ohio, 1964), p. 345. My italics.

6 Royden Harrison, in *The English Defence of the Commune, 1871* (1971), p. 23.

7 *The Typology of Scripture* (Philadelphia, 1852), p. 122.

8 *The Ruskin Family Letters*, ed. Van Akin Burd (Ithaca, N.Y., 1973), pp. 150–1.

9 On Ruskin's typological analysis of Tintoretto see George P. Landow, *William Holman Hunt and Typological Symbolism* (New Haven and London, 1979), pp. 2 ff.

10 See chapter 5, *The Aesthetic and Critical Theories of John Ruskin*

(Princeton, 1971), and 'There Began to be a Great Talking about the Fine Arts', in *The Mind and Art of Victorian England*, ed. Josef L. Altholz (Minneapolis, 1976).

11 The network of texts and interpretations suggested by Ruskin's reference to 'vile figs' illustrates the allusive nature of his quotations from works, especially the Bible, that he constantly reread and knew virtually by heart. For an extensive analysis of text and sub-text in Ruskin see William Arrowsmith's chapter in this volume.

12 'John Ruskin's Unpublished Letters to his Oxford Tutor on Theology', ed. John Hayman, *Etudes Anglais*, XXX (1977).

13 *Letters of John Ruskin to Charles Eliot Norton*, I, ed. Charles Eliot Norton (Boston, 1905), p. 132.

14 *The Open Society and its Enemies* (1966), 5th ed., I, p. 32.

15 *Geology and Mineralogy considered with Reference to Natural Theology* (1836), p. 22.

16 See *Letters to Norton*, p. 116 ff, for one of many letters on this theme.

17 Ruskin's editors attempt to sort out his various interpretations of this allusive title in 27.xx ff.

18 F. Max Müller, *Lectures on the Science of Language*, First Series (New York, 1869). The lectures were delivered in 1861.

19 Robert Hewison discusses these oppositions in *John Ruskin. The Argument of the Eye* (Princeton, 1976), p. 141 ff.

20 Dixon was indeed a cork cutter, but he was an independent tradesman who earned enough from his business to retire and give generously to others. He was also the English 'discoverer' of Walt Whitman. That such a man was to Ruskin 'a working man' indicates that whatever problems Ruskin may have had in maintaining contact with his audience in *Fors* he was not, as has so often been alleged, ignorantly or wilfully addressing a proletarian audience above its collective head.

21 In 'Ali Baba and the Forty Thieves' Morgiana dances that she may have the chance to save her master by plunging a knife into the disguised thief at his table. For further exploration of Ruskin's habit of pressing the materials of childhood into the service of his mature arguments see John Dixon Hunt's chapter above.

22 Ruskin's letters to Lawton are reprinted in 37.14–7, but his name is not given. It survives, however, on the envelope of one of the letters now in the Pierpont Morgan Library.

23 Considering Ruskin's insistence on handling the distribution of *Fors* himself and selling it at a fixed price, the letters were remarkably successful. Both as individual pamphlets and as bound volumes some went through several editions and the 'Notes and Correspondence' section Ruskin began in 1872 records responses from as far away as California. Ruskin's method of distribution evolved in 1882 into what has become 'the net book system', a major innovation in publishing from one whose name is almost a byword for visionary unpracticability. See 27.lxxxii ff, and Brian Maidment's chapter below.

24 *Purgatory*, XXIX, 11.122–3, trans. Dorothy L. Sayers (Baltimore, Penguin, 1955).

25 'Afterward Jesus findeth him [the man he healed at Bethesda] in the temple, and said unto him, Behold, thou art made whole: sin no more, lest a worse thing come unto thee.' (John 5:14.)

Interpreting Ruskin 1870–1914

BRIAN MAIDMENT

In an editorial conclusion to Arthur Severn's memoir, James 1
Dearden suggests that 'the greatest blank in our knowledge of
Ruskin occurs between the end of his active life in 1889 and his
death in 1900'.[1] I have always been drawn by the sad reversal of
Ruskin's last years—the torrential writings stilled, the thunderous
voice reduced to an occasional whisper from a bath chair. At a less
impressionistic and more scholarly level, it is entirely clear that these
years were nowhere near as inactive for Ruskin's works, ideas and
reputation as they were for their author's life. Through the last
thirty years of the century several important transformations were
taking place in his life and work—his books became, for the first
time, widely popular; his use of literary genre (the lecture, the serial
article, the letter to the press, *Fors Clavigera*) became so advanced
and experimental that his audiences and readerships, as well as
his literary style, became totally and uniquely redefined; and,
largely through illness, he was forced to abandon his active and carefully created presence and to become represented by a canon of
literary works instead of being an active and visible controversialist.

These factors created a noteworthy, but not necessarily inexplicable, paradox. Ruskin, whose work had depended on his public style and his presence as much as on its content for its survival as a focus of debate, became a really significant intellectual force only after that presence had, by force of circumstance, been withdrawn. This paradox can be explained in several ways—by an account of his development of active relationships with his readers through the use of experimental kinds of literary discourse, by a study of the influence of his guardians and advisers on the public understanding of his work, by looking at the distribution of his works between 1870 and 1910, and by examining some aspects of the Ruskin 'industry' and the subsequent transformation of Ruskin from a radical author into a public monument. With such a broad subject it is necessary to proceed through a sequence of suggestive incidents rather than detailed factual evidence.[2]

11   Any collector of Victorian first editions will have a totally different conception of Ruskin from the scholar raised on Cook and Wedderburn's Library Edition of the *Works*. The *Works* edition is, of course, a magnificent scholarly achievement, and, as one critic has rightly noted, the index alone is worth a Ph.D. The textual editing in particular is exemplary in providing all the variants necessary to discriminate, for example, between the various elements which were conflated to make *The Queen of the Air*, or to show the relationship between *Fors Clavigera* and *Praeterita*. Equally, Cook and Wedderburn enable scholars to distinguish between hastily written part-issue periodical texts and carefully revised volume format republication—a difference which is central to any interpretation of a book like *Time and Tide*, where the work's significance lies not so much in the originality of what is said as in the extraordinary mode of publication and original readership which Ruskin constructed for the book. The different discourses which he used, then, can be reconstructed from the bibliographical notes of the *Works*, but even in the process of describing the occasional differences in Ruskin's works Cook and Wedderburn show a marked, and understandable, preference for revised volume texts against the topicality and improvisation of unrevised lectures or part issues.

Such a belief that his work had to be organised into a tidy body of coherent writing is entirely plausible to any editor confronted with the quantity and variety of Ruskin's works, and it offered many advantages. Cook and Wedderburn were enabled, for example, to put together, 'for the first time' as they rightly claim, all Ruskin's works on political economy, together with related public letters and private correspondence, into one volume, 17. This kind of thematic organisation, widely practised in the *Works*, places a great deal of emphasis on the logical internal development of Ruskin's thought—in this case on the transition from the theoretical and controversialist arguments of *Unto this Last* and *Munera Pulveris* to the utopianism of *Time and Tide* and then to the practical attempts to enact an ideal commonwealth which dominate *Fors Clavigera*. Such transitions, heavily stressed by Cook and Wedderburn's conscious editorial policy, are further to be seen against the broader, but implicitly logical, slide from the analysis of 'work' and 'worth' in the 'Nature of Gothic' chapter of *The Stones of Venice* to the political economy and social ethics of the later works. More recent psychologically informed study of Ruskin has also tended to concentrate, with justice, on the internal intellectual coherence in the development of his ideas, and on the slow evolution of his social concerns. Since Wilenski pioneered such accounts in 1933 other works by Rosenberg and Hewison have provided similarly succinct and cohesive versions of Ruskin's varied output without shirking the moments when coherence becomes very hard to identify.[3] Even Ruskin's literary styles can be accounted for within such critical orthodoxies, although there has been little recent work in this area. By 1900 the Oxford University extension course on Ruskin had embodied a belief, widely expressed in contemporary criticism,[4] in Ruskin's 'two styles'—an early 'gorgeous' style related to art criticism, and a later, simpler, more satirical but 'brutal' style related to social writings. As the *Handbook* has it, 'the beauty of Ruskin's "second manner" is not so greatly appreciated as that of the first',[5] and this general belief in a close relationship between the kind of content in Ruskin's books and the style he adopted has largely gone unquestioned ever since. Once again, the movement from art to society is accounted for as a logical progression.

Against this necessarily tidy and coherent view I think it is important to put the 'book collector's' Ruskin—heaps of pamphlets, unfinished projects, essays in popular genres, part issues and lecture texts. It must have been immediately apparent to any mid-Victorian reader that he was above all an *occasional* writer, and that the occasions of his writing were not to be predicted. Indeed, of all his works, only the three early art books, *Modern Painters*, *The Seven Lamps of Architecture* and *The Stones of Venice*, were written deliberately in *volume* format without Ruskin having any distinct sense of a particular readership. The vast bulk of his work comprises lecture texts published in a wide variety of formats (at least fifteen volumes), series of periodical articles, single articles, letters to the press, educational textbooks, popular guidebooks, books of popular science, exhibition catalogues, extended didactic dialogues, and a fairy tale. It may be possible to find an intellectual coherence or emotional unity in such works, but more immediately striking is the

vast variety and self-consciousness of the literary and social discourses in which Ruskin engaged. Far from being detached by class,
wealth or inclination from Victorian popular literary discourse, he
showed an awareness of formal and generic possibilities which was
far in advance of that of many of his contemporaries. The internal
compulsions of his psyche were offset by his realistic grasp of literary
possibility. The readerships which he chose, or even on occasions
created, for his works show a baffling diversity of literary and didactic intention. The 80,000 *Cornhill* readers of the serial issue of *Unto
this Last* form a very different group from the subscribers to the
Leeds Mercury to whom *Time and Tide*, a book on a very similar
subject, was directed six years later. Equally, the 'little housewives'
to whom *Ethics of the Dust* was dedicated are separated by more than
five years from 'the workmen and labourers of Great Britain' defined in the sub-title of *Fors Clavigera*. Ruskin's sharp awareness of
the range of contemporary literary audiences and their pressure on
readership, form and style do as much to explain the nature of his
work as does the internal logic of his psychological and intellectual
development.

Ruskin's knowledge of the literary market place and its forms
liberated his work from conventional literary contexts. He realised
that popular literary genres had both a readership and a form ready-
made which enabled a writer to utilise the vigour of the form without
necessarily using the genre for conventional purposes. For example,
he turned the idea of a utilitarian catalogue for the annual Royal
Academy exhibition into the place for a polemic on the state of contemporary painting. Thus the prescribed, but very specific and
quite substantial, readership created by the form had their expectations affronted by the unexpected use of a format more usually informative than argumentative. One of the most radical tendencies in
Ruskin's work is this ability to subvert conventional genres while at
the same time exploiting the readership and occasion already
established by that genre. His own version of the 'Cottage Library'
is an informative example. Such series were widely distributed in
cheap format through pedlars and market stalls, and aimed to combine the diverting, the devotional and the informative in super-
ficially attractive volumes meant as much for cultural ornament as
widely read texts. Ruskin's own *Bibliotheca Pastorum* ('Peasants'
Library'!) was an almost parodic realisation of the format, for it was
produced with exquisite care, at great expense, and was difficult to
obtain through his own deliberate marketing methods. The idea of a
cheap, permanent, improving series for the respectable working
classes was retained, but negated by Ruskin's perverse insistence on
aristocratic standards of production and morally defensible, but
practically inept, notions of distribution. The series was halted after

three volumes. Many critics have seized gleefully on Ruskin's unpractical and paradoxical betrayal of a recognised need for cheap and
easily available editions of his works, focusing attention particularly
on the wilful difficulties of *Fors Clavigera*. But it is equally important
to stress his splendidly pragmatic and successful development of
other popular genres. As early as 1857 the text of *The Political
Economy of Art* had appeared in a 'Cheap Series of Original and
Standard Works of Information and General Interest' clad in glazed
canvas boards and published at the very low price of 2*s* 6*d*. The
existence of such a series at all in the deeply respectable list of Smith
Elder and Co. in the 1850s is itself a recognition of the widespread
and various markets available in mid-Victorian England. Others of
Ruskin's books, notably *Unto This Last*, had never been expensive.
But perhaps the most graphic example of his quick grasp of the
potential of popular genres is his pragmatic and successful development of the guidebook genre in *Mornings in Florence* and *St Mark's
Rest*. There is obvious good sense and practical virtue in the original
part issue of *Mornings in Florence* (1876–77). The six stout canvas-
backed pamphlets, each containing a morning's activities, are both a
charming and a perceptive response to the need for a popular port-
able guide. Such persuasive use of a popular format is clearly lost by
subsequent bulky volume reprint.

Whether these experiments were entirely successful or not, they
point to the extremely advanced self-consciousness which Ruskin
had gained of the modes and occasions for literary expression available to him. And if there is one tendency identifiable in his increasingly sophisticated use of Victorian publishing methods, it is a
movement away from *statement* towards *discourse*, that is, a crucial
shift from the idea of the book as a kind of interior monologue
describing the relationship between a sensibility and its political,
social and psychological stimuli to a belief that books are rather ex-
plorations of the relationships between writer and reader. I have
described elsewhere (see note 2) the elaborate construction of this
belief in Ruskin's work, culminating in the extraordinary discourse
of *Fors Clavigera*. It can be argued that his literary modes and
unusual methods of publication made him unprecedentedly accessible to his readers, and thus in unique relationship with his public.
Such extreme sensitivity to readership and context in fact defies the
notion of a literary canon—permanent, unchanging and open to
detached scrutiny. It also changes Ruskin from being a digressive
eccentric, compelled by psychological pressures into writing volume
after volume, into an urgent, witty writer using literary opportunity
in a startlingly open and original way. Having thus developed a huge
range of literary discourses which were totally dependent on his
presence for their progress, he was forced by illness to retreat from

his numerous dialogues. What happened to his life and work when his dramatic presence was removed?

III   In the twenty-odd years of illness that preceded his death, Ruskin's interests passed into the hands of his guardians, his second cousin Joan Agnew Severn and her husband, the artist Arthur Severn. Ruskin himself has paid tribute to the devotion of Joan Severn in *Praeterita*, and recent books, especially Sheila Birkenhead's *Illustrious Friends* (1965), have drawn proper attention to the true extent of 'Joanna's care'. Ruskin's illness was sometimes violent, a fact carefully concealed from his many friends and correspondents, and considerable effort must have been exercised by the Severns in order to create and preserve the image of the silent, peaceful, sad old man. Ruskin had in fact proved an extremely difficult patient, and there had been major disagreements within the Brantwood household. It would be ungracious to doubt the motives of the Severns in their guardianship, even though the querulousness and even outright ingratitude of Arthur Severn's view of Ruskin in *The Professor* is difficult to forget. That Ruskin's estate became largely the legal property of the Severns during this period has also to be kept in mind, but the main difficulty that arose between the Severns and Ruskin's friends, supporters and readers was more one of incomprehension than wilful malevolence. The Severns never understood the activity generated by Ruskin's works and, on the often necessary pretext of preserving him from anxiety or excitement, completely cut off the wide-ranging discourse which he had created with a vast range of journals and correspondents.

Under the Severns large-scale changes in Ruskin's public presence took place. These changes were largely changes of manner, and can most easily be illustrated by turning to his semi-public letters. Ruskin's response to correspondents was always unpredictable but entirely calculated. If he refused requests for translation rights his arguments were spelled out in full. If he refused to sanction cheap and easily available editions of his works he referred his correspondent to his sustained attacks on cheap literature in *Sesame and Lilies* and *Munera Pulveris* (8.85 and 17.59). All correspondents were met with vigorous, witty, unpredictable and allusive replies which were designed to produce a creative mixture of aggravation and fresh insight in the recipient. A poor Glasgow clerk, much influenced by Ruskin's work, wrote to him pointing out the expense of his books and the impossibility of interested working men obtaining them. Ruskin might well have been expected to respond with warmth and sympathy to such an appeal, but his reply gives an immediate impression of callous and perverse indifference:

... I don't want any poor people to read my books. I said so long ago, in *Sesame*. I want them to read these letters *Fors* which they can get, each for the price of two pots of beer; and not to read my large books, nor anybody else's, till they are rich enough, at least, to pay for good printing and binding. Mr Grant Duff says they are all to be rich first, and only next to be intelligent; and I am happy in supposing it needs a great deal of intelligence to read *Modern Painters*.[6]

Ruskin's archness here, the seemingly deliberate abuse of his superior rhetorical power, seems to be unnecessarily belligerent unless one sees the serious argument—that the urgent discourse must be economic rather than aesthetic. During the writing of *Fors* Ruskin consistently directed his readers away from his other works, and his stubborn refusal to conciliate his readers created the tone of the letter to the Glasgow clerk, in which an underlying seriousness of purpose is only just visible beneath a startling verbal aggression.

Such a carefully intended and stylistically complex reply has to be put against the hundreds of brusque letters sent by the Severns, or by Ruskin's publisher George Allen on the Severns' behalf, which totally failed to convey the spirit and manner of Ruskin's own combative replies. One long-standing and devoted Ruskinian was told that his request for help with a Ruskin exhibition in Manchester was not only refused but had been motivated solely by the hope of commercial profit—a deeply wounding reproach for a volunteer, unpaid member of the committee responsible, made even more wounding by the abrupt condescension of Severn's tone, entirely un-Ruskinian in its lack of concern.[7] Ruskin too could be cutting, but always in pursuit of some nobler motive or intended instruction. An even more graphic example of the total lack of sympathy between his manner and that of the Severns is to be found buried in the papers of the Manchester Ruskin Society.[8] The society, on its inauguration, had written to Ruskin asking his permission to use his name in their title. He wrote back a detailed reply, outlining his anxiety at the spread of 'Ruskinism' when more urgent matters needed to be studied—a justifiable anxiety, as I hope to show, and one widely expressed to dismayed admirers throughout his career. Typically, Ruskin was willing to use such a casual occasion as a vehicle for the wider explanation of his ideas. But accompanying his letter is a brief note from Mrs Severn saying, in effect, that Ruskin was not entirely rational and that of course the society must use his name. Such evidence points clearly to the prodigious discrepancy between Ruskin as an active force in intellectual life and Ruskin as an institution, or even a name, which needed to be protected from criticism or exploitation. The transition from Ruskin's uniquely public articulacy to silence was the product both of his illness and of the Severns' care.

IV   My argument, then, is that those closest to Ruskin, and those most concerned with the production and sale of his works, changed utterly the sense of what his books represented and of the readership at which they were to be directed. Both the Severns and ultimately George Allen believed the books to be a commodity rather than an expression of idealism or part of a continuing intellectual debate, and the period between 1885 and 1900 saw a gradual sapping of the energy and radicalism of the books through the growth of conventional commercial success. The development of Ruskin's publishing venture, George Allen and Co., provides a telling image for this process. George Allen had become his publisher in 1870. Ruskin's decision to take charge of his own publishing arose directly out of the arguments he had been developing in the 1860s, which had provided the underlying themes of *Fors*. The most noteworthy of these was his attack on a commodity economy, with the concommitant growth of entrepreneurs and middlemen. Thus the founding of his own publishing firm was a way of both exemplifying and publicising his views—an extension of his polemical methods to practical business. Allen was to operate from his home in Kent—initially Keston, and then 'Sunnyside', Orpington—and sell Ruskin's books direct by post to customers, avoiding booksellers altogether, and refusing any discount. On Ruskin's directive, the firm was to advertise his work only by simple informative notices in the back of books, and by equally simple circulars which were not to quote from reviews or notices. The whole venture was thus underpinned by an analysis of contemporary commercial abuses, and embodied a three-pronged attack on the specific wrongs of bookselling—the discount system, underselling, and the monopoly of London-based business. While Ruskin remained well and interested his publishing firm off-set commercial failure (he certainly lost money on the first few years of *Fors Clavigera*) or at best moderate success against an enormous opportunity for him to pursue his teaching in the pages of *Fors*, in letters to the press, in conversation and in essay. The idealism and opportunity for controversy stressed by the firm were thus more important to Ruskin than its commercial success.

Yet the history of George Allen and Co. after Ruskin's own personal supervision was removed by illness in the early 1880s runs in a contrary direction.[9] Of the three specific wrongs in bookselling which he attacked in the beginning, ultimately none was seriously challenged by George Allen & Co. The rural home of the business survived uncomfortably for twenty years, but then a move to London was made in order to allow Allen to compete on equal terms with his more orthodox rivals. In other words, Allen's capitulation on this issue, admittedly under heavy pressure from the Severns, directly reversed Ruskin's intentions, and brought the firm into line

with the protectionist attitudes of most other contemporary pub-
lishers. Underselling and the discount were also problems which
Allen never really solved, although his eventual concessions to con-
vention brought him to a logical and constructive compromise. He
fixed the *selling* price of Ruskin's books but still allowed a set discount to the trade. Later writers, especially E. T. Cook,[10] have
seized upon this aspect of Allen's work as directly preceding the net
price agreement. There is an element of truth in this, yet Allen's
slight influence in this direction must be weighed against his and
Ruskin's failure to render the bookseller altogether redundant. It is
surely not unfair to either to say that the idealistic commercial
adventurousness which was expressed in the beginnings of George
Allen and Co. was eventually so largely modified that all the radical
force was lost. This is not to deny the originality, sophistication and
accuracy of Ruskin's analysis of the corruptions and failings of bookselling in the late nineteenth century, but rather to point to the way
in which his illness and retirement from public controversy ensured
that his plans could never be developed in the way that he wished.

Economically, too, the success of George Allen and Co. is questionable. Ruskin, it is true, was earning £4,000 a year from his books
in the last few years of his life, but there is still a strong sense of lost
opportunities in the story of his publishing firm, opportunities lost
largely through the caution and misunderstanding of the Severns.
The commercial prosperity of George Allen and Co. around the
turn of the century, based largely on huge sales of Ruskin's books, is
a clear but misleading fact. By 1900 Allen was fully exploiting a vast
market which the policies he and the Severns had adopted over the
previous twenty years had largely frustrated, or at least delayed.
The great heyday for the sale of Ruskin's books (which was of
course not entirely dependent on publishing policy) was very short.
I would limit the years in which Allen's editions of Ruskin's books
could be described as selling widely to those between 1886, when
Allen began to issue his 5*s* green octavo reprints in quantity, and
1907, the year in which he died and many of Ruskin's most important books began to come out of copyright. Although Allen had introduced a 'Pocket Edition' of Ruskin's works in the early years of the
century at an even cheaper price than the 5*s* edition, the sales of his
books, under pressure from 'non-copyright' editions after 1907,
declined rapidly from 1907 to 1914, when George Allen and Co.
went bankrupt. Thus the years between 1886 and 1907 seem to be
the only time for which it can be said that Ruskin's books enjoyed a
truly wide circulation under Allen's imprint, and for many of them
even this period is a generous one—*Modern Painters*, for example,
only became a popular success after the first cheap edition, which
appeared as late as 1896. It is important to remember that the cor-

relation between sales figures and influence can be only a hypothetical one. Even so, there is no doubt that, however admirable Ruskin's
idealism as a publisher might have been, when his own presence was
withdrawn from the firm the continually conservative interpretation
of business practice by his guardians, especially in the matters of
cheap editions, translation rights and permission to reproduce
extracts, frustrated both the commercial success and the wide
dissemination of his ideas, and delayed the general appreciation of
his theories by at least a decade.

The role of the Severns in the dissemination of Ruskin's works is
ambiguous. On the one hand, they wished to ensure Ruskin an ade-
quate income from his books, and they presumably wanted his ideas
to be more widely understood and discussed. On the other, they
were prepared to justify their opposition to such things as translation, advertising and cheap editions by reference to passages of his
works written many years before in a totally different context and in
the heat of public debate or occasional pressure. As this context
inevitably changed, Ruskinian pronouncements, robbed of their
proper function, became lame and fossilised, even absurdly and
irrelevantly dogmatic. What Ruskin had originally balanced in his
publishing activities had been an occasion for argument and demonstration against commercial necessity. But the entire logic of this
balance had been destroyed by the loss of his actual presence—the
ideals became the dead relics of a once vigorous intellect, the commercial successes became the property of the uncomprehending
Severns. Deliberate provocativeness gave way to downright in-
convenience. The most tactful way of describing the Severns' effect
on the diffusion of Ruskin's ideas would be to say that their powers of
opposition to the complacency and expectations of the Victorian
reading public were totally insignificant in comparison to those
available to a fit, alert and polemical Ruskin.

v   Further evidence is available to explain how a radical writer like
Ruskin was turned into a public monument, and rendered respectable as a kind of institution. Perhaps the best way to describe the
process is through an examination of the ways in which his works
were mediated into public consciousness through the activities of
the Ruskin Reading Guilds and Societies, through a close study of
the individual proponents of Ruskinism and their work as publicists,
lecturers and writers (I am thinking of the versions of Ruskin
presented by William Morris, W. G. Collingwood, J. A. Hobson,
C. R. Ashbee, and so on), and through the changing consciousness of
Ruskin expressed in periodical and fictional accounts of his work.[11]
The results of such a survey are still impressionistic and inadequate
—the presence of a public figure is not easily quantifiable. Yet the

overall movement from 'Ruskinian' to 'Ruskinism' is clear enough
—that is, a movement from a precisely focused and deliberate attack
on Victorian social and economic organisation to the use of Ruskin's
authority to authenticate any eccentric social view which anyone
wanted to hold. The Severns had given the precedent for this process in their method of interpreting the Ruskin canon without
reference to the public discourse which his works had enacted with
such urgency. These kinds of transformation can be suggested by
some typical examples.

The magazine of the Birmingham Ruskin Society, *St George*,
which ran from 1898 to 1911, gives a glimpse of the problems and
weaknesses of Ruskin discipleship. The production of the magazine
created an immediate tension between social usefulness and artistic
aspirations. Ruskin's own views on book production, as we have
seen, were themselves muddled—a love of fine books could be partly
justified by a socially concerned writer on the grounds of service-
ableness, especially if their subject was a serious one whose 'worth'
demanded a permanent format. However, the nagging need to reach
wider and wider audiences had led him into many popular, though
never poorly produced, literary modes. What kind of magazine,
then, was appropriate to a Ruskin Society? Under J. H. Whitehouse
the Birmingham society instinctively opted for something worthy of
Ruskin's most fastidious taste—thick uncut hand-made paper, a
beautifully designed Walter Crane title page, superb layout, and, in
volume form, a decorated bevelled-board binding. The overall
effect is that of a private press book rather than a club news-sheet:
nothing could focus attention more precisely on the clash of values
between the production and the content of the magazine—the one
aspiring to Arts and Crafts aestheticism, the other earnestly directed
to the abolition of social privilege and injustice. A further contradic-
tion is apparent in the content and discourse adopted by the magazine. Were the lecture meetings, the magazine-making, the endless
interpretation of Ruskin's works, the accumulation of Ruskinian
anecdote, the public statement of personal respect to a great man,
really the forms of social action demanded by Ruskin? Was the
common interest social group really the way to enact 'Fors in deed
not words'? The Ruskinian study group or magazine, as Ruskin had
so aptly reminded the Manchester Ruskin Society, was not the kind
of discipleship he had intended. With these awkward distinctions
between appreciation and social action in mind, it is not surprising
that the content of *St George*, at first firmly directed towards Ruskin
and his teaching, slowly slipped away in many directions, led by
Whitehouse's own growing interest in education. By the last issues
the magazine was even printing stories and plays, diverting subscribers from the severe attention of Ruskin's own discourses.

Without Ruskin's presence his works became a source of authority for almost any kind of anti-industrial social melioration, a rallying place for an extraordinary diversity of ruralist, progressive, liberal, reactionary or anti-Victorian views, many of them never remotely mindful of the original intentions of his work. The Ruskin canon had become open to interpretation without fear of the awful recrimination of Ruskin himself.

As well as being used for various kinds of reformist or anti-industrial social attitudes, Ruskin's work also began to be associated with a new kind of self-improvement wholly removed from the earnest and largely altruistic social concern of men like the Sunderland cork cutter Thomas Dixon, for whom, and to whom, Ruskin had written *Time and Tide*. In late Victorian and Edwardian England a cultural status was accorded to his works which would have been impossible with the author himself present and active. Ruskin's writings became associated with the aspirations of the new clerkly classes which inhabit the novels and stories of Pett Ridge, Wells and Kipling. It is not surprising that Edwardian novelists laughed at him, for all they saw was the display of his ideas and sensibility as a cultural possession. Thus Forster satirised Lucy Honeychurch for needing her Ruskin to tell her which Florentine tomb to admire most.[12] So Kipling mocked the pretentious schoolboy posturing of reading the subversive *Fors Clavigera* during prep in *Stalky & Co.*[13] Even the bookshelves of the aspiring clerks and shop assistants are embellished with gilt cloth *Sesame and Lilies* in *Kipps* and *Love and Mr Lewisham*.[14] Such instructive shifts of attitude clearly require more detailed examination. The debased version of Ruskin expressed in Edwardian fiction, however, comments on the poignant transformations of his urgent dialogue with Victorian England into a canon of half understood attitudes which were used to justify many varieties of social concern and cultural pretension.

NOTES   1 Arthur Severn, *The Professor*, ed. J. S. Dearden (1966), p. 138.

2 This essay is part of an interlocking and occasionally overlapping group of three with common origins in a paper given at the 1977 'Ruskin as Critic' Conference at Leicester University. The others have, or will, appear in *Ruskin. Twelve New Essays*, ed. R. Hewison (1981) and in *The Victorian Periodical Press*, ed. M. Wolff and J. Shattock (1981).

3 R. H. Wilenski, *John Ruskin* (1933); J. D. Rosenberg, *The Darkening Glass* (1961), and R. Hewison *John Ruskin. The Argument of the Eye* (1976). Hewison rightly comments in his foreword that his book is 'not the first attempt to see Ruskin's work in terms of the mind that made it'.

4 Interesting accounts of Ruskin's style are found, for example, in C. Waldstein, *The Work of John Ruskin* (1894), and R. de la Sizeranne, *Ruskin and the Religion of Beauty* (1899).

5 W. Hudson Shaw, *The Life and Teaching of John Ruskin* (Oxford University Extension Lectures Syllabus, Oxford, n.d.), p. 13.

6 Quoted in F. A. Mumby and F. H. S. Stallybrass, *From Swan Sonnenschein to George Allen & Unwin Ltd* (1955), pp. 68–9. An extended discussion of Ruskin's attitudes towards cheap books is to be found here.

7 Unpublished letter in the possession of Mrs D. M. M. Betts, Norwich, and quoted with her permission.

8 The collections relating to the Manchester Ruskin Society are in the Local History Library in Manchester Central Reference Library. Much remains to be discovered about the nature and composition of the societies and the way in which they reflect late Victorian attitudes towards social change.

9 The surviving archives of the firm have been published on microfilm (1973). Mumby and Stallybrass's book and my own unpublished Leicester Ph.D. thesis, 'John Ruskin and George Allen' (1973), give more detailed accounts of the development of the firm.

10 E. T. Cook, 'Ruskin as the Father of the Net Book System', *Book Monthly*, 1907. See also 30.358–62.

11 Surprisingly little work has been done on Ruskin's followers, perhaps because of the difficulty of assessing 'influence' in any systematic way. One exemplary essay in such study is F. D. Curtin, 'Aesthetics in English Social Reform: Ruskin and his Followers', in *Nineteenth Century Studies*, ed. H. Davis, W. DeVane and R. Bald (Ithaca, N.Y., 1940), pp. 199–245. Curtin discusses Morris, Hobson and Patrick Geddes.

12 E. M. Forster, *A Room with a View* (1908), chapter 2. Forster is of course satirising the way in which guidebooks deaden the imagination and preclude individual judgement. Unwittingly, though, he is paying respect to the success of the Ruskinian guidebook, still influential forty years after being written.

13 R. Kipling, *Stalky & Co.* (1899), 'Slaves of the Lamp', Part I. '...young M'Turk reads Ruskin for his amusement.' 'Nonsense! He does it to show off....' 'He does nothing of the kind. I went into the study the other night, unofficially, and M'Turk was gluing up the back of four odd numbers of *Fors Clavigera* ...'

14 H. G. Wells, *Kipps* (1905), chapter II, section I; *Love and Mr Lewisham* (1901), chapters XVI and XVIII. Both books provide interesting accounts of the cultural possessions of their characters in which Ruskin features 'in bulk'.

Proust on the margins of Ruskin

RICHARD A. MACKSEY

... je m'apercevais que ce livre essentiel, le seul livre vrai, un grand écrivain n'a pas, dans le sens courant, à l'inventer, puisqu'il existe déjà en chacun de nous, mais à le traduire. Le devoir et la tâche d'un écrivain sont ceux d'un traducteur.

Vacationing at Evian-les-Bains in September 1899, the twenty-eight-year-old Marcel Proust writes to his mother, asking her to send him his copy of Robert de La Sizeranne's *Ruskin et la religion de la beauté*.[1] This is the first reference in the Proust correspondence to the English author who was to engage his imagination and energies over the next six years. Proust, whose relationship to Ruskin during these years of apprenticeship was by turns that of disciple, translator and critic, was to become the great clinician of human love in a French tradition that extends from Racine and Stendhal to *A la recherche du temps perdu*. The novelist's literary affair with Ruskin could serve as a paradigm for the trajectory of all those passions chronicled later in his life's work. And, like the fictional affairs, the relationship achieved its ultimate meaning as an incitement to reading, a reading not of a master's texts but rather of the 'inner book' composed of past moment, places and events recovered in the architectural programme of memory.

A week after the first letter, on 2 October, Madame Proust receives a renewed plea from her son for La Sizeranne's 'presentation' of Ruskin, that he may 'voir les montagnes avec les yeux de ce grand homme'.² Thus Ruskin, who found 'the world of literature more or less divided into Thinkers and Seers', is first invoked by Proust as an instrumentality of sight; this is the Ruskin who conconcluded in *Modern Painters* that 'the greatest thing a human soul ever does in this world is to *see* something, and to tell what it *saw* in a plain way.... To see clearly is poetry, prophecy, and religion—all in one' (5.333). And significantly, Robert de La Sizeranne, who was to be Proust's Galeotto at this stage in the affair, chooses to begin his study of Ruskin, in a chapter entitled 'La Contemplation', with the recreation of a moment in the summer of 1833 when the fourteen-year-old Ruskin arrived with his parents and cousin at the gates of Schaffhausen, about to discover for himself the Alps.³ He quotes the aged Ruskin of more than fifty years later, engaged in a final heroic effort to 'bind and blend' the lost moments and occluded sights of a lifetime into a book of recollection, *Praeterita*:

> Thus in perfect health of life and fire of heart, not wanting to be anything but the boy I was, not wanting to have anything more than I had; knowing of sorrow only so much as to make life serious to me, not enough to slacken in the least its sinews; and with so much of science mixed with feeling as to make the sight of the Alps not only the revelation of the beauty of the earth, but the opening of the first page of its volume,—I went down that evening from the garden-terrace of Schaffhausen with my destiny fixed in all that was to be sacred and useful. To that terrace, and the shore of the Lake of Geneva, my heart and faith return to this day, in every impulse that is yet nobly alive in them, and every thought that has in it help or peace. [35.116]⁴

Ruskin recognises, from the gathering silence of his last years, that this precocious first vision of the Alps was already refracted through authors who had transformed man's relations with the landscape—Rousseau and Wordsworth; and he adds in the MS that the same day he recorded his memory of the garden-terrace of Schaffhausen he had been reading Ernest Chesneau's account of the boyhood of Géricault, which in its sunless deprivation contrasted so markedly with the natural and human vistas of his own earliest years.

Proust came down from his vision of the mountains, from his brief stay at the Splendide Hôtel d'Evian, far from a confirmed traveller of the Ruskin variety; his subsequent 'pilgrimages' were few and usually anxious, though nearly all of them were in some way marked by his encounter with Ruskin. Instead, he came down from the Alps to return to Paris, to Maman, to a characteristic bout of asthma, and then to busy weeks at the Bibliothèque Nationale studying the texts of Ruskin then available in French. Soon he was turning to the librarian of the Ecole des Beaux Arts for editions of Ruskin in English as well.[5] He was also corresponding with Reynaldo Hahn's Manchester cousin, Marie Nordlinger, who was to be his guide to Ruskin's grammar, seeking additional books and translations; by February 1900, when he is asking her for fragments of letters and passages from the works dealing with the cathedrals of France ('excepté celle d'Amiens'), he quickly adds that she need not bother with references to *The Seven Lamps of Architecture*, *The Bible of Amiens*, *Val d'Arno*, *Lectures on Architecture and Painting* and *Praeterita*, since he already knows these books 'par coeur'.[6] Ruskin was already beginning to circulate in Proust's veins; the younger writer had by this stage already moved beyond La Sizeranne as his cicerone and had consciously conceived his vocation as translator and critic of the Sage of Coniston. In addition to Marie Nordlinger he now enlisted other friends for help with his Ruskin studies, notably the 'fidèle et compréhensif' François d'Oncieu, to whom he had earlier lent his copy of La Sizeranne.

On 20 January 1900, after a decade of silence, John Ruskin died at Brantwood. Proust, as he records in a letter to Marie Nordlinger, was immediately moved to write an obituary, which appeared over the signature 'M.P.' a week later in *La Chronique des arts et de la curiosité*, a supplement to the *Gazette des Beaux-Arts*.[7] He introduced this brief notice with the lugubrious observation that, with Nietzsche mad, with Tolstoy and Ibsen at the end of their careers, the death of Ruskin marked a turning point: Europe was losing, one after the other, its great 'directeurs de conscience'. He also seized the opportunity to announce that the *Gazette des Beaux-Arts* would publish in its next number a more extended impression of Ruskin's achievement. This critical project, which appeared in the April and August numbers of the journal under the title 'Sur Ruskin', was later reworked into the preface to Proust's translation of *The Bible of Amiens* (pp. 48–61 and 61–77, constituting chapter III of the preface). This early evaluation of Ruskin was further qualified by the 'PS' (pp. 78–95) added to the 1904 translation, the point at which he finally raised the question of Ruskin's 'idolatry'. These three texts taken together were again published by Proust as the third part of 'En Mémoire des églises assassinées' in *Pastiches et Mélanges* of 1919 (pp. 148–97).[8]

Even before the appearance of the essays in the *Gazette des Beaux-Arts*, Proust had found a new vehicle for his Ruskinian passions. He had met, probably through Léon Daudet, Gaston Calmette, who had recently assumed the editorship of *Le Figaro*. This was a literary relationship that was to extend over the years, forming for Proust (as for the narrator of his novel) a considerable beach-head in Parisian letters. 'Pèlerinages ruskiniens en France' appeared in *Le Figaro* of 13 February 1900.[9] It is a pendant piece to the original obituary notice, but it marks an important turn in Proust's relations to Ruskin. Moving from the library to the places that informed Ruskin's imagination, Proust quotes him as confessing, 'Pendant toute ma vie, ma pensée a gravité autour de trois centres, Rouen, Genève et Pise.' ('There have been, in sum, three centres of my life's thought: Rouen, Geneva, and Pisa. All that I did at Venice was bye-work. . . . But Rouen, Geneva, and Pisa have been the tutresses of all that I know, and were mistresses of all I did, from the first moments I entered their gates.' *Praeterita*, 35.156) Proust concentrates his attention on the first of these 'thought-centres' and proposes to Ruskin's French friends a pilgrimage not to his grave at Coniston but to Rouen and the other cathedral cities of France that 'gardent son âme.' The pilgrim is urged to visit and read the 'Stones' of the great medieval monuments that are the pretext and inspiration of so many pages of Ruskin, including, as Proust remarks, pages of those books that Ruskin did not have time to write, the projected volumes on the cathedrals of Rouen (*The Springs of Eure*) and Chartres (*Domrémy*) that were to succeed *The Bible of Amiens*. For Ruskin, one structure and architectural programme reads another (thus Proust echoes his judgement of Abbeville, 'qui est comme la préface et l'interprétation de Rouen'), but all are woven into the texture of the author's thought, determining what Proust elsewhere calls 'l'optique de Ruskin'.

Proust himself undertook the rôle of pilgrim at precisely this stage in his apprenticeship. Having reread on the day of Ruskin's death a passage in the fifth chapter of *The Seven Lamps of Architecture* that described one of the more than three hundred small beasts and grotesques populating the intervals of the reliefs and outer pedestals of the North Portal of Rouen, Proust journeyed with Madeleine and Léon Yateman to the cathedral in order to get this tiny figure that had captured Ruskin's imagination 'right', much as Bergotte in *A la Recherche* makes his final pilgrimage to Vermeer's *View of Delft* in order to comprehend the 'petit pan de mur jaune' (*A.R.T.P.*, III, 187–8). This tiny brooding figure, emblem for Ruskin in its individuality of the 'noble vitality' of Gothic art, is but a detail of a portal commonly known as that of the 'Book-sellers' (cf. *A.R.T.P.*, III, 116); but following his pilgrimage with the Yatemans (some time after 20 January and before the appearance of the article in *Le Figaro*), Proust chose it as the graphic emblem with which to conclude the second of his essays in the *Gazette des Beaux-Arts*. Significantly, this little grotesque with the wrinkled cheek, discovered among a wealth of detail by his friend Madeleine Yateman, is facing the typanum of the 'portail des Libraires' where the Resurrection of

the Dead is enacted; and it elicits from Proust the following observation, one that anticipates his comments on Bergotte, Elstir, and
Vinteuil:

> L'artiste mort depuis des siècles a laissé là, entre des milliers d'autres,
> cette petite personne qui meurt un peu chaque jour, et qui était morte
> depuis bien longtemps, perdue au milieu de la foule des autres, à
> jamais. Mais il l'avait mise là. Un jour, un homme pour qui il n'y a pas
> de mort, pour qui il n'y a pas d'infini matériel, pas d'oubli, un homme
> qui, jetant loin de lui ce néant qui nous opprime pour aller à des buts
> qui dominent sa vie, si nombreux qu'il ne pourra pas tous les atteindre
> alors que nous paraissons en manquer, cet homme est venu, et, dans
> ces vagues de pierre où chaque écume dentelée paraissait ressembler
> aux autres, voyant là toutes les lois de la vie, toutes les pensées de l'âme,
> les nommant de leur nom, il dit: 'Voyez, c'est ceci, c'est cela.' Tel
> qu'au jour du Jugement, qui non loin de là est figuré, il fait entendre en
> ses paroles comme la trompette de l'archange et il dit: 'Ceux qui ont
> vécu vivront, la matière n'est rien.' . . . Et la petite figure inoffensive et
> monstrueuse aura ressuscité, contre toute espérance, de cette mort qui
> semble plus totale que les autres, qui est la disparition au sein de l'infini
> du nombre et sous le nivellement des ressemblances, mais d'où le
> génie a tôt fait de nous tirer aussi. . . . J'ai été touché en la retrouvant
> là, rien ne meurt donc de ce qui a vécu, pas plus la pensée du sculpteur
> que la pensée de Ruskin. [C.S.B., 126–7]

The artist and the critic are united, across the centuries, in an act of
attention; the integrity of the anonymous craftsman and the clarity
of the confirming vision survive the insults of time and the 'levelling'
of similarity through that act which was to become for Proust a
model of the reader's task. As with another passionate pilgrim, the
survival of the artistic expression depends upon the double function
of the intensity of 'felt life' and the collaborating eye of the critic.
Significantly, the passage from Ruskin that motivated the pilgrimage to Rouen appears as a bridge between chapters entitled 'The
Lamp of Life' and 'The Lamp of Memory'.

In addition to suggesting the rôle of critic as pilgrim, the *Figaro*
essay also announces Proust's assumption of the rôle of critic as
translator. Here he alludes to the project that will not be completely
realised until four years later, with the publication of the complete
introduction to and translation of *The Bible of Amiens*. Meanwhile,
the translation begun, Proust's 'pèlerinages ruskiniens' would extend by April 1900 across the Alps to Venice, where, accompanied
by his mother, he met Reynaldo Hahn, his mother and her niece,
Marie Nordlinger, to explore the monuments memorialised by Ruskin. With *The Stones of Venice* and *St Mark's Rest* as his guides to
the city, he could continue the work on the Amiens translation with
Marie as his guide to the mysteries of a new language. This Venetian
pilgrimage, with an excursion in Ruskin's footsteps to Padua for

Giotto's frescoes in the Arena Chapel and Mantegna's in Eremitani, would only be translated, many years later, into Marcel's thwarted Italian dream (themselves a tissue of phrases drawn from Ruskin)[10] in *Swann*, and—much later in the narrative—the actual voyage to Venice and Padua in *La Fugitive*. Outside his fictions Proust returned to Venice but once, in October the same year, this time without his mother—a much more mysterious and perhaps sombre visit.

The brief essay in *Le Figaro* concludes with one final prophetic note: summing up the range of Ruskin's concerns and gifts, the renunciation of his fortune and dedication of his talents, Proust likens him to the figure of Charity in Giotto's cycle of the Virtues and Vices at the Arena Chapel. While this rather surprising image evokes memories of Ruskin's own discussions of Giotto's allegorical figures (especially in *Fors Clavigera*), it anticipates the familiar passage in *Swann* where Giotto's Charity (translated into the humble *fille de cuisine* of Combray) introduces a complex sequence of meditations on the reading of allegory and the allegory of reading.[11] Marcel is at first mystified by the chasm between the *name* 'Caritas' and the *reality* of the humble, energetic figure with which it is associated—whether in the fresco or in the pregnant servant girl whom Swann had dubbed 'la Charité de Giotto'. He concludes, however, that this is but an instance of the general case, of the gulf between the 'idea' and the precise material of observation resolved only by the greatest artists (like the anonymous sculptor of the Rouen portal):

> Mais plus tard j'ai compris que l'étrangeté saisissante, la beauté spéciale de ces fresques tenait à la grande place que le symbole y occupait, et que le fait qu'il fût représenté, non comme un symbole puisque la pensée symbolisée n'était pas exprimée, mais comme réel, comme effectivement subi ou matériellement manié, donnait à la signification de l'oeuvre quelque chose de plus littéral et de plus précis, à son enseignement quelque chose de plus concret et de plus frappant. ... Il fallait que ces Vertus et ces Vices de Padoue eussent en eux bien de la réalité puisqu'ils m'apparaissaient comme aussi vivants que la servante enceinte, et qu'elle-même ne me semblait pas moins allégorique. [A.R.T.P., I, 82]

This respect for the precision of vision and for 'real things, actually felt or materially handled' in the service of artistic truth, is the first lesson that Proust learned from John Ruskin. He appropriated from Ruskin the insistence on the priority of observed impressions, of the 'literal' and the 'concrete'. This theory of aesthetic perception in which the artist's act of seeing takes precedence over any received 'ideas' or 'symbols' or the exactitude of scientific 'description' clearly descends from Ruskin's analysis of Turner's perceptual 'impressionism'; thus, in *The Harbours of England*, he writes in terms that Proust was later to translate to Elstir, 'He always painted, not the place itself, but his impression of it, and this on steady principle; leaving to inferior artists the task of topographical detail; and he was right in this principle . . . when the impression was a genuine one' (18.51). But this lesson in 'seeing' was supplemented for Proust, as for Ruskin, by the artist's burden of 'reading,' of discovering through the clarified reality of the creation the 'allegorical' dimension of the quotidian actuality. We learn to 'read' the sprawling world around us through the resolving optic of the artist's personal vision. 'La Charité de Giotto' is transfigured by the architecture of the novel in which she plays a small but significant rôle. (It is not irrelevant that the passage cited above, where the frescoes of the Arena Chapel and the *fille de cuisine* are imbricated, forms the prelude to one of Proust's most complex—and paradoxical—discussions of the act of reading.)

Meanwhile, through the spring and summer of 1900, Proust had published those articles, already prefigured in the obituary and the *Figaro* piece, that were to establish his claims as a serious critic of Ruskin. Dedicated to Léon Daudet, 'Ruskin à Notre-Dame d'Amiens' had appeared at the beginning of April in the pages of the *Mercure de France*, which was later to provide the imprint for his two volumes of Ruskin translations. This essay, which was redacted as the second part of the preface to *La Bible d'Amiens* and subsequently published as the second section of 'En mémoire des églises assassinées: II. Journées de pèlerinage' in *Pastiches et Mélanges* (*C.S.B.*, 69 ff), extends Proust's notion of the spatial work of art as a book and its converse. Proust insists on the necessity in reading Ruskin, as in 'reading' an architectural programme, of being able to juxtapose related texts and compositional elements. In a note he underlined the initial task of the critic as an aide to this juxtaposition:

> Au fond, aider le lecteur à être impressionné par ces traits singuliers, placer sous ses yeux des traits similaires qui lui permettent de les tenir pour les traits essentiels du génie d'un écrivain devrait être la première partie de la tâche de tout critique. [*C.S.B.*, 76n]

The image of the work of art as a book and the achieved book as a temporal multiplicity of panels resolved into a unity of vision will persist long beyond Proust's apprenticeship to Ruskin and finally resonate in the concluding pages of *Le Temps retrouvé*.

But addressing what Ruskin styles 'The Bible of Amiens', the sculptural programme of the West Portal, Proust remarks that we are asked to read a very specific book: 'Le porche d'Amiens n'est pas seulement, dans le sens vague où l'aurait pris Victor Hugo, un livre de pierre, une Bible de pierre: c'est "La Bible" en pierre' (*C.S.B.*, 88–9). After a brief flight into a visual evocation of the western façade of Amiens seen for the first time (and at successive hours—after Monet's experiment at Rouen), Proust returns to the Ruskinian image of the cathedral as text, the first Text of the Western imagination and the first text of the critic's own childhood:

> Mais une cathédrale n'est pas seulement une beauté à sentir. Si même ce n'est plus pour vous un enseignement à suivre, c'est du moins encore un livre à comprendre. Le portail d'une cathédrale gothique, et plus particulièrement d'Amiens, la cathédrale gothique par excellence [an allusion to Emile Mâle], c'est la Bible. Avant de vous l'expliquer je voudrais, à l'aide d'une citation de Ruskin vous faire comprendre que, quelles que soient vos croyances, la Bible est quelque chose de réel, d'actuel, et que nous avons à trouver en elle autre chose que la saveur de son archaïsme et le divertissement de notre curiosité. [C.S.B., 89]

Proust then ranges extended quotations from the third chapter of *The Bible of Amiens* ('The Lion Tamer'), where Ruskin presents Jerome as the translator who initiated European literature, his work of translation the 'library of Europe' wherein '"The Book of Books" took the abiding form of which all the future art of the Western nations was to be an hourly enlarging interpretation' (33., 109–10). The quotations include Ruskin on the Psalms as the sum of personal and social wisdom, on the range of historical and didactic writing encompassed in the Bible, but most significantly for Proust's own quest there is Ruskin on the rôle of the Bible as a first Book in his own affective life, as the speculum by which he first approached other cultures and, in fact, the experience of reading itself:

> I am no despiser of profane literature. . . . But it was from the Bible that I learned the symbols of Homer, and the faith of Horace: the duty enforced upon me in early youth of reading every word of the gospels and prophecies as if written by the hand of God, gave me the habit of awed attention which afterwards made many passages of the profane writers, frivolous to an irreligious reader, deeply grave to me' [33.118–19; cf. *Praeterita*, 35.39–41]

Any casual reader of the Library Edition of Ruskin is immediately struck by the constant orchestration of the author's prose to a continuo of biblical quotation and subterranean allusion (all faithfully recorded in the footnotes). The sound of the Bible and the evocative weight of the texts, learned in childhood, supply the distinctive tone as well as the moral directions of Ruskin's prose; they also give some clue to what Proust was later to sense as 'idolatry'. Each present text is, for Ruskin and Proust, a palimpsest of remembered texts.

   The way in which the biblical figures—prophets, kings and apostles—animate the sculptural work of Amiens, the way in which the moral dimensions of the embodied narratives organise the structural relations of the building seem to have suggested to Proust the power of the architectural image that was to supply a recurrent metaphor for his work as a novelist. Thus in a letter to Jean de Gaigneron of 1919 he confesses to a presiding ambition in his composition, one that was to become much more overt in the metaphorics of the concluding volume:

> Et quand vous me parlez des cathédrales, je ne peux pas ne pas être ému d'une intuition qui vous permet de deviner ce que je n'ai jamais dit à personne et que j'écris ici pour la première fois: c'est que j'avais voulu donner à chaque partie de mon livre le titre: *Porche*, *Vitraux de l'abside*, etc., pour répondre d'avance à la critique stupide qu'on me fait de manquer de construction dans des livres où je vous montrerai que le seul mérite est dans la solidité des moindres parties. J'ai renoncé tout de suite à ces titres d'architecture parce que je les trouvais trop prétentieux, mais je suis touché que vous les retrouviez par une sorte de divination de l'intelligence.[12]

The sculptural programme of the cathedral supplies a key to the composition; the architectural elements physically provide for its structural integrity. Through the design of the builder the opposed piers of the Gothic arch were enlisted so as to sustain the great mass of the towering edifice. And just as in the cathedral moral directions were embodied in space, so the extremes and the aspiration towards unity of Proust's life work are suggested in his system of structural oppositions—the two 'ways', the two 'moments', the two methods (of metaphor and memory), the two 'truths' (*générales* and *essentielles*), the two experiences (of disillusion and vision)—which form the piers of his building.

For Proust as for Ruskin originality was a quality of 'vision', a way of seeing the world whole and unique; the novelist saw his task as that of enclosing his world in a new structure, which, like the great cathedrals or the humbler parish church of Saint-Hilaire, would include in its unity 'un espace à quatre dimensions—la quatrième étant celle du Temps' (*A.R.T.P.*, I, 61). The vocabulary of Proust's extended architectural metaphors frequently recalls the descriptions he translated from Ruskin, but two insistent points in such comparisons are peculiarly characteristic of the novelist's own vision: the possibility of creating a dialectic between inside and outside, a living space within which the artist can construct the world, a book within that can be translated into articulated composition; and the possibility, usually represented by the Gothic arch or the rose window, of bringing into immanent contact two apparently opposed views or ways of life.

At the conclusion of 'Notre-Dame d'Amiens' ('Journées de pèlerinage') Proust returns to his own education before the Gothic cathedral, 'une sorte de livre ouvert, écrit dans un langage solennel où chaque caractère est une oeuvre d'art, et que personne ne comprend plus' (*C.S.B.*, 104). As pilgrim and student faced with the challenge of deciphering these hieroglyphs of an old language based on an even older Text, Proust first alludes to Emerson's advice about hitching one's wagon to a star ('Civilisation') and then confesses how Ruskin stands for him among the Major Prophets as the gateway to this new language and mode of feeling:

> Comprenant mal jusque-là la portée des arts religieux au moyen âge, je m'étais dit, dans ma ferveur pour Ruskin : Il m'apprendra, car lui aussi, en quelques parcelles du moins, n'est-il pas la vérité ? Il fera entrer mon esprit là où il n'avait pas accès, car il est la *porte*. Il me purifiera. . . . [C.S.B., 104]

> Et maintenant nous avons beau nous arrêter devant les statues d'Isaïe, de Jérémie, d'Ezéchiel et de Daniel en nous disant : 'Voici les quatre grands prophètes,' il y en a un de plus qui n'est pas ici et dont pourtant nous ne pouvons pas dire qu'il est absent, car nous le voyons partout. C'est Ruskin : si sa statue n'est pas à la porte de la cathédrale, elle est à l'entrée de notre coeur. Ce prophète-là a cessé de faire entendre sa voix. Mais c'est qu'il a fini de dire toutes ses paroles. C'est aux générations de les reprendre en choeur. [C.S.B., 105]

While the essay on Amiens in the *Mercure* is probably the clearest prefiguration of Proust's metaphorics of the cathedral and the book, the long essay that concludes this stage of his critical apprenticeship, 'John Ruskin', is an extended discussion of the character and obligations of the artist-critic; it is also the most compelling record, as we move from the first to the second part of the essay, of the ways in which Proust's reading had progressed from an initial reliance on his French predecessors—Milsand and La Sizeranne[13]—to an immersion in the interactive life of the original texts, the point where the words of the dead Englishman find a new resonance in the imagination of the French apprentice. 'John Ruskin', which had been announced in both the obituary notice and the *Figaro* article, appeared in successive numbers of the *Gazette des Beaux-Arts*, the journal founded by Charles Ephrussi, one of the precursors of Swann. The first part, published in April, possibly written as early as the preceding summer, stays close, with due acknowledgement, to texts available in the French translations of Milsand and La Sizeranne (the two exceptions being quotations from a passage in *The Bible of Amiens* and another from *The Seven Lamps*). The second part, published in the August issue of the *Gazette*, ranges much more widely over Ruskin's *oeuvre* and includes passages available only in the original texts of *The Pleasures of England*, *Lectures on Architecture and Painting*, *The Seven Lamps of Architecture*, *The Stones of Venice*, *Val d'Arno*, *Lectures on Art* and *St Mark's Rest*. Proust had clearly passed through the portal into the freedom of

Ruskin's writings. The two sections of this essay (called 'Sur Ruskin' in the original periodical form) were combined, as noted above, into the third chapter of the preface to *La Bible d'Amiens* (with some minor corrections and a number of supplementary notes—pp. 48–61; 61–77). They later formed the third part of 'En Mémoire des églises assassinées' in *Pastiches et Mélanges*, with the suppression of some of the quotations from Ruskin and the addition of an important four-page note (*C.S.B..*, 105–15; 115–29).

Proust begins the essay with a critical discussion of Ruskin's aesthetics as presented by Milsand and La Sizeranne. He contrasts the death of the artist with the survival—and translation—of his works, apparently reflecting his reading of Emerson (whom he had considered translating) and the doctrine of representative men: 'Car l'homme de génie peut donner naissance à des oeuvres qui ne mourront pas qu'en les créant à l'image non de l'être mortel qu'il est, mais de l'exemplaire d'humanité qu'il porte en lui' (*C.S.B.*, 106). While he acknowledges his debt to his French predecessors, he is anxious to liberate Ruskin from the epicurean or dilettante overtones that may attach to the titles of the books by his French disciples—*L'Esthétique anglaise* and *La Religion de la beauté*. While accepting their emphasis on the primacy of perception in Ruskin and his favourite artists, Proust is anxious to place the stress in 'the religion of beauty' on the first term:

> Que l'adoration de la Beauté ait été, en effet, l'acte perpétuel de la vie de Ruskin, cela peut être vrai à la lettre; mais j'estime que le but de cette vie, son intention profonde, secrète et constante était autre, et si je le dis, ce n'est pas pour prendre le contre-pied du système de M. de La Sizeranne, mais pour empêcher qu'il ne soit rabaissé dans l'esprit des lecteurs par une interprétation fausse, mais naturelle et comme inévitable. [C.S.B., 110]

Ruskin's religion was, Proust insists, 'la religion tout court'. For him happiness can be achieved only by looking beyond happiness; the aesthesis is but a by-product of a consecration of the author's powers to values that are quite other than those of immediate pleasure. He associates Ruskin with the breed of genius whom Carlyle saw as deciphering and translating an 'inner reality':

> Et, très loin d'avoir été un dilettante ou un esthète, Ruskin fut précisément le contraire, un de ces hommes à la Carlyle, averti par leur génie de la vanité de tout plaisir et, en même temps, de la présence auprès d'eux d'une réalité éternelle, intuitivement perçue par l'inspiration. Le talent leur est donné comme un pouvoir de fixer cette réalité à la toute-puissance et à l'éternité de laquelle, avec enthousiasme et comme obéissant à un commandement de la conscience, ils consacrent, pour lui donner quelque valeur, leur vie éphémère. [C.S.B., 110]

This is the sort of genius dedicated to the reading of that 'inner book' that was to play such a seminal rôle in Proust's own aesthetics. While written the first time by experience, it could achieve, in the artist's translation, a coherence and permanence that could gather together the innumerable glosses and marginal inscriptions in a 'message' that was, for Ruskin as for Carlyle, transpersonal and enduring:

> Le poète étant pour Ruskin, comme pour Carlyle, une sorte de scribe écrivant sous la dictée de la nature une partie plus ou moins importante de son secret, le premier devoir de l'artiste est de ne rien ajouter de son propre cru à ce message divin. De cette hauteur vous verrez s'évanouir, comme les nuées qui se traînent à terre, les reproches de réalisme aussi bien que d'intellectualisme adressés à Ruskin. . . . Il y a dans ces critiques erreur d'altitude. La réalité que l'artiste doit enregistrer est à la fois matérielle et intellectuelle. La matière est réelle parce qu'elle est une expression de l'esprit. [C.S.B., 111]

This insistence on 'realism' and 'intellectualism' in a very special sense comes close to the mature formulations of Proust's own aesthetic, at once rooted in affective experience and, freed from extraneous intrusions *de son propre cru*, translated into an architecture accessible only through the imagination. Speaking of the range of Ruskin's writings, both achieved and left incomplete, Proust speaks of their startling novelty and underlying identity: they give 'l'idée de quelque chose de plus qu'humain, ou plutôt l'impression que chaque livre est d'un homme nouveau qui a un savoir différent, pas la même expérience, une autre vie' (*C.S.B.*, 115). But this recurrent novelty is bound together and blended in the memory of the attentive reader.

As already noted, the second part of the essay draws much closer to the texts of Ruskin themselves and to the author's unique way of seeing. While proclaiming the primacy of vision, Ruskin has a retrospective as well as a prospective dimension; often the object can be fully comprehended by the imagination only when it is absent, adumbrating the 'law' that Proust suggests in *Le Temps retrouvé*: 'on ne [peut] imaginer que ce qui est absent':

> If the imagination is called to take delight in any object, it will not always be well, if we can help it, to put the *real* object there, before it. The imagination would on the whole rather have it *not* there;—the reality and the substance are rather in the imagination's way: it would think a good deal more of the thing if it could not see it. Hence that strange and sometimes fatal charm, which there is in all things as long as we wait for them, and the moment we have lost them; but which fades while we possess them. [5.181–2]

Things have to be seen, and seen clearly, but they are often fully accessible to the Scribe *after* they have been seen. Proust recognised that Ruskin's career was one of compounding losses, renunciations and final, occluding vision; but he also recognised the peculiar powers that these departures liberated; it could be said of *Praeterita* as well as of Combray that the only true paradises are those we have lost.

The concluding pages of 'John Ruskin' are devoted to a moving account of the pilgrimage that Proust had made with the Yatemans to Rouen in search of the tiny figure on the Portrail des Libraires, a figure given a certain kind of immortality, as noted above, by Ruskin's attentive recreation of it in *The Seven Lamps*. Through the happy intervention of his Madeleine (Yateman), the pilgrim is able to translate the art of the anonymous sculptor and the English critic into his own imaginative redaction: 'J'ai été touché en la retrouvant là; rien ne meurt donc de ce qui a vécu, pas plus la pensée du sculpteur que la pensée de Ruskin' (*C.S.B.*, 127).

The essay, which opens with a meditation on the mortality of artists and the immortality of their works, closes with Proust appropriating Ruskin's tribute to Turner, dead in 1851, to the master who had died at the opening of the new century: 'C'est par ces yeux, fermés à jamais au fond du tombeau, que les générations qui ne sont pas encore nées verront la nature' (*C.S.B.*, 129).

The appearance of the second part of 'John Ruskin' in the August 1900 issue of the *Gazette des Beaux-Arts* marked the end of the first, intensive phase of Proust's apprenticeship to Ruskin. The major work that lay ahead was the patient labour of the translator (and his network of collaborators), first the text of *The Bible of Amiens* (appearing in part serially during 1903 and as a book in February 1904) and then that of *Sesame and Lilies* (the first essay appearing serially during 1905 and the book in 1906). This labour was complicated and enriched by Proust's characteristic scrupulosity in enriching the texts with a web of footnotes, not only clarifying the references but also serving as an 'improvised memory' of *other* passages from Ruskin in dialogue with the primary text. The years of these labours were difficult ones for the author still without an *oeuvre*; they were darkened by the death of his father (1903) followed by the death of his mother and collaborator in the translations (1905), by the progressive deterioration of his own health, and finally by the traumatic removal from the family apartment to the 'temporary' settlement in his cell at 102 boulevard Haussmann.

But Proust like Ruskin could not bear to let a text enter the world without trying to recapture it through revision, marginal alteration, or cannibalisation into some later project. We have seen the outline at least of the rather complicated bibliographic history of the essays from 1900—footnotes added, citations suppressed or substituted in the successive incarnations of the text. The most important critical essay to appear during the years of translation, 'Sur la lecture' (the preface for *Sésame et les lys*) begins, in fact, with an extended passage evoking a child's world of reading in a proto-Combray; and this passage, where the most 'unnoticed' details are most vividly remembered, is actually cannibalised from the pages of the abandoned novel, *Jean Santeuil* (1895–99), that had preceded the discovery of Ruskin. There were also some occasional reviews of Ruskiniana that allowed him to rework or reiterate the arguments first raised in the essays of 1900: these briefer notes included reviews of Marie von Bunsen's *John Ruskin, sein Leben und sein Wirken*, which appeared in the *Chronique des arts et de la curiosité* for 7 March 1903; and again in the *Chronique* reviews of Charlotte Broicher, *John Ruskin und sein Werk. Puritaner, Künstler, Kritiker* and the same author's German translation of *Modern Painters I* and *II*, both under the date 2 January 1904; as well as a review of a French translation by Mathilde Crémieux of *The Stones of Venice* in the *Chronique* of 5 May 1906. To these should be added the much more substantial article on his friend and sometime patron Robert de Montesquiou, published in *Les Arts de la Vie* (15 August 1905) under the title 'Un Professeur de Beauté', since this exercise in literary politics includes some extended commentary on Ruskin's clarity of vision (a gift that he allegedly shared with Montesquiou). (These minor specimens of Ruskiniana have more recently been supplemented by a publication in quite another key—a pastiche of the earnestly didactic Ruskin apparently intended for inclusion in the cycle of 'L'Affaire Lemoine'; something of its tone comes through in the full citation of the title: 'La Bénédiction du sanglier. Études des fresques de Giotto représentant l'affaire Lemoine à l'usage des jeunes étudiants et étudiantes du Corpus Christi qui se soucient encore d'elles, par John Ruskin'. (*C.S.B.*, 201–5).

By far the most important 'revision' or gloss on the Ruskin essays of 1900 is, however, the 'Post-Scriptum' written for the publication of *La Bible d'Amiens* and following in the preface immediately on the 'John Ruskin' essay from the *Gazette des Beaux-Arts* (*C.S.B.*, 129–41). This text, which strenuously raises the question of Ruskin's 'idolatry', is frequently taken as Proust's recantation of his earlier passion for Ruskin and the precise end of his discipleship to the Sage of Coniston. His discussion of what he identifies here as a pervasive failure of 'sincerity' on Ruskin's part is not, however, so easily adjudicated. At the simple biographical level any reading of a definitive break with Ruskin leaves the important question of why his critic, in the more than two years following the completion of the 'Post-Scriptum', continues his Ruskin studies and undertakes the translation of another major work, *Sesame and Lilies*, after this 'repudiation'. (Walter Strauss suggests that the continuation of the

Ruskin projects was an act of piety to please his mother; George Painter, on the other hand, argues that the persistence was an effort to exorcise a spiritual 'father'.)[14]

Actually, taken within the context of the complete preface to *La Bible d'Amiens*, Proust's indictment of Ruskin's motives seems less final when measured against the earlier defence of the same author against a charge of *naive* 'aestheticism' in the discussion of Milsand and La Sizeranne. More significantly, however, his description of an interior struggle between the rival claims of aesthesis and truth is cast in such a way as to suggest that it is an inevitable division for any deeply serious artist. And in the course of the commentary the reader with the retrospective advantage of Proust's own novel realises that he is also describing under the rubric of 'idolatry' the great temptation of his own narrator.

Proust characteristically begins his 'Post-Scriptum' by allowing Ruskin to draw up the terms of the indictment himself, in language —as indicated earlier in the preface—that is inescapably religious. Both Ruskin and Proust are fully aware of both the seductiveness of the temptation and the rigour of the charge. ' "Sous quelles formes magnifiques et tentatrices le mensonge a pu se glisser jusqu'au sein de sa sincerité intellectuelle . . ." ' he takes as his text his own words from the now adjacent essay of August 1900, a qualification within an encomium, and then quickly adds, 'Il y a une sorte d'idolatrie que personne n'a mieux définie que Ruskin dans une page de *Lectures on Art*':

> Such I conceive generally, though indeed with good arising out of it, for every great evil brings some good in its backward eddies—such I conceive to have been the deadly function of art in its ministry to what, whether in heathen or in Christian lands, and whether in the pageantry of words, or colours, or fair forms, is truly, and in the deep sense, to be called idolatry—the serving with the best of our hearts and minds, some dear or sad fantasy which we have made for ourselves, while we disobey the present call of the Master, who is not dead, and who is not now fainting under His cross, but requiring us to take up ours. [*Lectures on Art*, 20.66; quoted by Proust, C.S.B., 129]

The tragedy of misplaced priorities was, in Ruskin's doctrine of sacrifice, always a present danger. In the simplest sense Proust had already underlined this risk as early as the *Mercure* essay (which became an integral part of the preface), where he sought to distinguish his notion of Ruskinian pilgrimage from mere fetishism: 'un fétichisme qui n'est qu'illusion' (*C.S.B.*, 70). (And no Ruskinian could contemplate the extraordinary incremental clutter—illustrating what was perhaps the widest-ranging mind of the century—of the museum at Coniston without weighing the word 'fetishism'.) But in the 'Post-Scriptum' the interrogation of motives, the possibility of the aesthetic asserting a subtle priority over the ethic, is much more deeply and universally put:

> Mais il est un dilettantisme plus intérieur que le dilettantisme de l'action (dont il avait triomphé) et le véritable duel entre son idolâtrie et sa sincerité se jouait non pas à certaines heures de sa vie, non pas dans certaines pages de ses livres, mais à toute minute, dans ces régions profondes, secrètes, presque inconnues à nous-mêmes, où notre personnalité reçoit de l'imagination les images, de l'intelligence les idées, de la mémoire les mots, s'affirme elle-même dans le choix incessant qu'elle en fait, et joue en quelque sorte incessamment le sort de notre vie spirituelle et morale. Dans ces régions-là, j'ai l'impression que le péché d'idolâtrie n'ait cessé d'être commis par Ruskin. Et au moment même où il prêchait la sincerité, il y manquait lui-même, non en ce qu'il disait, mais par la manière dont il le disait. [C.S.B., 130]

Having thus implicated Ruskin in a struggle faced by every writer at the innermost arcanum of his imaginative life, Proust suggests that Ruskin never successfully resolved this duel between sincerity and idolatry, despite the unambiguously moral character of his own teachings:

> Les doctrines qu'il professait étaient des doctrines morales et non des doctrines esthétiques, et pourtant il les choisissait pour leur beauté. Et comme il ne voulait pas les présenter comme belles, mais comme vraies, il était obligé de se mentir à lui-même sur la nature des raisons qui les lui faisaient adopter. [C.S.B., 130]

This is expecially poignant because, for Proust, Ruskin had clearly chosen the terms of his own 'religion de la beauté' and his own greatest gifts as a critic were grounded in his intense perception of the beauty of objects. The indictment is also intimately related to the special rôle that 'texts' (visual as well as literal) enjoyed in Ruskin's development. (Proust himself had earlier emphasised the significance for Ruskin in the work he was translating of the Bible taken literally rather than figuratively as a 'first text'.) Ruskin had, however, in the discussion of 'idolatry' in *Aratra Pentelici*, identified a source of contemporary 'frivolity' as 'two forms of deadly Idolatry which are now all but universal in England' (20.240). The first of these is 'the worship of the Eidolon, or the Phantasm of Wealth', which was hardly a serious temptation for Ruskin himself. The second transgression, however, cuts much closer to Proust's indictment of Ruskin; it is 'the Worship of the Letter, instead of the Spirit . . . the apprehension of a healing sacredness in the act of reading the Book whose primal commands we refuse to obey' (20. 240). The examples of Ruskin's 'idolatry' that Proust brings forward are significantly drawn from 'misreadings' for rhetorical purposes of the Bible itself (Egypt as 'l'éducatrice de Moïse et l'Hôtesse du Christ', *C.S.B.*, 134) and of 'misreading' of Venetian history figured against the biblical pageantry of her art ('Jamais cité n'eut une Bible plus glorieuse', *C.S.B.*, 131).

At this crucial point, however, Proust implicates his own affective history while introducing the difficult question of how far aesthetic pleasure is imbricated in any discovery of truth. The event, which ultimately judges Proust rather than Ruskin, involves the former's reading of precisely the seductive passage in *The Stones of Venice* (10.141–2), based itself on a 'misprision' of a verse from Ecclesiastes, that formed part of the 'text' of St Mark's; having submitted Ruskin's ringing denunciation of the sins of the Venetians to an ethical deconstruction, Proust then confesses to the suspect pleasure that this very text brought him when he first read it, within the figured confines of St Mark's itself. Speaking of the page marred by 'idolatry', he allows:

> Elle est elle-même mystérieuse, pleine d'images à la fois de beauté et de religion comme cette même église de Saint-Marc où toutes les figures de l'*Ancien* et du *Nouveau Testament* apparaissent sur le fond d'une sorte d'obscurité splendide et d'éclat changeant. Je me souviens de l'avoir lue pour la première fois dans Saint-Marc même, pendant une heure d'orage et d'obscurité où les mosaïques ne brillaient plus que de leur propre et matérielle lumière et d'un or intense, terrestre et ancien, auquel le soleil vénitien, qui enflamme jusqu'aux anges des campaniles, ne mêlait plus rien de lui; l'émotion que j'éprouvais à lire là cette page, parmi tous ces anges qui s'illuminaient des ténèbres environnantes, était très grande et n'était pourtant peut-être pas très pure. Comme la joie de voir les belles figures mystérieuses s'augmentait, mais s'altérait du plaisir en quelque sorte d'érudition que j'éprouvais à comprendre les textes apparus en lettres byzantines à côté de leurs fronts nimbés, de même la beauté des images de Ruskin était avivée et corrompue par l'orgueil de se référer au *texte sacré*. Une sorte de retour égoïste sur soi-même est inévitable dans ces joies mêlées d'érudition et d'art où le plaisir esthétique peut devenir plus aigu, mais non rester aussi pur. [C.S.B., 133]

While Proust has indicted Ruskin for his reading of the Venetian and biblical texts earlier, he has here summoned himself to judgement in the profoundly ambiguous act of reading Ruskin; the temptation of 'le texte sacré' (whether that of others or one's own) and the 'joies mêlées' of reading will remain central concerns of Proust and his fictional narrator down to the last pages of the novel which had become their common life.

Proust's post-scriptural reproof of the master is thus inseparable from a self-questioning of the disciple and translator. Proust, in translating a sentence from Ruskin on the hazards of interpreting Scripture ('There is no possibility of attaching the idea of infallible truth to any form of human language in which even these exceptional passages have been delivered to us', 33.116), gives the duplicity of language an even more overt formulation: 'Il y a pas de forme de langage humain où l'erreur n'ait pu se glisser' (*C.S.B.*, 135).

Again, touching yet another affinity that he shared with Ruskin, he speaks toward the end of the 'Post-Scriptum' of the profound materiality and topographical specificity of the latter's thought. (This can be, of course, both a rectifying 'realism' and an occasion of 'idolatry'.)

> Car la pensée de Ruskin n'est pas comme la pensée d'un Emerson par exemple, qui est contenue tout entière dans un livre, c'est-à-dire un quelque chose abstrait, un pur signe d'elle-même. L'objet auquel s'applique une pensée comme celle de Ruskin et dont elle est inséparable n'est pas immatériel, il est répandu çà et là sur la surface de la terre. Il faut aller le chercher là où il se trouve, à Pise, à Florence, à la National Gallery, à Rouen, à Amiens, dans les montagnes de la Suisse. [C.S.B., 138]

The last instance returns us to where we first found Proust in pursuit of Ruskin, writing for his copy of La Sizeranne so that he could experience the Alps 'through the eyes of this great man'. By this stage in his development he has not so much parted company with his English mentor as discovered that, distant as they are in certain formal doctrinal ways, they share common temptations as well as common affections. Thus Proust, who continually slips into the first person singular, asserts that despite his love for the hawthorn (which he shared with Ruskin and Walter Pater), a key to his affective *temps perdu*, 'sincerity' compels that he distinguish the subject-matter of a work of art from its more profound 'content', that he frequent objects but not idolise them:

> Non, je ne trouverai pas un tableau plus beau parce que l'artiste aura peint au premier plan une aubépine, bien que je ne connaisse rien de plus beau que l'aubépine, car je veux rester sincère et que je sais que la beauté d'un tableau ne dépend pas des choses qui y sont représentées. Je ne collectionnerai pas les images de l'aubépine. Je ne vénère pas l'aubépine, je vais la voir et la respirer. [C.S.B., 137]

The same might be said, on balance, of Proust's attitude at this stage of his career towards masters and 'directeurs de conscience'. In discerning the rounds that Ruskin lost in the continuing struggle against idolatry, Proust acquired insight into his own susceptibilities —his penchant for 'sacred texts' and idolatrous pursuits; whether under the guise of *snobbisme*, or love, or erudition, or a mystified conception of art, the analysis of these temptations was to become the major deconstructive activity of the novel he was yet to write but was already gathering into the 'inner book'. The last pages of the preface return to the question of discipleship, taken not as burden but as a liberation. ('Les personnes médiocres croient généralement que se laisser guider . . . par les livres qu'on admire, enlève à notre faculté de juger une partie de son indépendance. "Que peut vous importer ce que sent Ruskin: sentez par vous-même."' This line of argument is founded, Proust argues, on a basic psychological error common to those ignorant of genuine discipleship; they fail to recognise that those who have accepted 'une discipline spirituelle sentent que leur puissance de comprendre et de sentir en est infinie-ment accrue, et leur sens critique jamais paralysé' (*C.S.B.*, 140). These last pages do not read like an act of repudiation. Rather than 'exorcising a father' in Ruskin, Proust seems to have found a deeper insight into himself—in his weaknesses as well as his potential. The ultimate paragraph of the preface is a complex and precursal meditation on the power of memory to resurrect that which is absent and seemingly lost for ever. As noted above by Ruskin himself, certain powers of the imagination seem to operate effectively only in the absence of the object. In one sense Ruskin had become a part of Proust's own past; in another sense the master was removed just far enough for the task of translation to begin: 'C'est quand Ruskin est bien loin de nous que nous traduisons ses livres et tâchons de fixer dans une image ressemblante les traits de sa pensée' (*C.S.B.*, 141).

The translation of the *La Bible d'Amiens* was completed in 1901, save for some late revisions. According to Marie Nordlinger, Proust relied on the literal versions of the Ruskin text that his mother pre-pared during the daylight hours as the point of departure for the accomplished translations that he laboured over through the night. The circle of his collaboration extended further when it came to the pursuit of nuances, including as well as Mlle Nordlinger, Robert d'Humières, Reynaldo Hahn, Robert de Billy and François d'Oncieu among his informants. Georges de Lauris in the preface to his collection of Proust correspondence, *A un ami*, tells the anecdote of the Prince de Brancovan, who was the editor of *La Renaissance latine* which published parts of *La Bible d'Amiens* serially, approaching the translator in some bewilderment: 'Com-ment faites-vous, Marcel, puisque vous ne savais pas l'anglais?'[15] Lauris adds that, although Proust would have had difficulty ordering a mutton chop in an English restaurant and knew all the other English authors whom he loved only in French translation, he did indeed know the one who mattered most with genuine intimacy: 'De fait, il ne connaissait que l'anglais de Ruskin mais alors dans toutes ses nuances.'

The labour, however, which delayed the publication of *La Bible* and occupied more than a year of additional research was the creation of what Proust styled 'an improvised memory', a gloss on the single text of Ruskin that brought into play the resonances of echoes from the rest of the *oeuvre*. Recognising that Ruskin above all other writers seemed to require this 'echo chamber', he constructed through his footnotes an internal lexicon for reading in context. In a long footnote that begins with a passage from *Praeterita* he outlined the rationale for his system of echoing footnotes in terms that sound like the compositional system of repetitions finally articulated in *A la recherche*:

> En mettant une note au bas des passages cités de *La Bible d'Amiens*, chaque fois que le texte éveillait par des analogies, même lointaines, le souvenir d'autres ouvrages de Ruskin, et en traduisant dans la note le passage qui m'était ainsi revenu à l'esprit, j'ai tâché de permettre au lecteur de se placer dans la situation de quelqu'un qui ne se trouvait pas en présence Ruskin pour la première fois, mais qui, ayant déjà eu avec lui des entretiens antérieurs, pourrait, dans ses paroles, reconnaître ce qui est chez lui, permanent et fondamental. Ainsi j'ai essayé de pourvoir le lecteur comme d'une mémoire improvisée où j'ai disposé des souvenirs des autres livres de Ruskin,—sorte de caisse de résonance, où les paroles de *La Bible d'Amiens* pourront prendre quelque retentissement en y éveillant des échos fraternels. Mais aux paroles de *La Bible d'Amiens* ces échos ne répondront pas sans doute, ainsi qu'il arrive dans une mémoire qui s'est faite elle-même, de ces horizons inégalement lointains, habituellement cachés à nos regards et dont notre vie elle-même a mesuré jour par jour les distances variées. Ils n'auront pas, pour venir rejoindre la parole présente dont la resemblance les a attirés, à traverser la résistante douceur de cette atmosphère interposée qui a l'étendue même de notre vie et qui est toute la poésie de la mémoire. [Préface du traducteur, *La Bible d'Amiens*; C.S.B., 75–6]

Elsewhere Proust speaks of Balzac and Wagner as 'self-contemplating' artists who gave their work retrospective unity through the interplay of echoes and anticipations. But Ruskin is even more clearly an artist who is constantly escaping unity—both through incompletion and through accretion; even his most retrospective and radically selective effort, *Praeterita*, not only reached back towards his origins through a palimpsest of text but generated an ongoing commentary in the margin through the uncompletable *Dilecta*. The same need for a 'memory' to contain the absent texts, to achieve through juxtaposition the simultaneity that eludes the linear text, is stressed again in one of Proust's liminal notes for the second volume of translation, *Sésame et les lys*:

> Mais c'est le charme précisément de l'oeuvre de Ruskin qu'il y ait entre les idées d'un même livre, et entre les divers livres des liens qu'il ne montre pas, qu'il laisse à peine apparaître un instant et qu'il a d'ailleurs peut-être tissés après coup, mais jamais artificiels cependant puisqu'ils sont toujours tirés de la substance toujours identique à elle-même de

sa pensée. Les préoccupations multiples mais constantes de cette pensée, voilà ce qui assure à ces livres une unité plus réelle que l'unité de composition, généralement absente, il faut bien le dire.[16]

At the end of his affair with Odette, after years of suffering and dedication to his 'grand amour', Swann reflects that all his sacrifices were made 'pour une femme . . . qui n'était pas mon genre!' The reader of Proust as dévoté, translator and critic of Ruskin may be tempted to look back over the six years of intense work that punctuates his long apprenticeship to the English writer and conclude similarly that this passionate affair, too, was all offered up to an author who was, in the final analysis, not his type. The superficial differences in background and temperament separating Proust from Ruskin are all too obvious: Ruskin's puritanical, Scottish evangelical inheritance, his moralising, his ultimate rôle as a prophet of social and ethical renovation, all contrast markedly with Proust's Mediterranean and Cartesian heritage, his indifference to doctrinal concerns, his detachment as a demi-Juif in a profoundly secular society, his rôle as the worldly chronicler of the Faubourg Saint-Germain, the pitiless, illusion-free critic of human passions and obsessions—all these persistent lines of character suggest an unbridgeable chasm between the two authors. Even the external records of their careers tend to reinforce this distance: Ruskin the restless traveller, dedicated until late in life to annual circuits of the Continent and its monuments; Proust, after a brief period of 'Ruskinian pilgrimages', withdrawing with almost monastic consecration to the exploration of his own cork-lined cell; Ruskin, the author of a large and diverse body of writings that does not easily yield its essential unity; Proust, the architect of a single vast text into which he attempted to draw all that he had earlier experienced and written.

Beneath these dramatic differences, however, lie bonds of consanguinity that both account for the initial appeal across language and culture and explain as well those aspects of Ruskin's achievement that were permanently and subtly assimilated into Proust's imagination. These affinities are much more profound than the memories of a childhood organised and extended by over-protective parents; they touch a community of feeling that goes beyond a common love for the cathedrals of France, for Venice, for Giotto, Tintoretto and Turner. These deeper affinities that bind their careers, the lessons that the French writer garnered from his English predecessor, can be broadly summarised in terms of three characteristic modes of the imagination: similar ways of seeing (precisions of the critical eye), similar ways of feeling (resonances of the literary and affective memory), and similar ways of writing (a constant struggle with digression, a syntax of complex subordin-

ation, 'the cadence of mitigated authority', and a proliferating network of interactive images). During his apprenticeship to Ruskin,
Proust discovered that he saw, that he felt, and—ultimately—that
he wrote like Ruskin. Like the author of *Praeterita*, he was to be
engaged in a constant search to unite through successive revisions
the living self and the writing self. Both strove ultimately to bring
together the associative and penetrative imaginations in a single
critical act.

And whatever the vast distances that separated their careers, both
writers were marked by similar division and haunted by common
fears. Both Ruskin and Proust bear a resemblance to Isaiah Berlin's
characterisation of that other great 'directeur de conscience', Leo
Tolstoy: a polymathic 'fox' in search of a vocation as unifying
'hedgehog'. Both were plagued by demons of incompletion and
digression; both were tempted, in the comprehensive sense suggested in Proust's 'Post-Scriptum', by the artist's sin of idolatry.
Both had, in Leo Spitzer's characterisation of the mature Proust, the
double face of calm sage and nervous seeker. Maurice Blanchot
spoke of Proust's life work as 'une oeuvre achevée-inachevée'. The
same might be said of the vast monument assembled by Cook and
Wedderburn. Many of Proust's most perceptive critics have remarked of his great novel, which must be read both 'tour à tour' and
'à la fois', that it is the product of a double discourse, one undoing (or
completing) the work of the other. Walter Benjamin speaks of
Proust's 'Penelope-work' of weaving and unweaving, of recollection
and forgetting; Ernst Robert Curtius, in terms reminiscent of
Proust on Ruskin, speaks of the 'braiding' of 'intellect' and 'impression'; Roland Barthes describes the two discourses in more
purely linguistic terms as that of the 'decoder' and the 'encoder';
Gérard Genette argues that *A la recherche* must be seen at once
'comme oeuvre' and 'comme approche de l'oeuvre'. All these deeply
duplicitous characterisations could, with important qualifications,
be applied to Ruskin's work as well. It is these resonances that perhaps go furthest towards explaining the affinities between the two
writers, how the example of the English prophet was assimilated into the sensibility of the French novelist.

Both writers had to come to terms with incompletion. By project-
ing the 'texte sacré' into the future, beyond the provisional monument of his immense novel, Proust (in his prospective stage) finally
escapes the 'idolatry' of provisional origins, making of his work's
very incompleteness its over-arching virtue. This may have been a
strategy that he learned from Ruskin's occluded example. But
Proust also situated, close to the end of his 'unfinished', probation-
ary monument, a 'coup de théâtre' that evokes his apprenticeship to
Ruskin and the scene where he first read *The Stones of Venice*. The

narrator, desolate of any hope of redeeming the time and achieving his vocation, passes through the courtyard of the Hôtel Guermantes and stumbles against an uneven pavingstone. Suddenly, out of the wastes of lost time, he recovers 'un peu de temps à l'état pur' (III, 872), and the simultaneous experience in the present of a moment before the façade of St Mark's in a Venice long since fallen into the oblivion of his own past. This experience is the beginning of a series of centripetal 'moments' that bring together the strands of a life seemingly frayed beyond repair. It is the Venice of John Ruskin that contributes to this resurrection (tentative, to be sure), and it was the author's 'pèlerinage ruskinien' that first made a place for the stone that is at once a stumbling block and the keystone of the novelistic arch. In the same subtle and almost forgotten way Ruskin himself had become a part of Proust's life and emerged, translated into aspects of his portraits of the artist (Elstir, Vinteuil, Bergotte, the narrator himself). 'The duty and the task of a writer,' Proust observes in a page that follows this event, 'are those of a translator.'

NOTES   1 *Correspondance de Marcel Proust,* II, ed. Philip Kolb (Paris, 1976), p. 348. Robert de La Sizeranne's book was published by Hachette in 1897; portions of it had appeared serially in the *Revue des Deux Mondes* from December 1895 to April 1897. Proust seems to have read it soon after its appearance, since Douglas Ainslie, an English friend of Robert de Billy, records conversations at the Café Weber during 1897 on the respective merits of Ruskin and Walter Pater in which Proust was a partisan of the former. See *Correspondance,* II, pp. 220–2. That Proust had at least some second-hand knowledge of Ruskin dating from an even earlier period seems likely. His professor of philosophy at the Ecole Libre des Science Politiques, Paul Desjardins, published brief translations from Ruskin in his journal, the *Bulletin de l'Union pour l'Action Morale,* every year from 1893 to 1903 (save for 1894 and 1901). Robert de Montesquiou, whose portrait had been painted by Whistler, gave Proust an elaborately bound copy of *Le Gentil Art de se faire des ennemis* and opinions on the Ruskin–Whistler trial. In later letters Proust argued that one of Whistler's *mots* at the trial was in fact pure Ruskin. (Proust never quite mastered the painter's name, always referring to him in the correspondence as 'Wisthler'.)

Jean Autret in *L'Influence de Ruskin sur la vie, les idées et l'oeuvre* de Marcel Proust (Genève: Droz, 1955), pp. 16–17, advances an earlier date, following Robert Vigneron, for the first appearance of Ruskin in Proust's correspondence 'En décembre 1897, Proust écrit à Pierre Lavallée: "Si tu va à la bibliothèque, aie la gentillesse de regarder si vous possédez *The Queen of* [*the*] *Air* par Ruskin et mets-moi un mot chez mon concierge."' The *carte-lettre* to his friend from the Condorcet, now a librarian at the Ecole des Beaux-Arts, has been, however, positively dated by Philip Kolb in *Correspondance* II, pp. 375–6, as 'jeudi soir 30 novembre 1899'; the note bears a postmark of the following morning: 'PARIS DEPART N/1 DEC 99'. Thus, this reference, rather than anticipating all others, dates from the period of intense Ruskin studies in late 1899, when Proust was moving from reliance on La Sizeranne to an exploration of the original English texts.

2 *Correspondance*, II, p. 357. Later in the month of October Proust wrote to his mother asking her to translate for him some passages from *The Seven Lamps of Architecture: Correspondance*, II, p. 365. Proust's attitude towards La Sizeranne (1866–1932) as a guide to Ruskin was obviously not without its ambivalences; thus, in an unpublished letter written many years later (31 January 1917), he remarks, 'Il y a chez Ruskin trop de génie obscurci et captif au milieu de théories caduques, pour qu'un ruskinien non encore complètement initié doive lire autre chose que des *Pages choisies*, ce qui pour Ruskin pourrait s'appeler plutôt des pages délivrées. J'avais fait un recueil de ces pages, mais je l'ai détruit à la prière, ou plutôt sur l'injonction—car c'est plutôt sa manière —de M. de la Sizeranne qui avait fait lui-même un receuil de ce genre non encore publié alors et ne voulait pas se laisser 'damer le pion.' Je me suis fait un cas de conscience, ruskinien si vous voulez, d'obéir à quelqu' un que je ne tiens nullement pour un maître, mais qui, en ce qui concerne Ruskin tout au moins, était pour moi un ancien avec qui je tenais à garder les distances, les distances qui sans aucune fausse humilité de ma part, sont très grandes. Ayant le chemin libre, alors, il a fait paraître un receuil chez Hachette.' To Jacques Hébertot.

3 *Ruskin et la religion de la beauté* (Paris, 1897), pp. 11–23.

4 For a life finally oppressed by clouds, consider the first sight of the Alps: 'There was no thought in any of us for a moment of their being clouds. They were clear as crystal, sharp as the pure horizon sky, and already tinged with rose by the sinking sun. Infinitely beyond all that we had ever thought or dreamed,—the seen walls of the lost Eden could not have been more beautiful to us; nor more awful, round heaven, the walls of sacred Death' (35.115). For Ruskin's contemporary response see 'The Alps! the Alps!—it is no cloud', 2.367. (Cf. Marcel's first attempts at literary creation after seeing the spires of Martinville from Dr Percepied's carriage, *A.R.T.P.*, I, 180–2.)

5 By late November he had progressed to seeking out Ruskin titles in English. Thus he wrote to Pierre Lavallée, the librarian at the Beaux Arts, for a copy of *The Queen of the Air* ('mets-moi un mot chez mon concierge (je ne m'éveille guère avant 2 heures)'); *Correspondance*, II, p. 375. He apparently later secured Marie Nordlinger's annotated copy of the book; *ibid.*, p. 385.

6 *Correspondance*, II. p. 387. The correspondence with Marie Nordlinger from the autumn of 1899 to 1905 affords a continuing record of Proust's struggles as a reader and translator of Ruskin. He was delighted to discover that she came from Rusholme, the Manchester suburb where Ruskin had delivered the two lectures of *Sesame and Lilies* that became his second volume of translations.

7 'John Ruskin' in *Contre Sainte-Beuve*, précédé de *Pastiches et mélanges* et suivi de *Essais et articles*, ed. Pierre Clarac et Yves Sandre (Paris, 1971), pp. 439–41. This edition hereafter indicated as *C.S.B.*. For the letter to Marie Nordlinger, *Correspondance*, II, pp. 384–5.

8 *C.S.B.*, 69–141. The component elements of this palimpsest are discussed below. The earliest parts of the *Gazette des Beaux-Arts* essay

may date from an unfinished (or at least unpublished) article commissioned by Louis Ganderax for the *Revue de Paris* at the earliest stage of
Proust's acquaintance with Ruskin. In a letter to Jean-Louis Vaudoyer
(*Correspondance Générale*, Paris, 1933, iv, 42–6) written in March 1912
Proust offers an amusing account of the fate of this first venture at Ruskin
criticism: 'L'étude sur Ruskin a failli paraître parce que Ruskin ayant fini
par vieillir et mourir dans l'intervalle, le manuscrit détestable comme
littérature se trouvait admirable comme actualité. Tel autre critique se
récusa. Le directeur-ami étant pris en ce dilemme de laisser sa Revue sans
nécrologie de ce grand homme ou de faire paraître ce qui a été ensuite ma
préface à la *Bible d'Amiens*, préféra encore le premier désastre. Et la raison
que, pour tous ces écrits, il me donna uniformément, tristement, affectue-
usement, de ses refus, était "qu'il n'avait pas assez de temps à lui pour les
refaire et les *écrire*"'. (44–5.) As Bernard de Fallois has observed, however, 'l'oeuvre inédite de Proust n'existe pas'. Everything was recuper-
ated, redacted or rescued for some later use. But however much of the first
section of the *G.B.A.* article may descend from the Gandarax commission,
the author had carefully reworked it to reflect the death of Ruskin.

9 *C.S.B.*, 441–4. This text is to be distinguished from what was to
becomes the central panel of 'En Mémoire des églises assassinées' in
Pastiches et Mélanges (*C.S.B.*, 69–105): 'Journées de pèlerinage'.
Proust, with characteristic scrupulosity, bothered a number of friends in
order to determine what had become of Shelley's heart.

10 *A.R.T.P.*, 389–93. This passage on the evocative—and deceptive
—power of names is one of the great set pieces of the third part of *Swann*,
'Noms de Pays: Le Nom'; significantly, the Italian trip that provokes this
rêverie, a synesthetic anthology of images drawn from Ruskin's texts, is
unrealised but leaves an indelible mark: 'Ces images irréelles, fixes,
toujours pareilles, remplissant mes nuits et mes jours, différencièrent
cette époque de ma vie de celles qui l'avaient précédée . . . comme dans un
opéra un motif mélodique introduit une nouveauté qu'on ne pourrait pas
soupçonner si on ne faisait que lire le livret' (*A.R.T.P.*, 390).

11 Cf. Paul de Man, *Allegories of Reading* (New Haven, 1979), pp.
57–76. De Man's radical reading of the Giotto passage and the ensuing
scene of reading as inescapably founded on error and a 'deferral' of
meaning is, oddly enough, based on a minor misreading of Ruskin interpreting the Charity allegory. (Ruskin actually gives *three* successive
readings of the figure's emblematic gesture.) The quotation from Ruskin
is itself not quoted exactly (75).

12 Quoted by André Maurois in *A la Recherche de Marcel Proust*
(Paris, 1949), p. 175. In this and other exfoliations of Proust's cathedral
image it is interesting to compare his remarks on fictional composition
with Ruskin's distinction between architecture and building in the first
chapter of *The Seven Lamps of Architecture*.

13 Joseph-Antoine Milsand (1817–86), critic and philosopher,
author of *L'Esthétique anglaise. Etude sur M. John Ruskin* (Paris, 1864);
Robert de La Sizeranne (1866–1932), critic and author of *La Peinture
anglaise contemporaine* (Paris, 1895) and *Ruskin et la Religion de la Beauté*
(Paris, 1897) cited above.

14 Walter Strauss, *Proust and Literature. The Novelist as Critic*
(Cambridge, Mass., 1957), pp. 184–6; George D. Painter, *Marcel Proust*.

A Biography, II (London, 1965), pp. 1–2.

15 Georges de Lauris (ed), *Marcel Proust. A un ami: correspondance inédite, 1903–1922* (Paris, 1948), p. 22.

16 John Ruskin, *Sésame et les lys*, trans. Marcel Proust (Paris, 1906), p. 62n.

Ruskin's fireflies

WILLIAM ARROWSMITH

In his essay on *Hamlet* T. S. Eliot observed that both Hamlet and
Shakespeare are dominated by feelings in excess of the apparent
facts and situation and therefore inexpressible. The feelings of poet
and protagonist alike are too inchoate, too complex or violent to find
an 'objective correlative'—appropriate words, events, situations in
which to embed themselves:

> The intense feeling, ecstatic or terrible, without an object or exceeding
> its object, is something which every person of sensibility has known; it
> is doubtless a subject of study for pathologists. It often occurs in
> adolescence: the ordinary person puts these feelings to sleep, or trims
> down his feelings to fit the business world; the artist keeps them alive
> by his ability to intensify the world to his emotions.[1]

A psychological critic might speak of obsessions or neurotic motifs:
Eliot puts the accent instead on the *imagistic* quality of obsessive feelings in the writer's work. Reality is heightened in order to accommodate the poet's emotional provocation, the feelings that lack an
objective home or focus; alternatively they are enlarged or 'sub-

limated' into something else. Images and motifs endowed with this kind of special intensity Eliot later termed 'saturated'—a phenomenon involving not only the poet's reading and possession of (and by) literary texts but his whole sensitive life since early childhood:

> Why, for all of us, out of all that we have heard, seen, felt, in a lifetime, do certain images recur, charged with emotion, rather than others? The song of one bird, the leap of one fish, at a particular place and time, the scent of one flower, an old woman on a German mountain path, six ruffians seen through an open window playing cards at night on a small French railway junction where there was a water-mill: such memories may have symbolic value, but of what we cannot tell, for they come to represent the depths of feeling into which we cannot peer.[2]

Around and over these mysterious personal images, layer on layer, gathered the cumulus of literature—the intricating associations of other texts, themselves saturated in earlier texts, as Dante is saturated in Virgil, and Virgil in Homer and the Greek tragedians.

Ruskin put it differently, but the emphasis is remarkably similar. Of *Hamlet* (had he agreed with Eliot's adverse judgement) he might have said simply that the play lacked what he called the 'Imagination Penetrative':

> there is in every word set down by the imaginative mind an awful under-current of meaning, and evidence and shadow upon it of the deep places out of which it has come. It is often obscure, often half told, for he who wrote it, in his clear seeings of the things beneath, may have been impatient of detailed interpretation, but if we choose to dwell upon it and trace it, it will lead us always securely back to that metropolis of the soul's dominion from which we may follow out all the ways and tracks . . . [4.252ff.]

The poet's material is precisely this obsessional, life-saturated larval core; and the penetrative imagination, claw-like, seizes directly and intuitively upon it, but in such a way that its mystery and power—its *natural* obscurity—are preserved inviolate. The imagination reveals—but only in its diverging ramifications—the matrix from which everything else springs; we intuit the source as we might intuit a cold from its constellated symptoms. Providing it is clearly stamped as *the* source by the penetrative imagination, obscurity is a quality to be respected, a guarantee of emotional complexity and wholeness, of the poet's respect for the organic, germinal mystery, which could be revealed only by suggestion of its intricating products:

> Will you undertake to convey to another person a perfectly distinct idea of any single emotion passing in your own heart?
> You cannot—you cannot fathom it yourself—you have no actual

expression for the simple idea, and are compelled to have instant recourse to metaphor.

You can say, for instance, you feel cold, or warm, at the heart; you feel depressed, delighted, dark, bright: are any of these expressions competent to illustrate the *whole* feeling? If you try to reach it you must heap metaphor after metaphor, and image after image, and you will feel that the most mysterious touch nearest and reach highest, but none will come up to the truth. In short, if you banish obscurity from your language you banish all description of human emotion, beyond such simple notions as that your hero is in a fury or a fright. For all human emotions are obscure, mysterious in their source, their operation, their nature; and how possibly can the *picture* of a mystery be less than a mystery?

But, farther—were it possible, it is not desirable to banish all obscurity from poetry. If the mind is delighted in the attainment of a new idea, its delight is increased tenfold if it be obtained by its own exertion—if it has arisen apparently from its own depths.

The object in all *art* is not to *inform* but to *suggest*, not to add to the knowledge but to kindle the imagination. He is the best poet who can by the fewest words touch the greatest number of secret chords of thought in his reader's own mind, and set *them* to work in their own way. [1.441–2]

This aesthetic doctrine is obviously Ruskin's attempt to describe and rationalise his own artistic practice, above all his lifelong strategy of using ramifying association and textured complexity of image in the effort to reveal the mysterious nature of reality and human emotion. It is also a remarkable anticipation, in its main points, of the Symbolists; and in its feeling for reality as a continuous, flowing, organic whole, it comes uncannily close to Bergson.[3]

My immediate purpose is to examine one of the more prominent instances of a 'saturated' image or obsessional metaphor in Ruskin— the famous fireflies. There are, of course, numerous other, often interrelated, clusters or obsessions. One thinks, for instance, of his lifelong fascination with pure-running water, blue water above all, with sinister depths or with undarkened clarity like the Rhone's,[4] water in all its forms, hellish or paradisal—wave gathering for the fall, brook gliding, river rushing. Or his contagious delight in natural or man-made filigree, all the intricate entanglements of *la divina foresta*, from the arabesques of acanthus scrolls drifted by the wind around the capitals from which they rise, to the instinctual textures of birds' nests and the uncurling 'Greek life' disclosed by a fern spiral or the curve of a calligrapher's uncial.[5] Or his passion, geological and moral, for fragmentation and formation of stone, stresslines, folds and cleavages in layered rock (and even blanc-mange), all flawing and growing of crystal, and analogous formations of human virtue. But none of these, except possibly his preoccu-

pation with serpents, is so unmistakably obsessive as the fireflies.
Here, in no particular order, are the more striking examples:

I have just come in from an evening walk among the stars and fireflies.
One hardly knows where one has got to between them, for the fires
flash, as you know, exactly like the stars on the sea, and the impression
to the eye as if one was walking on water. They dazzled me like fireworks, and it was very heavenly to seem them floating, field beyond
field, under the shadowy vines. [35.562]

An account of Orcagna's Fiesole:

The Dominican convent is situated at the bottom of a slope of olives,
distinguished only by its narrow and low spire; a cypress avenue
recedes from it towards Florence . . . No extended prospect is open to
it; though over the low wall, and through the sharp, thickset olive
leaves, may be seen one silver gleam of the Arno, and, at evening, the
peaks of the Carrara mountains, purple against the twilight, dark and
calm, while the fire-flies glance beneath, silent and intermittent, like
stars upon the rippling of mute, soft sea. [12.233–4]

A more ominous example, in a letter of 1870 to a friend:

A climate like the loveliest and purest English summer, with only the
somewhat, to me, awful addition of fire-flies innumerable which, as
soon as the sunset is fairly passed into twilight, light up the dark
ilex groves with flitting torches, or at least, lights as large as candles,
and in the sky, larger than the stars. We got to Siena in a heavy thunderstorm of sheet-lightning in a quiet evening, and the . . . showers
of fire-flies between, made the whole scene look anything rather
than *celestial*. But it was very lovely by morning light . . . [20.liv]

In a letter to Carlyle (1867) the emphasis is on the splendour of the
fireflies by night:

I hope . . . the weather has found you still in Italy; and that you will
outstay the Firefly time. I always think that nothing in the world can
possibly be so touching, in its own natural sweetness, and in the
association with the pensive and glorious power of the scene, as the
space of spring time in Italy during which the firefly makes the mea-
dows quiver at midnight. [36.527]

In a letter to his mother (1870) the fireflies seem, by comparison,
almost threatening:

The stars burning like torches all over the sky, the fireflies flying all
about, literally brighter than the stars. One came into the railroad
carriage and shone clear in full lamplight, settling above my head . . .[6]

In another letter to his mother (also dated 1870) the sinister spectacle of the fireflies is revealingly contrasted with the goodness of the

Sienese *contadini*:

> The fireflies are almost awful in the twilight, as bright as candles, flying in and out of the dark cypresses. The people are *so* good too—I mean the country people. [37.9]

Ruskin clearly regards the fireflies with something resembling awe; he was visibly shocked when his friend Charles Eliot Norton invited him to come and 'look at the lightning-bugs' (36.xcii). But the 'bracketing' is ambivalent, producing, according to Ruskin's mood or emotional needs, either foreboding or delight.

In *The Ethics of the Dust* (1865) he describes, in manifestly Dantesque terms, an allegorical 'Valley of Diamonds'. The scene and the symbolism are saturated in Dante. A rough road winds its way beside a river of blood; the river runs over diamond sands, through harsh, rugged ground, a waste of wild vines said to be 'the grape of Eshcol', bitter as gall; the spiny brambles are thick with ruby berries; and high in the contorted trees nest crimson-crested serpents. Wherever one looks there are fireflies:

> And the fireflies fly round the edge of the forests all the night long; you wade in fireflies, they make the fields look like a lake trembling with reflections of stars; but you must take care not to touch them, for they are not like Italian fireflies, but burn, like real sparks. [18.214 ff]

At the end of this infernal valley—the Earthly Paradise inverted and run wild—one approaches the throne of its king, Mammon, on whose canopy in fiery letters is written *Pape Satan, Pape Satan Aleppe* (18.215).

The Old Lecturer who recites this tale—clearly Ruskin surrounded by the girls of Winnington School, raptly listening—refuses to unpack his own allegory, saying, 'I hate explaining myself.' But then he adds:

> You girls ought to be little fireflies yourselves, and find your way in twilight by your own wits.
> But you said they burned, you know?
> Yes; and you may be fireflies that way too, some of you, before long, though I did not mean that . . . You can scarcely guess that I meant them for the light, unpursued vanities, which yet blind us, confused among the stars. One evening, as I came late into Siena, the fire-flies were flying high on a stormy sirocco wind,—the stars themselves no brighter, and all their host seeming at moments, to fade as the insects faded! [18.368]

As self-explanation this is less than convincing, as the Old Lecturer suggests. In the slightly deprecatory tone ('You can scarcely guess . . .') Ruskin appears to disavow his own early interpretation of the fireflies as images of his own lost illusions, all those fitfully glimmering 'false fires' and 'phosphor lights' one finds everywhere in the early poetry and prose.[7] In the youthful drama *Marcolini*, for instance:

> Is it then come to such a pass with me
> That this undying hope, this dreamy thing
> That flickers in a quick and changing fire
> Like to a crown about the brow of madness—
> That fixes its far gaze on throne and clouds,
> And fills the night of misery with stars
> Of thought, which mock with their cold quivering
> Of light unreachable . . .
>   I do love that hope—
> As I have loved the beautiful in death . . .   [1.505]

The youthful fireflies are simply *ignes fatui*, the traditional images of vanished hopes, cherished illusions. The Old Lecturer dismisses these youthful illusions and nostalgia for unlived life, writing off with something like distaste the 'fatuous fires' and 'sputtering illusions' by whose feeble light he had once walked.[8] Old associations are stripped away, and the essential details—twilight, stars, storm cloud, the thick-set background of cypress, ilex or vine—are inflected afresh, at a deeper level, saturated with new experience. In *The Ethics of the Dust* we witness the saturation taking place; the fireflies are now saturated with Rose La Touche (the firefly as unattainable love, a love that *burns*) and also Dante, to whose Inferno, human and cultural, Ruskin now sees himself condemned. But there is also a hint of pride in the thought that the damned must find their own way, glow by the inward light of their own courage and mother-wit, in a dark world. Dryden's famous lines (which Ruskin may be echoing here) come pat to the point:

> My thoughtless youth was wing'd with vain desires,
> My manhood, long misled by wandring fires,
> Follow'd false lights; and when their glimps was gone,
> My pride struck out new sparkles of her own.
> Such was I, such by nature still I am,
> Be thine the glory, and be mine the shame.[9]

It is important to stress the ambivalence which Ruskin, like Dryden, implies. The 'shame' is mixed with a 'glory' in these 'new sparkles' struck by pride—the pride of courageous selfhood.

In the overtly Dantesque setting of Ruskin's fable, the fireflies which, unlike Italian fireflies, 'burn, like real sparks' are immediately identifiable as the flakes of fire falling on the sinners in hell:

> Sovra tutto 'l sabbion, d'un cader lento
>   piovean di foco dilatate falde,
>   come di neve in alpe sanza vento . . .

tale scendeva l'etternale ardore;
  onde la rena s'accendea, com' esca
  sotto focile, a doppiar lo dolore.

Sanza riposo mai era la tresca
  de le misere mani, or quindi or quinci
  escotendo da sé l'arsura fresca . . .   [*Inf.* 14, 28 ff.]

Per li occhi fora scoppiava lor duolo;
  di qua, di là soccorrien con le mani
  quando a' vapori, e quando al caldo suolo:

non altrimenti fan di state i cani
  or col ceffo or col piè, quando son morsi
  o da pulci o da mosche o da tafani.   [*Inf.* 17, 43–51]

Over all the sand huge flakes of fire were falling slowly, like snow in the
mountains without a wind . . . so did the eternal burning descend there,
and the sand was kindled by it like tinder under the flint, to redouble
the pain. The dance of the wretched hands was ever without repose,
now here, now there, as they beat off the fresh burning . . . Their grief
was bursting forth through their eyes; with their hands they defended
themselves, now here, now there, sometimes from the flames, some-
sometimes from the burning ground; not other wise do the dogs in
summer, now with muzzle, now with paw, when they are bitten by
fleas, or flies, or gadflies. [*Trans. Singleton*]

The fire-bitten sinners of Canto 17 are of course Dante's usurers,
their pouches tied around their necks. And Ruskin naturally
annexes the figure in the service of his own anti-industrial allegory
of Mammon's ruined world. Through economic avarice and usury,
industrial greed and natural impiety the Earthly Paradise has been
transformed into the polluted wasteland of the Fall, wild with thorn,
thistle and serpent, whose rivers run with the blood of wounded
Nature and Man, and whose true Lucifer is Mammon. The gospel
task of redeeming this hellish waste, purifying the polluted rivers of
Paradise, and waging war against thorn and serpent, is unmistakably the great, all-absorbing prophetic mission of Ruskin's later
years—the source from which sprang all those furious jeremiads
against spoilers and vandals (restorers!) of Europe's cities; which
fuels the tirades of *Fors Clavigera* and the frantic energies devoted to
the Guild of St George; and which, in *Sesame and Lilies*, with
gentle sternness, reproves English womanhood for its religious
indolence and, raising the banner of justification through works,
adjures women to stir themselves, to work with *their own hands*. It is
their duty, their birthright even, he tells the girls of Winnington, to
become *fireflies*: to walk through the darkness by their own inner
light ('Let your light so shine . . .') until they become, like Dante's
poetic tongue, individual sparks of God's glory, transfigured
fireflies:

ch'una favilla sol de la tua gloria[10]

All this, looming and inchoate, lies within the penumbra of Ruskin's efforts to explain—or rather to *suggest* what he cannot yet, or will not, explain—his metaphor here. But the image is personal as well as cultural and economic; in the figure of the firefly who burns he is alluding, delicately but clearly, to Rose La Touche and his own burning pain. Ruskin's Inferno is the public hell of a world ruled by Mammon, and the private hell of his love for Rose. *Above*, she is, like Beatrice, one with 'the Love that moves the stars', a part of Dante's divine Rose. *Below*, she is a flake of falling fire, she *burns*; she is spine and thorn, she *hurts*. These years were, for Ruskin, years of despair and, often intense bitterness; the feeling of having wasted his youth becomes increasingly strong; and his tragic love for Rose coincides with his rejection of his youthful religion. As his world darkens, the image of the firefly changes from celestial to infernal, from *ignis fatuus* to an image of fleetingly incandescent mortality. The cypresses, ilexes and olives become a funereal backdrop[11]—the *selva oscura* of his, and human, life, against which the firefly flickers like felt pain, a hurt that is no longer simply literary. The pain is, if anything, intensified by contrast with the paradisal memories of the past—the sign of something celestial making its brief epiphany in the world below. The firefly season brings with it the sadness and ecstasy of memory, and the ecstasy intensifies the torture, as with Dante's Francesca:

> Nessun maggior dolore
> che ricordarsi del tempo felice
> ne la miseria.[12]

In Ruskin's hell the task is to cope with the darkness, in him and around him; to find within himself the light he needs to make his way out. In short, to strike his own spark and generate his own light; to become autonomous firefly. This at any rate is exactly how he seems to have thought of the matter. In 1875, several months after Rose's death, Ruskin tried via spiritualist seances to make contact with her:

> Heard from Mrs. Ackworth, in the drawing room where I was once so happy, the most overwhelming evidence of the other state of the world that has ever come to me; and am this morning like a flint stone changed into a firefly, and ordered to flutter about—in a bramble thicket.
> [D.876, 14 December 1875]

The imagination, brooding on its material and searching associations, now with the joy of recognition annexes the *flint* (cf. Dante, *Inf.* 14, 39) from which the firefly's proud 'new sparkles' will be struck. Ruskin's joy—I paraphrase the passage—transforms him from unfeeling flint into ecstatic, illuminated firefly; which passes in turn, after the revealing dash, into the old feeling of being lost among the brambles (all that's left him of his Rose—Ruskin's own metaphor) of the familiar 'dark wood'.

Yet, as Ruskin certainly knew, that 'dark wood' is, in Dantesque terms, simply the 'sign' of 'the other state of the world'—the sacred grove of the Earthly Paradise, and the invisible Paradise beyond. Hell and the world are sown with 'signs' pointing beyond themselves, towards their own transfiguration in a higher anagogical realm. Demons point to angels, torture to joy, thirst to its slaking, flint to fire. Ruskin's own passion for geology would have supplied the idea of *silex scintillans*,[13] the flint-born spark. At any rate, the idea of the flint gestates and breeds; before long we find him writing:

> the aspect of my life to its outward beholder is of an extremely desultory force—at its best—confusedly iridescent—unexpectedly and wanderingly sparkling or extinct like a ragged bit of tinder. Only by much attention—if any one cares to give it . . . could the spectator of me at all imagine what an obstinate little black powder of adamant the faltering sparks glowed through the grain of. [35.608-9]

Accretion on accretion, the image complicates.

If Ruskin now stresses not the unfeeling flint but the adamantine toughness of it, it means that he has found in himself the self-reliance he commended to the girls of Winnington when he told them to become fireflies and find their way by the light of their own wits. *The Ethics of the Dust* is an unabashed moral geology, Ruskin's sermons in stones and primer of the 'crystal virtues'. *Deucalion*, written in July 1875, just after Rose's death, is a far darker book in the same moral vein. In a chapter revealingly titled 'The Iris of the Earth' he discourses on the quality and virtue of flint:

> It is made of brown stuff called silicon, and oxygen, and a little iron; and so any apothecary can tell what you all . . . are made of:—you, and I, and all of us, are made of carbon, nitrogen, lime, and phosphorus, and seventy per cent or rather more of water; but then, that doesn't tell us what we are . . . And so, in knowing only what it is made of, we don't know what a flint is.
>
> To know what it is, we must know what it can do, and *suffer*.
>
> That it can strike *steel into white-hot fire*, but can itself be *melted down like water, if mixed with ashes*; that it is subject to laws of form . . . that *in the fulfilment of these it becomes pure,—in rebellion against them, foul and base*; that it is appointed on our island coast to *endure* for countless ages, fortifying the sea cliff; and on the brow of that very cliff, every spring, *to be dissolved*, that the green blades of corn may drink with the dew;—that *in its noblest forms* it is *still imperfect*, and *in the meanest, still honorable*,—this, if we have rightly learned, we begin to know what a flint is.[26.167-8]

In the italicised words (my emphases) I mean to suggest the general lines of Ruskin's sub-text, the way in which his imagination confronts his own (and human) suffering and the fact of death, his own sense of 'flinty' human nature. The crucial point is the ambivalence of this 'flinty virtue': adamantine in endurance and courage, in grief vulnerably soft; lowly, yet capable of celestial fire and 'immortal longings'; capable too of radical self-transformation, the highest formal law of its being which, being evinced, becomes (as in the great design of Sophocles' *Oedipus at Colonus*[14]) the life and meaning —intermittently firelit—of the earth itself. Implicit in the figure of flint lies the pattern and hope of recreating the earthly paradise. As always, Ruskin is *teaching*. Teaching himself to become himself, to accept his nature but also purify it, with the hope, through his own self-taught example, of teaching others. As he changes, the obsessive image of the firefly changes, becoming more and more subject to the shaping, controlling imagination, less and less obsessive.

We *see* it happening. Before Rose's death Ruskin wrote to a mutual friend that Rose, in her treatment of him, had *not* acted like a flint:

> Alas, if only she did behave like a flint! My flints *comfort* me. When I've said all that's in my mind against religion generally, I shall settle myself quietly to write the 'history of flint' [here is the germ of what became *Deucalion*]—long intended,—headed by the species, 'Achates Rosacea'—I gave her such a pretty piece of rose-quartz ages ago— little thinking . . . when I told her laughing—it was a type of her (which made her very angry, *then*) that she would ever say so with her own lips.[15]

Ruskin means that Rose is quartz because she is hard and beautiful; she *glitters*, but persistently, not intermittently and humanly, like a struck flint. She is all crystal, blazing with the love of God and hence unresponsive to her human lover (who loved God in *her*[16] and later complained to a friend (37.117), 'I wanted my Rosie *here*. In heaven I mean to go and talk to Pythagoras and Socrates . . . What will grey eyes and red cheeks be good for *there*?'). Hence his desire to speak his mind 'against religion' generally, which had robbed him of Rosie.

The final 'firefly' passage is the most renowned, the famous closing words of *Praeterita*, his last and best book. The passage—the matrix from which the final image, under intensely converging pressures conveyed by apparently randomly linked associations and happy memories—deserves to be cited entire:

> I draw back to my own home, twenty years ago, permitted to thank Heaven once more for the peace, and hope, and loveliness of it, and the Elysian walks with Joanie, and Paradisiacal with Rosie, under the

peach-blossom branches by the little glittering stream which I had paved with crystal for them. I had built behind the highest cluster of laurels a reservoir, from which, on sunny afternoons, I could let a quite rippling film of water run for a couple of hours down behind the hayfield, where the grass in spring still grew fresh and deep. There used to be always a corncrake or two in it. Twilight after twilight I have hunted that bird, and never once got a glimpse of it: the voice was always at the other side of the field, or in the inscrutable air or earth. And the little stream had its falls, and pools, and imaginary lakes. Here and there it lost itself under beads of chalcedony. It wasn't the Liffey, nor the Nith, nor the Wandel, but the two girls were surely a little cruel to call it 'The Gutter'! Happiest times, for all of us, that ever were to be; not but that Joanie and her Arthur are giddy enough, both of them yet, with their five little ones, but they have been sorely anxious about me, and I have been sorrowful enough for myself, since ever I lost sight of that peach-blossom avenue. 'Eden-land' Rosie calls it sometimes in her letters. Whether its tiny river were of the waters of Abana, or Euphrates, or Thamesis, I know not, but they were sweeter to my thirst than the fountains of Trevi or Branda.

How things bind and blend themselves together! The last time I saw the fountain of Trevi, it was from Arthur's father's room—Joseph Severn's, where we both took Joanie to see him in 1872, and the old man made a sweet drawing of his sweet daughter-in-law, now in her schoolroom; he himself then eager in finishing his last picture of the marriage in Cana, which he had caused to take place under a vine trellis, and delighted himself by painting the crystal and ruby glittering of the changing rivulet of water out of the Greek vase, glowing into wine. Fonte Branda I last saw with Charles Norton, under the same arches where Dante saw it. We drank of it together, and walked together that evening on the hills above, where the fireflies among the scented thickets shone fitfully in the still undarkened air. *How* they shone! moving like fine-broken starlight through the purple leaves. How they shone! through the sunset that faded into thunderous night as I entered Siena three days before, the white edges of the mountainous clouds still lighted from the west, and the openly golden sky calm behind the Gate of Siena's heart, with its still golden words, 'Cor magis tibi pandit,' and the fireflies everywhere in sky and cloud rising and falling, mixed with the lightning, and more intense than the stars. [35.560–2]

How things bind and blend themselves together! [17] The intricacy of the binding here, whether these concinnities are deliberate or the work of 'dream-gifted' association in a mind nearing madness, is close to miraculous. Ruskin's *things* ('How *things* bind and blend...') suggests that here *things*—active memories—*are* in control; that the narrator's mind is merely a chain on which these memories thread themselves and collect, imposing their own apparently adventitious unity on the musing mind whose past they casually glean. This may be artifice, of course, a narrative strategy for this most improbable of autobiographies. But this seems unlikely. Ruskin rather seems—or wants to seem—resigned to writing according to the concerted rush of things crowding into his mind, speaking through him as their chosen vessel. At least, this is the effect: obsessive themes, images, memories appear to lift into a new life of their own, twining uncontrollably into an autonomous new whole, with a texture of its own making.

Memory laps into memory; they coalesce, expand, annex another memory or image. We get, as it were, a montage of paradisal rivers and waters, all converging into a single celestial Rhone.[18] From Nith to Wandel we move with the rememberer to the putative rivers of Ruskin's Eden-land, sweeter to the parched throat than the fountains of Trevi or Branda. Thoughts of the giddy Severns recall the older Severn in his room, overlooking the Fontana di Trevi, with its Baroque river gods and splashing waters, all liquid life and exuberance—living water in the city of the dead.[19] This in turn recalls Severn's 'Marriage in Cana', the sculptured scene set beneath the vine trellis (those 'purple leaves' of the firefly passages, the thick-set hedge of shade, olive, ilex, cypress or bramble), and *showing forth*, in its own artistic miracle, the natural miracle of water becoming wine, the miracle happening *now*. *Now*—this is the effect of Ruskin's verbs—'the *changing* rivulet of water out of the Greek vase *glowing* into wine'; we note the way in which the present participles indicate the intensity of a continuous present, the happening now of things of the past, miraculously quickened. Fontana di Trevi melts into Fonte Branda (associated in Ruskin's mind with Fonte Gaia), recalling happy days spent with his friend Charles Eliot Norton—and then Norton, via a footnote, multiplying into five other friends, other associated memories). But Fonte Branda also recalls Dante's Tuscany and the events associated by Dante with Fonte Branda—the story of the famous forger of the *Inferno*, Maestro Adamo. Ruskin's narrative guides, and is in turn guided by, the Dantesque association. Ruskin and Norton, their thirst quenched, walk uphill, back to the sources in the hills of Casentino where the waters of Fonte Branda begin as brooks. Fusing in memory with these brooks are the paradisal streams and waters of Ruskin's childhood life and later:

> ... the Tay, Erne, and Wandel, as early familiar rivers—Loch Leven and Queen's Ferry, Derwent Water and Coniston Water . . . and later . . . Matlock and Bristol . . . the open sea beach at Sandgate . . . [35.609]

In this way Ruskin's lost paradise—the Eden-land he spent his life trying to reconstruct and rescue from pollution, even to the 'little glittering stream' where he walked with Rosie and Joan—glancingly attaches Maestro Adamo's situation in the polluted ditch. The result is greater depth and dimension, a pathos that is no longer purely private. The whole Dante episode crowds into Ruskin's memory, and then, by means of further associations, carries him forward to the final image of the fireflies, itself profoundly saturated in Dante, as we shall see.

But here, first, is Master Adam:

> O voi che sanz' alcuna pena siete,
>   e non so io perché, nel mondo gramo,'
>   diss' elli a noi, 'guardate e attendete
>
> a la miseria del maestro Adamo;
>   io ebbi, vivi, assai di quel ch'i volli,
>   e ora, lasso!, un gocciol d'acqua bramo.
>
> Li ruscelletti che d'i verdi colli
>   del Casentin discendon giuso nel Arno,
>   faccendo i lor canali freddi e molli,
>
> sempre me stanno innanzi, e non indarno,
>   ché l'imagine lor vie più m'asciuga
>   che 'l male ond'io nel volto mi discarno.
>
> La rigida giustizia che mi fruga
>   tragge cagion del loco ov'io peccai
>   a metter più li miei sospiri in fuga.
>
> Ivi è Romena, là dov'io falsai
>   la lega suggellata del Batista;
>   per ch'io il corpo sù arso lasciai.
>
> Ma s'io vedessi qui l'anima trista
>   di Giudo o d'Alessandro o di lor frate,
>   per Fonte Branda non darei la vista . . .'

[*Inf.* 30, 58–78]

'Oh, you who are without any punishment, and I know not why, in this dismal world,' he said to us, 'behold and consider the misery of Master Adam. Living, I had in plenty all that I wished, and now, alas! I crave one drop of water! The little brooks that from the green hills of Casentino run down into the Arno, making their channels cool and moist, are always before me, and not in vain, for the image of them parches me far more than the malady that wastes my features. The rigid justice that scourges me draws occasion from the place where I sinned, to give my sighs a quicker flight; there is Romena, where I falsified the currency stamped with the Baptist, for which on earth I left my body burnt. But if I could see here the miserable soul of Guido or of Alessandro or of their brother, I would not give the sight for Fonte Branda.' [*Trans. Singleton*]

A few lines later, Master Adam is reviled by his fellow sinner, Sinon the Greek, and cursed with the curse most appropriate to the sinner who, born among pure streams, had, by defacing the coinage stamped with the Baptist, desecrated 'the water of life':

'E te sia rea la sete onde ti crepa,'
   disse 'l Greco, 'la lingua, e l'acqua marcia
   che 'l ventre innanzi a li occhi si t'assiepa!'

                         [*Inf.* 30, 121–3]

'And to you be torture the thirst that cracks your tongue,' said the Greek, 'and the foul water that makes your belly thus a hedge before your eyes.'

That Ruskin perceived himself in these Dantesque terms, and here and elsewhere has Master Adam constantly in mind, there can be no doubt.[20] Again and again the aging Ruskin sets himself among Dante's damned or living dead, those who, like Sordello, have never lived at all; a man who has for ever lost the light and the living water. He stands instead in Master Adam's *acqua marcia*, or among the sinners on whom the rain of fire-flakes descends. *There* he remembers the unpolluted streams of his childhood, the radiance and purity of Mont Blanc, and the forbidden fruit of his Herne Hill Eden:

[a garden] . . . possessing also a strong old mulberry tree, a tall white-heart cherry tree, a black Kentish one, and an almost unbroken hedge, all round, of alternate gooseberry and currant bush; decked, in due season . . . with magical splendour of abundant fruit: fresh green, soft amber, and rough-bristled crimson bending the spinous branches; clustered pearl and pendant ruby joyfully discoverable under the large leaves that looked like vine.
    The differences of primal importance which I observed between the nature of this garden, and that of Eden . . . were that, in this one, *all* the fruit was forbidden . . . [35.36]

Behind Ruskin stands Dante's Master Adam, and, behind both, fallen Adam himself. In 1867 he wrote to Norton:

Dante's *Vita Nuova* falls in much with my own mind—but, when death or life depends on such things, suppose it should be *morte nuova* day by day. [36.545]

But, until the last years, *morte nuova* always. On one of his final trips to Venice, looking out on the polluted canals of 'the world's most splendid city', he wrote:

. . . This green tide that eddies by my threshold is full of floating corpses, and I must leave my dinner to bury them, since I cannot save . . . This green sea-tide!—yes, and if you knew it, your black and sulphurous tides also—Yarrow and Teviot and Clyde, and the stream, for ever now drumly and dark as it rolls on its way, at the ford of Melrose. Yes, and the fair lakes and running waters in your English park pleasure-grounds—nay, also the great and wide sea, that gnaws your cliffs—yes, and Death and Hell also, more cruel than cliff or sea. [28.77–8]

As for his paradisal Alps ('the seen walls of Lost Eden could not have been more beautiful to us . . .'), they were gone for ever. The late Ruskin is full of the melancholy, sometimes the rhetoric but often the rage, of *ubi sunt*. At times his sadness is little more than liverishly brilliant elegy or jeremiad; at others it reaches greatness, as in his 1882 letter to Charles Eliot Norton:

> . . . I couldn't draw the ridge, and there was no Mont Blanc, any more than there was any you; for indeed the Mont Blanc *we* knew is no more. All the snows are wasted, the lower rocks bare, the luxuriance of light, the plenitude of power, the Eternity of Being, are all gone from it—even the purity—for the wasted and thawing snow is grey in comparison to the fresh-frosted wreaths of new-fallen cloud which we saw in the morning light—how many mornings ago? [27.408]

It is this experience of a shared paradise, taken for granted in youth (as Paradise usually is), followed by expulsion into lonely damnation—and perhaps this very letter to Norton—that Ruskin is recalling in the final paragraphs of *Praeterita*. With Norton he shared a consuming passion for Dante; together they had shared Dante's Tuscany, and in Siena drunk of Fonte Branda together. This memory of former happiness shared and lost is intensified in the perspective of Master Adam, alone in the 'stinking water', burning with thirst as though enveloped in fire, remembering.

The perspective is anything but bookish. Ruskin's personal experience actively attaches the literary text passively acquired in earlier years; Dante's vision informs his experience. If the early Ruskin was *par excellence* the observer, the late Ruskin is the prophet of committed action, *himself* committed to action, working frantically against time, always reminding himself, 'I must work the works of him that sent me, while it is day: the night cometh, when no man can work.'[21] All his innumerable projects—rescuing threatened buildings, rooting out thistle wastes, saving the Rhone, ditching swamps and rebuilding roads, cleansing polluted springs and streams, restoring to the routine-numbed worker of industrial England the true craftsman's joy in his work, resurrecting the old crafts and the craftsman's virtue, redeeming the selfish economics which had contaminated the 'waters of life'—all these projects, however unpractical or grandiose, were his conscious effort to recreate the Earthly Paradise. The virtues they required were not primarily intellectual or literary, but rather the moral virtues he had praised in flint: endurance, the capacity to strike sparks from one's own inward nature, humility, kindness and compassion, patience. They also required—what has been too seldom noticed in the late Ruskin's strangely Nestorian Christianity—a sympathy with the earth, with one's own animal nature and powers. His symbol for this is St Theodore of Venice, standing on his crocodile, 'the human spirit in true conquest over the inhuman, *because in true sympathy with it . . .* being strengthened and pedestalled by the 'Dragons and all Deeps''. 'The animal gods of Egypt and Assyria', he proceeds darkly but grandly, 'the animal cry that there is *no* God, of the passing hour, are, both of them, parts of the rudiments of the religion yet to be revealed . . .' (24.303). This was the Ruskin who wanted his Rosie '*here*', and who, in his last years, worked so hard to reform *himself* as the first step in persuading others to recreate the Garden.

It was too late, of course, and Ruskin knew it. But *Praeterita* deserves to be read as something more than nostalgia, a commemoration of 'golden times'. It is that, but it is also paradisal autobiography—a life revised backwards in order to create, through Imagination Penetrative, what the hands could no longer accomplish. *Praeterita* shows us how Ruskin—having never lived at all, or having started too late—*might* have lived, *could* have lived, had he only known how, known earlier. There are few sadder or more revealing reflections on his own life than these:

> nothing prevails finally but a steady, worldly-wise labour—comfortable—resolute—fearless—full of animal life—affectionate—compassionate. I think I see how one ought to live, now, but my own life is lost, gone by. I looked for another world, and find there is only this, and that is past for me: what message I have given is all wrong: has to be all resaid, in another way, and is, so said, almost too terrible to be serviceable. For the present, I am dead-silent. [36.381]

The dead silence was broken by *Praeterita*, his last effort to renew, in a wholly new way, his prophetic ministry by putting to fullest verbal use just those flinty virtues he praises as alone prevailing. These virtues, in others but also implicitly in himself, are what *Praeterita* is so beautifully and compellingly about. In short, a book of deliberate preterition: a disregarding of matters best forgotten or not worth remembering; or a memorial of important matters wrongly neglected in the writer's earlier years. The struck flint strikes new sparks; and these sparks—luminous, iridescent natures shining bravely and fitfully against the leaves of this world, *selva oscura* or darkening Garden as the case may be—are the fireflies the book remembers. But that commemoration is itself a deliberate *act*. The writer rewrites himself by conscious preterition, according to his own 'lights', and, by so doing, brightens the darkness himself.

Ruskin's language, when he speaks of the paradisal loveliness of the unpolluted world he once knew, is so powerful that there is real danger of forgetting that this power, at least in the late works, is intended to effect reform. The prose is missionary, but what gives it special urgency is his own involvement in practical (or unpractical) reform. The preacher's text has been blooded by *praxis*; and the text takes on a fresh power and concentration of energy. In the earlier Ruskin the language, for all its splendour, is finally that of the pulpit, of the vicarious observer. The astonishing power of the late prose— *Fors Clavigera, Praeterita*, the letters, *The Bible of Amiens*, parts of *Deucalion* and *St Mark's Rest*—has its source in Ruskin's experience of the depths, in despair and pain, but above all in his efforts to re- make himself, to practise what he preached. The reader who sees in the allusion to Dante's Master Adam in his dirty ditch, thirsting for the living water of Fonte Branda, only literary embellishment misses the whole point. Misses the point that the allusion is govern- ed not by passive or 'dream-gifted' association but by selective memory, itself galvanised by purposive action. The association has been actualised, is so saturated in ways of feeling, seeing and acting that it is one thing with them. It is 'second nature'.

As in this remarkable passage with which *The Crown of Wild Olive* (1873) begins:

Twenty years ago, there was no lovelier piece of lowland scenery in South England, nor any more pathetic, in the world, by its expression of sweet human character and life, than that immediately bordering on the sources of the Wandel, and including the low moors of Aldington, and the villages of Beddington and Carshalton, with all their pools and streams . . . The place remains (1870) nearly unchanged in its larger features; but with deliberate mind I say, that I have never seen any- thing so ghastly in its inner tragic meaning,—not in Pisan Maremma, —not by Campagna tomb—not by the Torcellan shore,—as the slow stealing of aspects of reckless, indolent, animal neglect, over the delicate sweetness of that English scene . . . Just where the welling of stainless water, trembling and pure, like a body of light, enters the pool of Carshalton, cutting itself a radiant channel down to the gravel, through warp of feathery weeds, all waving, which it traverses with its deep thread of clearness, like the chalcedony in moss-agate, starred here and there with the white grenouillette; just in the very rush and murmur of the first spreading currents, the human wretches of the place cast their street and house foulness; heaps of dust and slime, and broken shreds of old metal, and rags of putrid clothes; which, having neither energy to cart away, nor decency to dig into the ground, they thus shed into the stream, to diffuse what venom of it will float and melt, far away, in all places where God meant those waters to bring joy and health. And, in a little pool behind some houses farther in the village, where another spring rises, the shattered stones of the well, and of the little fretted channel which was long ago built and traced for it by gentler hands, lie scattered, each from each, under a ragged bank of mortar, and scoria, and bricklayer's refuse, on one side, which the clean water nevertheless chastises to purity; but it cannot conquer the dead earth beyond: and there, circled and coiled under festering scum, the stagnant edge of the pool effaces itself into a slope of black slime, the accumulation of indolent years. Half-a-dozen men, with one day's work, could cleanse those pools, and trim the flowers about their banks, and make every glittering wave medicinal, as if it ran, troubled only of angels, from the porch of Bethesda. But that day's work is never given . . . [18.2–4]

The art critic's narratively graphic eye recreates as it moves over the scene the unfolding reality of paradisal river in pollution, its frustrated efforts to recreate its purity, to cleanse itself. The prose is especially passionate because it is Ruskin's own childhood Paradise, the springs of Wandel at Carshalton, that are at stake. Disgust and anger jostle memory—memory outraged. Beneath the rising gorge of his anger, we can sense the implied challenge to himself ('one day's work . . . could cleanse those pools . . . But that day's work is never given') and the gathering determination to act. And act he did. In homage to his mother Ruskin repeatedly cleaned the springs and trimmed the weeds of 'Margaret's Well' at Carshalton.[22]

As for art and art history, it led, inevitably, to the same effort to 'purify the sources' and halt the pollution—economic, industrial, moral—that had contaminated the 'waters of life':

> The beginning of art is *in getting our country clean* . . . How can the artist paint a blue sky, if he cannot see the sky because of the smoke, or how can he paint the harbour at Folkestone, if the harbour is polluted? [27.159]

> I have . . . spoken of the flowing of streams . . . as a partial image of the action of wealth . . . The popular economist . . . declares that the course of demand and supply cannot be forbidden by human laws. Precisely in the same sense . . . the waters of the world go where they are required. But . . . whether the streams shall be a cure or a blessing, depends upon man's labour, and administering intelligence . . . The stream which, rightly directed, would have flowed in soft irrigation from field to field—would have purified the air, given food to man and beast—now overwhelms the plain and poisons the wind; its breath pestilence and its work famine. No human laws can withstand its flow. They can only guide it: but this, the leading trench and limiting mound can do so thoroughly, that it shall become water of life . . . or, by leaving it to its own lawless flow, they may make it . . . water of Marah —the water which feeds the roots of all evil. [17.60–1]

It is because Ruskin is engaged by the actual meanings of his own metaphors, whether economic or artistic or broadly cultural; because he insists upon living his text, purifying it by action, that his late prose achieves a power and energy and clarity that distinguish it from the earlier work.

Having drunk of Fonte Branda, Norton and Ruskin left Siena and 'walked on the hills above'. The text of Dante has been so internalis- ed, is so much a part of Ruskin's mind that he can suppress precisely the one element—the story of Master Adam—which links Fonte Branda with the stroll in the Tuscan hills. The suppressed detail controls the narrative sequence; but it can do this only because it has already been absorbed by his life.

The point is central. Ruskin's intense bookishness in early life meant that for him literature, the great got-by-heart texts of his childhood—the Bible he read daily with his mother;[23] Shakespeare; Scott; and, later, Dante—acquired the authority of real experience, the intensity of unlived life. As Eliot acutely observed, 'One feels that the emotional intensity of Ruskin is partly a deflection of some- thing that was baffled in life.'[24] Track Ruskin as far as you can, and you will almost always come upon a text from one of his major sources, or several overlapping and recombined texts, capable of combining in new ways as experience demands. And this is especi- ally the case with a mind like that of the youthful Ruskin, with scant knowledge of the world, an over-protected, imaginative boy of astonishing observational energy, prodigious memory and, not least, a desperate and hardly recognised emotional need.

Ruskin's mode of thinking is clearly complex. But the essential component is association. Typically, an observation roots itself, for enhancement of emotional force or generalising power, in an earlier text, preferably a classic, of apposite form and/or meaning. This text is often concealed. Not for deceptive reasons, to deny an influence, but because the writer is unaware of the associations—I speak of the *early* Ruskin—by which he is guided. He may control the text im- perfectly; or he may simply fail to realise that the text has him in its grip; or because, as with the Master Adam passage, he has made the text so thoroughly his own that he can no longer tell the difference between it and his own thought. The dangers of unawareness are obviously compounded when the critical text is one which, at an early age, has been committed to memory—the deeper kind of memory which, in music and rhythm, lies *below* the meaning. Such texts govern us more deeply perhaps than those whose meanings we consciously acquire; uncritically acquired, they often assert an authority out of all proportion to their meaning. Ruskin insists, of course, that his Bible was critically acquired. Even so, his acquisition at a very early age of the Bible whole, most of Shakespeare, much of Scott, provided him with an enormous storehouse whose complex textual meanings he could have mastered only *after* committing them to memory. The text, so committed, then returns in later years to inform and, unless the writer is very vigilant, to guide, influence, shape, even control the diction, rhythm and sense of his own 'con-

scious' thought. Elevate this influence or authority of the remembered text to the level of a principle, and you authorise a certain passiv-
ity before tradition. For the remembered, the got-by-heart, text is
always the traditional text; why otherwise memorise it in childhood?
What this means in practice is that the writer who consciously
assents to the tradition he has uncritically acquired consents to what
may be real confusion or unrecognised multiplicity of purpose. He
is, let us assume, intellectually his own man; yet, given the shaping
of ear and tongue and even mind in his formative years, he may
become the unwitting vehicle of all those potent ghosts still active in
him or the acquired tradition. If he believes on theory that the writer
is a kind of vessel or voice for all these ghosts, and if his own experience is limited, he may not always know whose hand is guiding his
pen, or to what purpose.

His account of Turner's mode of painting is perhaps the most
accurate account of Ruskin's own way of thinking and writing, at
least for much of his working life. Turner's composition, he asserts,
may in fact not be composition at all but *an arrangement of associated
memories*:

> It is this very character which appears to me to mark it as so distinctly
> an act of dream-vision; for in a dream there is just this kind of con-
> fused remembrance of the form of things which we have seen long ago,
> associated by new and strange laws ... whenever Turner really tried to
> *compose*, and made modifications of his subjects on principle, he did
> wrong, and spoiled them; and that he only did right in a kind of passive
> obedience to his first vision, that vision being composed primarily of
> the strong memory of the place itself he had to draw; and secondarily
> of memories of other places ... with all great inventors I know not, but
> with all those whom I have carefully studied (Dante, Scott, Turner,
> and Tintoret) it seems to me to hold absolutely; their imagination
> consisting, not in a voluntary production of new images, but an
> involuntary remembrance, exactly at the right moment, of something
> they had actually seen.
>
> Imagine all that any of these men had seen or heard in the whole
> course of their lives, laid up accurately in their memories as in vast
> storehouses, extending, with the poets, even to the slightest inton-
> ations of syllables heard in the beginning of their lives, and, with the
> painters, down to the minute folds of drapery, and shapes of leaves and
> stones, and over all this unindexed and immeasurable mass of treasure,
> the imagination brooding and wandering, but dream-gifted, so as to
> summon at any moment exactly such groups of ideas as shall justly fit
> each other ... Turner's mind is not more, in my estimation, distin-
> guished above others by its demonstrable arranging and ruling
> faculties than by its demonstrably retentive and submissive faculties;
> and the longer I investigate it, the more this tenderness of perecption
> and grasp of memory seems to me the root of its greatness ... I am
> more and more convinced ... respecting the imagination, that its true
> force lies in its marvellous insight and foresight ... and ... because in

its work, the vanity and individualism of the man himself are crushed, and he becomes a mere instrument or mirror, used by a higher power for the reflection to others of a truth which no effort of his could ever have ascertained. [6.41–4]

Elsewhere in *Modern Painters* Ruskin remarks in a way which vividly anticipates, and perhaps influenced, Eliot's doctrine of poetic 'impersonality':

> The power of the masters is shown by their self-annihilation. It is commensurate with the degree in which they themselves appear not in their work . . . Every great writer may be at once known by his guiding the mind far from himself to the beauty which is not of his own creation, and the knowledge which is past his finding out. [3.23]

In sum, precisely the aesthetic posture of the Ruskin who asserts in *Praeterita*:

> My entire delight was in observing without being myself noticed,—if I could have been invisible, all the better. I was absolutely interested in men and their ways, as I was interested in marmots and chamois, in tomtits and trout. If only they would stay still and let me look at them, and not get into their holes and up their heights! The living inhabitation of the world—the grazing and nesting in it,—the spiritual power of the air, the rocks, the waters, to be in the midst of it, and rejoice and wonder at it, and help it if I could,—happier if it needed no help of mine,—this was the essential love of Nature in me, this the root of all that I have usefully become and the light of all that I have rightly learned. [35.166]

A tender submissiveness of mind as opposed to the governing intellect, with the stress on the involuntary combination of memory and dream; the censure of doctrinal composition and intellectual revision—these precepts tell us a great deal about Ruskin's perception of his own work, as well as the way in which that apparently 'dream-gifted' book *Praeterita* may have been written. Add to this his consistent counsel of humility towards the greatest masters, of making oneself invisible by steeping the mind in the tradition, and we have a set of principles which, despite obvious differences, are those advocated by Eliot in 'Tradition and the Individual Talent'. There too the poet proposes to divest himself of his own personality in order to become the continuing voice of 'the changing mind of Europe'. The past is crowded with ghostly presences who, through his voice, recover life but also quicken him into individual fulfilment; tradition is precisely this living larval inhabitation of the present by the past. The tradition possesses the poet, who, in turn, struggles to master what possesses him—to become the active rather than the passive bearer of his tradition, or at least to balance submission with mastery. What came to Ruskin through daily family readings of the Bible, Shakespeare and Scott was achieved by Eliot only through arduous labour. The difference is felt as a difference in control, as a degree of effort. The traditional text seems at times to possess Ruskin as though he were unaware of the possession, whereas in Eliot the possession smells at times of the lamp.

An example of such 'possession' in Ruskin. In 1875 he wrote to his friend Susan Beever about, among other things, Scott's *Waverley*:

> Do you recollect Gibbie [*sic*][25] Gellatly? I was thinking over that question of yours, 'What did I think of the things that shall be here-after—J. R.?' But my dear Susie, you might as well ask Gibbie Gellatly what *he* thought. What does it matter what any of us think? We are but simpletons, the best of us, and I am a very inconsistent and wayward simpleton. I know how to roast eggs, in the ashes, perhaps—but for the next world! Why don't you ask your squirrel what *he* thinks too? The great point—the one for all of us—is, not to take false words in our mouths, and to crack our nuts innocently through winter and rough weather. [37.158]

The allusion to Davie Gellatly in Scott's *Waverley*, the feeble-minded boy who could at least roast eggs in the ashes, is here abruptly enjambed, with the last words from Amiens's song in *As You Like It*. But look again at the Shakespeare text and the abrupt-ness becomes ellipsis. Amiens's song ended, Jacques says, 'I can suck melancholy out of a song as a weasel sucks eggs.' The weasel turns into Susan Beever's pet squirrel, and Jacques disappears. Not because Ruskin planned it that way, but because his mind associated in this way, with lightning rapidity collapsing the two works to-gether (along with Scott's *Old Mortality*, cf. note 25) and suppress-ing the pivotal term—Jacques and the image of the egg-sucking weasel—in order to conclude on the squirrel's 'steady, worldly-wise' innocence. Ruskin's thought, while concentrated, is simple; it acquires range and power by his talent for finding appropriate 'correlatives' in which to embed itself—though in a clear sense the rote mastery of the tradition is the condition of the talent it 'posses-ses'. The possessed text bides its time, waiting for the precise moment in which to precipitate itself into the imagination of its possessor. But it may also, as with the firefly image, be precipitated by the active imagination of its engaged possessor.

Look back, from this perspective, at the firefly image. Given the quite incredible degree of Ruskin's immersion in Dante[26]—an immersion matched among English writers only by Eliot—it would, I think, have been quite impossible for him, while musing on the spectacle of the fireflies, there in Dante's Tuscany, *not* to have recalled the great metaphor, in Canto 26, of the peasant and the fireflies, who stand for the fire-enveloped sinners. Here is the passage:

> Quante 'l villan ch'al poggio si riposa,
>   nel tempo che colui che 'l mondo schiara
>   la faccia sua a noi tien meno ascosa,
>
> come la mosca cede a la zanzara,
>   vede lucciole giù per la vallea,
>   forse colà dov'e' vendemmia e ara:
>
> di tante fiamme tutta risplendea
>   l'ottava bolgia, sì com'io m'accorsi
>   tosto che fui là 've 'l fondo parea.
>
> E qual colui che si vengiò con li orsi
>   vide 'l carro d'Elia al dipartire,
>   quando i cavalli al cielo erti levorsi,
>
> che nol potea sì con li occhi seguire,
>   ch'el vedesse altro che la fiamma sola,
>   sì come nuvoletta, in sù salire:
>
> tal si move ciascuna per la gola
>   del fosso, ché nessuna mostra 'l furto,
>   e ogne fiamma un peccatore invola.
>
> Io stava sovra 'l ponte a veder surto,
>   sì che s'io non avessi un ronchion preso,
>   caduto sarei giù sanz'esser urto.
>
> E 'l duca, che mi vide tanto atteso,
>   disse: 'Dentro dai fuochi son li spirti;
>   catun si fascia di quel ch'elli è inceso.'

[*Inf.* 26, 25–48]

As many as the fireflies which the peasant, resting on the hill—in the season when he that lights the world least hides his face from us, and at that hour when the fly yields to the mosquito—sees down along the valley, there perhaps where he gathers grapes and tills: with so many flames the eighth ditch was all agleam, as I perceived as soon as I came where the bottom could be seen. And as he who was avenged by the bears saw Elijah's chariot at its departure, when the horses rose erect to heaven—for he could not so follow it with his eyes as to see aught save the flame alone, like a little cloud ascending: so each flame moves along the gullet of the ditch, for not one shows its theft, and each steals away a sinner. I was standing on the bridge, having risen up to see, so that if I had not laid hold of a rock I should have fallen below without a push; and my leader, who saw me so intent, said, 'Within the fires are the spirits; each swathes himself with that which burns him.'

The figure is extremely vivid, above all in the likening of the seamless flame enclosing the sinners with the *ascending* blaze of Elijah's cloud-like chariot. Small wonder that Ruskin, in his own imagination already an inhabitant of the depths, should find the fireflies in *this* perspective 'anything but celestial'. The correspondence between the various firefly passages and the Dantesque image are simply too close to be coincidental; they are Dante-saturated. Detail for detail: hills and/or valley at dusk; the glimpse of the vineyards against whose leaves the fireflies glow; the heat of the summer season; the astonishment of the spectator, *tanto atteso*; and, most important of all, the revelation of the fireflies—beautifully delayed in Dante, the infernal world improbably unfolding from the simple pastoral image—as the flame-enveloped sinners. In Canto 17 the usurers defend themselves from the flakes of falling fire; the image is then intensified, transformed, in the later canto, with the developed image of the sinner-*as*-flame, the firefly itself.

But not all Ruskin's fireflies are infernal or funereal; in the earliest instance, it was 'very heavenly to see them floating, field after field, under the shadowy vines'. And the language of the *Praeterita* passage is clearly designed to avoid all sinister suggestion ('*How* they shone! moving like fine-broken starlight through the purple leaves!'). But how, we may reasonably ask, can the same passage—one spectacle repeatedly re-seen, with modest variation of details but drastic differences of feeling-tone—how can the same image indicate moods so antithetical? Clearly, the viewer's mood changes with experience. Still, the ambivalence remains. In part, because Ruskin's sources are multiple. But also, as Ruskin would have known, the 'sign' in Dante is inherently polyvalent. The *Commedia* is a vast and intricate structure of exact correspondences between the poem's three realms; sign for sign, image for image, the Inferno is anagogically transformed in Purgatory and Paradise. Take, for instance, the passage in the *Paradiso* which clearly corresponds to the image of the firefly or flaming sinner in the *Inferno*. Beatrice describes in Canto 30 (38 ff.) how it is that angelic sparks—glittering angels—rise from, and fall back into, the great river of heavenly light (in which alone the thirsting sinner, like Master Adam, can finally quency his thirst):

> . . . Noi siamo usciti fore
> del maggior corpo al ciel ch'è pura luce:
>
> luce intelletüal, piena d'amore;
>   amor di vero ben, pien di letizia;
>   letizia che trascende ogne dolzore . . .
>
> e vidi lume in forma di rivera
>   fulvido di fulgore, intra due rive
>   dipinte di mirabil primavera.
>
> Di tal fiumana uscian faville vive,
>   e d'ogne parte si mettien ne' fiori,

quasi rubin che oro circunscrive;

poi, come inebrïate da li odori,
   riprofondavan sé nel miro gurge,
   e s'una intrava, un'altra n'uscia fori.

[We have issued forth from the greatest body to the heaven which is
pure light: light intellectual full of love, love of true good full of joy,
joy that transcends every sweetness . . . And I saw a light in form of a
river glowing tawny between two banks painted with marvellous
spring. From out this river issued living sparks and dropped on every
side into the blossoms, like rubies set in gold. Then, as if inebriated by
the odours, they plunged again into the wondrous flood, and as one
was entering, another was issuing forth.]

Beatrice then proceeds to address Dante as one whose desire for the
heights and for heaven has enveloped him in flame and whose thirst
for God can be quenched only in the river of light:

L'alto disio che mo t'infiamma e urge,
   d'aver notizia di cio che tu vei,
   tanto mi piace più quanto più turge;

ma di quest' acqua convien che tu bei
   prima che tanta sete in te si sazi.   [*Par.* 30, 70 ff.]

[The high desire which now inflames and urges you to have knowledge
concerning that which you see please me the more the more it swells;
but first you must needs drink of this water before so great a thirst in
you be slaked.]

Infernal fireflies and Master Adam here fuse anagogically into the
flame-enveloped Dante, himself an angelic spark by virtue of his
poet's tongue (. . . *una favilla sol de la tua gloria*) about to plunge into
the great stream of light from which he came, to quench the thirst
that can be assuaged only in God. That it is *this* image that Ruskin
has, among others, in mind in *Praeterita* seems probable if we simply
set Beatrice's account of the sparks rising and falling back into the
great flood of light against Ruskin's final clause, with its skyscape of
heaven and cloud, 'and the fireflies everywhere . . . rising and falling,
mixed with the lightning, and more intense than the stars'.

Behind Dante, of course, stands the Bible, in which Ruskin's mind
was even more saturated than it was in Dante. Hence it is not surprising that Ruskin's fireflies should have biblical origins also. In the
apocryphal *Wisdom of Solomon* (3:1), for instance, the godly are
compared to sparks in the stubble:

And in the time of their visitation they shall shine and run to and fro
like sparks among the stubble.

Godly and *good* because tested by the fire of suffering. These sparks, in turn, derive from the great image of suffering mankind in Job (5:7): 'Yet man is born unto trouble, as the sparks fly upward.' Ruskin, citing this figure elsewhere, immediately links it with Dante:

> I know that there are many who think the atmosphere of rapine, rebellion, and misery which wraps the lower orders of Europe more closely every day, is as natural a phenomenon as a hot summer. But God forbid! There are ills which flesh is heir to, and troubles to which man is born; but the troubles which he is born to are as sparks which fly *upward*, not as flames burning to the nethermost Hell. [11.261]

The intricate linking of association here—from 'hot summer' to the fireflies seen at Siena, to the *upward*-rising sparks of Job, which are contrasted with the *falling* rain of fire in Canto 17—is wholly typical of Ruskin's metaphorical habits.

Even more impressively remembered, I believe, is the great passage from Isaiah (50:2–3, 10–11), which combines a number of Ruskin's most obsessive themes, from the desecration and pollution of the earth to the Last Judgement, to Jehovah's awful anger with those spiritual leaders who have led their followers astray, preferring their own illumination and refusing God's light—and who are therefore condemned to walk for ever in the light of the fires they have kindled:

> Wherefore, when I came, was there no man? when I called, was there none to answer . . .? Have I no power to deliver? Behold, at my rebuke, I dry up the sea, I make the rivers a wilderness: their fish stinketh, because there is no water, and dieth for thirst.
>
> I clothe the heavens with blackness, and I make sackcloth their covering.
>
> Who is among you that feareth the Lord, that obeyeth the voice of the servant, that walketh in darkness, and hath no light? let him trust in the name of the Lord, and stay upon his God.
>
> Behold, all ye that kindle a fire, that compass yourselves about with sparks: walk in the light of your fire, and in the sparks that ye have kindled. This shall ye have of mind hand: ye shall lie down in sorrow.

Ruskin took his role as prophet seriously, and also his Guild of St George, of which he was founder and spiritual leader. Increasingly he came to feel that he had failed those who had looked to him to lead them out of the wilderness; that he had neither solace nor wisdom to offer. In this mood he wrote to a friend:

> You say, in losing the delight I once had in nature, I am coming down more to fellowship with others. Yes, but I feel it a fellowship of blindness. I may be able to get hold of people's hands better in the dark, but

of what use is that, when I have nowhere to lead them, but into the ditch? [36.83]

The ditch here is Inferno itself, Master Adam's polluted *fosso*; and Dante's fire-cloaked sinners are, in fact, the Evil Counsellors— those who, by unwise advice, had like Ulysses destroyed themselves and those they led. Ruskin too had failed, walking by the sparks he had kindled; but the failed prophet refuses to abandon his own inner light. Determined to strike new sparks from his own flinty nature, he rejects the biblical text while annexing the image. To a young girl he loved he wrote:

> . . . surely your statement of the things that torment me is just as terrible as my own. It is just because I am one of those flakes of chaff who 'with all light and all vision *will* not strive to the ideal set before them'—that I fear the winnowing.[27]

His flinty nature, he knew, was ambivalent. At one moment it was outwardly desultory and unreliably iridescent; but the gleams rose from 'an obstinate little black powder of adamant the faltering sparks glowed through the grain of' (35.609). In love, he said, he was all adamant:

> When I have once loved any creature, I am true to them to the death— theirs or mine—through whatever decay of body or soul . . . *I* change not.[28]

He could praise, but also *be*, the crystal virtues he commended: hard work, dogged courage, loyalty. There was genuine pride and self-knowledge in this. 'Man is born to trouble, as the sparks fly upward.' But *upward*—hellfires no longer—towards the light and the stars which they resembled and, in the *Praeterita* passage, outshone. Pain had ripened him; he knew the darkness now; he could assess with something like pleasure his ability to strike a spark against the cold and the darkness:

> . . . perhaps one use of all that I most mourn, is to fit me to see the darks in things that *are* dark—and of which others forget the existence—in the joy of their own quiet lamp and light of their room by its sufficient love—though all around—without—*is*—the 'outer darkness,' and the cold.[29]

If he was not a *fixed* star, like Shakespeare's Caesar,[30] he could claim nonetheless that his own sparks, no less than those of others— Joanie, Arthur, Rose, etc.—still shone star-like against the dark sky and the gathering storm to the west of Siena. Ruskin knows now where the light rises and sets, and what it means: 'I shall not mistake light in the West for light in the East—now. I know the Evening and the Morning.'[31]

Knowing his nature, its weaknesses and strengths, he could now devote his remaining light and time to the project most fitted to his nature, art and convictions—the effort to recreate here on earth, with whatever light he could strike from his mixed nature, the only paradise to which he thought human nature could practically aspire. He had wanted his Rosie *here*; and his paradise too was here and now—under threat of imminent destruction, but still miraculously *there*, suspended in the precarious present.

This, at any rate, is how Ruskin puts it in one of his most remarkable letters:

> It is impossible for me ever to be as I was in the days of my youth again,—and, believe me, I am better—as I am, for all *I* have to do, *now*. But that is so with many men's lives. They lose the best that was in them, but another good of an opposite kind—equally theirs, takes its place, or may take it if they do their best. Meantime—be as religious as you please—but do not let yourself be lulled into the great heresy of this age—that God will put things right—though He lets little things go wrong—if only we trust in Him. The great things—like the little—will turn out finally ill—or well according to our own human care—and are properly to be called 'ill' or 'well' according to human perceptions. If the Cook makes the Pudding heavy—through her trust in Providence—she is even a more capable Cook than if she had done her poor impious best—and failed. And a Heavy Pudding is a Bad and not a Good Pudding, and there an end—and that's what *I've* got to preach—*now*.[32]

Combining in different ways, with different emphases, certain elements in the firefly passages constantly, obsessively recur. A Tuscan twilight, hills and valley, a vineyard (or ilexes, olives or cypresses), the quivering pulsation of fireflies constantly likened to starlight; and the sense of buoyance, of walking on water; a thunderstorm gathering; sheet lightning, celestial or infernal as the case may be—we recognise the feeling of meaning in possible excess of the situation, the obsessional overload; or, alternatively, the combination of unconscious memory and consciously controlled recall in the effort—the effort of all art, according to Ruskin—to *suggest* the mysterious quality of human feeling and life. What is he finally getting at?

I suggested earlier that the *Praeterita* passage seems devoted to eternising, or at least suggesting the indefinite suspension of the present. *Something* is about to happen; the moment is pregnant with looming change. But the change is suspended; Ruskin keeps the focus of his gaze on the eternity of the moment: *now*. We feel this ephemeral eternal as a vibration or oscillation—the trembling of the present, suggested by the shimmering and pulsing of the fireflies.

The dusk is poised precisely at the intersection time: *twi*light. An interim world: the white masses of Alpine clouds piled up in the thunderous but still illuminated night building in the west, the golden afternoon behind the Gate with its words of golden welcome, *Cor magis tibi Sena pandit*.[33] The sky is calm, 'openly golden', as expansive as the Latin words. (Everywhere in Ruskin, except in the economic tracts, 'golden' is paradisal, *good*). Golden, because this *now*, this poised and hovering present, is also good. The visual image of this golden present is of course Severn's 'Marriage in Cana'. His last painting, it is itself a miracle, made more miraculous because the subject is suspended in time, that 'instant of forever' when a sacred order intersects with a temporal one. Past and present are fused, in perfect balance', one simultaneous thing. The tense is all preterita-present. The fireflies *shone* fitfully in the *still undarkened* air; the fireflies shining *now* fuse with those of three days past, just as all the waters, paradisal brooks and streams, and the fountains of Trevi and Branda converge in the single goodness of water—water of life—drunk in the light of the fireflies, hinting, in their Dantesque way, of paradise lost and infernal pain, but also of pain overcome, transcended, moving upward, like sparks or self-ignited light, brighter than the stars. A time, a place, of looming meaning. 'Still undarkened' hints of darkness to come; 'still golden' is faintly ominous, the language of a man who has seen golden times, golden things vanish. The *mountainous* clouds—those same cloud-like paradisal Alps the youthful Ruskin first glimpsed, in ecstasy, from Schaffhausen—are still lit with the last light of the westering sun. Three 'stills' in as many lines, and then, capping them, the delicate vibration of the crystal-fragile present in the participles closing the passage, confounding the fireflies with lightning and starlight. 'How things bind and blend themselves together!' The fireflies flicker like 'fine-broken starlight'. The idea is fragmented eternity—the pulsing, iridescent, intermittent, transient life-lights against a background of advancing darkness. And finally the fireflies move, rising and falling, like Dante's angelic *faville*, towards the floodstream of heavenly light, fireflies everywhere, eclipsing even the stars in their bright intensity.

Intensity: the precariousness and fragility of present joy; the image of the present as doomed but vivid iridescence; the shining and warmth of human courage and love against the 'cold' and the 'outer darkness' as against the warmer darkness of the Earthly Paradise with its 'scented thickets'. The evoking of these things, of the Edenic world, *this* world with its ordinary *daily* miracle—water into wine[34]—in rapt, partly 'dream-gifted', but mostly composed, temporal montage and miraculous prose, is, I believe, the main purpose and astonishing achievement of this passage in which the whole book converges. A fallen man if ever there was one, Ruskin here writes in secure possession, for the first time, of the Garden he has recovered by remaking himself. He writes, as I suggested, in manifest control of the images which had for so many years obsessed and, to that degree, controlled him. He writes at last, on his own, echoing the Bible and Dante, not to annex their authority and experience, but in the service of his own vision. *These* fireflies may borrow the language and ideas of their biblical and Dantesque contexts; but, unlike the earlier fireflies, they are Ruskin's own possession. The great texts speak through him and guide his associative memory still; but they are finally subject to his own Imagination Penetrative.

Even more remarkable perhaps is the new moral and human control the book reveals. Above all in its *charity*, its manifest love for other human beings. Late in life, very late, Ruskin had learned to love. 'I find myself totally changed,' he wrote to a dear friend, 'and that living people are now everything to me.'[35] In this respect *Praeterita* is not an autobiography at all but an exemplary memorial, commemoration, of those he had come to love. Ruskin proposes to remember both the past and the persons omitted or scanted elsewhere—*personae praeteritae*—and, in the course of so doing, to recreate himself. To revise himself: not perhaps as he was, but as he is, *now*. To be reborn; to memorialise the Severns who were good to him; to make amends to the past he has not lived, for the virtues he has lacked or failed to evince—this is the heart of his project. The charity is not indiscriminate; of his wife, Effie, there is not a word. Ruskin's charity was human, not divine.[36] But it is an impressive charity, all the same, especially if his age and mental condition are taken into account. How many men in their late sixties propose to remake themselves completely and succeed so well—if I understand *Praeterita* rightly—as Ruskin did? The effort was wholly conscious. To his friend Susan Beever he wrote:

> And we will make more and more of all the days, won't we, and we will burn our candles at both beginnings instead of both ends, every day beginning two worlds—the old one to be lived over again, the new to learn our golden letters in. Not that I mean to write books in that world. I hope to be set to do something, there. [37.545]

But *here*? Here he means to write books. Books like *Praeterita*: 'the old [life] to be lived over again, the new one to learn our golden letters in'. He had dreamt his first life badly; now he would dream it well. Charitably, truthfully. In a sense *Praeterita* is a golden dream, a real dream; the memory, wandering 'dream-gifted', re-enacts the past as present, the present as past. Ruskin never came closer to writing poetry than in this book. So far as I can judge, its compositional principles belong not to prose but to poetry. If Ruskin lacked, as Matthew Arnold thought,[37] the *ordo concatenatioque veri*, it is because Arnold's criterion is that of discursive prose.

Look one last time at the final firefly passage. Here everything converges. The tangible subject is an enclosed garden, the *hortus inclusus* of the present. Over the wall, in the background, we can see what the garden excludes—everything which impends upon, which threatens, the precarious present implied in those three 'stills', in the evanescent fireflies, the lingering of the golden afternoon. Excluded, barely excluded, are the night and the storm, surely 'the great storm-cloud of the nineteenth century', with its devil winds and wrath-scourged skies. This, I hardly need to add, is also the storm cloud of Ruskin's most dreaded nightmare, the 'serpent-dream', the Last Judgement of a God who, for a while at least, became for Ruskin 'a raging enemy':

> ... I am driven more and more to think that there is to be no more good for a time, but a Reign of Terror, of men and the elements alike; and yet it is so like what is foretold before the coming of the Son of Man that perhaps in the extremest evil of it, I may some day read the sign that our redemption draws nigh ... [37.127]

One has merely to glance through the standard biblical accounts of the Judgement or God's Wrath to recognise that the whole idea and vocabulary of Ruskin's lunatic clarity in 'The Great Storm-Cloud of the Nineteenth Century' are firmly traditional. Ruskin's night, here and elsewhere, echoes the languages of the prophets and the gospels:

> I clothe the heavens with blackness, and I make sackcloth their covering. [Isaiah 50:3]

> The sun shall be turned into darkness, and the moon into blood, before the great and notable day of the Lord come. [Acts 2:20]

> Multitudes, multitudes in the valley of decision: for the day of the Lord is near in the valley of decision. The sun and the moon shall be darkened, and the stars shall withdraw their shining. [Joel 3:14–15]

> For as the lightning cometh out of the east, and shineth even unto the west: so shall also the coming of the Son of Man be. [Matthew 24:27]

No need to labour the point. Ruskin's 'storm cloud' in the *Praeterita* passage and the famous 'Storm cloud' lectures is simply the worldly or secular form of the great thunder cloud on which the Lord comes to judge the world. In the last poised enchantment of the dusk—the day-world still visible, the night-world moving in—the fireflies shine in the darkening, but 'still undarkened', air. The stress is on their shining: '*How* they shone!' Intense evanescence is in that shining: what is more ephemeral than the glimmering of the firefly?

The fireflies' dance—like broken starlight—fills the foreground, brighter than the stars. Who are these fireflies if they are not simply Dante's sinners? Surely the 'shining' firefly-girls of Winnington; Rose too, once in death she had lost her hard living glitter; and other girls of his childhood who had died or disappeared, 'glittering' in memory; and Giorgione's nudes moving 'among the trees like fiery pillars, lying on the grass like flakes of sunshine' (4.195–6); and Carlyle; and Adèle Domecq; and little Constance Hilliard, who 'glittered about the place'; and many, many more. But above all the Severns, Joan in particular. Joan and Arthur, wrote Ruskin, were 'giddy enough'—and by 'giddy' he meant, as the context shows, giddy with happiness and gaiety. ('Happiest times, for all of us, that ever were to be . . .'). And this giddiness of joy—contrasted with the Severns' sorrow and Ruskin's own—dissolves into the account of Joseph Severn, another firefly, with a gift for gaiety, gaiety wherever he was (a gaiety Ruskin associated with Mozart's Papageno),[38] shining with 'delight' in his painting of 'The Marriage in Cana', which then, by association with miraculous water, melts into the happiness of Ruskin and Norton, drinking together of Fonte Branda. A characteristic Ruskin footnote—born of the sense of time running out, the need to get everything down, *now*—adds more names, more happy days spent with all 'these friends, tutors, or enchantresses'. Can there be any doubt that it is these happy, giddy spirits, each enveloped in his vital flame ('Within the fires are the spirits . . .'), dancing, rising and falling, brave and good people, whom he writes to commemorate while he still can, in the short interval between the last afternoon light and the coming night? It was Ruskin's achievement here, in his last words, to have confronted his obsessions and tamed them into art: an intricately simple and powerful image of human courage, warmth, transience, pain transcended in joy, and daily decency, confronting the dark blank of eternity.

NOTES

1 *Selected Essays* (New York, 1960), p. 126.
2 *The Use of Poetry and the Use of Criticism* (London, 1933), p. 148.
3 Cf. F. Delattre, *Ruskin et Bergson* (Oxford, 1947), *passim*.
4 The most paradisal of all of Ruskin's many paradisal rivers, as the power and beauty of the prose, quoted above, p. 11, makes unmistakably clear.
5 See *Praeterita* [35.157n], where Ruskin speaks glowingly of his 'love of all sorts of filigree and embroidery, from hoar-frost to the high clouds. The intricacies of virgin silver, of arborescent gold, the weaving of birds' nests, the netting of lace, the basket capitals of Byzantium, and, most of all, the tabernacle work of the French flamboyant school . . .'.
6 Cited by R. H. Wilenski, *John Ruskin* (1933), p. 141, as coming from a letter Ruskin wrote to his mother from Siena on 25 June 1870.
7 See, for instance, 'On Adèle, by Moonlight' [2.16]; 'The Broken

Chain' [2.142–4]; 'The Last Song of Arion' [2.119–20]; 'Christ Church, Oxford' [2.125].

In several passages Ruskin links the fireflies with fireworks, in which he took great pleasure. Cf. R. H. Wilenski, *op. cit.*, p. 138 ff. Wilenski rightly, I think, regards the fireworks and the fireflies as *ignes fatui* and images of transient joys. 'But of all evanescent pleasures,' wrote Ruskin of a firework display in Rome [D.172], 'these spitfires are the quickest, for they are forgotten as soon as they are over. I *knew* it was fine, but I don't remember one bit of it.'

Wilenski's attempt to trace Ruskin's fireflies and fireworks to a common graphic obsession—a fascination with 'spots of light surrounded with darkness', and a deep dislike of Rembrandt because of his 'rushlight obscurity' strikes me as unconvincing. The dislike of Rembrandt, Ruskin makes quite clear, is precisely the domination of his paintings by shadow and darkness; they lack the intricate play of light and dark, textured in background and foreground, which fascinated, and usually delighted, Ruskin.

8 The expression and images here, of considerable importance for Ruskin's imagery of light, come from the famous disaparagement of Rembrandt: 'It was the aim of Rembrandt to paint the foulest things he could see—by rushlight. By rushlight, observe: material and spiritual . . . If that light within became but a more active kind of darkness;—if, abdicating the measuring reed of modesty for sceptre . . . we dip it into such unctuous and inflammable refuse as we can find, and make our soul's light into a *tallow* candle, and thenceforward take our guttering, sputtering, ill-smelling illumination about with us . . . perhaps by such fatuous fire, the less we walk, and by such phosphoric glow, the less we shine, the better it may be for us and for all who would follow us' (19.109–10). The imagery here, needless to say, tells us a great deal more about Ruskin than about Rembrandt.

9 'The Hind and the Panther', I, 72–7.

10 *Paradiso* 33, 71, '. . . but a single spark of Thy glory'.

11 Cypresses are of course traditionally funereal, but for Ruskin intensely so, since he saw Italy as a beautiful 'land of the dead'. In an early prose piece entitled 'Velasquez' (1.542), later reworked in *The Poetry of Architecture* (1.19), he evokes this darkly sepulchral background, against which he will later see, glimmering in the foreground, points of firefly-light—the intermittently glowing dance of doomed mortality: 'I meant that the cypress befits the landscape of Italy, because she is a land of tombs, the air is full of death—it is the past in which she lives, the past in which she is glorious—she is beautiful in death, and her people, her nation, are the dead; and the throne of her pride is the *hic jacet*. The echoes of her mountains are like the voices of the departed; the blue of her heavens seems brightened with spirits; the desolation of her palaces full of a life in death. Every nation has its tree . . . and Italy, whose people are the dead, hath her cypress. Oh, it is beautiful to me, the tall and melancholy trees watching over the sepulchre of her earth.'

The spectacle of fireflies against dark cypresses is repeatedly compared to stars shining against a dark sky, and for similar reasons. The dark night sky, which Ruskin usually spoke of as *cold*, appears as a kind of celestial *selva oscura*, an overhead thicket or roof, against which the stars flicker bravely in the foreground: 'For the sky of night, though we may know it boundless, is dark; it is a studded vault, a roof that seems to shut us in and down' (3.81).

12 *Inferno* 5, 121–3; 'There is no greater sorrow than to recall, in wretchedness, the happy time.'

13 Cf. Henry Vaughan, 'Authoris (de se) Emblema'. But Ruskin's knowledge of Vaughan appears to have been slight.

14 Ruskin's favourite (i.e. most frequently cited) Sophoclean play. See the allusions cited at 39.572.

15 J. L. Bradley (*ed.*), *The Letters of John Ruskin to Lord and Lady Mount-Temple* (Columbus, Ohio, 1964), p. 255. The letter is dated 19 January 1870.

16 *Ibid.*, pp. 330–1, letter dated 18 August 1872.

17 A strong theme in Ruskin's work throughout, but intensified in the bouts of madness of the later years. Cf., for instance, 'For a Birthday in May' [1.243]or 'Twist Ye, Twine Ye' [1. 248–9]:

Twist ye, twine ye! even so
Mingle shades of Joy and Woe,
Hope and Fear, and Peace and Strife,
In the thread of human life . . .

in which Ruskin adapts Meg Merrilees's song from Scott's *Guy Mannering* to his own purposes. In *Praeterita* the same thought is expressed by 'arborescent' intertwining of life and death, triumph and defeat, joy and sorrow in the sculptured foliage and 'death-light' of Scott's Roslyn Chapel: '. . . in the deaths of the creatures whom I had seen joyful, the sense of deep pity, not sorrow for myself, but for them, began to *mingle* with all the thoughts which, founded on the Homeric, Aeschylean, and Shakesperian tragedy, had now begin to modify the untried faith of childhood. The blue of the mountains became deep to me with the *purple of mourning*,—the *clouds that gather round the setting sun, not subdued, but raised in awe* as the harmonies of a *Miserere*—and all the strength and framework of my mind, lurid, like the vaults of Roslyn, when weird fire gleamed on its pillars, *foliage bound*, and far *in the depth of twilight*, 'blazed every rose-carved buttress fair.' (35.233; my emphases.)

In his madness Ruskin experienced, clearly with visionary and hallucinatory exaltation, the same mingling of opposites: 'I really look back to all those illnesses . . . with a kind of regret to have come back to this world. Life and death were so wonderful, *mingled together* like that—the hope and fear, the *scenic majesty* of delusion so *awful*—sometimes *so beautiful*. In this little room . . . last year, at this very time, I saw the stars rushing at each other—and thought the lamps of London were gliding through the night into a World Collision. I took my pretty Devonshire farm-girl Nurse for a Black Vision of Judgement; when I found I was still alive, a tinkling Italian organ became to me the music of the Spheres . . .' (37.442).

18 See note 4 on the Rhone, and above p. 11.

19 To Ruskin, who disliked Rome and thought of it as a dead and polluted city, Fontana di Trevi suggested purity and life: 'When I say water, I mean legitimate Roman springs . . . fresh from the rocks of the Apennines—bubbling up in every street and marketplace in abundant gushings, or poured in a roaring torrent under the arches of gigantic fountains; the only thing in Rome that does not look diseased or cursed—

dying or dead—plague or terror-struck—falling, fallen, or to fall—desolate—desecrate—dismal—dull—or damnable . . .' [1.445]

20 See 23.29–30. 'Without engineers' art, the glens which cleave the sand-rock of Siena flow with living water; and still if there be a hell for the forger in Italy, he remembers therein the sweet grotto and green wave of Fonte Branda.'

Also 17.551–2: 'But she [Italy] does not need us. Good engineers she has, and has had many since Leonardo designed the canals of Lombardy . . . Her streams have learned obedience before now: Fonte Branda and the Fountain of Joy flow at Siena still; the rivulets that make green the slopes of Casentino may yet satisfy true men's thirst.'

See also 5.308; 'Ugolino, in his dream, seemed to himself to be in the mountains, 'by cause of which the Pisan cannot see Lucca'; and it is impossible to look up from Pisa to that hoary slope without remembering the awe there is in the passage; nevertheless, it was as a hunting-ground only that he remembered those hills. Adam of Brescia, tormented with thirst, remembers the hills of Romena, but only for the sake of their sweet waters:

The rills that glitter down the grassy slopes
Of Casentino, making fresh and soft
The banks whereby they glide to Arno's stream
Stand ever in my view . . .'

21 John 9:4. For Ruskin's numerous citations of this verse, cf. references in 39:70.

22 Cf. 22.xxiv, 531. 'At Carshalton, in Surrey,' wrote Ruskin in *Fors Clavigera* [28.204], 'I have indeed had the satisfaction of cleaning out one of the springs of the Wandel, and making it pleasantly habitable by trout; but find that the fountain, instead of taking care of itself when once pure, requires continual looking after, like a child getting into a mess . . .'

According to Cook (*Life*, II, p. 222), Ruskin in 1876 'restored a spring of water between Croydon and Epsom, and erected a tablet over it, bearing the following words: 'In obedience to the Giver of Life, of the brooks and fruits that feed it, of the peace that ends it, may this Well be kept sacred for the service of men, flocks, and flowers, and be by kindness called MARGARET'S WELL. This pool was beautified and endowed by John Ruskin, Esq. . . .'''.

23 Cf. 35.40: 'She read alternate verses with me, watching, at first, every intonation of my voice and correcting the false ones, till she made me understand the verse, if within my reach, rightly and energetically. . . . In this way she began with the first verse of Genesis, and went straight through, to the last verse of the Apocalypse . . . and began again at Genesis the next day.'

24 Essay on 'Francis Herbert Bradley', *Selected Essays*, p. 395.

25 Faith Holland informs me that Ruskin's 'Gibbie Gellatly' should in fact be 'Davie Gellatly'. Ruskin has, revealingly, confounded the simpleton boy Davie Gellatly of *Waverley* with the crack-brained Gibbie Goose of *Old Mortality*.

26 Cf. the extremely numerous citations listed in 39.149–54.

27 *The Gulf of Years. Love Letters from John Ruskin to Kathleen Olander*, ed. Rayner Unwin (1953), p. 34. Ruskin's allusion characteristically blends two texts: Luke (3:17) and Deuteronomy (4:24). And it almost certainly glances at the passage cited from Isaiah (50:2–3, 10–11).

28 *The Letters of John Ruskin to Lord and Lady Mount-Temple*, p. 104. The letter is dated 4 November 1866.

29 *Ibid.*, pp. 215–16.

30   If I could pray to move, prayers would move me;
      But I am constant as the northern star,
      Of whose true-fix'd and resting quality
      There is no fellow in the firmament.
      The skies are painted with unnumber'd sparks,
      They are all fire, and every one doth shine;
      But there's but one in all doth hold his place.
      So in the world: 'tis furnish'd well with men,
      And men are flesh and blood, and apprehensive;
      Yet in the number I do know but one
      That unassailable holds on his rank,
      Unshak'd of motion; and that I am he . . . [III, i, 58 ff.]

Elsewhere ('Notes on the Life of Santa Zita': 32.73) Ruskin makes a distinction between those fireflies who are, as it were, of permanent brilliance, and those who, like himself, shine intermittently: 'The saintly virtues, humility, resignation, patience (in the sense of feeling no anger) . . . obedience . . . fortitude against all temptation of bodily pleasure, and the full-flowing charity which prevents a selfish love . . . are all conditions of mind possible to few, and manifestly meant to furnish forth *those who are to be seen as fixed lights in the world*;—*and by no means to be the native inheritance of all its fire-flies*.' See also the interesting comments ('. . . in the cloud of the human soul there is a fire stronger than the lightning . . . ; though of good and evil it shall one be said alike, that the place that knew them knows then no more, *there is an infinite separation between those whose brief presence had there been a blessing* . . . and those whose place knew them only as a drifting and changeful shade . . .') in *Sesame and Lilies*: 18.147.

In *The Bible of Amiens* Ruskin speculates sadly on what might have been, had he possessed the courage to live by 'his own lights': 'How far my mind has been paralysed by the faults and sorrows of life,—how far short its knowledge may be of what I might have known, had I more faithfully walked in the light I had, is beyond my conjecture or confession' (33.118–19).

One other source, at least for the *transience* of the firefly, may have been Shelley's 'The Triumph of Life' (though Ruskin never cites the poem at any point):

Maidens and youths fling their wild arms in air;
As their feet twinkle; they recede, and now
Bending within each other's atmosphere

Kindle invisibly—and as they glow,
Like moths by light attracted and repelled,
Oft to their bright destruction come and go,

Till like two clouds into one vale impelled
That shake the mountains when their lightnings mingle
And die in rain—the fiery band which held

Their natures, snaps—while the shock may tingle,
One falls and then another in the path
Senseless—nor is the desolation single,

Yet ere I can say *where*—the chariot hath
Past over them—nor other trace I find
But as of foam after the ocean's wrath

Is spent upon the desert shore . . .

31 *The Letters of John Ruskin to Lord and Lady Mount-Temple*, p. 219.

32 *Ibid.*, p. 241.

33 'More and more does Siena open her heart to you.'

34 In *Fors Clavigera* (29.343–5) Ruskin cites a long letter from a correspondent dealing with the real meaning of the miracle at Cana. In an earlier Fors [29.285] he had written, 'They have no wine? and the command is, "Fill the water-pots with water."' His correspondent comments by observing, 'I am greatly averse to what is called improving, spiritualizing—i.e. applying the sacred text in a manner other than the simple and literal one . . . In every grape that hangs upon the vine, water is changed into wine, as the sap ripens into rich juice. *He* had been doing that all along, in every vineyard and orchard; and that was His glory.' On which Ruskin remarks approvingly, 'Seldom shall you read more accurate or more noble words . . .'.

35 *John Ruskin's Letters to Francesca, and Memoirs of the Alexanders*, ed. Lucia Grey Swett (Boston, 1931), p. 177.

In a letter of 25 September 1885 Ruskin (*ibid.*, 95–6) writes to Mrs Alexander: 'It is the chief thing that gives me any hope of myself—next to Joanie's love of me, that you and *Sorella* care so much for me, and that I have indeed an intense sympathy in all your pleasures, though my own, for the time are ended. Every word you write—each of you is joy and strength to me; and you are the more to me because my life has been so strangely loveless till now. I have taken the chance of the people who came in my way—and never sought for friendship—till at last it has come to me—if only I may be spared in its possession.'

The Alexanders, mother and daughter, were, I assume, two more of Ruskin's close-of-life fireflies, whom he doubtless would have commemorated in the uncompleted sections of *Praeterita*.

36 'All great Art is Praise' So is all faithful History, and all high Philosophy. For these three, Art, History, and Philosophy, are each but one part of the Heavenly Wisdom, which sees not as man seeth, but with Eternal Charity; and because she rejoices not in Iniquity, therefore rejoices in the Truth' (33.23–4).

37 *Letters of Matthew Arnold, 1848–1888*, ed. George W. E. Russell (1904), I, p. 67.

38 'But there is nothing in any circle that ever I saw or heard of, like what Mr. Joseph Severn then was in Rome. He understood everybody, native and foreign, civil and ecclesiastical, in what was nicest of them, and never saw anything else than the nicest. It was the nature of things that the Pope should be at St Peter's, and the beggar on the Pincian steps. He forgave the Pope his papacy, reverenced the beggar's beard, and felt that alike the steps of the Pincian, and Araceli, and the Lateran, and the Capitol, led to heaven, and everybody was going up, somehow; but might be happy where they were in the meantime. Lightly sagacious, lovingly humorous, daintily sentimental, he was in council with the cardinals today, and at picnic in Campagna with the brightest English belles tomorrow; and caught the hearts of all in the golden net of his good will and good understanding, as if life were but for him the rippling chant of his favourite song,—*Gente, e qui l'uccellatore*' (35.278).

'*My darling Charles*': selections from the Ruskin–Norton correspondence

JEFFREY L. SPEAR

It was on a little steamer crossing between Vevey and Geneva in the summer of 1856 that a young New Englander, recognising the Ruskins across the cabin, introduced himself, his mother and sisters. 'And thus,' Ruskin wrote in *Praeterita*, 'I became possessed of my second friend, after Dr John Brown; and of my first real tutor, Charles Eliot Norton' (35.520). Ruskin's account both flattered and embarrassed his old friend, who felt compelled to insist that he could never have trespassed 'on the privacy of a gentleman with whom I had no right to speak'.[1] In truth the previous autumn Norton had been one of the many armed with letters of introduction to be shown the Denmark Hill Turners—an encounter Ruskin had forgotten. Their friendship began on Lake Geneva and as far as Ruskin was concerned they met there. In this as in so much *Praeterita* is more true than factual.

Norton was prepared to give in full measure the apparently contradictory responses Ruskin required from his close friends: admiration and admonition. Son of Andrews Norton, the orthodox opponent of Emerson, himself a puritan grown sceptical, Norton had the culture, scholarship and moral rectitude to make his praise valued and his correction at least respected. An admirer of contemporary English writers, a scholar of medieval Italian art and literature, a student of *Modern Painters*, he could understand Ruskin's religious turmoil and sympathise with his social conscience, if not his economics. Their friendship survived disagreement over the American Civil War and was forever cemented when Norton, who had married in 1862, returned to Europe with his family in 1868. Ruskin had feared marriage would come between them: 'Yes—I don't want any messages from Mrs Norton—If she's not jealous of me—I am of her.'² But Susan Norton captured the affection and respect of Norton's entire circle of English friends, and Ruskin was no exception. When she died in Dresden in 1872 after the birth of her sixth child (in ten years of marriage) the loss proved a further bond between the two men. The people and places he had shared with his wife remained special in Norton's memory.

Following Ruskin's example, Norton buried his grief in work. Home from London in 1873, he began teaching at Harvard, where he set an example for the Cambridge humanists of the next generation. Not until he visited Brantwood in 1883 did he see Ruskin again, but they corresponded regularly. Not even their angry disagreement over Froude's handling of the Carlyle papers stopped the flow of mail. When Ruskin died Norton was left with one of the most extended and detailed series of his letters to anyone outside the Ruskin family. Returning to England in 1900 as one of Ruskin's literary executors, he joined Mrs Severn in burning Ruskin's letters to Rose La Touche and at the same time recovered and, evidently, destroyed most of his own letters to Ruskin. Norton seems to have felt that Ruskin's letters to him, however, were at once too valuable to destroy and too personal to publish—at least in his lifetime.

Convinced that in his years of mental instability Ruskin had published too many letters, too much of everything, Norton opposed the creation of the now invaluable Library Edition—fortunately to no avail. Knowing the value of his collection to Ruskin's editors, but unwilling to surrender editorial control of it, he determined to publish his own selections, first in the *Atlantic Monthly*, then in book form. Although the *Letters of John Ruskin to Charles Eliot Norton* fill two volumes, Norton eliminated enough letters to fill a third, besides cutting words, lines, entire pages out of the letters he printed, sometimes without acknowledgment. Emotional passages were printed with their motive suppressed; references to deleted passages were let stand to become needlessly mysterious. Contemporary readers recognised some of what had happened. William James protested:

> I wish that your modesty had not suppressed certain passages which evidently expressed too much regard for yourself. The point should have been *his* expression of that sort of thing—no matter to whom addressed!³

The acute sense of propriety that found in Ruskin's pellucid account of their meeting in Switzerland the implication that thirty-two years earlier he had improperly introduced himself led to the elimination of far more than the personal references—flattering and derogatory—to Charles Eliot Norton. Gone are most familiar references to Susan Norton, to their children, to Ruskin's girl favourites, particularly Constance Hilliard,⁴ and, of course, to Rose, though Ruskin had made his love for her, like his attacks of mania, public knowledge.

While most of Norton's cuts in the letters are at least explicable, there are some for which there is no apparent rationale. Having published Ruskin's reservations about his eulogy of Dickens, there seems no reason to have eliminated the anecdote in which Ruskin links him to the fashion for 'sensation' drama and fiction and, by the way, gives a glimpse of Dickens's public readings.

> I heard him read the death of Nancy—and the pursuit of Sykes. —Nothing that he has done is more truly tender and deep in pity. After it was over—a respectable bald headed gentleman got up on his seat—and begged to protest in the name of the audience against 'such an utter piece of abomination.' There was a titter on the part of the audience—but I believe that nearly every one of them there liked it—if they liked it at all—only for the 'sensation' and were at heart of the old gentleman's opinion—. . . .⁵

Norton's editorial discretion, and that of his daughter in her edition of *Norton Letters*, preserved family privacy, but at the expense of the full humanity of both men. Only a complete new edition of the correspondence can fully repair the damage,⁶ but the following selection, taken primarily from Ruskin's active years, will restore the integrity of some of the best known letters and give the flavour of the whole.⁷

NOTES   1 Norton to S. C. Cockerell, 7 April 1892, in *The Letters of Charles Eliot Norton*, ed. Sara Norton and M. A. DeWolfe Howe (Boston, 1913), vol. 2, p. 211; hereafter cited as NL. Norton had protested directly to Ruskin when the passage appeared in 1888; see 35.519 n.
2 Sentence excised from the letter of 10 February 1863 as printed in *Letters of John Ruskin to Charles Eliot Norton*, ed. C. E. Norton (Boston, 1905), vol. I, 136; hereafter cited as N.
3 James was responding to the selections in the *Atlantic*, which seemed to him 'immortal documents'. NL. 2, 348
4 Born 1852, daughter of the Rev. J. C. Hilliard and Lady Trevelyan's sister, 'Connie' became a favourite of the Nortons as well as Ruskin and corresponded with Norton at least into the 1880s.
5 From the letter of 8 July 1870. For the context see N, II, 10. Ruskin wrote to C. A. Howell, then his factotum, on 30 September 1868, asking him to obtain tickets 'for the David Copperfield readings—and the Mrs Gamp'. 'John Ruskin and Charles Augustus Howell: Some New Letters', ed. Jay E. Caliborne, *Texas Studies in Language and Literature*, XV (fall 1973), 492.
6 Professors John L. Bradley and Ian Ousby are planning such an edition.
7 Passages restored to the published letters have been keyed, first, to Norton's text at the relevant page and then to the Library Edition of Ruskin's *Works*. Passages quoted from Norton's text have been checked against the manuscripts and silently corrected. I have restored Ruskin's characteristic dash and ampersand, but supplied a full stop at the ends of sentences. Where crossed-out words seem significant they have been so printed (but, for the printer's convenience, not above or below the line as in the original). Norton's elisions are enclosed by square brackets;

Ruskin's insertions from the margins shown by */ . . . / at the point he indicates they belong; editorial insertions are in angled brackets. Unpublished letters appear by permission of Ruskin's Literary Trustees, Allen and Unwin, and the Houghton Library, Harvard University, whose friendly and efficient staff deserve all praise. My thanks as well to the Princeton Committee on Research in the Humanities and Social Sciences and Miss Elizabeth Billington for aid in preparing draft transcripts of the letters.

My dear Norton 〈Denmark Hill,〉 25th February 61   1
. . . It seemed to me, that to keep any clear headedness—free from (N,I.103;36.355) intellectual trouble & other pain, no life would do for me but one as like Veronese's as might be, and I was seriously—and despairingly—thinking of going to Paris or Venice & breaking away from all modern society & opinion and doing I don't know what. Intense scorn of all I had hitherto done or thought—still intenser scorn of other peoples doings & thinkings!—especially in religion—the perception of colossal power more & more in Titian, and of weakness in purism—:[1] and almost unendurable solitude in my own home— only made more painful to me by parental love which did not & never could help me, and which was cruelly hurtful without knowing it; and terrible discoveries in the course of such investigation as I made into grounds of old faith—were all concerned in this: and it would have been, but for the pain which I could not resolve to give my parents. I don't in the least know what might have been the end of it, if a little child (only 13 last January) had'nt put her finger on the helm at the right time; and chosen to make a pet of herself for me; and her mother to make a friend of herself. [Very oddly—this mother is the sister of my first college acquaintance of the opposite kind—the man at whose table I first sate, at Christchurch—beginning my initiation into Evil. Not that he was wicked, her brother could not be—but the wildest, noblest in look— and on the whole most interesting to me—of all the men of my time. I have not seen *him* since I left college. Her, I have known about three years:[2]] certainly the ablest and I think the best—woman I have ever known. [She has been watching me carefully; and I've promised her that I'll never do anything to vex her, or make little Rosie sorry in her after life that she had once been my pet. They're just going away to Italy: and I—stay here, and draw—I doubt if I shall ever see much more of them.—The father—a staunch— narrow—unimprovable evangelical of the old school ~~cannot bear~~ fears my influence over Rosie: Her mother does *not* at small cost—nor unconsciously as her husband bids her, however this is all probably for the best—for *me*; now that they've done their work.[3] The issue of which is for the present, for me, that] I settle down to mine,

without the least farther care as to what is to come of it—having no pleasure in it & expecting none, but believing that I am in a better state than I was, understanding a few things about Angelico again, which I had lost, and do not think I shall now lose any more.

You have also done me no little good,—in the same way, and I don't feel alone, now that I've you on the other side of the Atlantic, and Rosie & her mother by the Mediterranean—all wishing me well; and I don't think there's any chance now of my going all to pieces. You see I answer letters more prettily than I used to—don't I . . .

NOTES   1 For Purism, Naturalism and Sensualism in painting see 10.224 ff.

2 Rose's mother, Mrs John La Touche, was the half-sister of J. O. O. Cuffe, third Earl of Desart. 'Lord Desarts card party (wherein not a card was touched—nothing but dice) was by no means interesting,' Ruskin wrote to his father from Oxford, 26 February 1835. *The Ruskin Family Letters*, ed. Van Akin Burd (Ithaca, N.Y., 1973), II, p. 439.

3 Passage partially quoted in *John Ruskin and Rose La Touche. Her Unpublished Diaries of 1861 and 1867*, ed. Van Akin Burd (Oxford, 1979), p. 42. Hereafter cited as *JRRL*.

11
(N,1.119;36.381)

Holyhead, 26th Aug. 1861

. . . I have been staying at Boulogne nearly two months. I went out mackerel fishing and saw the fish glitter and choke—and the sea foam by night. I learned to sail a French lugger—and a good pilot at last left me alone on deck at the helm in mid channel with all sail set, and steady breeze. It felt rather grand; but in *fact* would have been a good deal grander if it had been nearer shore—but I am getting on, if I don't get too weak to hold a helm, for I can't digest anything, I think. I tried Wales after that—but the moorland hills made me melancholy—utterly. I've come on here to get some rougher sailing if I can—then I'm going over to Ireland for a day or two [to see my little Rosie—who has been writing me little rosy sermons and scolds alternately all the while I've been at Boulogne.] Then I'm going straight to Switzerland, for the fall of the leaf, & what next I don't know. There's enough of myself for you.

[It gives me more pleasure to hear from you than I get in any other way—I've no other such friend among men. I was *so* glad you liked your missal leaves.[1]—I've been bothering Rossetti to send your drawing[2]—but vainly because feebly—like all else I do just now. Thank you for your beautiful letter—I mean the end of it, about the birds, especially, and] I'm so glad you think hopefully about the War. It interests me no more than a squabble between black & red ants. It does not matter whether people are free or not, as far as I can see, till when free they know how to choose a master.

Write to me, please, poste restante, Interlachen, Switzerland. I'm hoping to find out something of the Making of the Jungfrau, if the snows don't come too soon, and my poor 42-year-old feet will still serve me a little.

[Goodbye with all thanks for your love and help.—Remember me affectionately to your mother & sisters.]

Ever your affectionate

J Ruskin.

1 Taken from his 'St Louis' Psalter, see N, I.104; 36.356.   NOTES

2 Probably *Before the Battle* see *Ruskin: Rossetti: Preraphaelitism*, ed. W. M. Rossetti (London, 1899), Ruskin to Rossetti, 274; Rossetti to Norton, 296 ff; 311 and NL, 1, 207.

Dear Norton . . .   Denmark Hill, 6th Jan. 62.   III

I've been drawing—(painting) a little; with some self-approval. (N,I.122;36.403)
I've tired of benevolence and eloquence and everything that's proper, and I'm going to cultivate myself and nobody else, & see what will come of *that*. I'm beginning to learn a little Latin and Greek for the first time in my life—and find that Horace & I are quite of a mind about things in general—I never hurry, nor worry—I don't speak to anybody about anything; if anybody talks to *me*, I go into the next room. Sometimes I find the days very long—and the nights longer, then I try to think it is still at the worst better than being dead:—And so long as I can keep clear of toothache, I think I shall do pretty well.

Now this is quite an abnormally long and studied epistle, for me, so mind you make the most of it—and give my love to your mother and sisters & believe me ever affectionately yours,

J Ruskin.

[It's a shame to send a half written sheet to America. Now here's a question for you: Norton, did you ever hear of anybody being in this state of mind of mine. Imagine a youth of 17, suddenly waking on a winters morning and finding himself 43 years old, with rather less power—of every sort than a man of 43 should have—but with every wish of his youth, and mode of thought—the loss of the 25 years being accompanied with only one serious change of mind—that the expectation of future life should be cut off with the auspices of the present one. Fancy what a pleasant waking.[1]

Well—I feel *exactly* so.]

1 Cf. his letter to Dr John Brown, 16 January 1862, 36.404: 'Wrong at   NOTE
both ends of life . . .'

IV
(N,I.127;36.406)

Dear Norton   Denmark Hill 28th April, 1862
[You are a dear fellow, and your letters*/Deepest thanks for that Diary one. It was a great help & gift to me./ are the comfort of my life just now and I am glad with you and for you with all my heart. It used to be a sound heart enough, but has got shrivelled or pinched somehow lately, and is not much to give, but what is left of it, or in it, you have. Not that I shall have much of yours, now—whatever pretty speeches you may make—you will find the difference fast enough, and I shall find it faster. It is rather too cool and provoking of you to tell me your wife is to like me. I don't want her to.—I want her to be jealous of me, for ever so long yet.

It is so nice of you to want me to be at your wedding.¹ But there is little of good omen in me, and you had better not. I shall think of you, every May morning, and rise more cheerfully for the thought; but cannot come across the blue water to you.]
Where one's friends are, one's home ought to be, I know—whenever they want us; But every day finds me, nevertheless, sickening more and more for perfect rest—less and less able for change of scene or thought—least of all for any collision with the energies of such a country and race as yours. Nay, you will say it would not be collision —but communion—you would give me some of your life. I know you would if you could. But what could you do with a creature who actually does not mean to enter the doors of this Exhibition of all nations within five miles of his own door.

14th May.
I have kept this—hoping to be able to tell you some cheerful thing about myself, but few such occur to me. Tomorrow I leave England for Switzerland; and—whether I stay in Switzerland or elsewhere—to *England* I shall seldom return.—I must find a home— or at least the Shadow of a Roof, at least of my own, somewhere: certainly not here—May all good be with you & yours.

Ever your affectionate
John Ruskin.
Look in Fraser's magazine for next month—June, please.²

NOTES   1 Norton married Susan Ridley Sedgwick on 21 May 1862.
         2 For the first of the *Munera Pulveris* essays.

V
(N,I.129;36.423)

Mornex, Haute Savoie, 28th Aug. 62
... I can't work without bringing on giddiness—pains in the teeth— and at last—loss of all power of thought. The doctors all say "rest— rest—" I sometimes wish I could see Medusa.—
And you can't help me. Ever so much love can't help me—only time can, and patience. You say "does it give you no pleasure to

have done people good?"—No—for all seems just as little to me as if I were dying—(—it is by no means certain I'm not) and the vastness of the horror of this world's blindness & misery opens upon me—as unto dying eyes the glimmering square—(and I don't hear the birds.) [I am sure your wife must be nice, as you've chosen her; but it does not the least follow that *I* should like her. There are many noble and nice people whom I know & yet don't like, and I've been so disappointed by some of my friends' wives— that I never believe any of their descriptions any more. The photograph—as far as expression goes—is nice—but I've been trying to draw Titian beauties—& Luini's—and can't believe in a woman's head unless it has a wreath of hair behind it as thick as a coil of cable—or a wave over the shoulders as broad as a cloud—I don't think I should like her. *There*. I'm very fond of *one* of my friend's wives, however—Edward Jones's. They call themselves, both, my children, and love me very much, and I love them. They came with me to Milan on their way to Venice—stayed with me a little there, and were sorry to go—and I was sorry to let them go, a little. Georgie nestled close to me when she said goodbye and said "you nice thing"—so that I'm not quite horrid yet, I suppose— (but soon shall be.) I loved poor Rossetti's wife much, too: and bid *her* goodbye, very⟨?⟩ sorrowfully, with a kiss, in her coffin[1] —: but sometimes I take quite sharp antipathies to my friends' wives.]

As for your American war—I still say as I said at first—If they want to fight, they deserve to fight, and to suffer. It is entirely horrible and abominable—but nothing else would do. Do you remember Mrs Brownings curse on America.[2] I said at the time "she had no business to curse any country but her own." But she, as it appeared afterwards, was dying—and knew better than I against whom her words were to be recorded. We have come in for a proper share of suffering—but the strange thing is how many innocent suffer—while the guiltiest—Derby & d'Israeli, & such like—are shooting grouse.

Well—as soon as I get at all better, if I do ⟨,⟩ I'll write you again. And I love you always—& will. I'm so glad you liked Rossetti's banner so much. Remember me affectionately to your mother & sisters. Write to Denmark Hill. I stay among the hills, all winter, but don't know where, yet, so D. Hill is the only safe address.

Ever your affect [e].

J Ruskin.

1 Elizabeth Siddall Rossetti was buried on 17 February 1862.
2 See her poem, 'Curse for a Nation'.

VI
(N,I.166;36.533)

My dear Norton,   Ambleside, 8th August, 1867

I am *very* glad of your letter—[its sympathy is precious to me—I can speak of the thing to few, and of those few—whom in various ways I have been forced or tempted to trust—not even those who care most for me understand me—or the thing—or the meaning of it. All remains just as it did—I won't speak of it to night for] I want to say a word about the Turners,[1] which I am very thankful for all your kind thoughts about—but indeed the only "kindness" of *mine* is in putting you, as it were, ten years back, on fair terms of purchase. I wish I *had* the pleasure of giving—all my art treasures are now useless to *me*—except for reference; the whole subject of art is so painful to me, and the history of Turner — and all my own lost opportunities of saving his work, are a perpetual torment to me, if I begin thinking of them.

But this was what I wanted to say—Your American friends, even those who know most of art, may be much disappointed with the Liber Studiorum. For the nobleness of those designs is not so much in what is *done*, as in what is *not* done in them. Any tyro—looking at them first—would say, Why—*I* can do trees better than that—figures better—rocks better—everything better.

"Yes: and the daguerreotype—similarly—better than *you*"—is the answer, first. But the final answer—the showing how every touch in these plates is related to every other, and has no permission of ~~individual~~ withdrawn, monastic virtue, but is only good in its connection with the rest, and in that connection *infinitely* & inimitably good;—and the showing how each of these designs is connected by all manner of strange intellectual chords and nerves with the pathos and history of this old English country of ours; and on the other side, with the history of European mind from earliest mythology down to modern rationalism and ir-rationalism—all *this* showing—which was what I meant to try for in my closing work—I felt, long before that closing, to be impossible—and the mystery of it all—the God's making of the great mind[2]—and the martyrdom of it —[and the full and miserable pain & wreck of it]—and the uselessness of it all for ever, as far as human eyes can see or thoughts travel. All these things it is of no use talking about.

I am here among the lakes, resting, and trying to recover some tone of body. I entirely deny having lost tone of *mind* (in spite of all pain)—yet. And yesterday I walked up Helvellyn, & the day before up Skiddaw—(and walked twelve miles besides the hill work yesterday)—both of them 3000 feet of lift—so I think there may be some life in the old dog yet. [But I always enjoy being kind & being kindly treated; and nothing is such deadly poison to me as anger, or a state of non-charity with people—and now for four years I have lived in gradually increasing anger coming now at last into something very like the relation of the Master of Ravenswood to Lady Ashton—with a woman who was once my quite dearest woman-friend.³ Fancy the state this keeps one's soul (and body—) in?] All you say of religion is true & right, but the deadly question with me is—what next? or if *any*thing is "next"? so that I've no help, but rather increase of wonder and horror from that.

One word more about Turner. You see—every great man's work—(*his* pre-eminently)—is a *digestion* of nature, which makes glorious *human flesh* of it. All my first work in Modern Painters, was to show that one must have *nature* to *digest*. Not chalk & water for milk. [Well, then I came to treat of the absorption and found I couldn't explain it to other people—and now a great deal of artists work—done as they suppose, on my principles—is merely gobbling good food and *polluting* it a little and sending it out at the other end of them—and asking the public to admire the faeces—

Are you to be at Cambridge now any time. Write soon, and tell me if you really *do* like what I've sent you—or any of it—as much as you now affectionately think you will. Love to your mother and sisters—Tell me something of your life—]

Ever lovingly yours
J Ruskin

1 Some plates from the *Liber Studiorum*, and some pencil drawings. NOTES
[N.'s note.]
2 I.e. Turner's.
3 In Scott's *The Bride of Lammermoor*. The friend is Mrs La Touche.

My dear Charles   Denmark Hill, 22nd Aug. 68.   VII

Five of the little pebbles were sent yesterday to be polished, and (N,I.180;36.552)
will be sent, or brought, to you next week; if the children are *told* on "Saturday" next, they can't be disappointed. I have looked out to-day a few fossils of the chalk—flints and the like—of which I know—nothing, though I have them as illustrations of certain methods of mineralization. But they will show you what kind of things are now under your feet, & in the roadside heaps of stones, and the first time Darwin takes them in his hand they will become Prim-*Stones* to you, (I am glad to escape writing the other word after Prim¹)—and—Stones-Lips, instead of Cows. Not that they're worth his looking at, otherwise than as the least things have been.*/ They are worth carriage to America however—as you hav'nt chalk there./ But the little group of shattered vertebrae in the square piece of chalk *may* have belonged to some beast of character and promise. When is he going to write—ask him—the "Retrogression" of Species—or the Origin of Nothing? I am far down on my way into

a flint-sponge. Note the little chalcedony casts of spiculae in the sea-urchins—(wrapt up more carefully than the rest.)

Next—as Mrs Norton remembered that bird of Hunt's, I thought she might like to have one a little like it—which would otherwise only be put away just now—and I've sent it, and a shell and bit of stone of my own which I'm rather proud of—(I want Darwin to see the shell—only don't say I did, please!) I can do much better, but it looked shelly & nice, & I left it. [And, between them, there's an etching for you to *keep*, one of my duplicates of the Dunstanborough. It will let you see a great deal of care in the rocks, &c.—especially the distant promontory on the right—which is superb —and how quietly & thoroughly Turner prepares all his work in all its stages.

The two engravings of Ivy bridge are both fine.—The one is a proof, with much of the loveliness & richness of the drawing, but confused in general effect at a little distance. The other is the published plate, after Turners touches & alterations—which I leave you to amuse yourself by examining. They often seem to spoil or sacrifice *parts*, but you will see how the whole gains at a little distance. Still, I would rather for myself, have the transcript of the drawing, and so with all Turners much celebrated touched plates. They gain effect, but lose sentiment—purity—& peace. His first thought was always best. Both these are for you to keep. I'm done with them.

I enjoyed my day much on Thursday.—It is the first time I've not been disappointed in a friend's wife—(and this was when I expected the most.)

I could not help looking at her in a kind of dreamy wonder, she is so intensely like what my favourite "Lily" of the Ethics of the dust will be,[2] when she comes to that age—if she is as much—no— that she can't be—but if she is at all, among as nice people—or in proportion as she is among such. Love to you all.] Ever your affectionate,

J Ruskin

NOTES   1 Rose.
      2 Lily Armstrong, later Mrs Kevill-Davies. For her long correspondence with Ruskin see *The Winnington Letters*, ed. Van Akin Burd (Cambridge, Mass., 1969).

VIII   My dearest Charles   Abbeville, 11th September, 1868.
(N,I.183;36.555)   [I have your lovely letters—one to Denmark Hill long ago, the other now, here.] Come whenever it is most convenient to you—I shall have my work in a more comfortable state in about a week's

time than it is now, but come at your own time.

[The little stones ought to have come before my limiting Saturday
—They *were* finished, but I forgot I had not given directions for
sending them in leaving home. I am afraid Eliot[1] will not trust me
another time.

They would be too brittle, I fear, for a seal, but it might succeed.
If Eliot could find a few more, and send them to Denmark Hill,
directed "for Mr Rusch, care of Lucy Tovey" they would be
polished, if worth, in due time, & Mr Rusch would report on
engraveability.]

I have often thought of setting down some notes of my life.
But I know not how. I should have to accuse my own folly bitterly—
but not less—as far as I can judge—that of the fondest—faithfullest
—most devoted—most mistaken parents that ever child was blest
with—or ruined by. For myself, I could speak of my follies and my
sins—I could not speak of my good. If I did—people would know
the one was true—few would believe the other. Many of my own
struggles for better things I have forgotten—I cannot judge myself
—I can only despise—and pity. In my good nature, I have no merit
—but much weakness & folly. In my genius I am curiously imperfect & broken. The best and strongest part of it could not be
explained.—And the greatest part of my Life, as Life, (and not
merely as an investigating or observant energy—) has been [one
succession of Love-sorrow, which I could only describe by giving
myself up to do it hour by hour and pain by pain—by writing
another Nouvelle Heloise—which—even if it could be done
honourably to myself—or to others—would not be the *best* work I
could leave behind me,[2]—it seems to me? And—chief reason of all
—telling now against my ever setting down so much as would give
you conception of all—the whole life has been] a series of delights
which are gone for ever—and of griefs which remain for ever—and
my one necessity of strength or of being is to turn away my thoughts
from what they refuse to forget.

Some day—but not now—I will set down a few things [for
you—] but the more you understand—the less you will care for
me. I am dishonest enough to want you to take me for what I am,
to you, by your own feeling—not for what I am in the hollowness
of me. I bought a cane of palm tree a week ago—it was a delightful
cane to me—but it has come untwisted—it is all hollow inside. It is
not the poor cane's fault—it would let me lean upon it—if it could.

[Thanks for nice account of Darwin. Susan says you have been
tiring yourself—please don't. Give her my love & thank her for her
beautiful letters.

And pray give my respectful thanks to your mother for her
kindness in writing also.

And with affectionate regards to your sisters believe me—]

Ever your affectionate

J Ruskin

NOTES 1 Norton's eldest son.
2 Passage partially quoted in *JRRL*, p. 116.

IX
(unpublished)

My dearest Susan[1]   Denmark Hill. ⟨January, 1869?⟩

You gave me *no* pain—nothing that Charles or you ever do or say can give me anything but comfort—(—stop—provided Charles keeps off J.S.M.!!!)—but I'm very glad of your lovely little note.—I don't want to make faces and make you uncomfortable about me.—I shall do very well, as soon as I get settled to my work again—only I can't *play*, nor will years make any more difference than hours,—in that—and Christmas happens strangely to be the darkest day of the year to me—as yet.

Joan is passing to-day—so I send the flint & little Lily,[2] & am ever   your faithful J.R.

NOTES 1 Norton fell ill in October 1868 and Ruskin shifted his regular correspondence to Susan Norton through his period of convalescence. The reference in the third line is to John Stuart Mill.
2 Probably Elizabeth Gaskell 'Lily' Norton, their second daughter.

X
(unpublished)

My dearest Susan,   Denmark Hill ⟨Feb 2, "69⟩

This is a book indeed—and so was your face on Friday night, and I could easily read in it all you would have said if I could'nt have read it. It is a great strength to me that I give you pleasure. But this Lowell book is marvelous. I opened at the cloudbergs in p. 73*/In "An Invitation"[1]—that and the next six stanzas are to me more delicious even than Tennyson being less artificial—and without a peculiar frankincense-like musky sweetness, which always makes me feel a little sick in Tennyson, like the smell of grape-hyacinth—have you got the grape hyacinth in America?—It's like honey and plums distilled into something richer than attar of roses—but this Lowell is so fresh & so comforting—Tennyson only makes one whine worse than before.

The "All saints" is a heavenly one.

It was so nice Charles going to see the pictures, & finding out all my tricks

Ever your loving JR

1 In James Russell Lowell's *Under the Willow and Other Poems* (1868): NOTE
Where, as the cloudbergs eastward blow,
From glow to gloom the hillsides shift
Their plumps of orchard-trees arow,
Their lakes of rye that wave and flow,
Their snowy whiteweed's summer drift.

There's nothing at all but firefly's work, sent to-day   XI
       Denmark Hill,   Thursday ⟨Feb. 10, 1869⟩   (unpublished)
My dearest Susan
That is so nice about the Japan things—I'll come to see them
tomorrow at 2, but must see them quickly as I have an appointment
in Hanover Sq. at $\frac{1}{2}$ past 3.[1]
              Ever your loving   JR.

You *are*—all—probably much more in my life than I am in yours;
—only you are nerve and support to me—not mere pleasure—for
I cannot *have* pleasure: whereas I am no support to you but—as
I must believe you—pleasure—and sometimes a little firefly of
dim light.
    But the support is far the graver & nobler gift.

1 Ruskin's Diary for 10 February records a 'meeting of Pauperism NOTE
society.' . . . In evening with Joan and Connie at Norton's.' On the 13th,
'bought Japan vases . . .' (D.664).

My dearest Charles   Denmark Hill   26th April 1869   XII
    Unless at risk of fulfilling my testament forthwith, I could not (unpublished)
stay longer in town, but I will draw up the new one quickly when
I am over the water, and send it from Paris or Neuchatel.—When
drawn up it can be sent to Venice for me to sign—meantime
keep this—If my next of kin go into chancery, fight them *until* there's
no money left—and *then*, give up the Turners for my drawings—
it will be a lovely lesson to the nation on the beauty of law—far
more useful to them than any Turners.[1]
    I've a great mind—now that I think how I should laugh, (—if I
knew anything about it down below—)—to leave this will as it is—
only for the nuisance it would be to *you*. But I'll write another as
soon as I can.
    Now—look here—I know you'll read this new-old-book of
mine—so you may just as well read it unbound—and with pen in
hand. I have not been able to revise it rightly—please give it one
current⟨?⟩ glance through from end to end—the printers will

send it you—tomorrow evening I believe in as clear form as I can get it. They are to receive your corrections as mine, and you have carte blanche to alter anything unintelligible or awkward, and put ~~minor~~ little wrongs right—not *big* wrongs, you know:—for then you might as well re-write it.[2]

The *Preface* will come to you for nearly *all* its revises—I can't get it into shape at all before leaving, & must send it in M.S. from Paris. Finally—Mr Williams, the managing partner of Smith & Elder is referred to you to take final instructions about binding & lettering.

—If there's the least pleasure in angelic minds in having things all their own way, you won't mind doing this for me—I don't think you will—even if the angelic mind only cares about giving relief to others*/In fact—it's a mere beginning of editing post-humous works—for *all* my work now is posthumous./

Ever with dear love to Susan—
Your faithfully and thankfully loving
J Ruskin

Denmark Hill is left as it usually is—and you & your mother & sisters & Susan may often I think have pleasant times in the garden and library with my dear Mrs Scott[3]—and Lucy has the keys of *all* the Turners.

NOTES　1 Ruskin had begun to think of himself as leading a posthumous existence early in 1869, perhaps because his rejection by Rose at that time seemed final. He persuaded Norton to act as his agent in drawing up a new will.

2 *The Queen of the Air*, which Norton saw through the press.

3 Ruskin left his mother in the company of Mrs Alexander Scott and her daughter, Susan, one of his Winnington School pets, while he travelled in Europe.

XIII
(unpublished)

My dearest Charles　　　　　　　　Vevay　1st May, 1869

I am very sorry to have given you this fever-fit of law-panic—pray destroy or otherwise treat the present will just as you like, and get me this simple bequest to Acland, Simon[1] and you, drawn up at once, and sent to post office, Venice. I go on, the day after to-morrow, and hope to be at Venice before the end of next week: and Fate must decide if the hope is to be vain.—

I think that is a lovely simple notion of the plain bequest—it will save all manner of trouble and chance of lawsuit, and mistake in detail.

The weather has been lovely, but too hot in sun, with cold wind on heights.

Have you read Tyndalls lecture in last number of proceedings of Royal Institution?—²

It is marvellous, and must modify my preface a little—I have to apologise first for rude observations—and then say how wonderful this putting the sky in a bottle is; and then say—for last word—that I'll thank *them*—the men of science⟨—⟩and so will a wiser future world—if they'll return to old magic—and let the sky out of the bottle again, and cork the devil, *in*.

Ever your loving   JR

Is it not curious that looking out on the blue water where I first met you—I should be writing this letter?³

1 Dr Henry Acland, the Regius Professor of Medicine, Ruskin's NOTES dearest friend from his Christ Church days; Dr John Simon, the public health reformer.

2 John Tyndall's 'On Chemical Rays, and the Light of the Sky'; see preface to *The Queen of the Air* (19.292).

3 In his reply, 3 May, Norton reported the will cancelled; suggested additional bequests, and that he be given control of Ruskin's copyrights should the worst come to pass (profits to go to Oxford University, then Ruskin's chief beneficiary, at least of works of art). He concludes: 'How well and tenderly I recall the day we first knew each other (we had met before) on the Lake of Geneva.' All unpublished Norton letters are in the Houghton Library unless otherwise noted.

My dearest Charles   Verona, 16th May   **XIV**
I am getting a little anxious at not hearing from you—I trust you (unpublished) got my letter—authorizing you to draw up the will of simple bequest to Acland Simon & you.—it will be very provoking if by any chance that letter miscarried.

I am settled to my work now—and will soon write about it, & about some plans.

Please—some day, ask Miss Scott¹ to read you a letter I wrote her, three days ago—about some Americans, whom I travelled from Venice with, here.

Love to you all.
Ever your affectionate JR.

1 Susan Scott. The letter, dated 14 May, appears in *The Solitary* NOTE *Warrior*, ed. J. H. Whitehouse (London, 1929), pp. 113–15.

XV
(N,I.210;36.571)

My dearest Charles   Verona, 21st June 69.

. . . I wish I could give you, for an instant [—Or say "twenty minutes" (the time necessary for doing my will)] my sense of sailing on lonely sea—and your writing to me from far away—about things so very practical & important—on the shore—which of course I ought to care for—and to leave all properly arranged—fin che il mar sia sopra me richiuso.[1] But I don't care about them. Or take the comic side of it—Jonathan Oldbuck leaves Lovel—who is sensible & practical—to bring out his essay on the Praetorium. Lovel doesn't bring it out—and writes its title page calling it "an attempt at identification of the Kaim of Kinprunes, with the landing place of Agricola—" and keeps teasing Jonathan to write his will![2]

["Don't be Wilful"—My dear Charles—it's the very thing I *don't* want to be—now—I've had so little of my Will—in Life—that I do not care much for having it— when I shan't know whether I have it or not.—]

And indeed—if I were to die now—

*/24th June/

the life would have been such a wreck that you could'nt even make anything of the drift wood.—It really is *more* important and practical for me to try before I die—to lead two or three people to think "whether there be any Holy Ghost"—than even to make sure that you have my watch and seals to play with—though I *should* like you to have them.—Only I'm not sure after all whether it is really me, or an ideal of me in your head, that you love. I don't believe anybody loves *me*, except my mother and poor little Joan.

[I've got your last note—very pretty—but let me finish what I had to say.]

I really *am getting* practical. Last night—full moon—the metal cross on the tomb summit—which I have named in the Stones of Venice—as "chief of all the monuments of a land of mourning,"[3]—reflected the moonlight as it rose against the twilight, and looked like a cross of real pale fire—for the last time I believe from the old roof, for they take it off to-day—or to-morrow—to "restore" it.

Well—in old times, I should have thought that very pretty: whereas now I reflected that with four tallow candles stuck on the cross-ends, I could produce a much brighter effect.

And I'm thinking of writing Hamlet's soliloquy into Norton-&-Mill-esque. "The question which under these circumstances must present itself to the intelligent mind, is whether to exist, or not to exist," &c.

[—Well—I really tried to look at that will—to please you—and got wondering why the bequests to the servants were all wrong—and got into a general reflection upon my servants lives—and things

connected with them—till I lost all my afternoon and all my equan-
imity—and the next morning also—in growling and swearing—
tacitly—and much time since in the same way.]

Don't send me any letters that will require any sort of putting up
with or patience—because I have n't got any. Only this I'll say—
I've suffered so fearfully from *Reticences* all my life that I think
sheer blurting out of all in one's head is better than silence.

[I never got the least help from a woman who loved me with all
her heart in the perfectest way—because she always chaffed me so
that I thought she didn't really care a bit—And Lear is always
being played over again—with the silent breath at last not able to
move a feather⁴] . . .

Ever your loving
JR

1 Cf. Dante's *Inferno*, 26, 142, Ulysses's last voyage.   NOTES
2 Scott's *Antiquary*, chapters 4 and 16. See 36.571.
3 The Castelbarco tomb, 9.177.
4 Lady Trevelyan, who died in the presence of her husband and Ruskin at Neuchâtel on 13 May 1866. Ruskin was perpetually grateful to her
for standing by him at the time of the annulment of his marriage.

My dearest Charles   Venice—9th August 1869 XVI
I am just leaving Venice for Verona—your letter just in time— (unpublished)
I will write from Verona—I have been overwhelmed with strange
immediate needs for doing this and that, but have kept well—
except for the bitter horror in which all things keep heart and mind
—the more I see—the more I know them—as they are, now.

Of natural history, I have found an important thing, exquisite
drawings by a Venetian of *1415*, which show that *no trace* of change
is visible in wild species, during 400 years.—An important fact—
any way.

Love to you all—Ever your affect.
JR

My dearest Charles   Verona, 9th August 69. XVII
[The dream was curious—for] several things have concurred (N,1.216;36.576)
lately in furthering my preparation for the plan I told you of about
the Valais . . .¹

[Perhaps I have told you all this in the continued dream—surely
at least—I went as far as the restraint of the glacier waters on the
north side. I cannot at all events—go on to that tonight.

Thank you for the bit about Longfellow, and sweet⟨?⟩ extract from Appleton's letter[2]—It—& your comment on it, are both delightful but—do you know what *my* feeling was after the Long-fellow visit?[3]—the most cruel sense of utter loneliness I ever had yet in my life—in seeing that men even of that intellect and virtue were to all intents and purposes—apathetic to evil, unless it touched some personal feeling. There is nothing in Dante more loathsome—more obscene—more terrible—than the present state of Italy—but Longfellow saw it all as he had all winter, seen with a fixed serenity of quietly sad contemplation—as if it were a scene in a play and didn't matter—and Appleton, without the slightest apparent diminution of his emjoyment.]

Omar is very deep and lovely [—a far more noble form of resigna-tion.] But the Universe is not a shadow show nor a game—but a battle of weary wounds and useless ~~roar~~ cries—and *I* am now in the temper that Omar would have been in—if somebody always stood by him to put mud into his wine—or break his amphora. You don't quite yet understand the humour of thirsty souls, who have seen their last amphora broken—and "del suo *vino* farsi in terra laco"[4].
. . .

NOTES 1 He goes on to describe his scheme to restrain alpine torrents.
2 Thomas Appleton, Longfellow's brother-in-law.
3 Ruskin met Longfellow and Appleton in Verona on 4 June; see 19.liv.
4 'Delle mie vene farsi in terra lago': *Purgatorio*, 5,84. [N.'s note.]

XVIII My dearest Charles, Giesbach, 18th August.
(N,1.235;36.583) I have your letter from Lugano. [—I am afraid—though it is a horribly ~~conceited~~ proud thing to *say* however one may be sure of it —that you will all be dreadfully disappointed when you get my last two letters—but I can't help it—Fate closes steadily round me in all kinds of ways, small and great.]

I must get that book on Italian irrigation[1]—strangely enough— I have just finished and folded a letter to the banker Carlo Blumen-thal at Venice, with some notes on a pamphlet he lent me by the engineer who has the management of the lagoons . . .

[My poor sick girl here is—*very* sick—She is the second whom I've seen in the irrevocable doom—both of them so *perfectly* good and right and precious—both living in vain—and dying bitter deaths. When I was here three years ago—she was bright & strong —17—and as good as gold—and Joan & Connie and she and I were very happy among the rocks—I had my "three years" to "wait"[2]—then—which I thought very hard—but could be happy meanwhile.

Now *I've* nothing to wait for—and poor Marie is waiting for death.[3] And the rocks are all there—looking as if I had only left them yesterday—I could fancy the moss still with my footprints.]

Ever my dear Charles
your affectionate
JR

1 The book, on Italian irrigation by Captain (afterwards Colonel) R. NOTES
Baird Smith, one of the ablest officers of the corps of Bengal Engineers . . .
[N.'s note.]

2 When Rose turned eighteen in January of 1866 she said she would answer Ruskin's proposal of marriage in three years.

3 Marie of the Giesbach (Marie Schmidlin) was to be the focus of a chapter of *Praeterita* Ruskin never reached: 35.633. Marie does not seem to have died in 1869; see letter of 6 March 1872, below.

[My dearest Charles   Dijon   30th August 1869   XIX
I strangely did not ask you to write anywhere. I hope your next (N,1.238;36.586)
line to me—a lovely series of lines—will find me at home, and tell me that you are better—or at least that your coming to Brientz has not harmed you. I was glad that you came—and for many reasons—chiefly because I saw more clearly the ways in which I have at different times hurt you—and can avoid them for the future.

But remember—you never could wound, however you may teaze—or provoke, me. *I* shall never think *you* ungrateful—Never rude—never in what you choose to say or choose not to say, wrong. —I may be in a violent state of irritation against you for being what you may sometimes be—to me. But never for doing what you at anytime may do, to me.

It is true that I have every cause to trust in your affection—and you hardly any to trust in mine;—But you ought always to trust in it so far as to know that when such ideas come into your mind as the having to "take, from me, what you would not take from anyone else"—you must have misinterpreted me. You will never have to take anything from me but what is in its purpose loving and courteous, whatever its aspect may be.]

I do not know what it was in my last letters that gave you the impression of arrogance. I never wrote with less pride in my heart. Was it my comparing myself to the Antiquary and you to Lovel? Is not Lovel, throughout, the more sensible of the two?

It was very natural that you should think me ungrateful in the matter of the will. But remember, in all that you did for me in that, you were really working for the feelings of others after I am dead—not for me. *I* do not care two straws what people think of me after

I am dead. [And those who love me most—my mother, Joan—Dora[1]—if I were now to die, would also care very little, for the talk of me. But neither you—nor any creature living—could keep that talk from being painful to them—as far as it went. I must live longer, to do that.]

But I *do* care, and very much, for what is said of me while I live. It makes an *immense* difference to me *now*, whether Joan and Dora find a flattering review of me in the morning papers, or one which stings and torments them, and me through them. And the only vexation of my life which you have it really in your power to allay—is the continual provocation I receive from the universal assumption that I know nothing of political economy, and am a fool—so far—for talking of it.

[And I think that the trouble you would have in doing this, would both be infinitely less than the trouble you are so anxious to have in arranging my old journals—and would be wholly beneficial to yourself also.]

For—(Now I *am* going to write arrogantly—if you like—but it is right that you should know what I think, be it arrogant or not.) [—I think your life passes too much on the surface of things—and that you would be made stronger in many ways by going quite to the bottom of *one* thing.]

I came yesterday on a sentence of Ste.-Beuve's—which put me upon writing this letter—(it is he who is your favorite critic—is it not?) "Phidias et Raphael faisaient admirablement les divinités, et n'y croyaient plus."

Now this is the sentence of a quite incurably and irrevocably *shallow* person—of one who knows everything [—and nothing—] who is exquisitely keen and right—within his limits—sure to be fatally wrong beyond them. And I think your work and life force you to read too much of, and companion too much—with, this kind of polished contemplation of superficies—so that I find that I have influence over you, and hurt you, by external ruggednesses of some of which I was wholly unconscious; and did not fancy that those I was conscious of, would be felt by you.

But—whether this be so or not—there is really no question but that a man [of your influence, and occupied as you are and will be, in deep historical inquiries,] should once for all master the *real* principles of political economy—know what its "laws" are—for it *has* its laws—as inevitable all as gravitation—know what national poverty really means—and what it is caused by—and how far the teachings of present professors are eternally false or true. And then I want you to say publicly, in Atlantic monthly,[2] or elsewhere what you then will think respecting my political economy, and Mill's.

And what I meant by saying that I could not love you rightly till
you did this, was simply that until you did it—you were to me what
many of my other friends and lovers have been—a seeker of my
good in your own way—not in mine. If I had asked my father to
give me forty thousand pounds to spend in giving dinners in
London—I could have had it at once—but he would not give me
ten thousand—to buy all the existing watercolours of Turner with
—and thought me a fool for wanting to buy them. I did not misun-
derstand his love for me—but I could not love him as much as if he
had done what I wanted.

So—I know perfectly well that you would work for five years, to
write a nice life of me.—But I don't care about having my life
written—and I know that no one *can* write a nice life of me—for
my life has not been nice—and can never be satisfactory.

But if you work for one year, at what will really be useful to you
yourself,—(though I admit some discourtesy in my so much leaning
on *this*—yet I should not urge you to help me if it would be all lost
time to you)—you can ascertain whether I am right or wrong in
one of the main works of my life; and authoritatively assist, or
check me . . .

Ever, with faithful love to you all
Your affectionate J Ruskin.

1 Dorothy Livesey, one of Ruskin's Winnington pets and, as Mrs Lees,
a founding member of the Guild of St George. See *Winnington Letters*,
p. 268 and *passim*.

2 Norton wrote regularly for the *Atlantic* between 1859 and 1861,
when Lowell was its editor.

My dearest Charles   Geneva,   4th May 1870   XX
(unpublished)

Your little packet with the photograph came from Rome—but
I chance this to Florence, to say I am getting a little rest now, and
am better, but that I am very anxious about you, especially after the
account I had at Paris from Francois.¹ I did not know that you ate
so very little—and he spoke of you as having been anxious lately, and
sometimes sad.

I was really ashamed to write to you lately, till I had got that
will made. I signed it—after much amazing and disgusting Mr.
Martineau by obstinately refusing to hear it read—(as I saw he
understood what I wanted—)—and it is safe in my banker's safe in
the Union, Chancery Lane. It leaves you, besides my books &
MSS.—a Turner or two—Florence from Fiesole,—Turin from
the Superga—& Vesuvius in action & repose—the former to be
evermore typical to you of what your friend was, and the latter of

what you vainly tried to make him. Simon & Acland the executors.
Love to Susan, and to all your gracious circle.
A line would find me at Baveno, Lago Maggiore

Ever your loving JR.
Do not be angry with poor Rose.[2] She has done all she could.—
My life was entirely at an end in a certain sense—before—it never
could have been what you hoped—And she has made it now—far
better than it was.[3]

NOTES   1 Norton's servant.
    2 'I feel how much you must have suffered, and I find it hard to under-
stand, & if understanding, to be patient with her who has, as it seems to
me, needlessly renewed your suffering & broken the current of your days
with a new trial. . . . I would not believe in the God of the good' (Norton to
Ruskin, 31 March 1870). See *The Letters of John Ruskin to Lord and Lady
Mount-Temple*, ed. J. L. Bradley (Columbus, Ohio, 1964), pp. 246 ff and
JRRL pp. 119–23 for Rose's rejection, return to, and rejection, of Ruskin
in 1870.
    3 Passage partially quoted in *JRRL*, p. 121.

22nd April.
Joan married on 20th.
Everything went nicely.
Denmark Hill   15th April ⟨1871⟩.
XXI   My dearest Charles
(unpublished)   I have yours from Venice of the 9th April. I am so dead with
monotony of work here, always more or less for others, and never
carried out with any satisfaction except that it is the best I can do—
so dead, I say that I can hardly fancy you at Venice—nor think of
any possibility that I could be there.—Joanna is busy with her
presents and her bridesmaid, and her house and her invitations—
it is all a dream to me, from which I shall be glad to escape—for my
head scarcely serves me—and my heart much dis-serves me.

A package came the other day containing four Greek vases of a
late time: white figures on a black ground. I do not remember your
telling me of these.—The case meant first for America described
in yours of March 13th has not yet appeared—the one you now
speak of as at Leghorn is the one with the marble statue, is it not?[1]

Give my dear love to Mr Brown whenever you see him.

The St John in clay is lovely—but I can't buy it—clay things are
no good to me

Your loving JR

NOTE   1 Norton had an open commission from Ruskin to buy antiquities while in the south of Italy, and his surviving letters to Ruskin during 1871 record a string of purchases, including: 'thirty small Greek vases, cups, etc. from Corfu or Samos, but one from Athens,—. . . and a lovely little Greek statue found in a Temple of Neptune . . . of a wingless Fortune, standing on a globe' (29 March 1871). This statue became a treasure of Brantwood: see 20.328 and Ruskin to Norton, N,II.34.

My dearest Charles   13th Dec. 71   XXII

I can't write you much for the last month has just been one (unpublished) ghastly monotony of indescribable shadows.[1]

—All the real sorrow of my life about human creatures—is not connected with any manner of relationship. Which I suppose is horrid—& I dare not say it, but to you—who are no relation! yet whom I like. People wanted to show respect and came in a crowd to the burial yesterday. Lunched afterwards—and stunned */ unlucky word, inevitable/and horrified me all day long.

If it had been Rosie or Joan I was burying—I should have pitched gravel in their faces—and sent them all to the worst place I could devote them to.

As it was, I did the best I could but am horribly stupid this morning.

And very tired—

Shall be better soon, I hope.

I am going to stay here till Oxford meets—then lecture there on the relation of science & art.[2] John Simon says your mother may get much better.

                              Love to Susan
                        Ever your loving   JR

1 Ruskin's mother died on 5 December after a lingering decline.   NOTES
2 *Eagle's Nest*.

My dearest Charles   Denmark Hill, 23rd Jan. 72   XXIII

Perhaps you may like to have another portrait of Connie, to (unpublished) compare with the one en dishabille.

They're no use to me—except to teaze—I wonder whether that's why she does them.*/It's a piece of art, the graceful disorder-in-order of her touching is very wonderful to me. Titian could not have applied a given numbers of touches much more caressingly than the little wretch has done in her hair. Look at it through a lens./

—Why is Friedrich so melancholy to you? It is not half so melancholy as most of the facts of the world. There is at least— throughout a power, getting things right. In the world—it is now the battle of Vünersdorf—and no other. I hardly read any book now, with real enjoyment *except* Friedrich.[1]

I've been reading the Arabian nights again, with a little,⟨?⟩— the Caliph being able to hang forty Barmecides whenever he likes is balm to my wounded spirit. To be able to hang bad men—would be glorious—but to have the power to hang good ones—if one was in the humour to—what bliss![2]

—Don't you think the entire sum of Modernism is gathered in the brief statement in my daily Telegraph yesterday.

"The body of Colonel Fisk was interred with military honours"?[3] I expect to have bound copies of lectures for you now, literally, every carrier,—(that's three times a day)

Ever your loving   JR.

NOTES   1 Carlyle's *Frederick the Great*.
2 See 'The Tale of the Three Apples'.
3 James Fisk, the notorious manipulator of railroad stocks.

XXIV
(unpublished)

Corpus Christi College   Oxford
6th March, 72

My dearest Charles
What can I say to you.[1]—Life—and Death—have long been to me as horrible dreams,—both of them. If I thought we could wake out of them, I would try to make you think so too—but I think we only cease to dream. Day by day I think of *you*, and do no more. You know I cared for Susan—Will my saying so be any good to you? I am expecting—any day, to hear that Rosie is dead—It would be no good to me though all the world were sorry too.

—Are you going to stay in Dresden?—In Europe? It seems to me as if it would be better for you—to be anywhere than at home.

We shall be in Italy—God willing, this spring, but it would all be bitterness to you. Paris, I fancy, would be best for you. So much to think of. So little that she would have cared for.

Do you recollect Marie of the Giesbach? Her husband is just dead, and he was all in all to her.

And the primroses come out all the same. But I am thankful for them nevertheless.

If Susan and Lady Trevelyan meet in the next world, as they're sure to if there is any, they'll talk finely of you and me.

Ever your loving   JR.

NOTE   1 Susan Norton died in February, a few days after the birth of Richard Norton.

Corpus Christi College, Oxford,   **xxv**
Easter Sunday 72.   (N,2.51;37.52)

My dearest Charles,

I left my Denmark Hill study, to go back no more, on Thursday,[1] and have passed my Good Friday & Saturday here, quite alone—finding, strangely, one of my Father's diaries for my solace,—giving account of all our continental journies—from the time I was six years old, when he & my mother, and I, and a cat, whom I made a friend at Paris, and an old French man-chambermaid, were all very happy (yet not so much in degree as completeness)—at Paris—my Father some twelve years younger than I am now.

[And I have your lovely letters, and we will all do in Italy as you say.—Chiefly what you tell me about dear Siena, where you showed me Nicola[2]—and fireflies—and the heart of poor living Italy—and of—the not living.

And I think I shall be able to give you some little rest and even pleasure, of a weary kind—among my Coniston hills—at least it is a sanctifying of the new home to me that you should come there.]

We leave England, D.V. on Tuesday the 9th a line to care of Arthur Severn, *Herne* Hill, London, would find me probably sitting writing before breakfast at the window of my old nursery—*whence* I visited Paris for the first time.

[I have no notion how letters find people in Rome. But we shall be at Turin certainly on our way, and a letter there, any time within the next fortnight telling me where to address to you, will be answered with full detail of journey planned. I've promised Connie to be at Venice on her birthday, 26th May. So Hotel Danieli there will be safe then.]

I am going to sell my Venice Rialto by Turner. It is too large for Brantwood, and I have enough without it, & it makes me sad. [I have told Mr Kay to send you my last weeks letters about it—which will answer all questions in an entirely hard and ~~unfriendly~~ business manner.—But if your friend wants it, I will answer differently—only I don't yet know what the value of it is—in market.]

I am so tired that this, which I have written in the idea of its being quite a slow and careful & proper letter, looks as slovenly as if I cared nothing for you. But I care for you, though I can't write—

Ever your,
J Ruskin

[The Yorkshire drawing is not a good one, or I should have told you.]

NOTES   1 Ruskin was moving to Brantwood.
2 Nicola Pisano. Ruskin joined the Nortons in Siena in June 1870; see the end of *Praeterita* (35.562) and William Arrowsmith's chapter above.

XXVI   Brantwood, Coniston   Sunday, 1873
(unpublished)   My dearest Charles,
Read the enclosed letter that you may understand what terms I am on with Merritt,¹—the best and honestest fellow I know in London,—then send it and go and see him as soon as you can.

Yes. London *must* be changed to you. It has ~~always~~ been to me for the last seven years what it is to you now, and I had got so used to walk in it as a city of the dead that when suddenly I was taken out of the grave for three days,² I could do nothing but wander about wonderingly and dreamily from Street to Street seeing all the places that had been hung with black, hung with golden tapestry.

The inkstand has come: but is too black for me, now,—my brains are addled, and I have, for the time wholly forgotten what Susan had it made of for me.³—I know I was greatly pleased when I first heard of it—tell me again.

I shall still be a fortnight here—It is very beautiful at this time, and I think would be worth your running down for a day or two.

You could help me immensely with some lectures I'm doing on Sandro Botticelli.

—If you came quickly—you would find Joan and her husband and Lily Armstrong here—but they'll be gone I suppose, by the 17th or 18th.—I am digging & making courses for springs, and you might be a little amused.

Ever your lovingest   JR

The best way to come is to sleep at Kings Arms Lancaster—then take 11. morning train to Ulverston, (the line separates at Carnforth)—where I would meet you, and drive you here by the lakeside.

Your pictures are in charge of Snell, 27 Albemarle St.—I'll send you a letter to him if you can't come here.

NOTES   1 Henry Merritt (1822–77), a restorer of paintings, art critic and writer, whose 'A Story of a Flower' Ruskin reprinted in *Fors*, 37.486 ff.
2 His brief reconciliation with Rose in August 1872.
3 'The inkstand will come to you before very long. Ebony was not at first to be found here' (Norton to Ruskin, 19 December 1871).

Bath Hotel   Picadilly   XXVII
Thursday, 13th Feb. 73   (unpublished)

My dearest Charles,

I have just got your note back from Coniston—I knew this was the first Returning Time to you—and did not quite know if to come & see you—also to me the streets are so heavy with purple snow of eternal winter that I can scarcely walk in them. I am going back to Coniston on Saturday.

I am very thankful you like those drawings. The two of St Nicholas are the best—the thing itself—in each—was wholly lovely, and I was hindered by time from trying to do more than I could. The Baden sketch is also of a beautiful *thing* but the one I fancy you will ultimately care most for is the evening⟨?⟩ sketch from San Miniato,—as connected with our Fiesole time there &c. and now Dante's fast.

My mind is terribly divided between the perplexity of six or seven years more of sketching—now, I hope at last free from torment of trying to do what I could not—and from luxuriousness of indolence in what I do—between this, I say and the seeming duties of Oxford.—

Colvin's[1] appointment to Cambridge so mortified my pride that I have since every day been tempted to resign for that reason only. The other would be—I think—a just one, my sense of the *in*justice of the other militates against that.

Ellis the bookseller dines with me at six tomorrow to talk over putting copyrights of all my books before 1870 up to auction.

—I am on the way to a very pretty quarrel with S⟨mith⟩ and E⟨lder⟩.

If your cold is better, you might much help me by joining us. But as you will help me—I know—anyhow, before anything is settled, don't *think* of coming out if you have still cold.

Love to you all
Ever your loving   JR

I am not drunk—though this note looks like it—but partly tired, partly over-excited by hearing that the Germans have ascertained St Paul to be Simon Magus.[2] The Infinite Lark I shall have out of this, if I live. It was competent authority I had for it. To think of the faces of the Evangelicals!

The articles in this mornings Times—on Railroads and Seamen —greatly interesting to me.[3]

1 Sidney Colvin had just been named Slade Professor at Cambridge.   NOTES
2 A theory of the Tübingen school; see 27.509.
3 Ruskin refers to the inquest into a collision off Dungeness in which

290 people were drowned and, perhaps, to the refusal of the directors of the Metropolitan Railway to install mechanical safety devices on their trains. (*Times*, 13 February 1873, pp. 6, 7.)

XXVIII
(unpublished)

⟨March 1873⟩

My darling Charles

I couldn't come to see you.—For one thing I quite recoil in a sort of insane way from getting west of the British museum—all the streets are so terrible to me—but also—I need to *seize* what afternoons I can—when fine, for walks, and I got away into the country. —I've had to say goodbye to Lily, too.—She *would* come—and so that took up a little time & wasn't very cheerful.

—You've never told me a word whether you enjoyed my *letter* about Connie[1] and whether you read any of it to her.

—I'm off to Coniston in an hour, D.V.—but I don't take the ivy with me, as you enjoy it a little & may like to show it a little to London people—; what I have to do to it can be quite easily done here in May, if you lend it me a day or two then.

Love to Sally.[2]

I liked her prim "the drawing is lovely, and I like it" greatly. Very dear love to your mother & much to your sisters

and I am your own poor   JR

NOTES   1 When Ruskin asked for a copy of his letter about Connie, Norton confessed that he had burned it, as he did all letters in which 'confidences are given to which no third person should be privy'. Norton's justification of his action clearly anticipates his role in the controversy over Froude's handling of Carlyle's papers and in the destruction of Ruskin's letters to Rose La Touche. 'I have burned some of the sweetest love letters ever penned, because I would make sure that no eyes but mine should ever see them. I have burned letters with the tears blinding me,—but I keep the memory of them safe in my heart. Sometimes I have burned letters from you,—those in which you told me of sorrowful experiences in love, for they were secrets between you & me. No man or woman shall have to reproach me with violating the trust they have given me. And only yesterday afternoon, I read & reread your letter about Connie, and questioned with myself, & wanted to keep it, and then thought, *no*. I alone can interpret it perfectly, it is a little *scène de la vie entime* for me. I shall not forget it, I shall not leave it to chance, & to cold eyes. . . . It sparkled & shone for a minute—like a symbol of itself,—and then burned grey & fell to ashes, like a symbol of so much else.' (Unpublished letter of 2 April 1873, reproduced by courtesy of The Ruskin Galleries, Bembridge School, Isle of Wight.)

2 Norton's eldest daughter, Sara, for whom Ruskin drew the ivy.

Dearest Charles   Herne Hill   8th May ⟨1873⟩   **XXIX**
Can I come and see you tomorrow about two o'clock? I must be   (unpublished)
at the Arundel Society, Bond St at 4, and back at Oxford in evening.

You are a great burden on my mind!

Emerson came to my rooms a day or two ago—I found his mind
a total blank on matters of art; and had a fearful sense of the whole
being of him as a gentle cloud,—intangible—

What *can* you do by going back among a people whose best are
only this. You are not of them.

Your children ought not to be of them. They are *not* a nation.

Emerson said of the whole North, "They fought for *existence*."
—What 'infinite deal of nothingness' does that saying not tell of
them?—As if a man ~~could~~ did not exist—essentially,—do what he
~~would~~ could, or suffer what he ~~would~~ might—(Bother the tenses)
                        —Your Siena is at Oxford.
                            Ever your loving   JR.

C⟨orpus⟩ C⟨hristi⟩ C⟨ollege⟩   2nd Dec 1873.   **XXX**
[My dearest Charles   (N,II.68;37.74)

It is one good to me, of the many which rise out of pain, that you
are able to write to me about Susan, knowing that I know what pain
means; and can understand all you can say, and give you the comfort
of faithful listening, and silent—such as it is.

I am very thankful to have those extracts from her letters.

For all the rest of the letter—every sentence in its own way, I
would thank you one by one, if I could. I am especially glad to
hear of Mr Moore,[1] and will do all I can—and that you can direct
me in doing, to assist him.—Your requests to Burgess shall all be
directly seen to; he comes here this week.

I am glad you are upon Florence.—I write by this post to my
printer to send you the ten lectures on it this term—they are still
scarcely corrected but I shall be glad you see them before the final
revise.]

I often hear your sermons over again.—I attend to them very
much indeed. I think my steady resistance to them the most heroic
of all the efforts I make in the service of my poor—"lower than the
angels." Sometimes, when I'm tired in the evening, they nearly
break me down, and I'm so proud next morning of not having been
beaten.

But I am very sure you will be better pleased with the Fors's for
next year, if I live.

I go to Assisi early in the Spring to work there, with what help I can gather, on a monograph of it.

I am surprised to find how well my health holds, under a steady press of work; but my sight begins to fail and I shall begin with spectacles this next year.

I will find a bit of architecture for you however—or—even with my old eyes, do you a bit, that won't be copiable by the 'bold' scholars.

[Holman Hunt's picture (reviewed to-day in Times) seems to me a little bit of good 'co-operation'.[2] By the way, I'm going to have some larks out of Master Agassiz. If Adam & Eve Agassiz ~~dislike~~ think their little boy's ~~getting into a mess~~ clever, they'll be in a state worth seeing soon.—I do think of all the human stupidities and meannesses I've come across in my life,—the Agassiz letters to Forbes about the Riband structure beat.[3]

—Then—how the whole herd—Faraday even as foolish as the rest!—go on trying experiments in icicles—and don't even know so much as what the words brittle—viscous—and plastic—*mean*. They don't know so much as the mechanical facts of Honey & Butter.—Use the words viscous & plastic as if they had never known the difference. Tyndall seems actually never to have seen hot glass break!—That's the way *I* shall go to pieces.

Love to you all—

Ever your loving   JR.

NOTES   1 Professor Charles H. Moore, a friend and colleague of Norton's at Harvard. He accompanied Ruskin to Venice in 1876. See letter XL (14 March 1877) below.

2 *The Shadow of Death.*

3 See 27.735 ff. for Ruskin's defence of James Forbes' theory of glacial motion.

XXXI
(N,II.69;37.80)

My dearest Charles   Herne Hill 11th February, 74

I am sitting in my old nursery, in the afternoon of a clear, *very* cold frosty day,—wind outside sharp. I a little numb and weary, after drawing on Giotto's tower for a drawing example, (I am pushing them now, at last). The view through the bars put to keep me from falling out when I was little is much as it was,—only the Crystal palace is there, and a group of houses on the ridge of the hill, where the Xl ⟨Crystal⟩ palace Hotel is,—where my father and mother used to go when they could'nt travel any more with me. [Rosie is there, now—very ill, and come to London for physicians. She proposed the XI palace Hotel to Joan,—'for the dear old lady used to like it.'[1] But she won't write to me, nor let me see her. She can't live with her own people any more, just now—goes wandering about the world with her maid—and is as I say at this moment on yonder ridge of hill, where *my* people used to be.

I'm going back to Oxford on Saturday. I hope to lecture on glaciers. I enclose you a letter from Forbes' wife.—I think you will be touched by the calm relation of the death of her two daughters.—I've had great comfort in fighting for them—you saw the glacier Fors, I suppose.]

Send me all the remarks you can on Val d Arno—they will be in plenty of time.

I shall go down to Brantwood for a month, and then start straight for Assisi, about end of March. I have no pleasure whatever in the thought of going but perhaps may find more than if I expected it. But I shall think of Siena, and many sad things, and present Italy is saddest of all. [I had a half offer of Connie to go with me, with her brother for chaperon—but refused, thinking my Giotto work had better be steady, however sad. I want to work on Arnolfo and him, for an unbroken six months,—then go & do some geology in the cool, (if there's any now left on the Alps now a days.)

Love to you all—especially to Sally I carried her pincushion in my waistcoat pocket a long time but found it merely a sentimental form—for I could'nt pin anything.

—Well—I shall not make you more cheerful by writing, but I wanted to, sadly, this long time

Ever your loving   JR]

1 Mrs Ruskin.   NOTE

My dearest Charles   Herne Hill, 13th Feb. 74   XXXII
Your letter came to-night, after dinner,—on one side of the tray (N,II.70;37.81)
on which letters are brought up, [—on the other side, lay, for Joan one from Rosie. I was very thankful for yours,—and I shall have great pleasure in those Florentines—and most rejoiced shall I be when Merritt writes to me for a cheque and says he has found something for you. I answer at once—to say this—and I *have* enclosed the note to Merritt and addressed it for the mornings post. I shall probably call in Devonshire Street on my way to the Western Station tomorrow—for I must go to Oxford—the wistful looking up at the Xl ⟨Crystal⟩ palace hill is unendurable.

—She says in her letter to Joan—"Oh Joanie,—under the pain—and fasting, and opium last night, I had such dreams of the old teas—and crumpets—and shrimps."

Fancy crumpets and shrimps becoming pathetic!

But those teas are fifteen years ago—when I was first called

'Crumpet'—(because their governess was 'Bun')—and my special privilege was to have my shrimps shelled all by Rosie.]

I am so glad you like those Brantwood photographs. It was a terrible disappointment to me, your not coming. No photograph can give you the least idea of the sweet greys and greens;—the intense English richness of the moss vegetation,—or the almost Italian beauty of the lower end of the lake, all the photographs lose it in mist.—I will send you a little sketch or two this next month—God willing [—and if that child does not die. I am trying vainly to fancy what I shall feel if she does. I thought I knew, beforehand, what I should feel for father and mother; so I did, for the first six months—but now! I had no idea of now.]

Saturday morning, St. Valentine's [—I'm too anxious to leave for Oxford without hearing, so Joanie's] going to drive me up the hill to the Xl Palace, and I shall play some games of chess with the automaton chess player,* while she goes and sees Rosie and sings to her, if she's well enough. That's to be my Valentine's gift.

Love to you all.

* I get quite fond of him; and he gives me the most lovely lessons in chess. I say I shall play *some* games, for I never keep him waiting for moves, and he crushes me down steadily,—and my mind won't be all in my play, to-day—any more than Henry 8th at the end of the play—only the automoton won't say ⟨")Sir, I did never win of you before⟨."⟩[1]

Ever your affectionate JR.

Thanks for the words about Fors.

NOTE   1 *King Henry*. Charles, I will play no more tonight; my mind's not on't; you are too hard for me.
    Suffolk. Sir, I did never win of you before.

Henry VIII, v.i. [N.'s note].

XXXIII
(N,II.72;37.81)   [Dearest Charles   Corpus Christi College   Oxford,
                                                  15th Feb. 1874.

I'm greatly puzzled by the address of the enclosed scrap,—will you kindly send word to the writer where & how to get Fors.—You know Allen is now at Sunnyside, Orpington, Kent.]

I played three games with the automaton—not bad ones considering. Two other people played him also;—an hour and a half went in the five games [—then Joanie came back. She had found R a little better; and up, on her sofa—but it will be a week or more before we can know how she will bear the fasting.

She was greatly delighted with my two drawings—and a book I used to read when I was a boy, Mrs Sherwood's Henry Milner. We had got her some other books, too, and she was very happy hearing Joan sing.]

I came away here in the evening—and am going down to Brant-wood [,till the crisis is over—] I shall make you a little drawing of myself, positively before I go abroad. Write for the present to Brantwood.

I have just put up half a dozen proofs of Turner's Rivers &c. for you—all but one have some scratching or pencilling of his own on them. [In the early etching, his important spotting⟨?⟩ is of the cleavage over the engravers shapeless rock

⟨Sketch with comment "Turner pencil"⟩

and his exquisite outline of Monk Rock, at the side with 'the lobster pot' below will I think interest you. The others are unimportant.

—I've put a lot of Professor ⟨Rood's?⟩¹ drawings with them which I don't know how to send back to him.

Ever your loving   JR]

1 Perhaps Ogden Rood, Columbia physics professor and founding NOTE member of the American Water Color Society, who cites *The Elements of Drawing* in his *Modern Chromatics* (1879).

Brantwood, Coniston,   XXXIV
My darling Charles,   23rd February, 1874   (unpublished)

I got your letter inclosing General Cesnola—¹(copy) this morn-ing, and have sent off a cheque for 200, promising 800 more, accord-ing to compact in great Russell St.

The excitement and interest come opportunely—for I have a hard time of it and curious Dragon battle, about Rosie.—I was nearly beaten yesterday,—lance in worse splinters than Car-paccio's²—and not at all so well through the back of the throat—but it holds, I am thankful to say. I look with great interest and hope—need I say so—to this new work of yours.

The two pages of your letter contain the sum of all teaching in the purest truth.

Forgive, the seventy times seventh time, my remissness in sending you drawings,—and in setting Burgess on his mettle. Please God—I'll do better now.

Ever your loving & grateful
John Ruskin

1 Ruskin helped to finance one of Count di Cesnola's archeological NOTES expeditions to Cyprus. In 1872 the New York Museum of Fine Art

outbid the British Museum for an earlier collection. See NL, 1, 440; 29. 563.

2 His *St George* in San Giorgio degli Schiavoni, Venice. See 24.340–1.

Brantwood, Coniston.

Dearest Charles   28th Dec. 74

I have just got your letter of 14th, an immense comfort to me, in days of frost—solitude & fatigued langour—even to lying in bed to breakfast—after two months of unusual labour & excitement.

With your letter came one in pencil from poor Rose—praying me to deliver her from her father—(who has driven her mad and is shutting her up with a Doctor in Dublin.)—I am of course helpless —and proceed to correct press⟨?⟩ and study saxifrages—which in my botany are to be called Francescas.[1]

Francesca stellaris.

———— hypnoides—&c.—I'm going to change every name that has any unworthy or unclean association. The saxifrage is to be called Francesca because it is essentially the flower whose poverty-stricken beauty depends on its stigmata. It is the flower which introduces my general essay on Spots.

I shall give a French (& generally also a German—) synonym "Francoise etoilée" &c. for my French or German pupils—and the new name will be always given under the authority not of Ruskin but of 'Schol. Art Oxon.'

—All you say of Val d Arno illustrations is true—but the difficulty is to get *any* illustrations.—If I set to engraving them or drawing them—I should be dead before my books came out.

—They are only the best available makeshifts—these present ones.

But I'm going to do something prettier.

—No more time to-day

Ever your loving   JR.

NOTE   1 Passage partially quoted in *JRRL*, p. 130.

Ashbourne, Derbyshire

My dearest Charles,   27th Jany, 75

I think I sent some rag of an answer to yours of November 9th. Perhaps not, for, as you feared, I had rather a bad time just then, [but more of amazement—horror, and such forms of indignation as *diseased* wickedness may justify, than actual grief, for, even in this renewed hope of getting some remnant of what I had so much wished, I had seen much to dread.[1]

But—at any rate, I had much anxiety—and astonishment,—]
and was again somewhat seriously injured in health, going down to
Brantwood in a state of torpor and feebleness from which I am
but now slowly recovering . . .

1 As Rose neared death Ruskin was given permission to see her.   NOTE

Dearest Charles   Broadlands,[1] 15th Oct. ⟨1875⟩   xxxvii
    I must not get into that bad habit again. You will like to know (unpublished)
how I get on here.—Poor Crawleys[2] wife has become deranged, and
he is at Oxford where Dr. Acland is going to put her into an asylum.
—I am going to establish Crawley as a servant of the Oxford drawing
school; permanently and I have got for my valet a nice old Dutch-
man, who has a pretty room next mine, here, and gets on well with
the servants, being very modest and very funny. The Temples are
very kind to me—and I am not yet finding how salt another's
bread is. I cost them a good deal in candles, for I insist on having my
evening as well as morning to myself, and like light everywhere. I
breakfast at ½ past 8 with the children (a little girl they adopted,
called Juliet, five or six years old, and another who is being with her
for a while to teach her French;) and the sister of poor Munro[3] the
sculptor, who is their governess and very nice. None of the three are
particularly pleasing to me; but Miss Munro is entirely worthy,
sensible—and quiet—and Juliet is amusing, and not the least
troublesome. Then I disappear till lunch—and find my work
go ⟨es⟩ well with the quiet park lawn, and shades.—I am now on my
elementary drawing at last, very seriously, as you will see by
November Fors—and am therefore drawing for the plates, which
are to be given in Fors, *as well as I can*. It is a strange feeling for
me to do this,—all my work, hitherto, having been beneath my
real power, almost without exception merely memorial, or tentative.
But I shall do some bits of feather, leaf, and rock, now—with the
utmost strength I have. If I can get them engraved, well—if not, the
drawings will be there, when I'm not, to show that I could do something besides talk.
    I'm doing an analysis of the geology of Yorkshire in the limestone
district, which is coming out very interesting to myself, and I've
taken lodgings for Christmas at Brighton: to study the fish & sea.
I take care now not to overwork, and hope to make a good end, yet,
of life, more or less.—Well here's my tea knocking at the door—
good night my dear friend.

                              Ever your loving   JR

NOTES   1 The Cowper-Temple estate.
2 Ruskin's valet.
3 Alexander Munro the sculptor, one of the many artists Ruskin aided:
see 36.510.

                                        Corpus Christi College   Oxford
XXXVIII   Dearest Charles,   10th Nov. 75
(unpublished)   I am at once in comfort and consternation, by finding your letter
with Mr Moore's and the drawings.
      The parcel arrived in my confusion of leaving: (I heard of Rosie's
death on Friday;[1] had to dine by command with Princess of wales
~~of~~ on Saturday—and to show the schools to her and the other
Princesses in the following week. I did the best I could; but my
parcels weren't opened.
      And now—my response ⟨to⟩ the drawings is—they are full of
admirable purpose and have many fine qualities. But Mr Moore
has no perception yet, of light and shade, and there are points of
erring taste in the drawings, which makes me anxious that Mr
Moore should now quickly see the beginning of our Oxford series.
—Give me just a week more of patience—and you shall have a
parcel that both he and you will like to see.
                                        Ever your loving   JR.
      I have separated Mr Moore's drawings into two parcels—of
good, and inefficient (—His chief failure is in the ornamental
work—he does not know noble from ignoble grotesque.)¶—I've
actually put aside some bits of sketches to be sent you, at last,—
and they shall be posted to you certainly this next week—21st—to
27th Nov.
      Shall I keep Mr Moore's drawings till he sees the Oxford ones?

NOTE   1 Cited in *JRRL*, p. 132.

XXXIX   [My dearest Charles   Broadlands, 1st Feb. 76
(N,II.128;37.190)   Before going down to breakfast "with the children"—according
to programme but of late the household have all come to the early
$\frac{1}{2}$ past eight breakfast instead of the fashionable 10—(I *think*—a
little because—*I*—forsooth am never visible after the childrens
time!) I must answer your most important questions about Mr
Moore. I am—as you must be, entirely glad of his coming to '
England. I see in his drawings the power of using all our advantages,
and quite drinking in and up whole rivers of knowledge—it is not
my schools,[1] but the national gallery and our cathedrals that will

be his places of scholarship. But even in my own schools, there is nothing now, I am happy to say, left dependent on me. Enough is printed and enough examples given to enable every man of sense to use them independently. Then the Chartres plan is excellent, but before he can feel thirteenth century sculpture he must get a better power of light and shade in drawing, for this I will find some means of study for him, if I am not in England. It is useless to look forward.]

I am being brought every day, now, into new work and new thoughts, and, whether I will or no, into closer contact with evidence of an altered phase of natural, if not supernatural, phenomena, the more helpful to me because I can compare now with clear knowledge, the phase of mind in which [you] John Simon and other noble Deists or infidels are, and in which I have been for ten years, with that which I am now analyzing in the earlier Florentines, and recognizing in some living Catholics.

To me, personally, it is no common sign that just after the shade of Rose was asserted to have been seen beside Mrs. Temple & beside me, here,[2] I should recover the most precious of the letters she ever wrote me, which, returned to her, when we parted, she had nevertheless kept, [with the long ago given tress of her hair; and which the friend who opened her little treasures when she was gone, brought back to me: while at the same time, I first saw her favourite aunt, a quiet maiden lady, now very grey and calm in age—withdrawn always from all the angers and errors of the rest of her family—and who wrote to me—on the 18th of last month—"You asked me if I had any *reason* for my conviction that you will be together hereafter; and when I answered, No—it was that I fancied you meant some supernatural reason. My conviction comes from belief in the efficacy of earnest prayer, such as you have been the object of, many a long year. Rose was very young when this longing took possession of her, and never left her."

In a former letter to Joan she says ⟨:⟩ "Truly she was worthy of all esteem, and that from her earliest childhood: perhaps my *extreme* admiration of her in all respects, warped my judgment, for I always felt, and almost always saw, that when she appeared to err it was in reality that she was not understood, and could not be judged by the same standard as other girls. (would there were more like her).— Her deep and constant regard for your cousin partook of the same peculiarity, for she never ceased praying for him. There are many who talk of praying for others. She *did*—in ardent hope, and fine trust. She cared for his soul in very truth & earnestness, and looked forward to endless happy companionship. May her prayer be granted—at her earnestly expressed wish. I have made it mine, and will continue to do so."

—Her judgment was not warped—Every error of the sweet child may now be seen in its root—in forms of the brain disease that killed her.

I would not have been thus talkative, but that I am not without hope of bringing you yourself some comfort, such as all this has already brought to me. Your complete understanding of Dante and his time cannot I think, permit you much longer to remain— with every speranza lasciata[3]—*out*side the golden instead of within the dark gate.

Do not fear, for *me*, the interruption of my own special work. I did yesterday the best bit of peacock's feather I've ever done yet.

I was nearly as hopeless as you about St George's work—but am able now to put a better life in it, gradually.

Ever your loving   JR.

My love to Lowell ⟨—⟩ I shall rejoice in ⟨the⟩ essay on Dante ⟨—⟩ and to Longfellow.

See *last* in this puzzle of prayer ⟨?⟩

I am more aghast at your giving six lectures a week than you can possibly be at my many candle ends.—If I could bear the thought of adding in any wise to your work I should snatch at the offer to abridge the Stones for me.

—I would buy some of the old plates—and have others, better, done.

NOTES   1 For the plan of Ruskin's drawing schools see Robert Hewison, *John Ruskin. The Argument of the Eye* (Princeton, 1976), pp. 170 ff.

2 At a seance at Broadlands.

3 'Lasciate ogni speranza, voi ch' entrate.' From the inscription on the Hell Gate, Dante's *Inferno*, 3, 9.

xl
(unpublished)

My dearest Charles   Venice 14th March 77.

I don't know how far your last letter was written in play:—but it still seems to me to need answer. For I *did* also speak of keeping Moore in Europe,—not, as you thought for *my* uses,—and still less, as you thought, that he might have the benefit of *my* teaching—but that, being a man of extreme tenderness of art power and extreme purity of heart, he might live with Luini and Carpaccio, and become a man precious to the whole world instead of a bad drawing master at Cambridge ⟨Harvard⟩.—Unless you are able to do without him—you can do no good *with* him. And further—you are yourself lost and sinking in that element—over working to begin with—hardening I perceive—and losing taste—for else, a man of your culture could never have thought of quoting such men as Mill and Garbett[2]—the last a poor mad wretch consumed with religious egotism—beside Plato & Aristotle—in a University examination paper. There is no possible excuse for doing such a thing. It may make the immediate teaching of the course more amusing to its students—but it is treason to the entire cause of classic literature —: and it is because you do not yet see the essential difference between divine work like Plato's—and such earthy gas vapour as Mill, that your sadness and darkness bears you down in heart. For to see true Good and Evil is to see Life. _This_ is the True God—and Eternal Life.

Ever your loving   JR.

1 Edward L. Garbett, whose _Elementary Treatise on Principles of_ NOTE _Design in Architecture_ was critical of _The Seven Lamps_; see 9.451 ff.

My dearest Charles   Venice, 15th April 77.   xl**i**
                                                         (unpublished)
Your grief at my letter[1] makes _me_ very sad,—but not in sympathy with it. Here is all Italy laid in final ruin by a horde of banditti—all Europe in the vilest harlotry and atheism—debating whether they shall begin universal murder—here is England once honest, a nation of rascals—here is your wife dead—my Rose—my Father —mother—nurse—my life gone all but a shred of it—here are the snows vanishing from the Alps—and God out of Heaven—and— forsooth—you are grieved!—because your friend sends you a cross letter! Are not you a very curious & wonderful Charles, when you think of it?

Ever your loving John Ruskin.

1 Presumably the letter of 14 March.   NOTE

                          Brantwood, Coniston.   xl**ii**
Darling Charles   ⟨4 February, 1880⟩   (unpublished)
I never felt more—(—though I often feel intensely—) the deep spirituality of Horace's question—"ignavis amicis,"[1] than when I read your question how I could bear the 'cant' of a man's calling me Master, who has been my faithful servant these thirty years! Nothing ever showed me the impossibility of the American mind ever understanding the deepest motives of the English one, so hopelessly. But 'Master' is now my _legal_ address by the members of the St G. Guild—as much as 'colonel' or 'captain' in the army or navy. The ex-mayor of Birmingham[2] writes to me so—as naturally & simply as my own servant. And if _you_ had learned how

to engrave from me, and had executed one of the plates in Fésole, *you* would call me 'Master' too.

Nor can I conceive how you expect to make the new M.P. useful—with that number of plates in it.—Not a single student could ever buy it, and few libraries could. I believe the only way is to issue a separate atlas, with photographs of my etchings, and the rest of the plates managed under Allen's care.³ I'll consult with him.

Ever your lovingest

JR.

Please give enclosed ⟨fragment⟩

NOTES   1 *Epistles*, II:2.210.

2 George Baker, Trustee and later Master of the Guild of St George.

3 George Allen, Ruskin's former pupil at the Working Men's College, now his publisher.

xlɪɪɪ   Lucca, Coffee time, (7 A.M.)
(N,II.179;37.413)   [Darling Charles   3rd Oct. 82

I got your lovely letter from Pisa yesterday—and if Sally's photograph comes there, she'll get it next week, and if I think it pretty I'll send her my love back for her's—and I haven't much to spare just now, for I've been getting a lot of new pets lately— "Full of music"!—but, now I think of it—I didn't know you had any music in America, except the wind in the pines—and the rivers in their falling—for I suppose they're too big and awkward to sing except when they're broken to pieces.—How I did pity you, at Geneva—a fortnight since—for having those big nasty rivers, instead of Rhones and Isises.

I like your impudence in saying "we're always of a mind when we meet."—How can I ever *tell* you my mind when we meet? You always say such a lot of pretty things to me that I've nothing to say but the fag-end of Miss Farren's song—"Thank ye—Sir—"¹ but you never get any of my 'mind'—whatever that may be.—As for giving up Froude! My dear Charles, he was C's only comfort for years and years before his death,² and during my own illness last spring was as tender as a sister—walking out from Onslow Gardens continually to come and sit with me and soothe me—for I would always let *him* in, whoever was kept out.] . . .—I'm so glad to hear what you tell me of the Emerson letters³—all the same—I don't see much good in Emerson—he is only a lot of cobweb over Carlyle.

Ever your loving John Ruskin

1 Nellie Farren. Her song was probably a musical hall version of NOTES 'Where are you going to, my pretty maid?'. See *The Oxford Dictionary of Nursery Rhymes*, ed. Iona and Peter Opie (Oxford, 1951), pp. 281-3.

2 For a brief account of the Froude controversy see K. J. Fielding, 'Froude and Carlyle: some new Considerations', in *Carlyle Past and Present*, ed. K. J. Fielding and Rodger Tarr (London, 1976), pp. 239 ff. Across his courteous reply to Ruskin's most angry letters on the subject Norton wrote: 'I burned these letters. They were sad, insane outbursts of unbridled resentment at my exposure of Froude's violation of the trust reposed in him by Carlyle' (Norton's letter of 28 June 1889). Copies of the letters survived, however, to be published by Helen G. Viljoen in *The Froude–Ruskin Friendship* (New York, 1966). They are angry letters, but not 'insane outbursts'. Froude was a subject on which Norton himself was not entirely rational.

3 Norton probably referred to his preparation of the Carlyle–Emerson correspondence, published in 1883.

My dearest Charles   Brantwood, Coniston. 18th Aug 86   xliv
You ought not to be so anxious during these monsoons and (N,11.215;37.568)
cyclones of my poor old plagued brains.—They clear off, and leave
me, to say the least, as wise as I was before. Certainly this last fit[1]
has been much nastier for *me* than any yet—and has left me more
frightened, but not so much hurt, as the last one. [This was wonderful for the quantity of things in it.—I recollect first one and then
another as my wits get into shape again. It began very prettily by
my fancying that a fit of moral rhyming which I fell into—of a
Byronic character (—e-g

> 'The Protestant is a peculiar sinner
> Who dines his God instead of his
>   dinner
> Who fasts in spite, when he ought to
>   eat
> And doesn't know his God from his
>   meat')

had offended my poor old Rose—who came alive again to lecture
me—and came over from Ireland and woke me suddenly in the
night with a candle!—Then she took command in the house—
but I thought everybody was frightened of her—because she sometimes wore a Death's head instead of her own!—Then I got up
into heaven with her—but was presently sent down again—and
lost in more confused horrors of earthly Death than I ever dreamed
yet. As I came back to myself I became more violent than usual!—
fought all my gardeners and broke windows and tumblers enough
for Alnaschar[2] himself. My wrist is sprained—and my ribs sore—

but for the rest I'm pretty well myself again (the gardeners rather dilapidated!)—and am going on with Praeterita rather prettily— very eager to come to you in the Vevay steamboat,—and again at the Giesbach—when you broke off my flirtation with Marie! I believe you were quite wrong,—it was all your stuck-upness and too fineness.—I might have been ever so happy over there with Marie— instead of fighting my gardeners here—annually.]

—Send me a line now & then still, please, whether I'm mad or not I'm

your loving   JR.

NOTES   1 In July 1886.
2 See 'The Barber's Fifth Brother' in *The Arabian Nights*.

xlv
(unpublished)

My dearest Charles   Sallenches, 9th Sept 1888
I have got back to my old home again; here from Geneva two days ago, but to-day only the Mont Blanc has cleared. I have been up the old ravine—under the hill we climbed together that first morning from St Martin's, and I wrote here this morning the enclosed two leaves which begin 3rd chapt^r of 3rd Praet. The introduction of my friend is in the end of the 2nd—but I want you to read *that* as it comes in clean type—it will soon reach you, I hope.

My eyes are stronger than they have been for years, and I am drawing well, and I think writing what will give many people pleasure. My own interests and joy in nature are greater than ever, but thwarted into more bitterness than I care to express to *you*, by the course of modern trade and war—and the changes in Switzerland following the track of Cook's and other tourists.

You would sometimes hear from Joan during the severest phases of my illness, in the early part of the year. They were chiefly brought on by rage at English filth & rascality—by the smoke which *always* hid the sunsets—and the lying, encouraged alike by the Folkstone authorities and the S⟨outh⟩E⟨astern⟩R⟨ailway⟩ directors—to conceal the real causes of collisons—just off Dover and Folkestone—in one of which 150 persons were drowned in ten minutes, in a perfectly calm sea. The collision was in the night—I painted the sunrise clouds, as it happened, with the smoke–fog at the base of them which was the cause of the collision—not of the unprepared state of boats, &c.

—There were other causes of illness, of course, pressing on me at the time—but *these* were primary. Gradually, with the most tender help from Joan at Midsummer, I recovered strength enough to cross into France—revived altogether in work on St Etienne of

Beauvais,—and am now bound for Verona, with a young architect[1]
who is gradually becoming confidential secretary, and has copied
these two sheets that I may send the originals to you.

What things—in both clauses, did you mean, when you wrote
there were some I should put into my life that you would omit, and
some that you would put in, which I should omit?
Write to Verona & tell me.

Prof[r] Charles Eliot Norton.

Ever your lovingest JRuskin

1 Detmar Blow. This journey was cut short by yet another attack of NOTE
mania, and Ruskin never travelled abroad again.

Marl.

(13)

Lignite

Gypsum

Sulphate of Lime

Loam.

(14)

Chalk —

15)   16)

17)

18)

(19) 20)

The most interesting geological phenomenon in the Val del Bove, are its dikes, which are mostly composed of blue basalt with olivine. They vary in breadth from 2, to 20 feet or upward and usually project from the face of the cliff, as is represented in N° 12. They are harder than the strata which they traverse, and therefore waste away less rapidly under the influence of that repeated congelation and thawing to which the rocks in this gorge of Etna are exposed. The dikes are, for the most part vertical, but sometimes run in a tortuous direction through the tuffs, and breccias; as represented in N° 13. From no point of view are the dikes more conspicuous, than from the summit of the highest cone of Etna. N° 14. The cone and crater a, and b, were formed during the eruptions of 1810, and 1811.

The most important member of the sub-apennine formation, is a marl, which varies in colour from greyish brown to blue. It is very aluminous and usually contains much calcareous matter and scales of mica. It often exhibits no line of division throughout a considerable thickness. It is elsewhere placed thinly laminated. Near Parma, 30 distinct laminae may be counted in the thickness of an inch. Beds of lignite are sometimes interstratified as at Melesano, four leagues from Parma. Subordinate beds of gypsum also occur in many places, as at Bargone, and Vigolena, in the Territory of Parma, where they are interstratified with shelly marl and sand. At Sognano in the Monte Ceris, the sulphate of lime is found in lenticular crystals, in which unaltered shells are sometimes included.

Loam often assumes very remarkable contortions, as in the cliffs between Cromer and Runton. Fig 15, and between east and west Runton. (16) where a central nucleus of sand is surrounded by argillaceous and sandy layers. That phenomenon is very frequent, and there are instances where the materials thus enveloped consists of broken flints, mingled with pieces of chalk, forming a white mass encircled by dark laminated clay. The diameter of these included masses, as seen in sections laid open in the sea-cliff, varies from five to 15 feet. East of Sheringham a heap of partially rounded flints, about 5 feet in diameter, is nearly enveloped by finely laminated strata of sand and loam and some of the loam is entangled in the midst of the flints (No 17) and in another part, the argillaceous beds a. (No 18) are cut off abruptly, and succeeded by the vertical and contorted series b, (sand and gravel, and c, (twisted beds of loam). The chalk, (between Mundesly and Trimmingham). Subject the strata are highly inclined, projects in a promontory (a, No 19) because it offers more resistance to the action of the waves than the tertiary strata which are in contact with it. where they are inclined at an angle of 45 and appear more disturbed than in other parts of the cliff, as if displaced by the movements in which the chalk was protruded. These strata are, gravel and ferruginous sand 3 feet, laminated blue clay, 8 feet d, dark blue clay with fragments of marine shells, 3 feet, d. yellow sand, 1 foot 6 inches

s. and g. yellow loam and flint gravel 3 feet h, light blue clay, 1 foot, c. sand and loam 12 feet, i, yellow and white sand, loam and gravel